The Third Republic from its Origins to the Great War, 1871–1914

JEAN-MARIE MAYEUR

and

MADELEINE REBERIOUX

Translated by

J. R. FOSTER

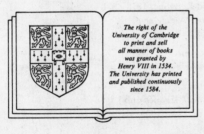

*The right of the
University of Cambridge
to print and sell
all manner of books
was granted by
Henry VIII in 1534.
The University has printed
and published continuously
since 1584.*

CAMBRIDGE UNIVERSITY PRESS

Cambridge
New York   New Rochelle   Melbourne   Sydney

**EDITIONS DE
LA MAISON DES SCIENCES DE L'HOMME**

Paris

Published by the Press Syndicate of the University of Cambridge
The Pitt Building, Trumpington Street, Cambridge CB2 1RP
32 East 57th Street, New York, NY 10022, USA
10 Stamford Road, Oakleigh, Melbourne 3166, Australia
and Editions de la Maison des Sciences de l'Homme
54 Boulevard Raspail, 75270 Paris Cedex 06

Originally published in French as *Les Débuts de la Troisième République 1871–1898*
and *La République radicale? 1898–1914*
by Editions du Seuil, Paris 1973 and 1975
and © Editions du Seuil, 1973

First published in English by Editions de la Maison des Sciences de
l'Homme and Cambridge University Press 1984 as *The Third Republic from its
Origins to the Great War, 1871–1914*

First paperback edition 1987

English translation © Maison des Sciences de l'Homme and
Cambridge University Press 1984

Printed in Great Britain at the University Press, Cambridge

Library of Congress catalogue card number: 83–15084

British Library Cataloguing in Publication Data

Mayeur, Jean-Marie
The Third Republic from its origins to the Great
War, 1871–1914.—(The Cambridge history of
modern France; 4)
1. France – History – Third Republic, 1873–1940
I. Title   II. Rebérioux, Madeleine
944.081   DC335

ISBN 0 521 24931 7 hard covers
ISBN 2 7351 0067 7 hard covers (France only)

ISBN 0 521 35857 4 paperback
ISBN 2 7351 0223 8 paperback (France only)

CE

Contents

A note on the translation*

The main problem in translating from French a book about French life and institutions lies in deciding what to leave untranslated. On the whole, I have translated names of institutions when the result made sense, and left them in French when it did not. A good example of the latter case is *bourse du travail*. It is no good translating this by 'labour exchange', as most dictionaries do, because a *bourse du travail* was a kind of trade union institution, not simply a job centre.

The terms *interpellation* and *rapporteur* also require a word of explanation. *Interpellation* is the formal term describing the right of members of parliament to interrupt the order of the day by asking from a minister an explanation of some matter involving his department. This right existed through the Third and Fourth Republics until 1958, when *interpellations* were forbidden: now votes of confidence or censure are employed as the means of attacking government ministers. A *rapporteur* is a member of parliament who writes the conclusions of parliamentary commissions which discuss legislative bills.

J.R.F

*The publisher wishes to record that the translator J. R. Foster died soon after proofs of this book became available, and that their correction was supervised by Dr Andrew Palmer.

Chronology

1871

16 April	Municipal law
15 April – 11 July	Laws on the press
10 May	Treaty of Frankfurt
21–8 May	The Bloody Week
29 June	Longchamp review
2 July	By-elections to the National Assembly
5 July	Manifesto of the comte de Chambord
	Failure of the merger
29 August	Law on the general councils
31 August	The *loi Rivet* defining the powers of Thiers
23 December	Formation of the Catholic Workers' Circles
	E. Renan, *La Réforme intellectuelle et morale*

1872

14 March	Law against the International
30 March – 25 April	Addresses of the general councils to Thiers
29 June	Agreement fixing the evacuation of the occupied departments
July	Protective tariffs
27 July	Military law (five years' service)
26 September	Gambetta's speech at Grenoble
6 October	National pilgrimage to Lourdes
	Jules Verne, *Round the World in Eighty Days*

1873

7 January	Death of Napoleon III
15 March	Agreement on evacuation of French territory
28 April	Election of Barodet in Paris
24 May	Resignation of Thiers. Appointment of MacMahon as President of the Republic, and Broglie as Vice-president of the Conseil (i.e., deputy premier)
24 July	Law declaring the public utility of the erection of a sanctuary at Montmartre

16 September	Liberation of French territory
September–October	Attempt at restoration
19 November	Septennial law
	Rimbaud, *Une saison en enfer*

1874

16 May	Broglie overthrown by coalition of extremes
22 May	Cissey as vice-president of the Conseil
	Monet, *Impression, soleil levant*; César Franck, *Rédemption*

1875

30 January	Wallon amendment
24 February	Law on the Senate
25 February	Law on the organization of the government (*pouvoirs publics*)
10 March	Buffet as Vice-president of the Conseil
12 July	Law relating to the freedom of higher education
16 July	Law on *les rapports des pouvoirs publics*

1876

30 January	Senate elections
20 February–5 March	Parliamentary elections
9 March	Dufaure as Prime Minister
2–10 October	First Workers' Congress in Paris
12 December	Ministry of Jules Simon
	Mallarmé, *L'Après-midi d'un faune*

1877

4 May	Gambetta's speech against clericalism
16 May	Dismissal of Jules Simon
17 May	Broglie government
18 May	Manifesto of the 363
25 June	Dissolution of the Chamber
14–28 October	Parliamentary elections
23–4 November	Rochebouët ministry
13 December	Second Dufaure ministry

1878

6 January	Renewal of the municipal councils
12 April	Amnesty for offences of a political nature in the period of 16 May
May	Opening of the Universal Exhibition
May	Start of the Freycinet plan

1879

5 January	Senate elections
30 January	Resignation of MacMahon

	Grévy elected President
4 February	Waddington ministry
21 June	Revision of the constitution
	Return of Parliament to Paris
	Death of the Prince Imperial
9 August	Paul Bert law on teacher-training colleges
20 October	Socialist Workers' Congress at Marseille
28 December	Freycinet ministry

1880

27 February	Law on the Higher Council for Public Education
9 March	Rejection of Article 7 by the Senate
18 March	Law on the granting of degrees and the freedom of higher education
29 March	Decrees against unauthorized religious orders
June	Execution of the decrees
July	Amnesty for the communards
12 July	Law abolishing the obligation to rest on Sunday
14 July	Official celebration of the national festival
25 September	Ferry ministry
21 December	Law on the secondary education of girls
	Rodin, *Le Penseur*

1881

12 May	Protectorate over Tunisia
16 June	Law on free primary education
30 June	Law on public meetings
29 July	Law on the press
21 August–4 September	Parliamentary elections
14 November 1881 – 26 January 1882	Gambetta ministry

1882

19 January	Crash of the Union Générale
30 January	Freycinet ministry
28 March	Law on compulsory education and secular character of education
29 July	Fall of the government in connection with the intervention in Egypt
7 August	Duclerc ministry
September	Congress of Saint-Etienne
	The Guesdists part from the possibilists
31 December	Death of Gambetta

1883

29 January	Fallières ministry
21 February	Ferry's second ministry
July	Ratification by the Chamber of the agreements with the railway companies
25 August	Protectorate over Annam
24 August	Death of the comte de Chambord

1884

21 March	Law on professional trade unions
5 April	Municipal law
27 July	Law on divorce
14 August	Revision of the constitution
	Opening of the Salon des Indépendants

1885

28 March	Protective duties on corn
30 March	Fall of Ferry
6 April	Brisson ministry
9 June	Treaty of Tientsin. China gives up Annam
4–18 October	Parliamentary elections with voting for lists of candidates
	Zola, *Germinal*
	Pasteur injects the first vaccine against rabies

1886

7 January	Freycinet's third ministry
January	Boulanger is Minister for War
January	Strike at Decazeville
13 March	*Interpellation* on the strike at Decazeville
29 March	Formation of Association Catholique de la Jeunesse Française (*ACJS*)
22 June	Law forbidding heads of families who had reigned in France to stay in France
11–16 October	First congress of the Federation of Trade Unions in Lyon
30 October	Law on the laicization of teaching staff in state schools
11 December	Goblet ministry
	Drumont, *La France juive*; Rimbaud, *Les Illuminations*

1887

20–30 April	Schnaebelé affair
30 May	Rouvier ministry. Boulanger leaves the government
2 December	Resignation of Grévy after the honours scandal
3 December	Election of Sadi Carnot
12 December	First Tirard ministry
	Antoine founds the *Théâtre libre*

1888

14 March	Boulanger put on the retired list
3 April	Floquet ministry
15 April	Boulanger deputy for Nord
December	First Russian loan raised on French market

1889

27 January	Boulanger elected in Paris
13 February	Reintroduction of voting by *arrondissement*
22 February	Second ministry of Tirard
1 April	Flight of Boulanger to Brussels
15 July	Three-year military law
22 September – 6 October	Parliamentary elections
	Universal Exhibition – the Eiffel Tower

1890

17 March	Fourth Freycinet ministry
October	Congress of Châtellerault
	Allemanist split
12 November	Cardinal Lavigerie's 'Algiers toast'

1891

1 May	Incidents at Fourmies
15 May	Encyclical *Rerum novarum*
23 July	Visit by the French fleet to Kronstadt

1892

11 January	Customs tariff
20 January	Declaration by the French cardinals
7–8 February	Constituent congress of the Fédération des Bourses du Travail at Saint-Etienne
20 February	Encyclical *Au milieu des sollicitudes*
27 February	Loubet ministry
July	Franco-Russian military agreement
19 November	Delahaye's *interpellation* on the Panama affair
6 December	Ribot ministry

1893

March	Creation of the republican right
4 April	Ministry of Charles Dupuy
20 August and 3 September	Parliamentary elections
3 December	Ministry of Casimir-Périer

1894

30 May	Second ministry of Charles Dupuy
24 June	Assassination of President Carnot
27 June	Election of Casimir-Périer to the presidency of the Republic
17 and 27 July	'Wicked' laws against the anarchists
17–22 September	The Corporative Congress of Nantes adopts the principle of the general strike
December	Conviction of Dreyfus

1895

17 January	Election of Félix Faure to the presidency of the Republic
26 January	Ribot ministry

23–8 September	Constituent congress of the Confédération Générale du Travail (*CGT*) at Limoges
1 October	French protectorate over Madagascar
1 November	Léon Bourgeois ministry

1896

29 April	Méline ministry
24 May	Congress of Christian Workers at Reims
30 May	Millerand's speech at Saint-Mandé
10 July	Law relating to the constitution of the universities
24 August	Ecclesiastical Congress of Reims

1897

December	Christian Democratic Congress at Lyon
	Barrès, *Les Déracinés*

1898

13 January	Emile Zola, 'J'accuse'
18–25 January	Violent demonstrations and anti-semitic pogroms in Algiers
9 April	Law on accidents at work
8 and 22 May	Parliamentary elections
4 June	League of the Rights of Man
28 June	Delcassé becomes Minister for Foreign Affairs
10 July	Marchand at Fashoda
31 August	Suicide of Colonel Henry
13 October	Failure of the railwaymen's general strike
1 November	Dupuy ministry
4 November	Evacuation of Fashoda
	Francis Jammes, *De l'Angélus de l'aube à l'Angélus du soir*
	Pierre and Marie Curie discover radium

1899

14 January	The Indo-Chinese loan is over-subscribed 36 times
15 January	Formation of the Comité d'Entente Socialiste
18 February	Loubet elected President of the Republic
23 February	Attempt at a *coup d'état* by Déroulède
21 March	Franco-British agreement on Africa
11 June	Republican demonstration at Longchamp
22 June	Waldeck-Rousseau ministry
5 August	Arthur Fontaine becomes Director of Labour
7 August – 9 September	Trial of Dreyfus at Rennes
9 August	Secret diplomatic convention with Russia
September	General Assembly of the Grand Orient eliminates anti-semitic lodges
10 October	First manifesto of the Sillon
19 November	Republican festival for the inauguration of the *Triomphe de la République* by Dalou

3–8 December	First General Congress of the socialist organizations
	René Bazin, *La Terre qui meurt*
	Eugène Le Roy, *Jacquou le croquant*
	Georges Méliès, *Le Miroir de Cagliostro*
	Foundation of the newspaper *Ouest-France*

1900

February	Jaurès: first instalments of *L'Histoire socialiste de la Révolution française*
14 April	Opening of the Universal Exhibition
6 May	Municipal elections
2 June	Strike and repression at Chalon-sur-Saône
19 July	First section of the métro opened
28–30 September	Socialist congress at Wagram
30 September	Millerand–Colliard law
1 December	The bar is opened to women
December	Secret agreements with Italy
	Edmond Rostand, *L'Aiglon*
	The Schola Cantorum becomes the Ecole Supérieure de Musique Nationale

1901

27 April	Insurrection at Margueritte in Algeria
6 May	End of the strike at Monceau-le-Mines
May	Foundation of the Alliance Démocratique
21–3 June	First congress of the Radical and Radical-Socialist Party
1 July	Law on associations
July	Foundation of the Action Libérale Populaire
December	Ratification of the new military Franco-Russian protocols
	Creation of the Banque Française pour le Commerce et l'Industrie (Rouvier)
	Paul Bourget, *L'Etape*
	Anatole France, *Crainquebille* and *M. Bergeret à Paris*

1902

27 February	*Pelléas et Melisande*
24 March	Formation of the French Socialist Party (*PSF*)
27 April – 11 May	Parliamentary elections
8 May	Martinique: eruption of Mount Pelée
6 June	Combes ministry
10 July	Secret diplomatic agreements with Italy
22–7 September	Montpellier congress of the *CGT*
26–8 September	Creation of the Socialist Party of France (*PS de F*)
November	Italian loan quoted on stock exchange
	André Gide, *L'Immoraliste*

Alfred Loisy, *L'Evangile et l'Eglise*
Romain Rolland, first volume of *Jean-Christophe*

1903

10–20 February	Parliamentary debate on the 'home distillers'
1 June	Bombardment of Figuig
3 July	Gas, state-owned, in Paris
July	First *Tour de France*
28 July	Turkish loan for the Baghdad Railway quoted on stock exchange
October	Workers' campaign against the employment bureaux

Ernest Lavisse, first volume of the *Histoire de France: Tableau de la géographie de la France*
Romain Rolland, *Le Théâtre du Peuple*

1904

January	Foundation of the Fédération Nationale des Jaunes de France
	Strikes by agricultural workers in Hérault and Aude
8 April	Entente Cordiale with Great Britain
18 April	First number of *L'Humanité*
12 June	Paribas enters the Moroccan market
7 July	Law forbidding all members of religious orders, whether authorized or not, to teach
30 July	Rupture of diplomatic relations with the Vatican
15 November	Resignation of André, Minister for War
20 December	First congress of Christian trade unions

Creation of the Banque de l'Union Parisienne
Léon Frapié, *La Maternelle*
E. Guillaumin, *La Vie d'un simple*

1905

24 January	Rouvier government
March	Military service reduced to two years
31 March	Wilhelm II at Tangier
23–6 April	Globe Congress: foundation of the Section Française de l'Internationale Ouvrière (*SFIO*)
6 June	Fall of Delcassé
29 June	8-hour working day in the mines
13 July	Law on compulsory assistance
July	First federation of Teachers' Trade Unions
November	Edouard Herriot becomes mayor of Lyon
9 December	Law on the separation of Church and State

Cézanne finishes *Les Grandes Baigneuses*

1906

17 January	Fallières elected President of the Republic

11 February	Encyclical *Vehementer nos*
10 March	Courrières disaster
14 March	Sarrien ministry
7 April	Algeciras Act
13 July	Obligatory weekly rest of 24 hours
August	Encyclical *Gravissimo officii*
8–14 October	Congress of the *CGT* at Amiens
25 October	Clemenceau ministry
December	Purchase of the Western Railway
	Creation of *La Guerre sociale*

Henri Bergson, *L'Evolution créatrice*

1907

8 March	First strike by Parisian electricians
April–May	Conflict between the government and civil servants belonging to trade unions
10–21 June	The 'beggars' revolt' culminates in Languedoc
3 July	Law on the protection of women's wages
11–14 August	*SFIO* congress at Nancy
11–14 October	Radical party congress at Nancy
8 December	Encyclical *Pascendi*

François Simiand, *Le Salaire des ouvriers des mines de charbon*
Picasso, *Les Démoiselles d'Avignon*

1908

3–10 May	Municipal elections
2 June – 30 July	Serious incidents at Draveil and later at Villeneuve-Saint-Georges
1 August	Arrest of the secretaries of the *CGT*
15–18 October	Unanimity at the *SFIO* congress in Toulouse

Jules Romains, *La Vie unanime*

1909

9 February	Franco-German agreement on Morocco
March	Strike of the postal workers
12 July	Jouhaux becomes secretary-general of the *CGT*
24 July	Briand ministry
25 July	Blériot flies the Channel
October	Foundation of *La Vie ouvrière*
10 October	Briand's speech at Périgueux
end of October	The Chamber rejects P.R.

League for the restoration of Vietnam
Maurice Barrès, *Colette Baudoche*
Diaghilev and the Russian ballet at the Châtelet theatre
Max Linder, beginning of the *Max* series
Matisse, *La Danse*

1910

5 April	Law on workers' and peasants' pensions
24 April – 5 May	Parliamentary elections
25 August	Pius X condemns the Sillon
10–17 October	General strike by the railwaymen
3 November	Second Briand ministry
14 November	Jaurès tables in the Chamber his plan for a 'New Army'
16 November	*Excelsior*: full page photos

1911

2 March	Monis government
April	Ngoko-Sangha scandal
	Demonstrations by the wine-growers of Aube
27 June	Caillaux ministry
1 July	German gunboat *Panther* at Agadir
28 July	Joffre becomes Chief of the General Staff
4 November	Franco-German convention (Morocco, Congo)

1912

14 January	Poincaré ministry
13 March	Arrest of the leaders of the 'Young Tunisians'
30 March	Treaty making Morocco a protectorate
5–12 May	Municipal elections
22 May	Paul Deschanel president

Paul Claudel, *l'Annonce faite à Marie*
Charles Péguy, *Les Tapisseries*
Louis Pergaud, *La Guerre des boutons*

1913

17 January	Poincaré elected President of the Republic
21 January	Third Briand ministry
22 March	Barthou ministry
29 May	*Le Sacre du printemps* at the Champs-Elysées theatre
7 August	The three-year law
9 September	State of siege in Tunisia
16–19 October	Congress of the Radical and Radical-Socialist party at Pau
9 December	Doumergue government

Alain-Fournier, *Le Grand Meaulnes*
Guillaume Apollinaire, *Alcools*
Maurice Barrès, *La Colline inspirée*
Blaise Cendrars and Sophie Delaunay, *Prose du transsibérien, premier livre simultané*
Maxime Leroy, *La Coutume ouvrière*
Ernest Psichari, *Le Voyage du centurion*
Marcel Proust, *Du côté de chez Swann*
Maurice Ravel, *Ma Mère l'Oye*
Gaston Leroux, *Le Mystère de la chambre jaune*

1914

13 January	Creation of the Fédération des Gauches
February	New Russian loan
16 March	Mme Caillaux kills the editor of *Le Figaro*
19 March	Big Turkish loan
26 April – 10 May	Parliamentary elections
9 June	Ribot government
13 June	Viviani government
20 June	Loan for national defence and Morocco
28 June	Sarajevo assassination
14–16 June	Special congress of the *SFIO*
15 July	Departure of Poincaré and Viviani for Russia
	Law introducing income tax passed
23 July	Austrian ultimatum to Serbia
27 July	Trade union demonstrations against war
28 July	Austria-Hungary declares war on Serbia
29 July	Poincaré and Viviani return to Paris
30 July	Russian mobilization. *SFIO* and *CGT* meet
31 July	German ultimatum to Russia and France
	Assassination of Jaurès
1 August	General mobilization in France
2 August	Invasion of Belgium
3 August	Germany declares war on France

Louis Feuillade, *Fantomas*
André Gide, *Les Caves du Vatican*

The origins of the Third Republic 1871–1898

Preface to Part I

The Republic born on 4 September 1870 out of the collapse of the Empire became, after some years of uncertainty, the legal régime: the first republican régime to take root and survive. Further, the Republic resisted crises, found a place in the concert of great powers and extended the colonial domain of France. French society did not change much, but it emancipated itself from the influence of the Church and acquired a more democratic look. Parliamentary government, free, secular, compulsory education, cheap newspapers, railways, and obligatory military service for all, once established in the early decades of the Third Republic, became lasting acquisitions.

In the last fifteen years the history of this period has been largely rewritten. The archives are now accessible and thoroughly utilized, and the field of investigation has been enlarged. The evolution of the economy and of social groups, regional differences and the major crises of the régime have formed the subjects of important books. Nevertheless, considerable areas of obscurity remain: political history and the history of ideas, subjects of excessive discredit, remain neglected. This observation, equally valid for other periods of history, applies particularly to the opportunist Republic. What we know best is the start, and the story of the struggles which led from the 'Republic of the dukes' to the 'Republic of the republicans'. After that come those 'obscure times' of which Daniel Halévy spoke. The years from the 1880s to the beginning of the century – a key period in the history of contemporary France – are relatively neglected. This liberal, anti-clerical world, 'democratic in the old-fashioned way' (Louis Girard), does not seem attractive, and no doubt suffers from having been elevated into a myth and from no longer suiting the dominant currents of our time. Significantly, historiography in France and Germany gives a privileged place to the Catholic or socialist movements which rejected the liberal society. This is a legitimate rehabilitation of people excluded from 'republican' history. But it should not lead to an anachronistic view of a régime, of an age and of a society apt to be dismissed as 'bourgeois'. This epithet does not adequately describe their originality.

We have tried to suggest the nature of this originality, while indicating the significance of the major events and the importance of the crises. An account of the general political history was all the more essential in so far as it must be rewritten with due regard to the contributions of social historians and political scientists. External policy and the colonial expansion have not been discussed *per se*, but have been tackled when they are linked to internal policy, in order to reveal the interaction, often unrecognized, between the two. The reader should not therefore expect to find the history of the colonial territories under French control, not even of Algeria. The colonial question only makes an appearance in connection with the attitudes adopted by metropolitan opinion or with international initiatives.

The story of the end of the notables and the victory of the republicans dominates the first chapter. Then follows a necessary picture of the economy and society of late nineteenth-century France. After recalling the work of the opportunist republicans, we were moved to enquire whether the values dear to the founders of the régime changed the spiritual and cultural world of the French. Around 1885 and in the following years the Republic seemed to be threatened by nationalism and socialism; the moderates seemed to have overcome those difficulties when the Dreyfus revolution suddenly appeared upon the scene ...

1

The end of the notables, 1871–1879

The Republic of M. Thiers: from the suppression of the Commune to 24 May 1873

After the disaster

Daniel Halévy, incomparable observer of the beginnings of the Third Republic, succeeded marvellously in *La Fin des notables* in conveying the atmosphere of the days following the defeat and the insurrection of the Commune:

> June 1871: what did Frenchmen feel? The Germans occupied their country from the frontier to Saint-Denis and Vincennes, and their dishonoured capital still smelled of blood and smoke. Lyon, Marseille, Toulouse, Bordeaux, Limoges, Périgueux were still armed and possibly primed to unleash a fresh explosion. Sadness, silence and stupor reigned everywhere. How was the order obtained by force to be fixed and stabilized? The precarious nature of the situation frightened people, and with the anguish and fatigue that they experienced was mingled a feeling of repentance.

Halévy assembles a number of different facts, over which we must linger briefly because of the tremendous effect long exerted by the double catastrophe of Sedan and the Bloody Week. The defeat, ratified, so to speak, by the annexation of Alsace and the Moselle, by the payment of an indemnity of 5,000 million francs, and by the presence of an army of occupation in some twenty departments, produced a common affirmation of patriotism and similarly a loyalty to the army, a 'sacred ark' kept beyond political arguments and worshipped by republicans and monarchists alike. On 29 June 100,000 men took part in a march-past at Longchamp; this was how Thiers acclaimed the rebirth of the army which had just crushed the Commune. The cry of 'Long live the Republic!' was mingled with that of 'Long live France!' The occasion created a rite in which both republicans and monarchists joined, unanimous in their desire to see the army strong again.

No doubt Thiers and the moderates, anxious to end a costly and hopeless war, were opposed to Gambetta and his friends with their obstinate pursuit of 'national defence'. In February 1871 the vast majority of the country had decided against the Gambettists. In Haute-Loire the friends of Thiers had clearly defined the available choice: 'Those who want war to the bitter end will vote for the Jacobin list, which ... wishes to have the last man killed and the last crown spent. Those who want an honourable peace will vote for the peace list.' One of the fundamental reasons for the conservatives' success in the elections to the National Assembly was that they had opted for peace. But this prudent realism went hand in hand with an intense patriotism which produced the desire to restore France and her army. The watchword of the régime in foreign policy was to be 'no bellicosity or provocation, but no pacifism or humiliation either'.

The words which best expressed the climate of the time were not only 'peace' but, equally, 'order' and 'work'. On this point, too, there was hardly any disagreement between republicans and monarchists. The most extreme republicans, even when they attempted to secure a reconciliation between Paris and Versailles, saw the Commune as an aberration or a utopia. Their conservative opponents strove in vain to make people see them as the allies of the communards; the country was not in the least deceived. In fact, the beaten Commune aroused only hostility and repugnance, and its supporters went into hiding. Public opinion was to favour those who, while asserting republican sentiments, knew how to keep their distance from the insurrection. Indeed, the Commune and its failure allowed the republicans to separate themselves from the revolutionaries, but the monarchist conservatives claimed to see in them the precursors of radicalism, socialism and communalism. On several occasions – for example on 24 May 1873 at the time of Thiers's fall, and on 16 May 1877 at the time of the dissolution of the Chamber – they tried to alarm public opinion and to play on people's fears. It has not been sufficiently remarked that such attempts did not have the expected consequences, probably because, as Gaston de Saint-Valry, a very clear thinker, noted at the time (*Souvenirs et réflexions politiques*, Paris, 1886), fear was quickly overcome – and far more quickly than after the insurrection of 1848. Then the social conflict had appeared to shake the ruling classes' system of values and had involved the optimism of the middle class. These do not seem to have been the feelings of the people – bourgeois, members of the middle classes, peasants – who were going to create the Republic. The will to found a republican order counted for more than fear. Their conservative opponents, on the other hand, though just as much attached to order, wanted a 'moral order'.

Here again we touch on one of the essential components of the spirit of the time. There was somehow or other a unanimous feeling in favour of establishing the reign, after the 'imperial holiday', of an austere, provincial morality. Such was certainly the tone of the first ten years of the régime. But, in the phrase 'moral order', 'moral' signified something quite different from morality. It was really a recall to a society dominated by religious principles; it asserted a desire for repentance, penance and expiation. Thus the apparently anodyne adjective which connoted the idea of order accepted by everyone brought in fact to the surface the line of division between two Frances, one republican, free-thinking and liberal, whose ideal was the secularized society that had emerged from the French Revolution, and one for which the Gospel was the guiding principle of societies and God the master of history. It is true that not all the conservatives were militant Catholics – far from it – but they all thought that the influence of religion was of capital importance for the destiny of societies and the defence of the social order. It is also true that there were irreconcilable differences between the intransigent Catholics, harbingers of the *Syllabus* and of papal infallibility, and the liberal Catholics, anxious for reconciliation with the modern world and regarded by their opponents as 'much worse than the communards'. But here again both sides shared the same picture of a France in which the Church would exercise a magistracy of influence and in which its precedence would be recognized.

Everyone in the conservative world strove to read 'the signs of the times'. Paris, they said, the modern Babylon, had surely expiated, in the flames of the siege and the civil war, the faults of sinful France. The hour of repentance had struck, and one might expect a regeneration which would see the return of France to religion and the restoration of the Christian monarchy. The time is approaching ... So spoke bishops and preachers. *Gallia poenitens et devota*: this return to the altar and the invitation to penitence are the normal accompaniment of great crises. But in 1871 the phenomenon benefited from the religious revival and the evolving spirituality of the 1860s. The religiosity which was asserting itself at the end of the Empire, with its sensitivity to the needs of the heart, its Marian piety, cult of the Sacred Heart and ultramontanism, blossomed after 1871. It was the time of pilgrimages to Lourdes, La Salette, Paray-le-Monial, and Pontmain, near Laval, where the Virgin had appeared in January 1871.

On the fringe of this great movement, but inseparable from it, came a spate of revelations, prophecies and miracles. In *Le Pèlerin*, only a few months after its foundation, Father François Picard, an Assumptionist, wrote in 1874:

> The supernatural and the marvellous have invaded society and are these days occupying the minds of those most recalcitrant to religious thoughts. From the prophecies of varying clarity which circulated in France throughout the war with Prussia to the apparitions of varying validity which are presently astonishing Germany and Alsace, everything reveals a new climate of society, everything demonstrates a positive fever for wonders and miracles.

Consequently the mouthpiece of the General Council for Pilgrimages (*Le Pèlerin* was in fact at first simply an information sheet), though it laid down prudent rules for guidance, was 'happy to echo the supernatural'. Things had gone so far that the cautious Mgr Dupanloup, Bishop of Orléans, thought it essential to publish at the beginning of 1874 a 'Letter on contemporary prophecies'. 'On all sides today, Gentlemen', wrote the Bishop, 'there is talk of nothing but miracles and prophecies', and he noted that a whole generation 'feeds on chimaeras'. This expectation of some sort of millennium was closely bound up with the hopes of a restoration of the comte de Chambord; it was an integral, if often forgotten, part of the mentality of the time.

To these observations on the state of mind prevailing in France of 1871 must be added one very important factor: the fluidity and mobility of public opinion. There is nothing surprising in this in a period of crisis, when people are as quick to forget as to enthuse, and full of contradictions. We shall meet many examples of it. For example, what a contrast between the elections of February to the National Assembly, which resulted in victory for the conservatives, and, some months later, the by-elections of July, which were a dazzling success for the republicans. What a contrast again between the discredit into which the Empire fell after Sedan and the victory of Bonapartist candidates at the by-elections in the spring of 1874, a victory that worried the Orleanist right so much that the result was the passing of the constitutional laws. Another surprise was the emotion of the people of Paris at the funeral of Thiers on 8 September 1877. Gambetta was amazed at 'this excited crowd of Parisians, bombarded, machine-gunned and bled white by M. Thiers six years ago, then finding in its rationality and patriotism the courage to pardon the victor and to award him an apotheosis'.

Thus in the confused period following the summer of 1871, success was to go to those who were able to respond to the successive waves of opinion.

The political forces

The elections of 8 February 1871 had taken place according to the provisions of the law of 1849, by simultaneous ballot for a list of names in each department. The campaign had been brief; the circumstances were dramatic. The conservatives had won a massive victory. The republicans, powerful in the east, the south-east and the big towns, were in a minority. Out of 645 persons elected[1] 400 were monarchists. The country people voted for the notables, whom they saw as guarantors of peace and order. Bonapartists numbered only about twenty. The membership of the National Assembly was new – only 27 per cent of the members had any previous experience of a legislative assembly – but hardly any more youthful; the average age was fifty-three. Nearly half those elected (250) were landowners. Thus it was certainly traditional France that returned to the helm. It was several months before the political physiognomy of the Assembly could take clear shape.

At the beginning of July 1871 two events – the by-elections of 2 July and the comte de Chambord's manifesto of the 5 July – were to give a clearer picture of the political forces at work and to make it possible to estimate more precisely both the relative importance of the different currents of opinion and the various attitudes to the fundamental question of the future of the régime.

Thanks to the multiple elections and to resignations, 114 seats in forty-seven departments had to be filled. More than half the country, including Paris, voted by simultaneous ballot for a number of names; the elections thus had a national dimension. The republicans were victorious in thirty-nine departments; they had about a hundred candidates elected, including thirty-five radicals, against twelve royalists. More than a third of the electorate abstained from voting. The republicans alone had fought an active campaign.

The country voted for the conservative Republic of Thiers, which gave the assurance of peace and order. But the ballot provided further lessons. It marked Gambetta's return to politics. He left Saint-Sébastien, where, resigning from his seat of deputy for the Lower Rhine, he had withdrawn after the peace preliminaries, and where he had remained silent during the Commune. On 26 June, in Bordeaux, where a few months earlier Jules Simon had divested him of his powers, the former head of the Delegation called on the republican opposition to be patient. The republican party, he said, must be a 'party of government', 'the enemy of chimaeras'; and it must undertake the political education of the countryside. The beaten man of February, the 'raging madman' denounced by Thiers, started on an astonishing re-ascent, and Paris was to elect him to the Assembly, together with four other radicals. The ballot-box demonstrated in fact, in spite of the Commune with which the conservatives strove to identify it, the strength of the extreme radical left. Hardly a month after the crushing of the insurrection, Paris elected predominantly friends of Thiers; but in southern and south-eastern France the radicals won some thirty seats. In general, and contrary to the monarchists' expectations, the Commune did no harm to the republican concept. On the contrary, its suppression demonstrated the Republic's capacity for maintaining order; and at the same time it made it essential to satisfy at least the fundamental claim of the rebels of 18 March.

At the very moment when the country was making its feelings known the monarchist alliance broke up. The laws enforcing exile had been repealed and the Orleanists had agreed to recognize the comte de Chambord; at his death the throne would return to them, since the comte had no heir. But the exile of Frohsdorf meant to assert his principles. Returning to Chambord, on 5 July he published a manifesto which was a provocation to the

Orleanists and a painful disappointment to the moderate legitimists. Its conclusion bore witness to the comte's romantic loyalty to the white flag: 'For me it has always been inseparable from my absent country; it waved over my cradle and I wish it to shade my tomb.' Quite apart from this symbolic assertion of divine right as opposed to a sovereignty based on popular assent, the whole document revealed hostility to the France that had emerged from the French Revolution, and a complete refusal to contemplate any compromise: 'One cannot escape eternal truths by means of expedients.'

The comte de Chambord certainly spoke of 'public freedom', but the term indicated, as in the thought of a man like Fénelon, a society based on the corporations, decentralization and 'local franchises'. The Orleanists were not unfamiliar with this ideal, but the prince did not say a word about the parliamentary government dear to their hearts. Even the reference to his study of the 'working classes' and the letter of 1865 about the workers were bound to worry them, for he had there shown himself favourable to corporations, thus going half-way to meet the ideals of economic liberalism.

On 9 July, at Falloux's request, most of the royalist members of the National Assembly, while asserting their 'respect' for the comte de Chambord, also asserted their loyalty to the tricolour, 'which has become, as opposed to the blood-red standard of anarchy, the flag of social order'. But the comte de Chambord preferred reaction and intransigence to conservation and compromise. A conflict of ideas, more bitter than any of the others, separated the two wings of the right. It was to exert a decisive influence on the outcome of the Assembly's labours.

It was only the elections of 2 July and those following the failure of the restoration that gave the National Assembly its true character. Until then, between the two extremes – 'Whites' and 'Reds' – the outlines of the various camps were not clearly defined; there was a search for a strong conservative bloc. Henceforth different groups were to form. It is true that these groups, which had no juridical basis, did not cover all members of the Assembly; double affiliations were possible. Nevertheless, these political friendships reflected fairly well the various shades of public opinion. Two points of view, however, were all but absent; those of the losers in the Commune and at Sedan. Socialism blended with radicalism was represented by men like Louis Blanc; Bonapartism counted only about twenty faithful supporters from the bastions of Corsica or the two Charente departments.

On the extreme right, some eighty legitimists did not follow the right on the question of the flag. They used to meet in a room in a blind alley called the rue des Chevau-légers (Light-horsemen). The name was marvellously apt for nobles such as Carayon-Latour, La Rochette and Cazenove de Pradines and Catholic bourgeois like Lucien Brun, a lawyer from Lyon, and the Béarnese Chesnelong. They formed the most resistant rock of monarchism and counter-revolution; they professed the ideal of a hier-archical society, based on intermediary bodies, which would have no truck with religious, political or social liberalism; they were connected with the Catholic Workers' Circles founded in December 1871 by Albert de Mun, a legitimist officer. Admirers of the *Syllabus* and ultramontane in their views, they vowed the same devotion to the exiled comte de Chambord, and to Pius IX, imprisoned in the Vatican. They wanted the restoration of the king and of the Pope's temporal power. Their strength was limited to the rural France which, in the wooded areas of the west and the mountains of the Massif Central, had not yet rejected the influence of the presbytery and the château. Men of principle to whom politics were alien, they were to be awkward elements in coalitions of the right. Accustomed to read events as the decrees of providence, they would not hesitate on occasion to follow the worst possible policy, being convinced that the renewal of Catholic France would only come about through catastrophe.

One can easily see how great a distance separated them from the moderate legitimists, men like Falloux, Charles de Lacombe,[2] and the vicomte de Meaux. In spite of their attachment to the legitimate branch, they were liberal conservatives like the Orleanists of the right, led by General Changarnier, or of the centre right, headed by the dukes – Broglie, Decazes, Audiffret-Pasquier. All these people wanted both order and freedom, considering, as Augustin Cochin put it, that parliamentary government and political liberalism represented the highest degree of civilization. They were readier than the legitimists to sit on boards of directors, for they had no doubts about the virtues of economic liberalism tempered by benevolence and charity. Many of them had given up the Voltairian tone of the 1830s and a certain number of them were liberal Catholics. The Rome of Pius IX had made an unfavourable impression on them with its proclamation of the *Syllabus* and of papal infallibility, which they considered inopportune, at the very least. In the review *Le Correspon-dant* and the newspaper *Le Français* they wrote finely modulated, middle-of-the-road analyses for highly cultivated readers. But that was their weakness: there was a legitimist electorate and a republican electorate, but there was no liberal Catholic or Orleanist electorate. Defeated by universal suffrage under the Empire, the dukes owed their election to the atmosphere of February 1871. The question was whether they would find enough voters in the centre to maintain the régime they wished to establish.

A small percentage of Orleanists formed the centre left group, whose rôle was to be decisive. It is difficult to see what divided this group from the centre right with the result that some historians have seen only a false appearance in these divisions; yet here we touch on one of the keys to the history of the régime. On both sides there was the same liberalism and the same faith in parliamentary government. Even if the centre left, with

Thiers, sceptical of the monarchy's chances, decided to support a conservative Republic, that in itself is not a decisive criterion by which to judge them, so true is it that Orleanism did not at first imply simply devotion to the dynastic principle but was rather a state of mind which could accept all kinds of alliances. In point of fact it was the religious question that divided the two groups. The men of the centre left, even the Catholics among them, had no desire that the Church should stamp its image on society or preserve 'the privilege of being deferred to' (D. Halévy). The liberal Catholics on the other hand, men like Mgr Dupanloup and Falloux, who were so powerful in the centre right, while accepting the 'modern freedoms' nevertheless took the view that the State should ensure that the Church was respected. At the end of 1871 the election of the positivist Littré to the Academy angered the Bishop of Orléans; the episode demonstrated the presence of a split in the Orleanist ranks. It explains the difficulty of any combination of centre groups; what is more, this split was to grow wider in the face of clerical agitation and radical agitation. A slow drift apart was to separate men apparently very close to each other, who were henceforth dedicated to difficult coalitions – unions of the left and right.

The 'left' group (about 150 members) consisted of the moderate republicans and was headed by Jules Grévy, Jules Ferry, Jules Simon and Jules Favre. They were in favour of peace and opposed to Gambetta. These successful bourgeois, with deep roots in their provinces, viewed with horror the loose living of the Gambettists, who in their eyes were upstarts, lawyers without briefs and journalists with no future, who had turned to politics under the Empire in the cafés of the Latin quarter. However, Gambetta settled down and grew more moderate on the advice of his friend Spuller and his mistress Léonie Léon, 'the wise Minerva'. With his friends in the Republican Union, which was also called the extreme left, he founded in autumn 1871 a serious newspaper with a soothing title, *La République française*. His closest colleagues were Freycinet, Challemel-Lacour, Ranc, Allain-Targé, Paul Bert and Scheurer-Kestner, the Alsatian industrialist who provided part of the funds and gave memorable sauerkraut dinners to the people who worked on the paper. Gambetta outlined a policy that was 'radical' but 'carefully weighed'; it was important, as Freycinet recalls in his *Mémoires*, 'not to make collaboration with the moderates in the party and even with the friends of M. Thiers impossible'. But let us make no mistake: at this time, although Gambetta had toned down his behaviour, he had not made any break with the radical group. He cut a figure as the chief radical, preaching the radical gospel throughout the country in speeches at public meetings or at banquets when meetings were forbidden. He fired the enthusiasm of the provincial militants, who were organized in committees and local societies like the Republican Alliance in Rhône, Loire and Var. For even if there was no national organization of radicals any more than there was of moderate republicans, one would be wrong to underestimate the rôle of these republican committees, which were much more active than the conservative committees and which, rather like the masonic lodges, brought together doctors, businessmen, small industrialists and craftsmen.

Thiers and his work

On 17 February 1871 in Bordeaux, the National Assembly had appointed Thiers 'head of the executive authority of the French Republic'. He was to exercise his functions 'under the control of the Assembly and with the collaboration of the ministers whom he chose and over whom he would preside'. It was thus a parliamentary régime, the common wish of all opponents of the Empire, monarchists, liberals and republicans alike, but it was only precariously a Republic. A preamble to the decree appointing Thiers stated that the National Assembly, 'repository of the sovereign authority', was acting provisionally 'until a decision was taken on the institutions of France'. Thiers had formed a government in which the Orleanist representatives were joined by three members of the government of National Defence who had opposed Gambetta's policy – Jules Favre at the Ministry of Foreign Affairs, Ernest Picard at the Ministry of the Interior and Jules Simon at the Ministry of Education. He called on the Assembly to carry out the task of reorganization before settling the question of the régime; this was the 'Bordeaux pact', which aimed at reassuring both royalists and republicans.

The failure of the royalists to merge after the comte de Chambord's manifesto of 5 July 1871 made it improbable that there would be any restoration in the immediate future. It was essential to put an end to a somewhat obscure situation. Thiers wanted the title President of the Republic, the prorogation of his mandate and guarantees *vis-à-vis* the Assembly, which distrusted him. He was supported by petitions from the republican municipalities; the initiative was taken by the municipal council of Toulouse as early as 20 June 1871. Rivet, a left-of-centre member of the Assembly and a friend of Thiers, tabled a motion giving Thiers the title of President of the Republic, but the Assembly asserted its 'right to use the constituent power'. Institutions remained 'provisional'. Thiers exercised 'under the authority of the Assembly, until it had brought its work to a conclusion, the functions delegated to him'. Thiers remained 'responsible to the Assembly'. In short, he was simultaneously President of the Republic, President of the Council of Ministers and a member of the Assembly. The law was passed on 31 August; the left, in the person of Gambetta, had opposed in vain the constituent power and demanded the dissolution of an Assembly which, so it said, no longer corresponded with the feelings of the country. The combination of all the centre groups ensured that the *loi Rivet* was passed by 491 votes to 94, mainly from the extreme right. The situation remained provisional, but the prolongation of the 'loyal attempt' begun in Bordeaux in fact strengthened the chances of the Republic. The conflict between Thiers and the Assembly soon broke out again.

Thiers strove to obtain the liberation of French territory as quickly as possible. The evacuation of the occupied departments was due to be carried out in step with the payment of the indemnity of 5,000 million francs, which had to be paid in full by March 1874. Thiers, who wished to end the risks of conflict involved in the presence of an army of occupation and to restore France's freedom of action, managed, thanks to the success of the loans floated, to anticipate the due date. The last 1,000 million francs were handed over between June and September 1873. By July Germany had evacuated the last occupied departments. This key aspect of Thiers's policy found unanimous support. On the other hand, when it came to reforming local government, changing military law or revising financial policy, Thiers found himself in conflict with the Assembly, which he forced to accept solutions that were less innovatory than the majority of members would have liked.

Under the Empire, both royalists and republicans had demanded the decentralization of government and the Nancy programme of 1865 had indicated that Ferry and the liberal conservatives subscribed to the same aim. The urgency, indeed the necessity, of responding to the Paris Commune involved the passing of the municipal law as early as 16 April 1871. Unlike the Assembly, Thiers wanted mayors to be appointed by the government. He had his way in the *chefs-lieux*, and in towns of over 20,000 inhabitants, but in the bourgs and villages the conservatives, confident of their own influence, obtained the election of the mayor, as in the Second Republic. The conflict was an important one, between the historian of the Consulate, the heir to the centralizing tradition, and the notables, who saw elections as a guarantee of a magistracy which appointment threatened to take away from them. The conflict flared up again in connection with departmental reform. Thiers strove to reduce the rôle of the departmental commission, elected by the general council to supervise the execution of its decisions, as in Belgium. Thiers saw in it 'a syringe in the backside of the prefects. They will not be able to govern.' In the final analysis, the law of 29 August 1871 – it remained in force all through the régime, and beyond – hardly gave any more powers to the general council, but the departmental commission did exercise a certain control over the prefect. Above all, the general council elected its secretariat and its president, its sessions were public and the minutes were published. Even if political resolutions were forbidden, the general councils were to form centres of political discussion, and the elections – the first, in

October 1871 confirmed the rise of the Republic – were an appreciable political test. However, the prefects certainly retained the real power.

The reorganization of the army was urgent; the German threat remained and, what was more, Bismarck made no bones about letting it be understood that he might take up arms again if it was necessary. The defeat had demonstrated the superiority of conscription over a professional army. Left and right agreed in seeing in obligatory military service, according to Freycinet, Gambetta's former deputy at the War Ministry, 'the best social training', and according to the duc d'Audiffret-Pasquier, 'the great training school for future generations'. France was to put an end to two institutions characteristic of the first part of the nineteenth century, the professional army and the National Guard. It is true that there were political reasons for disbanding the National Guard, which in towns other than Paris remained armed – universal suffrage and universal conscription condemned an institution bound up with qualified suffrage and the professional army. In August 1871 Thiers had reluctantly to accept the progressive disbandment of the National Guard, 'to the extent permitted by the progress of the army on the bases of the law of 1868'.

The military law, debated in May 1872, established the principle of obligatory military service: 'Personal military service is the duty of every Frenchman', but the application of the principle was not possible. Thiers wanted seven years' service; the Assembly was in favour of three and granted five. There was no question of enrolling the whole quota. Two sections of the quota were distinguished by drawing lots; one section had to serve for five years, the other for one; in fact, it did only six months. Dispensations were granted lavishly to civil servants, pupils of the *écoles* and the clergy. The sons of the bourgeoisie did only a year if they joined up before they were called to the colours, after the Prussian style. They had to be bachelors and pay the sum of 1,500 francs for their equipment. Thiers had twisted the principle to satisfy the liberal bourgeoisie. Equal military service, regarded as democratic, was to become one of the demands of the extreme republicans.

At the same time a military task of considerable size was undertaken. It was brought to a successful conclusion, after the fall of Thiers, by the passing on 24 July 1873 of the law dealing with the general reorganization of the army. It constituted reserves and established the conditions of mobilization. The replacement of equipment – the Gras rifle with a metal cartridge (instead of damp-prone cardboard) – the creation of a new artillery, with Colonel de Bange's steel guns with a removable breech, and the creation in 1875 of the Ecole de Guerre are some of the aspects of a task accomplished 'in an atmosphere of unanimous resolution' (Charles de Gaulle). There was the same unanimity in passing in 1874 the laws providing for the execution of the system of fortifications – entrenched camps and defensive lines – planned by the head of the engineers, General Séré de Rivière.

Financial policy was characterized by prudence and dominated by faithfulness to the bourgeoisie's golden rules. Loans were floated in 1871 and 1872 to pay the indemnity to Germany. The 1871 loan, of 2,000 million francs, should have been issued in March; because of the Commune, it was issued in June. The Minister of Finance, Pouyer-Quertier, an important Norman mill-owner, dealt with the big financiers of Paris and London backed by the Rothschilds. The income of 5 per cent, which the public bought for 82.50 francs, cost 'high finance' 77.70 francs. The merchant and deposit banks were not put in the picture. As Jean Bouvier says (Biblio. no. 109), 'the old firms meant to handle the business to be done with the French government in the style of the years 1815–18, without worrying about the new kinds of bank'. The most which the Crédit Lyonnais and its allies could manage to obtain was some share in the profits of the affair. The Crédit Lyonnais, besides a 'crumb' of guarantee commission 'dropped' by high finance, made nearly 3,900,000 francs at the end of 1871 from the sale at the average price of 91 francs of its 5 per cent, which had been issued at 82.50 francs. The loan had been covered nearly two and a half times. The deposit banks, except for the Société Générale, and the merchant banks made an agreement among themselves with a view to subsequent loans.

The Rothschild group and the credit establishments shared the loan of July 1872; 64.3 per cent of the commission profits went to the former and 35.7 per cent to the latter. The issue, subscribed at 84.50 by the public, was covered thirteen times. But this success for the national credit could not hide the reality, noted in a memorandum from the head office of the Crédit Lyonnais: 'Serious subscribers have been sacrificed to speculation in that "excessive facilities" were granted to the latter.'

The expenses of the war and the interest on the loans made new taxes necessary. The Assembly would have liked to impose a direct tax on personal fortunes. In company with the left, the landed proprietors, who were in a majority in the Assembly, numbers of them sitting on the benches of the right, favoured a tax on the incomes of commerce and industry. Casimir-Périer, the banker Henri Germain and the economist Léonce de Lavergne showed that a tax on income was operated in foreign countries, but their efforts were in vain. Thiers saw the 'socialist' peril in the obligatory declaration of incomes. Faithful to tradition, he did not touch the fiscal system inherited from the Revolution and raised indirect taxes. He also raised the rates of customs duties for fiscal reasons and to protect industry. Here, too, he encountered the hostility of the Assembly, which echoed the complaints of the chambers of commerce. But on this point, as on the others, Thiers was obstinate. Perhaps he expressed 'the profound instincts of the French peasantry and bourgeoisie' (D. Halévy). Thus there was a return to protectionism after the free-trade interlude during the Second Empire, and a refusal to institute fiscal inquisitions. Although they may have appeared routine, Thiers's formulas had the future on their side. Whether he was defending the 'four taxes' or the prefects, the former minister of Louis-Philippe maintained the framework of the beginning of the century through to the century's last quarter. He was to say, 'I was the real conservative.' His work was 'calculated to satisfy the holders of offices, of personal fortunes, of incomes from stocks', not the big capitalists, who often held bolder views. It reveals a France 'still largely tied to the old heritage of peasants and artisans' (R. Schnerb, Biblio. no. 104). But one could argue that it was also calculated to give a reassuring look to the republican institutions to which he had declared himself ready to give an 'honest trial', and that it showed an understanding of the deeply-rooted aspirations of those who, after him, were to found a moderate Republic.

The fall of Thiers

On 31 August 1871 the *loi Rivet*, without ending the provisional situation, had appeared to open the way for a conservative Republic with Thiers at its head. Less than two years later the Assembly failed to give Thiers a majority; the voting was 362 to 348. The 'combination of the centres' had failed; the right, from the legitimists to the centre right, was opposed to the left, from the centre left to the radicals. Rather than recount all the conflicts between the Assembly and the President of the Republic which marked these twenty months we shall simply indicate the reasons for them. The first was that Thiers and his friends of the centre left saw in the Republic 'the only form of government possible', while the right had not given up all hope of a restoration. But this is not the whole story. Neither the Bonapartists, who at the beginning of 1872 had formed with Rouher the group 'Appeal to the People', nor the Orleanists, who knew that nothing was to be expected from the intransigence of the comte de Chambord, thought that a restoration was near. The reproach incurred by Thiers went further: 'The President leans towards the republicans', people said. 'He governs with ministers and prefects incapable of stopping the progress of the "radicals"; in short, honest people are threatened.' On 9 June 1872 the by-elections in the departments of Nord, Somme and Yonne brought success for the extreme republicans. The *Journal des débats* saw in this result not only 'a defeat for the monarchy, but also and above all for the moderate Republic'. Radicalism was taking root in the countryside and north of the Loire. At Grenoble on 26 September Gambetta called on the 'radical party' to show 'wisdom'. This speech was meant to be reassuring, but what the conservatives noted with horror was the appeal 'to a new membership elected by universal suffrage', to the advent of a 'new social class'.

Albert de Broglie, who in May 1872 had resigned from the embassy in

London, headed the opposition to Thiers. An Orleanist and liberal conservative, he attached less value to the outward form of the régime than to the existence of institutions safeguarding the primacy of the ruling classes, the aristocracy and the clergy. The gradual transformation of Thiers into a republican threatened the structure of society. Broglie assumed the leadership of a coalition which the death of Napoleon III in January 1873 allowed the Bonapartists to support.

Thiers did not despair of arriving at a compromise; he agreed to communicate in future with the Assembly only by message, like a head of state in a parliamentary régime. But two events were to hasten his fall. First, the signing on 15 March of the evacuation agreement made Thiers's presence in the administration *vis-à-vis* foreign countries no longer indispensable; second, and more important, the election in the department of Seine of Barodet, the suspended mayor of Lyon, a radical who beat Charles de Rémusat, the Minister of Foreign Affairs, bore witness to Thiers's impotence in the face of radicalism. The people of Paris gave more than 180,000 votes to Barodet, as opposed to 135,000 to Rémusat and 26,000 to the Bonapartist Stoffel. There was consternation, even panic, among the conservatives. 'We thought we were seeing the resurrection of the Commune', wrote Broglie in his *Mémoires*. It was a 'legal Commune' denounced by all the right-wing press, from *L'Echo de la Dordogne* to *L'Espérance de Nancy*.

Thiers refused to remodel his ministry on more conservative lines; on the contrary, he gave it a centre-left bias. He introduced a draft law for the definitive organization of the Republic. The alliance with the centre right was over; Thiers was going to veer to the left. When the National Assembly met again after the holidays an *interpellation* demanded a 'resolutely conservative' policy. Broglie denounced the radical party as a 'social party' which 'threatened the foundations of present society'. He stigmatized these 'new barbarians' who would return to Paris 'to the acclamations of amnestied supporters of the Commune'. The defection of a small pivotal group, the Target group, fifteen strong, sealed the fate of Thiers. The *loi Rivet* allowed him to remain president, but, loyal to parliamentary custom, he resigned.

Moral Order and the restoration that fell through

Victory of the rightists over Thiers on 24 May; an attempt at a restoration of the monarchy and its failure; the passing, thanks to a renewed alliance of the centres, of the constitutional laws which established a conservative Republic; the notables final bid for power on 16 May 1877; the advent finally of the 'republicans'' Republic. These events formed, in a little less than six years – from the election of MacMahon to that of Grévy – a complicated drama in which the situation was constantly and abruptly

changing. These few years were decisive ones in the history of contemporary France; they provided the points of reference for French political life
for a long time. It is therefore essential to trace their course before
attempting to explain the reasons for the defeat of the conservatives and the
success of the republicans.

On the night that Thiers resigned Marshal MacMahon was elected
President of the Republic. A legitimist by origin but a stranger to political
conflicts, he appointed as Vice-president of the Council of Ministers
Broglie, who formed a ministry reflecting the majority. Two legitimists, de
la Bouillerie and Ernoul, joined the Orleanists, and Magne, who had been
a minister under the Empire, was given the Ministry of Finance. One of the
members of the Target group, the industrialist Alfred Desseiligny,
Schneider's nephew, was appointed Minister of Public Works. It was 'the
return to the Orleanist fold of a section of the businessmen' (J. Bouvier).
Straightaway some twenty prefects were dismissed or replaced. On 25 May
MacMahon defined the government's policy: 'With the help of God, the
devotion of our army, which will always be the slave of the Law, and the
support of all loyal citizens, we shall continue the work of liberating our
territory and of re-establishing moral order in our country.' Thiers could
have used this conservative language and he himself, on 12 July 1872, had
undertaken to defend this 'moral order' which was to be history's short-
hand definition of the new government. There were, however, two differences, slight but important, which help us to understand all that separated
the centre of the left from the centre of the right. Thiers gladly used the
adjective 'conservative', but he always applied it to the Republic; and
above all he said little about the help of God. Thiers was a liberal, like
Broglie; but the former embodied the anti-clerical liberalism born of the
Revolution, and the latter embodied an aristocratic, Catholic liberalism.

United in defence of the social hierarchy, the ruling classes and the
Church, the Moral Order coalition displayed a curious lack of unity. The
Bonapartists were unreliable allies, attached as they were to the cause of
the Prince Imperial. Those who were their adversaries under the Empire
feared the authoritarian tendencies of all of them and the democratic
tendencies of some of them. The Orleanists distrusted the exaggerated
ultramontanism and provoking religious displays of the intransigent
Catholics who adopted the legitimist cause. Although they wanted the
Church to exert an influence on society they distrusted 'a policy drawn
from Scripture'. Attached to the 'modern freedoms', they did not accept the
condemnation of these by the *Syllabus* in 1864, or rather they adopted the
discreetly critical observations published at that time by Mgr Dupanloup,
Bishop of Orléans, the friend of the most eminent among them. Loyal to
parliamentary government, they were not going to accept a restoration
which would mean going back on what seemed to them the highest mark of

civilization. To intransigent legitimists, these 'liberals' were the precursors of the Revolution; they compromised with evil. Did they not refuse to consecrate France to the Sacred Heart, as demanded by the baron de Belcastel at Paray-le-Monial on 29 June in front of 150 members of parliament? When the foundation stone of the church built on Montmartre as a mark of expiation was laid, were they not opposed to the Assembly's doing homage to the Sacred Heart in accordance with the wishes of Belcastel, and Cazenove de Pradines, the former pontifical Zouave, the hero of Patay? But these differences, considerable though they were, were scarcely apparent to the republicans, who noted the declaration that 'the construction of the church . . . in honour of the Sacred Heart' was a work of public utility, and who remembered Mgr Pie's phrases at Chartres, 'France awaits a leader, she awaits a master', or pilgrims singing 'Save Rome and France in the name of the Sacred Heart!'

Divided, the right united again to fight radicalism. Broglie struck at the republican press, making use of laws passed under the Empire and of the state of siege. He persuaded the National Assembly to authorize him to prosecute Ranc, who was accused of having taken part for a few days in the Commune. Gambetta's former colleague at the Ministry of Defence, who had just been elected deputy for Lyon, was condemned to death by default and went into exile in Brussels. The commemoration of 14 July was forbidden. In the 'Red' Midi, *Mariannes* – busts of the Republic – were banished from town halls. Civil burials were forbidden; in Lyon, the shrine of anti-clericalism, the prefect forbade by decree 'burials carried out without the participation of any religion recognized by the law' after seven o'clock in the morning. The right was confronting the Republic, socialism and free thought. To maintain its grip on the country, it gave up its ideals of decentralization. On 20 January 1874, in spite of the reservations of the majority of the Assembly, the Head of State and the prefects received the right to appoint the mayors in all the communes. This measure was very badly received in the rural areas; 'The mayoral law', Gambetta wrote to Ranc, 'has set the seal on the popularity of the men and ideas of our party.' Through its clumsy authoritarian measures the Moral Order government assisted republican propaganda.

However, on the initiative of the legitimists, the restoration of the monarchy, postponed for two years, was now attempted. Advantage was taken of the absence of the Assembly on holiday to undertake, from 29 July to 5 November, the negotiations which were to be decisive. The final failure of the enterprise does not suffice to demonstrate that it never had any chance of success; the 24 May and the advent of Moral Order had not provoked any very lively reactions in a country that was exhausted and tired of the transitory. The elections of 4 October 1874 for the general councils produced a slight success for the right, which held fifty-two presidencies. The moment was thus not unfavourable and the country, without being monarchist, would perhaps have accepted a restoration which did not call into question all the gains of liberalism. When the Orleanists and the men of the centre left who had abandoned Thiers to support MacMahon demanded guarantees – parliamentary government and the tricolour flag – they spoke in fact for the France of notables, lawyers, senior civil servants and soldiers which was ready to accept a king who would not govern and who would not be the champion of a religious, political and social counter-revolution.

But had the comte de Chambord's attitude changed? The duc de Broglie was not convinced of it; however, he let the project go ahead, without taking sides; if it failed, there would still be time to put forward the solution which he was keeping in reserve – the prolongation of MacMahon's presidency. On 5 August the comte de Paris went to Frohsdorf and recognized the comte de Chambord as 'representative of the monarchical principle in France'. In the case of a restoration the comte de Chambord would ascend the throne. As he had no children, a member of the house of Orléans would be his heir. But this 'reconciliation' did not put an end to the uncertainty; what was the situation with regard to the flag and parliamentary government? In response to the envoys who begged him to take account of the country's feelings, the prince refused to commit himself. Yet the weeks were passing and the absence of any decision was harming the plan. Chesnelong, a Catholic lawyer from Orthez who had become a legitimist, was despatched to the comte de Chambord by the royalist groups in the Assembly.

With Lucien Brun from Lyon, Carayon-Latour and Cazenove de Pradines at his side, he was received in Salzburg. After a very long interview Chesnelong noted the declarations which pointed in the direction desired, and not the others. On his return the combined committees of the monarchist groups approved the plan for a restoration and in a published memorandum affirmed the maintenance of the tricolour flag, which could only be changed 'with the agreement of the King and the Assembly'. The restoration seemed near, in spite of the hostility of the republican and Bonapartist groups. But on 29 October the comte de Chambord published in *L'Union* a letter intended to put an end to the 'misunderstandings'. He refused to inaugurate a régime of reparation by an 'act of weakness'. He rejected 'conditions' and 'guarantees' ... 'My person is nothing, my principles are all ... When God has resolved to save a people, he takes care that the sceptre of justice is placed only in hands strong enough to carry it.' Convinced that his mission was to re-establish the ideal Christian monarchy outlined by Cardinal Pie, Bishop of Poitiers, the exile of Frohsdorf persisted in awaiting the hour of providence...

Broglie then broke his silence. A skilful tactician, he took advantage of the legitimists' disarray to propose the prolongation of MacMahon's powers, a solution which left open in the long run the possibility of an Orleanist restoration. He was obliged to accept a compromise with the centre left – prolongation for seven years, not ten, with the title of President of the Republic, and the creation of a commission of thirty members to examine the constitutional laws. Thus it was a monarchical Assembly that instituted the seven-year period. During the discussions the comte de Chambord had travelled secretly to Versailles; he was hoping that Mac-Mahon would adhere to his cause and that the Assembly would recognize him as king. This ridiculous episode, which shows how blind the comte de Chambord was, was unknown to the legitimists, who, all except seven, voted for the seven-year period.

However, in the eyes of the most intransigent, Broglie and the Orleanists, responsible for the failure of the restoration, became the prime adversaries. In November the two legitimist ministers left the government, which was remodelled on Orleanist lines. Broglie had to fight on two fronts, against the republicans and against the extreme right. Veuillot's paper, *L'Univers*, was suspended for two months for publishing an address by the Bishop of Périgueux denouncing the *Kulturkampf*. Decazes, the Minister of Foreign Affairs, criticized the demonstrations in favour of the temporal power of the Pope, and vindicated the appointment of an ambassador to the King of Italy. In addition to the conflict about religious policy there was the conflict about the interpretation of the seven-year period. Broglie regarded it as 'above any contestation', while the legitimists saw it only as an expedient. On 16 May 1874 the *chevau-légers* voted with the republicans and the Bonapartists against the government, which was overturned by 381 votes to 317. They preferred a coalition of extremes to the union of all the right for the defence of the social order. The policy of choosing the worst alternative would produce, so they thought, the restoration. What it actually did produce was the Republic.

At that point some of the Orleanists began to think of an alliance of the centres, but the right was not ready to accept the immediate establishment of the Republic demanded by the centre left or to give up the policy of combating the republicans. MacMahon formed a right and centre ministry around General de Cissey, Minister of War. A by-election – that of the baron de Bourgoing, a former imperial equerry, in the department of Nièvre on 24 May 1874 – was to precipitate the realignment of political forces and the process of evolution towards constitutional laws. A year earlier, the election of Barodet had revealed the radical peril; now came the reappearance of the ghost of an Empire for which precisely four years earlier more than seven million Frenchmen had cast their votes. Bonapartism still retained considerable popularity in the rural areas, the army, the civil service and the magistracy. The failure of the attempt to restore the monarchy, the inability of the Assembly to take any but provisional

measures and the personality of the Prince Imperial all inclined a section of
public opinion towards a cause that had a new look. Between October 1873
and February 1875, at by-elections, six Bonapartists were elected against
one single monarchist and sixteen republicans. From Orleanists to republicans, all those opposed to the Empire joined forces to eliminate the
danger.

The ministers with Bonapartist sympathies – Magne, Minister of
Finance, and Fourtou, Minister of the Interior – had to leave the government in which the leading personality was the duc Decazes, Minister of
Foreign Affairs. The conservative majority broke up. On top of the attitude
of the *chevau-légers* and the Bonapartists came the division of the Orleanists:
Broglie remained the opponent of the centre left and wanted a law on the
Senate before any vote on the régime. It was only after some hesitation that
he agreed to vote for the constitutional laws. But the dukes Decazes and
d'Audiffret-Pasquier regarded this step as unavoidable; if the Assembly
continued to procrastinate, it would have to be dissolved, and that could be
extremely dangerous. At this point some waverers moved over to the
republican camp. On 29 January 1875 Laboulaye's amendment, 'The
government of the Republic consists of two chambers and a president', was
rejected by 359 votes to 336. The next day one of the moderates who had
come over to the republican camp, a Catholic university professor called
Wallon, proposed an amendment on the method of election of the president: 'The president of the Republic . . . is elected by the Senate and the
Chamber.' It obtained a majority of one, 353 votes to 352. The Republic
had been created.

A different majority was taking shape. It was confirmed by the passing of
a new amendment proposed by Wallon which subordinated the president's
right to dissolve the Chamber to the agreement of the Senate. The new
majority was formed by part of the centre right with the three left groups –
the Republican Union, the Republican Left, and the centre left – and the
Orleanist group headed by the economist Léonce de Lavergne. The
decisive debate was the one on the proposition dealing with the Senate.
Broglie saw the Senate as the base on which to build a constitution and had
conceived a grand council of notables comprising a certain number of
members belonging by right, a certain number appointed for life, and
finally a certain number elected by a college of notabilities. The left rejected
any scheme that did not require the election of senators by universal
suffrage – though not necessarily direct universal suffrage. Negotiation
among the centre groups ended in a compromise which gave wide satisfaction to the centre left: senators would be elected by colleges consisting of
one delegate per commune, deputies, local councillors (from the *arrondissements*) and general councillors. The 25 per cent of 'life members' would be
elected at first by the Assembly and later by the Senate. Broglie accepted

the scheme, in which his newspaper, *Le Français*, saw 'the firmest check administered so far to the omnipotence of numbers and the democratic activity of the towns'. Gambetta, until then against an upper chamber, persuaded the republicans to accept the scheme. He realised the necessity of making concessions to the centrists in order to make the Republic possible. Above all, he guessed that this 'Great Council of French communes' would help to give the Republic roots in the countryside and that the mode of electing the Senate would produce a ferment of political life in the smallest communes. The law on the Senate was passed on 24 February and that on the organization of the government on 3 and 4 March by the parties of the left and the centre right, including Broglie. The minority – the right, the legitimists, and the Bonapartists – only achieved 250 votes against 425. The law on the relationships between the various government departments was put to the vote on 16 July without provoking a major debate and approved by 502 votes out of 604. Four years after its election, and after many vicissitudes, the Assembly had carried out its mandate to give France a constitution. However, a long period of preparation had doubtless been necessary to make possible the brevity of the last act; with the monarchy shown to be impossible and the Empire detested, all the Assembly could do, as Wallon had said, was to take 'what exists' and organize the conservative Republic for which Thiers had foreseen a future as early as 1871.

The results of the National Assembly's labours were original in many ways. They demand fairly close analysis since they lasted until July 1940 and since the application of the constitutional laws gave them a meaning they did not necessarily possess at the outset. The absence of any preamble, of any declaration of rights or reminder of principles, is the first noteworthy characteristic; but what majority could have been found for any kind of agreed statement? To be accurate, it was not even a question of a constitution, but of constitutional laws, which could only be changed by a procedure of revision. These laws only tackled the essential aspects of the régime. And the sheer brevity of texts has made possible an extremely flexible interpretation.

The presidency of the Republic was an institution contrary to French republican tradition, which had always favoured a collegial executive. In fact the president of the Republic, elected for seven years by a Congress consisting of the Senate and the Chamber of Deputies, and accountable to neither chamber, possessed the powers of a constitutional monarch; a very slight revision would suffice to make a restoration possible. After all, the president had the right to grant pardons and to conclude treaties. He could propose laws, like the two chambers. He could adjourn and close the sessions of the chambers after five months of ordinary sittings. With the agreement of the Senate, he could dissolve the Chamber of Deputies. He appointed ministers.

Thus the upper chamber was the keystone of the system established in 1875. It had to form a counterweight to the Chamber of Deputies. The minimum age of forty, the replacement of a third of its members at a time, the appointment for life by the Assembly of seventy-five senators (who, it was hoped, would be conservatives), the distribution of seats and mode of election which perpetuated the dominating influence of rural France – these were all factors which were to make the Senate the bastion of traditional France. With the presidency of the Republic, it was to limit the influence of the Chamber of Deputies,[3] elected by direct universal suffrage inherited from 1848, on which it was impossible to go back.

The laws of 1875 established a representative form of government without sovereignty of the people, a parliamentary régime in conformity with the Orleanist ideal and accepted by the new republican generation, now converted to reality, but not by the intransigent republicans. 'Plurality of institutions, dual chambers, balance. Such are the characteristics of the Orleanist scheme, and they are all to be found, without alteration, in the texts of 1875' (R. Rémond). The presidency of the Council is not mentioned, but the decrees of the president of the Republic must be 'countersigned by a minister'. Thus there was a marked limit to the presidential power. 'The ministers are jointly responsible to the chambers for the government's general policy.' Responsibility of dissolution was intended to prevent parliamentary government from becoming government by Assembly. The control and balance of powers produced a complex system open to various different interpretations. However, in essentials, the constitutional laws, a piece of pragmatism that was the fruit of compromise, incorporated not only the practices that had originated under Thiers and MacMahon but also liberalism's constitutional contribution, 'the common right of free peoples', in the phrase of Laboulaye, the *rapporteur*.[4] Doubtless we should also include in this heritage Article 4 of the law of 25 February 1875, often neglected by commentators. It gave the president of the Republic the right to appoint the councillors of State. This constituted a modification to the law of 24 May 1872 which, against the wishes of Thiers, provided for the election of the councillors of State by the Assembly. This institution, under threat after the collapse of the Empire, now reassumed all its old importance. Nothing was said about its powers: the new régime did not touch the administration, its traditions or its legal status. The parliamentary Republic upheld the powers of the administration.

The constitutional compromise based on the 'combination of centres' was full of contradictions; the agreement on the constitutional question and on a 'middle-of-the-road' political and social philosophy should not be allowed to hide the profound disagreement on the religious question and the rôle of the Church in society. Above all, the reconciliation which was possible on the parliamentary level had no reality in the country, where each of the two centres looked towards its allies on the right or on the left.

After the constitutional laws had been passed, MacMahon, who did not mean to give up governing with the conservatives, called on the Orleanist Buffet to assume the vice-presidency of the Council. The centre right was dominant, but Dufaure and Léon Say were there to represent the centre left. The appointment to the Ministry of Finance of the liberal economist Jean-Baptiste Say's grandson and the appointment to an under-secretaryship of State of Agénor Bardoux, Montalivet's son-in-law, bear witness to the presence in the government of those 'bourgeois dynasties' who, after other régimes, co-operated to found the Republic. The ministry lacked unity; while Buffet wanted to pursue a 'clearly conservative' policy, his allies of the centre left, who did not forget their 'comrades-in-arms', wanted an end to the emergency laws on the press and the mayors, and the institution of a republican administration. In fact, it was the moment for the organization of the new régime and for the preparation of the elections. The conservatives, supported by the centre left, imposed voting for one name, a procedure which, so they thought, favoured the notables. The republicans, with Gambetta, wanted voting for a list as in 1848, a method abolished by the Empire. What was bound to be decisive for the political evolution of the Republic was the election of seventy-five senators for life in December. Broglie had hoped by this provision to make the Senate into a bastion of conservatism. But the legitimist extreme right and the Bonapartists came to an understanding with the republicans in exchange for the entry into the Senate of a few legitimists. 'I prefer', wrote La Rochette, deputy for Loire-Inférieure, 'those who fight us openly to those who have abandoned us ... and who today urge the King's abdication.' In the words of Seignobos, the Senate, which was supposed to be an Orleanist fortress, received a 'republican garrison'. At the time of the conflict with the Chamber less than two years later, MacMahon was not to find in the Senate all the support expected.

The first few weeks of 1876 were dominated by two decisive sets of elections, for the Senate and for the Chamber. Buffet had raised the state of siege, except in Paris, Lyon and Marseille, and proposed a law which allowed press offences to be tried by jury, not without numerous exceptions which came within the jurisdiction of the police court. Gambetta had striven to reassure the senatorial electors by pointing to the moderation of the republican programme. 'The true conservatives', he said, 'are the defenders of the present form of government.' In spite of the electoral system, the rightists had only a small majority – 119 safe seats, of which 40 belonged to the Bonapartists, whose hopes were not fulfilled. Universal suffrage suited them better than indirect suffrage. The centre left and the left obtained 92 seats. When account was taken of the life members the various tendencies were fairly well balanced in the Senate.

The conservatives had hoped that the return to voting for one name and the pressure exerted by the prefects and mayors would give them success in the elections to the legislature. The very first round brought them defeat, symbolized by the triple failure of Buffet. On the evening of the second round, on 5 March, the Chamber had about 360 republicans, while the conservatives had obtained hardly more than 150 seats, of which 75 were held by Bonapartists. The voting confirmed the results of the preceding by-elections and the growing rôle of the Bonapartists on the right. Eastern and south-eastern France voted in force for the republicans; the west and the north-west, except the towns, for the monarchists; and the south-west for the Bonapartists.

What was the President of the Republic to do? Form a ministry which governed against the Chamber by relying on the Senate? It was better to wait before opting for this eventuality. Call on Gambetta, who was cutting a figure as leader of the winners? MacMahon and his advisers could not make up their minds to do this. In any case Grévy and Ferry were not very much in favour of this solution. Ferry had just founded the group known as the Republican Left in order to prevent Gambetta from becoming leader of the 300 republicans who did not form part of the extreme left. Dufaure formed a centre-left cabinet; Léon Say remained at the Ministry of Finance. MacMahon reserved the right to appoint the Ministers of the Navy, of War and of Foreign Affairs. Dufaure took the title of President of the Council, thereby indicating that since the constitutional laws had come into operation the President of the Republic was no longer a member of the cabinet.

However, this former minister of Louis-Philippe, now nearly eighty, a Catholic and a liberal conservative, felt extremely ill at ease between the Elysée Palace, where the influence of the right was decisive, and the Chamber, where the republicans were starting on the fight against clericalism and the financial power of the Senate. He temporized on the reshuffling of the higher civil service. Confronted with a motion of the Chamber, he resigned on 2 December, faithful to parliamentary tradition. MacMahon called on Jules Simon. Apart from the change of prime minister, the government remained essentially unchanged. A moderate republican replaced an Orleanist who had given his support to the Republic. Perhaps MacMahon's advisers, who included Broglie, planned to divide the left; after all, it was Jules Simon who, in January 1871 at Bordeaux, had relieved Gambetta of his plenary powers. Jules Simon defeated Gambetta in the delineation of the financial powers of the Senate; it debated the budget after the Chamber, but on the same footing as the Chamber. However, the left maintained its unity. The presidents of the three groups – the Republican Union, the Republican Left and the centre left – affirmed this at the beginning of the 1877 session.

The Marshal's advisers did not wish to pursue the 'experiment'. Gambetta was no less desirous of putting Jules Simon in difficulties. The petitions of the Catholics and the directions of the bishops in favour of the temporal power of the Pope were the occasion of the crisis. Was it not in face of clericalism that the left would most easily unite? Jules Simon disapproved of the ultramontane agitation; this was not enough for the left and too much for the right. On 4 May Gambetta unleashed the enthusiasm of the left and the centre: 'You feel then, you admit then, that there is something which is as repugnant as the Ancien Régime to this country, to the peasants of France ... It is the domination of clericalism.' To be sure, he gave up the demand for separation and said that he was attached to the application of the Concordat, but at the time this shift of position passed unnoticed; what stayed in people's minds was the final sentence, which gave the republicans a common programme for decades: 'I am only expressing the deep feelings of the people of France when I say of clericalism what my friend Peyrat said of it one day, "Clericalism? That is the enemy."' Jules Simon, outflanked, had to accept a motion inviting the government to suppress 'ultramontane demonstrations'.

Unable to maintain a central position, Simon was becoming the hostage of Gambetta. MacMahon and his advisers Broglie and Mgr Dupanloup, who did not want to expose the Church, waited a few days. On 15 May Jules Simon opposed without much vigour the repeal of the penalties for press offences; on 12 May he had failed to prevent the municipal councils from holding their meetings in public; the right thought that the revolutionary societies were going to hold sessions in the rural areas. Early on the morning of 16 May MacMahon sent Jules Simon a request for an explanation; he was amazed at an attitude 'which makes one wonder if he has retained sufficient influence on the Chamber to make his views prevail'. MacMahon affirmed the responsibility of the President of the Republic to the country: 'I may not be responsible, like you, to Parliament, but I have a responsibility to France, with which I must concern myself today more than ever.' Jules Simon resigned.

The next day Broglie formed a government; after four years, almost to a day, it was a return to the union of the right. But the situation was reversed; then, in opposition to Thiers, the conservatives had been asking for a parliamentary régime; now they were claiming to defend the President of the Republic's responsibility *vis-à-vis* the Chamber, his 'constitutional right', as MacMahon asserted in a message on 18 May, to choose his 'advisers'. This 'affectation of personal power' was an absolute scandal to the republicans. But in this area Broglie himself and his Orleanist friends were ill at ease in a coalition of the right, champions as they had always been of parliamentary government. So for them there was no question of using force, a spectre evoked by all those who, scarcely a quarter of a century earlier, had lived through the 2 December. It was not even a question of imposing a literal interpretation of the constitutional laws, and Broglie was not very convincing when he tried to define a balance between the President, the Senate and the Chamber of Deputies. The real objective was in fact to prepare the way for successful elections, after the dissolution of the Chamber permitted by the agreement of the Senate. As on 24 May, it was necessary to defend the Church and the old ruling classes against anti-clerical radicalism and the 'new strata of society'. The dominant groups of the France of days gone by were opposing, for one last time, the rise of democracy. It was a difficult game and Broglie does not seem to have had many illusions, but he felt committed to MacMahon, whom he had persuaded to accept the seven-year period.

The 16 May sealed the union of the republicans, 363 of whom published on 18 May a manifesto drafted by Spuller, Gambetta's friend, denouncing a 'policy of reaction and adventures'. In his message the President of the Republic had adjourned the Chambers until 16 June. As soon as it resumed sitting the Chamber of Deputies passed a motion of 'no confidence' by 363 votes to 158. The Senate authorized dissolution by 149 votes to 130.

The Minister of the Interior, Fourtou, made ready to fight the election: he moved or dismissed seventy-seven prefects. He recalled the government's duty to 'enlighten' the electoral body and turned to administrative pressure. With the help of the management of the press, directed by Léon Lavedan, he undertook a substantial propaganda campaign, which included the organization of a Bulletin of the conservative alliance and the free distribution of brochures, manifestos and newspapers (P. Albert, Biblio. no. 137). The prefects fought against the peddling of republican newspapers and pamphlets, applying the law of 1849 which made the hawking of newspapers and printed matter subject to authorization. By virtue of a decree of December 1851 they shut bars which were subversive spots. Suspensions of municipal councils, dismissals of mayors, closures of masonic lodges and republican clubs, police-court summonses for press offences by virtue of the law of 1876, and distraints followed one another in quick succession. Today these measures may seem relatively limited: 1,743 dismissals of mayors, or scarcely more than 4 per cent; 3,271 prosecutions. They were sufficient to make the shadow of the Empire loom up again. The conservatives themselves regarded the action of the prefects, who in many cases had served under the Bonapartist régime, as excessive. Administrative pressure caused more unpopularity for the government than hindrance to its opponents.

Gambetta assumed the leadership of the republicans and showed just what a good strategist and organizer he was. He organized a central committee, consisting mainly of Senators, while the deputies campaigned in the provinces. He gathered and distributed funds and, as Freycinet notes in his *Souvenirs*, 'the subscriptions flowed in'. The 363 all stood as candidates unopposed by any republican opponent. There was thus a unified approach to the elections and a unified programme which made Gambetta a real party leader. The vote for one name acted in fact as a vote for a list.

The republicans called themselves the real conservatives, guarantors of peace and commercial prosperity. Their opponents, they said, dreamed of 'a return to an impossible past', and were leading the country into risky enterprises: the campaign in favour of the temporal power of the Pope would surely lead to war with the Kingdom of Italy, or with Germany.[5] Confronting the nobles and the clericals, the republicans took up the struggle of 1789 and 1830. Fear of disorder and crisis no longer worked in favour of the conservatives but against them. Moreover, the accusation of clericalism forced the latter to be very discreet in calling on the Church for support. In any case, intransigent Catholics, men like Veuillot or Cardinal Pie, were inclined to look down on an enterprise in which they could see only derisory expediency and in which the principal figures were their old liberal opponents, Broglie or, in the background, Dupanloup. MacMahon intervened in the struggle with a manifesto to the people of France, published on 19 September. Replying to the challenge issued by Gambetta in Lille a few weeks earlier, 'submit or resign', he asserted his intentions: 'I cannot become the tool of radicalism or abandon the post in which the constitution has placed me. I shall stay to defend, with the support of the Senate, conservative interests.'

The number of voters was greater than in February 1876 – 80.6 per cent of those registered on the electoral rolls[6] – which is an indication of the passions aroused by the campaign. The unified candidatures in each camp had the result that on the evening of the first round, which took place on 14 October, out of the 531 constituencies in metropolitan France, all save 15 were filled. The republicans lost a few seats in marginal constituencies won in 1876, but they retained a clear majority, with 323 seats to 208 conservative seats. In votes, the gap was not so big: 4,200,000 votes for the republicans, 3,600,000 for the conservatives. The voting by simple majority gave a premium to the victor. On the right, the Bonapartists belonging to the 'Appeal to the people' group came back in force – 104. There were about fifty legitimists. Thus the intransigent right and the authoritarian right had beaten the parliamentary right, which had not resisted the republicans so well. This fact is surely sufficient to demonstrate one of the major ambiguities of 16 May; its authors were fighting on dubious ground.

MacMahon toyed with the idea of resisting. The duc d'Audiffret-Pasquier, President of the Senate, refused him the support of the upper chamber, and the Orleanists shirked the issue. MacMahon formed a 'business government' headed by General de Rochebouët. The Chamber of Deputies refused to have any dealings with him. The budget was not passed. Was the government going to raise taxes by decree and return to a state of siege? Businessmen, whose feelings Pouyer-Quertier reported to the Elysée, were hostile, and the officer corps was divided (see F. Bédarida, Biblio. no. 94). Not without hesitation, MacMahon accepted the conditions made by Dufaure, who did not let him choose the ministers of the Navy and of Foreign Affairs. The centre left returned to power. Léon Say went back to the Ministry of Finance and Agénor Bardoux to Education; by his side, as Under-Secretary of State, was Jean Casimir-Périer, heir to a bourgeois dynasty. But the left entered the government; with Gambetta's agreement, Freycinet moved into the Ministry of Public Works.

According to Freycinet, it was Say, Bardoux and de Marcère, the Minister of the Interior, who drafted the message which MacMahon sent to the Chamber of Deputies and the Senate. The President of the Republic expressed his loyalty to the 'parliamentary rules' and agreed that the 'right of dissolution' could not be turned into a 'system of government'. 'The Constitution of 1875', he continued, 'founded a parliamentary Republic by establishing my irresponsibility, and instituting the joint and separate responsibility of ministers.' The interpretation of the constitutional laws was thus fixed for the future of the régime. The device of dissolution was to fall into disuse – president of the Republic had lost the weapon granted to him by the laws of 1875 against the Chamber, which received the real power. Another consequence of 16 May was that the republican party, the left, henceforth made parliamentary government their ideal, although they had accepted it with reserve in 1875, and distrusted any initiative by the executive. The notions of authority and democracy conflicted. For a long time in French political life the 16 May was synonymous with 'personal power', 'clericalism' and 'reaction'. Perhaps it had only been a struggle of the past carried on without great conviction – the last twitch of the old ruling classes.

Masters of the Chamber of Deputies, but not of the Senate or the presidency, the republicans knew how to consolidate and extend their victory. They knew how to temporize and how to put to good use the period of stability constituted by the ministry of Dufaure, who said, 'This country is tired of struggles; it needs calm and peace.' Five days after his arrival at the Ministry of the Interior, de Marcère dismissed, moved or retired eighty-two prefects. The pressure of 16 May came to an end. A programme of public works was launched to give a fillip to business and to gain supporters for the Republic. 'The influence of a minister who commissions major works', said Dufaure, 'is not negligible.' The Universal Exhibition was to make people forget the political crisis.

Nearly seventy election results were declared null and void because of

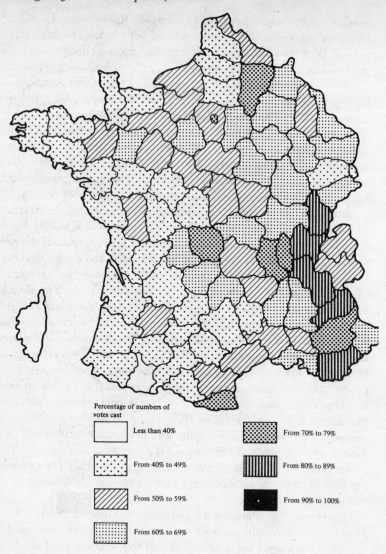

Percentage of numbers of
votes cast

☐ Less than 40%

⫶ From 40% to 49%

⫽ From 50% to 59%

⫶⫶ From 60% to 69%

⫶⫶ From 70% to 79%

║ From 80% to 89%

▦ From 90% to 100%

The conquest of the Republic by the republicans: republican votes in the general elections of 20 February 1876

Source: The maps here and on pages 33, 34 and 35 have been drawn by A. Lancelot after H. Avenel, *Comment vote la France. Dix-huit ans de suffrage universel, 1876–1893* (Quantin, 1894), and taken from the *Atlas historique de la France contemporaine 1800–1965*, edited by René Rémond (Paris, A. Colin, 1966).

Henri Avenel's identification of the candidates has not been critically examined. The chief value of the maps therefore is in the general impression they give and the movement they convey.

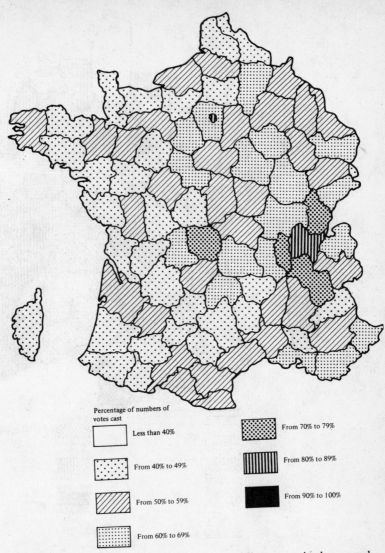

Percentage of numbers of
votes cast

Less than 40%

From 40% to 49%

From 50% to 59%

From 60% to 69%

From 70% to 79%

From 80% to 89%

From 90% to 100%

The conquest of the Republic by the republicans: republican votes in the general elections of 14 October 1877

administrative or clerical pressure. What is remarkable is that those disqualified were not usually re-elected; in Haute-Loire, where two results were declared null and void, the republicans won both seats. There were now nearly 400 republicans in the Chamber and the support of the centre left was no longer quite so indispensable. On 6 January the elections for the municipal councils produced a republican majority; and on 5 January 1879

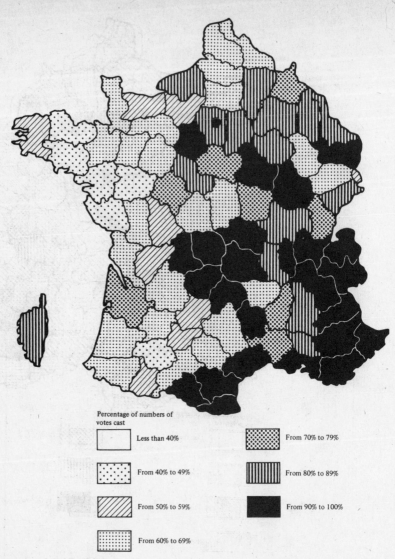

Percentage of numbers of
votes cast

☐ Less than 40%	▦ From 70% to 79%
⦂ From 40% to 49%	‖ From 80% to 89%
⫽ From 50% to 59%	■ From 90% to 100%
⦙ From 60% to 69%	

The conquest of the Republic by the republicans: republican votes in the general
elections of 21 August 1881

the elections following the retirement of the first third from the
Senate were a dazzling republican victory: of 82 seats, (75 retiring Senators plus the empty seats) the Republicans won 66. In the Forez, the
vicomte de Meaux, former Minister of Agriculture of the 16 May and
son-in-law of Montalembert, was beaten. The republicans had a clear
majority in the Senate.

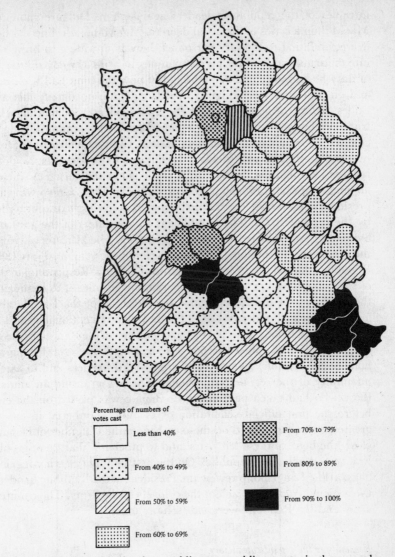

Percentage of numbers of
votes cast

☐ Less than 40%   ▦ From 70% to 79%

⬚ From 40% to 49%   ▥ From 80% to 89%

◩ From 50% to 59%   ■ From 90% to 100%

⠿ From 60% to 69%

The conquest of the Republic by the republicans: republican votes in the general
elections of 4 October 1885

The conquest of the legislature was to be reinforced by that of the
higher civil service. On 20 January the Chamber of Deputies, on a motion
put forward by Ferry, requested from the cabinet 'the legitimate satisfaction that it has long demanded in the name of the country, in particular so
far as the senior administrative and legal personnel are concerned'. Gambetta abstained; he preferred to postpone a crisis, being aware of the

intrigues of the republican leaders against him. Dufaure submitted to MacMahon a series of dismissal decrees. MacMahon declined to sign the decrees relating to military personnel; he was unwilling to bring politics into the army and to smite 'his companions-in-arms'. From a military sense of duty he had accepted everything, but now the limit had been reached and on 30 January he resigned. The Congress immediately met at Versailles. Before the vote was taken, the republican groups, creating a lasting tradition, had indicated that their choice was Grévy; senatorial weight had counted for a good deal in this nomination. Gambetta did not put forward his candidature; he was tired and did not seek to force events. No doubt he regarded his chances as only fair. A provincial, a reassuring character and an enemy of the presidency of the Republic in 1848, Grévy was the first president of the Third Republic to be elected according to the forms defined by the laws of 1875.[7] The republicans were masters of the government. Symbolic gestures bore witness to their victory. The Minister of War made the *Marseillaise* the national anthem. The following year, on 6 July 1880, the Republic adopted the 14 July as a national holiday. Responding to the call of the radicals and of Gambetta, the republicans meant to commemorate the memories of the Revolution – the storming of the Bastille and the festival of the Federation of 1790. (The 14 July was a national, civic, lay and popular holiday long shunned by the opponents of the Republic who closed their shutters and refused to put out any flags.[8]) By establishing a civic holiday the republicans wished to cross social barriers and to assert the unanimity of the régime's supporters. The law granting an amnesty to those who had taken part in the Commune was passed on the evening before the first official celebration of 14 July. Gambetta, in one of his greatest speeches,[9] called on the members of the Chamber of Deputies to close 'the book of these ten years' and to proclaim 'that there is only one France and only one Republic'. On the first 14 July the army regained its flags; at the Longchamp review the President of the Republic handed over the national colours to each of the colonels of the army. The country, the army and the Republic were indissolubly united.

Reasons for the republican victory

Why were the republicans victorious? The answer to this question is less obvious than it seems. It is true that the failure of the restoration is easily explained; the vicomte de Meaux summed up the reasons in one short sentence: 'We were monarchists and the country was not.' When the return of the comte de Chambord seemed near, the peasants in Haute-Loire, Ardèche or Seine-et-Marne were afraid of the return of the tithe and feudal rights. They were determined to defend against 'reaction' the egalitarian society based on the Civil Code, a society which, it should be remembered, was less than three-quarters of a century old. The Orleanist notables – and this was stated in so many words – were no less distrustful of a man so absolutely alien to the spirit of the age. The passing of the constitutional laws can be explained just as easily: they established a conservative, parliamentary form of government equally suitable for a Republic or a liberal monarchy, and thus preserved the chances of the Orleans line. In fact, the real question is this: why did this liberal, conservative régime based on the alliance of the centre groups and posing no threat to the traditional élites not last? The problem is happily avoided by explanations which insist *ad nauseam* on the profound agreement between the representatives of the bourgeois dynasties of the centre right and the centre left, and underestimate, or even regard as an ideological fiction, the conflict between the right and the left. This is to forget something that never ceased to provoke the astonishment of contemporaries such as the comte d'Haussonville, the nephew and collaborator of the duc de Broglie, when he reflected more than thirty years later on the origins of the Third Republic:[10] men who had so many ideas and interests in common had fought either in the coalition of the right or in the coalition of the left. On the electoral level, the fundamental division of the public mind into two camps and the impossibility of following a centre policy made itself obvious by 1876 – at the elections that followed the passing of the constitutional laws. The question that remains is what this confrontation between the right and the left, between the conservatives and the republicans, really signified.

The conflict which ended in the defeat of the men of 16 May was not a victory of the lower middle class over the upper middle class; the latter was in fact represented in the coalition of the left. Nevertheless, it was not a piece of shadow-boxing behind which the various interests pursued their strategies. In reality, the conflict of 16 May was first of all a conflict of ideas about the place of the Church in society, and the line of ideological division did not coincide with the social classes. The social significance of the 16 May was that, as in 1789 and 1830, it set up in opposition to each other the privileged few, who clung to a static, hierarchical conception of society, and the third estate as a whole, who accepted democracy – democracy defined, it is true, not as equality of means but as equality of opportunity. On this level the ideological and social factors met, for the republicans accused the Church of forbidding Man the 'enlightenment' that would liberate him. Thus the defeat of the men of 16 May in some ways brought to a conclusion the great movement which had begun in 1789.

This coalition of the third estate which formed the solid foundation of the republican party stretched from the upper middle class to the peasants. Together with the 'new layers of society', the latter were the infantry of the Republic. The workers formed only a contributory element; they were not a decisive factor. It would be easy to show that an appreciable fraction of the well-to-do bourgeoisie from the banks, business and industry was favourable to the republicans. It will be sufficient to mention Léon Say, Henri Germain, the founder of the Crédit Lyonnais and member of parliament for the Ain, Dorian, an iron-master from the Loire, Magnin, an iron-master from the Côte-d'Or, and Feray, the paper-maker from Essonnes. Dubochet, a former *carbonaro* who had become the great magnate of the gas industry, was the Maecenas of the republicans on the occasion of 16 May; he put his mansion in the faubourg Saint-Honoré at the disposal of the republican committee. Born at Vevey in 1792, he had come to France in 1811 and formed the link between the liberals of the time of the Restoration and the founders of the Republic. Gambetta, faithful to the ideas of Saint-Simon and Comte, did not fail to address himself to the 'real ruling classes, that is, those who think, those who work, those who amass wealth and know how to use it judiciously, liberally and in a way profitable to the country'.[11] He took the view that their entry into the Republic in conformity with the 'traditions' of the bourgeoisie of 1789 and 1830 would put an end to the antagonism between 'capital and workforce, which fertilize each other'.[12] From the upper middle class some 'producers' went over to the Republic, men who saw no contradiction between devotion to order and faith in progress, who, faithful to liberal optimism, remained convinced that the upsurge of the economy improved everyone's lot, who accepted an open society which rewarded talent and ability.

Gambetta distinguished between this 'upper middle class' and the 'more average middle class', the 'new social stratum' whose advent he had noted at Grenoble in September 1872. The republicans showed their political intelligence by adopting as their own the aspirations of these middle classes whose importance had been augmented by the economic and social changes of the Second Empire. No doubt the notion of 'new strata' or of 'middle classes' was vague; it stretched from the small-scale industrialists, the merchants and the members of the liberal professions to that huge 'virtually bourgeois' mass squeezed between the accepted bourgeoisie and the working and peasant population and consisting of shopkeepers, self-employed craftsmen, small building contractors, clerks and junior civil servants. But this very diverse world was animated by common aspirations – the desire to rise socially (here the faith put in the educational reforms was a crucial factor), and the desire for political advancement, which was displayed with particular intensity in the local assemblies. There, in the municipal councils and the general councils, a 'new set of people brought to the surface by universal suffrage' established themselves in less than a decade. The nobles, the old bourgeoisie, the notables and the landowners were succeeded, as Saint-Valry observes, by 'the party of the chemists and veterinary surgeons'.[13] Lawyers, doctors and teachers took their revenge on the conservative 'society' of the *chef-lieu*. They were to represent the common people; they liked to distinguish themselves from the latter, but they were much better equipped to satisfy their aspirations than the conservative 'gentry'.

It was in fact in this alliance between a section of the upper middle class, the 'new strata' and the working people of the towns and the countryside that the secret of the republican victory lay. All in all, the support of the peasants for the Republic could not be taken for granted. It is true that the peasantry had a revolutionary past; in 1849, in the south-east and the Midi, it had voted for the social democrats. But apart from these hotbeds of radicalism or the bastions of legitimist loyalty – western France, the eastern fringe of the Massif Central – the rural areas desired neither revolution nor reaction. To that extent they had found the Empire reassuring in that it was hostile both to the notables and to socialism. In the confusion of February 1871 they had elected the conservatives who promised peace and order.

Gambetta realized that it was essential to root the Republic in the rural areas, to found, as Ferry put it, 'a Republic of the peasants'. The republicans managed to create the image of a *Marianne* who was both wise and fraternal, both conservative and egalitarian. This image reassured the small and middling landowners without humiliating them. At Mazières-en-Gâtine,[14] a little *bourg* between Niort and Parthenay, the republican Eugène Proust, the son-in-law of the local doctor, was elected mayor in 1879; his predecessor, M. de Tusseau, relied on his farmers and the clergy. He practised benevolence and had bread distributed to the needy. His successor was cleverer; he established a newspaper depot and had a country house built for himself; he thus ensured that the new ideas spread, and created jobs without paternalism. The episode throws a revealing light on the 'town hall revolution' which struck a decisive blow at the influence of the traditional notables. By the services they rendered, by their moderation and by skilful propaganda the republicans succeeded in winning over country audiences who generally either adopted a policy of wait-and-see or who were indifferent to what did not concern them directly. They succeeded in raising fears of the restoration of the monarchy or of a clerical reaction, they denounced the appointment of mayors by the prefects, and they demanded free, secular, compulsory education and universal military service, which would put an end to the exemptions enjoyed by the middle classes. *L'Univers* could write at the beginning of 1874: 'The rural population – the country's reserve – hitherto almost intact, has now been tapped.'[15]

In the republican bloc the workers formed only a contributory element. Moreover, the republicans did not devote the special attention to them that they devoted to the peasants or the middle classes. This situation reflected the real situation in a France where the industrial proletariat remained very much a minority. It was also connected with the position of the

Workers' Movement after the defeat of the Commune. In addition to the state of siege and the legislation on the press, there was the law of 14 March 1872 that punished with a prison sentence affiliation to any international association whose 'aim was to incite to suspension of work, to the abolition of the right to own property, of the rights of the family, of religion or of the free practice of worship'. Strikes were harshly suppressed: 'the highest rates of judicial suppression in the half-century were attained in 1872, 1873 and 1874' (Michelle Perrot, Biblio. no. 126).

The first working-class organizations started up again in 1876. The workers' trade union societies took up reformist phrases again – association, co-operation, mutual assistance. Men like Barberet, who wrote the labour report in the radical newspaper *Le Rappel*, and de Vacquerie formed the link between the republicans and the working-class world. At their first congress, in Paris in 1876, the societies demanded democratic liberties and laicization. The craftsmen were the dominating force.

In any case, the workers voted for the advanced republicans, the radicals. It was they who in Paris, as early as July 1871, assured the success of four candidates of the radical committee, including Corbon, the author of the *Secret du peuple de Paris*; and it was they who voted for Barodet in 1873 and who, as was noted by someone in the Paris police headquarters, demonstrated their satisfaction in the wine-shops after the success of the former mayor of Lyon. Yet the social programme of the radicals remained modest; it was distinguished from that of the rest of the republican party by its egalitarian tone, by the appeal for a 'reform of taxation', which would facilitate, as Clemenceau wrote – he was a candidate in the *XVIIIe arrondissement* of Paris in 1876 – 'the improvement of the lot of the greatest number'.

The radicals also demanded an amnesty for those who had taken part in the Commune, but the rest of the republican party refused it until 1880. Yet when the workers had to choose between a conservative and a moderate republican they voted for the latter. There were frequent cases of workers voting for their boss if he had been won over to the republican cause. This must surely mean that ideological preferences rose superior to social antagonisms, that the power of the myth of the Republic was the decisive factor at Belleville or La Guillotière. Carried along by the city dwellers whose aspirations they shared, the workers put their hopes in the Republic. The memory of the French Revolution, that enemy of the 'great', the nobles and the priests, counted for infinitely more than the completely unknown reflections of Marx on the rôle of a workers' party. In 1876 Jules Guesde, exiled in Geneva after the Commune, returned to France; and the man who had introduced Marxism into France was still much closer to the radicals than to the collectivists.

Such was the coalition that made the Republic victorious. Its hetero-geneous nature is one more testimonial to the rôle of one man, to the political intelligence of Gambetta, to his tactical sense, his flexibility and discretion, his skill in choosing the right field of battle, that of 'clericalism' and of hostility to 'personal power'. Setting the seal once again on the union of the third estate, he won the day.

2

Economy and society

Our knowledge of the economic and social history of the first decades of the Third Republic has recently been enlarged by some important books. The process of growth, the banking system, the countryside and the workers' world, among other things, are the subjects of some very capable studies. There are some excellent monographs on French diversity. Yet many areas remain neglected. The spread of technical innovations has hardly been studied at all. The causes of the slowing-up of the process of growth are still a subject of debate. The monographs in particular, whether they deal with a social group or a regional entity, make one even more conscious of the incompleteness of our knowledge. The miners were a privileged profession, but what do we know about the textile workers or the metallurgical workers? We have some notion of the well-to-do bourgeoisie, but the middle classes remain a blurred area.

In this chapter we shall try simply to trace the main lines of a complex reality without failing to recognise the difficulty of isolating over two decades processes of evolution that lasted much longer.

Demography

The population of France numbered 36,103,000 in 1872 and 38,517,000 in 1886. The average annual increase was 89,700. This stagnation contrasts with the growth of the other countries of Europe. The birth rate fell regularly, from 26.2 per thousand in 1872–5 to 21.9 in 1896–1900. In 1896 the average number of children per family was 2.2. This figure does not reveal the very big inequality in fertility between one family and another and the contrasts between one region and another. Brittany, the north, and the eastern part of the Massif Central continued to record a large number of deaths. The death rate hardly varied from 1872–5 (22.4 per thousand) to 1891–3 (22.3 per thousand). Infant mortality remained high until the end of the nineteenth century, especially in the urban and industrial areas. It used to reach a peak in August and September as a result of summer toxicosis and accidents due to lack of supervision. The putting of children out to wet nurses remained another cause of infant mortality.[1] The death rate only started to fall from 1895 onwards thanks to the rise in the standard of living and advances in medicine which caused child mortality to fall. The fact that the death rate remained high while births were decreasing explains why from 1880 onwards the natural increase was less than 100,000 per year. From 1891 to 1895 there were, for the first time, more deaths than births.

The stagnation in the number of births was not peculiar to the towns; Aquitaine and Normandy were affected just as much. It reflected a new conception of life and a new picture of existence. The fertile family, as extolled by the Church, was confronted by the Malthusian family. Parents calculated and looked ahead, concerned to rise socially and to provide a good future for their children. This 'bourgeois' conception of the family spread progressively to all layers of society, reflecting the aspirations of individualism and egalitarianism. The movement particularly affected the lower middle class, the clerks and small employers. It corresponded to the aspirations of a whole society. Consequently those clear-minded people who uttered warnings were preaching in the wilderness.

Elisée Reclus, in his *Nouvelle Géographie universelle* in 1877, saw in the low birth rate a 'cause of weakness' and diagnosed 'a sadly routine attitude to the art of creating resources, a complete lack of confidence in the future'. There is a huge literature deploring the depopulation of the country; it forms an interesting contrast to the indifference of the authorities and of Parliament. In the age of liberalism the idea that the State may have a duty to protect the family was found surprising. Help for large families seemed contrary to equality between one citizen and another. For a long time the defenders of the family were mainly recruited from Catholic, traditionalist circles and their political and social philosophy sufficed to discredit them. The disciples of Le Play, in *La Réforme sociale*, combined the defence of the family with 'counter-revolutionary' demands; they blamed the Civil Code and compulsory sharing for the depopulation, and competed in extolling the authority of the father of the family. Their answer to revolutionary individualism was to praise the virtues of the family, the social unit *par excellence*. The school of *La Réforme sociale* exerted immense influence on the thinking of the conservative right and of 'social' Catholicism, but it remained an isolated current of thought. It was not until the end of the century that there was any real reaction, although it did not have much immediate effect: doctors and republicans in the administration, motivated by patriotism, denounced the dangers of depopulation; and in 1896 Dr Bertillon founded the 'National Alliance for the Increase of the French Population'.

The exodus from the countryside was a continuous phenomenon which affected all regions and all social categories: the small farmers followed the day-labourers. From 1871 onwards more than 100,000 people left the countryside every year. Between 1876 and 1881 the fall in agricultural prices and the phylloxera crisis accelerated the movement: there were more than 160,000 departures per year. On the other hand, after 1880 there was a relative decline. Aquitaine in the south-west, the plateaux of the east of the Parisian Basin, Brittany, and the Massif Central – a pole that was the reverse of magnetic – were particularly affected. There were many different reasons: the attractions of the towns, which offered higher and more regular wages, the difficulties involved in agriculture, the increase in agricultural yields which robbed some country people of their jobs, and the decline of rural industries. Converging factors positively encouraged the movement: better transport facilities, military service, and the part played by members of parliament whose intervention was decisive in finding jobs on the railways and in the post office.

Urban growth was regular but slow. The urban population formed 31.1 per cent of the total population in 1872 and 40.9 per cent in 1901; moreover, in the statistics, any agglomeration of more than 2,000 inhabitants was called a town. The growth, which in any case slowed down at the end of the century, was not comparable with that of neighbouring industrial countries. The salient facts to note are the small number of very big towns, the importance of the small and middle-sized towns and the growing size of Paris – and its suburbs, which now began to develop more quickly than the capital itself. And it is important to note that the development of the big towns was based as much on immigration from the small towns, which acted as half-way houses, as on immigration from the countryside. In Loir-et-Cher, *bourgs* and cantonal centres declined in population; local trade was affected by the vicissitudes of agriculture.

France, an area of low demographic pressure, was not a country from which many people emigrated. Such emigrants as there were often came from frontier regions – the Alpine districts, the Basque country – and were craftsmen or tradesmen, and in any case people moved not through poverty but through the wish to do something and to make their fortunes. On the other hand, there was considerable immigration. There were 800,000 foreigners in France in 1876 and 1,000,000 after 1876. The fact that their number stabilized is deceptive and does not take account of the naturalizations facilitated by the law of 1889. Italians, Belgians, Spaniards and Germans settled in the areas bordering on their homelands or in the big cities and the industrial regions. They were employed in the hardest industrial jobs rather than in agriculture. Competition with French workers, which was noticeable in crisis periods such as the 1880s in Lyon and Marseille, provoked xenophobic reactions.[2] However, these did not produce any measures limiting immigration, which was in fact vital to a country whose population was static.

The working population

	Percentage of the 3 big sectors of the working population (in millions)		Numbers of the 3 big sectors of the working population (in millions)	
	1876	1896	1876	1896
Primary sector agriculture, forests, fishing	49.3	45.3	7,995	8,463
Secondary sector industry	27.6	29.2	4,469	5,452
Tertiary sector	23.1	25.5	3,754	4,749
	100	100	16,218	18,664

Source: Taken from J. Bouvier, in G. Duby, Biblio. no. 35.

In percentage, the primary sector slowly contracted in favour of the secondary and tertiary sectors. But if we analyse the absolute figures, not the relative percentages, we find that the working agricultural population continued to grow in number. If we examine the data relative to the male working population of the primary sector, we should find that the tendency was comparable: 5,146 million in 1856, 5,777 in 1876 and 5,714 in 1896. This qualifies the notion of a rural exodus: 'The French land turns out in fact to have supported a large number of working peasants after more than half a century of industrial development' (J. Bouvier, in G. Duby, Biblio. no. 35). Moreover, the rural exodus affected not simply the peasants, agricultural workers or small farmers but also – and much more – craftsmen and the tradesmen from small *bourgs*: in short, the non-agricultural rural population.

What strikes us then is the rigidity of the working agricultural population and the disproportion between its share of the working population and of the material product. In the decade 1875–84, when the agricultural population accounted for 64 per cent of the population employed in productive activities, agriculture furnished only 43.8 per cent of the total product.[3] These figures demonstrate how poor agricultural productivity was. The purchase power of the agricultural world 'furnished industry with only a poor stimulus to growth'.[4] Thus agriculture acted as a brake on growth. This became particularly evident at the time of the big depression which affected the agricultural world from 1873 to 1896. The decline in productivity brought a drop in the demand for industrial products.

Slowness of growth

Even if they differ on the chronology and in their estimation of the breadth
and causes of the phenomenon, economic historians are agreed in thinking
that in the first decades of the Third Republic the growth of the French
economy slowed down considerably. Growth was rapid up to 1860, then it
slowed, although it remained higher than the average for the century until
about 1880. After 1880 the rate of growth is below the average for the
century; between 1883 and 1896 an incontestable 'tendency to stagnation'
(see F. Crouzet, Biblio. no. 114 and 115) is to be observed. It is true that in
the world economy as a whole prices were falling from 1873 to the end of the
century, but growth was not affected in Germany or the United States as it
was in France. France, once the second largest industrial power, slipped to
fourth place. It has often been said that this lag was due to demographic
stagnation. Yet no causal relationship can be detected between demographic stagnation and economic deceleration. Should we then blame an
insufficiency of investment partly explained by investments abroad, which
by 1880 had risen to 15,000 million? But would these savings have
otherwise gone into productive internal investments? Without doubt the
detrimental effect of the crisis in the agricultural sector should not be
ignored: it added to the problems of industry, which was no longer gaining
sufficient impetus from the urban centres – and urbanization was slowing
down at the end of the nineteenth century. Thus from the 1880s onward
'France was affected for more than fifteen years by one of the most serious
depressions that have ever marked the history of an industrialized nation.'[5]
The annual growth of exports slowed perceptibly after 1875: from 1875 to
1895 it was 0.86 per cent, and the balance of payments was in deficit.
Employers' profits, after growing rapidly in the good years of the Second
Empire, also slowed perceptibly before beginning to rise again from the end
of the nineteenth century (see Bouvier, Furet, Gillet, Biblio. no. 110).
Employers tried to reduce the effects of the drop in prices by increasing
productivity.

Against this background recurring crises stand out, such as that of 1882
which came after the three prosperous years that coincided with the
implementation of the Freycinet plan (see Y. Gonjo, Biblio. no. 117). The
crash of the Union Générale was the most spectacular event of a crisis
which, after that of 1846–51, was 'the most serious one of the nineteenth
century' (E. Labrousse). Backed by the legitimists, Bontoux, 'a poet of the
industrial world', had founded a merchant bank (see J. Bouvier, Biblio. no.
108); it extended its operations towards central Europe and the Danube
region in a somewhat risky fashion and in January 1882 had to suspend
payments. The French banking system was to reorganize itself with a clear
division between deposit banks and merchant banks. The Crédit Lyonnais,

which had been a victim of the consequences of the crash, became a deposit bank and never departed again from extremely cautious management. The metallurgical industry reduced its production. Métallurgie et Charbonnages de la Loire were stagnant. The textile industry was affected, both in Paris and in the rural areas of the west and north-west. In Paris again, the leather, wood and building industries felt the pinch. Ferry's second ministry, by increasing orders for school furniture and by having *lycées* and university departments built, strove to give a fresh impetus to the industry of the capital, where unemployment was spreading. This social malaise favoured Boulangisme and the disenchantment of the lower classes with the opportunist Republic.

However, neither the deceleration of the economy nor the periodic crises should lead us to underestimate the progress of production in absolute terms. Historians, familiar with other rates of growth, have highlighted the slowing-down of the economy. Contemporaries were more sensitive to the changes affecting the world in which they lived, whether it was a question of the very framework of the capitalist economy or of the progress of industry. People were seeing the 'flowering' (Guy P. Palmade) of the capitalist economy's institutions. The manipulation of money was easier. In December 1877 the fixed rate of exchange for the banknote established in August 1870 was abolished. Convertibility was reintroduced. It is true that people still turned for small transactions to the *louis d'or*, which was worth 20 francs, or to the silver crown, worth 5 francs, although since 1873 the minting of silver had been controlled. Although France was theoretically a bimetallist country, confronted with the depreciation of silver it in fact adopted the gold standard.

There was no note smaller than 50 francs in circulation. But for large payments the use of the note spread; there were 2,000 million in circulation in 1871 and 3,000 million in 1890. The circulation increased in step with the cash balance of the Bank of France: 2,000 million in 1882, 3,000 million in 1894. In spite of reservations, the use of written money, of the cheque, spread.

High finance no longer had absolute power but its influence remained considerable – its rôle in public loans has already been mentioned. We find the Rothschilds, the Hottinguers, the Neuflizes and the Mirabauds behind the merchant banks, such as the Bank of Paris founded in 1874. It was at this time that a division of functions – initiated as early as 1870 for the Crédit Lyonnais, but accelerated by the crash of the Union Générale – was established between the deposit banks, specializing in short-term credit operations, and the merchant banks, which concentrated on industrial development (J. Bouvier, Biblio. no. 109).

To the 'risks' of industrial enterprises the cautious Henri Germain preferred 'the results of trade and secured debts. These are the surest assets and the most easily realizable. They must form the counterpart to the deposits of the Crédit Lyonnais.'[7] This concept was to be generally adopted.

Bank deposits grew as a consequence of the development of industry, of the progress of stocks and shares (it was around 1890 that share assets overtook property assets) and of the extension of the banking networks that followed the railways. Banking unity meant the end of a partitioned economy; like the railway, the bank put local life in touch with national life. The Bank of France, the 'keystone' of the system, more and more took on the rôle of central bank for the credit establishments.

Savings were considerable – 2,000 million a year from 1875 to 1893. The low birth rate, an often modest style of life, and a stable currency were invitations to save. Although land and mortgages retained their prestige, stocks with a fixed rate of interest, and first and foremost government stocks, attracted the small saver. The ownership of these stocks was widely spread, thanks to the savings-banks. The more astute capitalist turned to shares with varying rates of interest. The fall in the cost of borrowing money stimulated people to look for foreign shares which brought in more – 5.5 per cent against the 4.1 per cent of French stocks in the 1880s. In 1880 foreign investments accounted for 12,000 to 15,000 million out of the total French personal fortune of 56,000 million (see Guy P. Palmade, Biblio. no. 124).

The physiognomy of French industry was much more like that of the end of the Second Empire than that of the beginning of the twentieth century when growth accelerated again and the chemical, electrical and car industries began to develop. The industrial geography of France in the 1880s was dominated by three groups of activity. In Paris the processing industries and craft activities remained pre-eminent. In the departments of Nord and Pas-de-Calais the coalfields grew rapidly 'without any industrial development on the same scale' (M. Gillet, Biblio. no. 116); but the textile industry – cotton and wool – retained considerable importance. The third group was centered on the Lyon/Saint-Etienne region: mines and metallurgy, but also 'Textile de la Loire' – textile industries dominated by the Rhône metropolis. From 1880–90 a decisive development set in: the centre of French heavy industry began to move from the Saint-Etienne area towards the north and north-east, owing to difficulties in working the Loire coal mines and to changes in the iron and steel industry. On the other hand, the Lyon silk industry remained important. At the end of the nineteenth century, after crises in regional silk-farming, it drew its raw materials from the Near East and the Far East. However, at this point the Lyon/Saint-Etienne agglomeration was in decline; from the 1880s the Lyons financial market lost its autonomy to the advantage of Paris.[6]

As well as these main industrial regions there were various scattered centres, their location dependent on ancient traditions or the presence of a coalfield or a good harbour.

Before 1890 the traditional sectors – textiles and the building trade – retained considerable importance. The metallurgical industries progressed slowly: the production of cast iron was 1.3 million tonnes in 1896, 1.7 tonnes in 1890 and 2.3 tonnes in 1896. Between that date and the beginning of the Great War it was to double. Steel production was 110,000 tonnes in 1869 and 800,000 tonnes in 1890. It reached 1.5 million tonnes in 1900 and was to more than triple by 1914. These figures, while indicating the undeniable size of the transformation after the turn of the century, demonstrate the modest growth of the iron and steel industry before 1900.

Coal production increased, rising from 19.4 million tonnes in 1880 to 33.4 million tonnes in 1900. The small fields of the Massif Central, expensive to work and also disadvantaged by high transport costs, were in relative decline, but Nord and especially Pas-de-Calais, against the prevailing tendency and in spite of the depression, doubled their output between 1873 and 1896. The fact remains that France was the only industrial country which had to import coal regularly in order to satisfy its needs – 9.9 million tonnes in 1880, 11.6 in 1900, or about a third of its total consumption.

Between 1800 and 1890 steel became very much more important than iron. It made the fortune of the metallurgical industry in the centre of the country, which in 1876 made a quarter of the cast iron and steel, 40 per cent of the sheet-iron, 60 per cent of the rails and almost all the high quality steels. Schneider's Le Creusot was the symbol of French metallurgy, 'the biggest factory in France and possibly in Europe', marvelled at by André and Julien, the two young heroes of the *Tour de France par deux enfants*. The first edition of that book came out at the same time as the Universal Exhibition of 1878, at which Le Creusot exhibited a power hammer which caused a sensation. But the price of steel remained high and its production low. Even in 1889 the Eiffel Tower was built of iron. The Thomas and Gilchrist process was to take France into the age of steel. A lining of dolomite on the sides of the converter purifies phosphoric molten iron and makes it possible to produce steel from it. Schneider and Wendel purchased the process in 1890 for 800,000 francs from a Belgian metallurgist who had obtained it for 1,250 francs. With the end of the century the deposits of iron ore in Lorraine were to be mined on a massive scale. Lorraine, which until then had produced poor quality iron for casting, threw itself into the production of cast iron and steel. In 1880 it produced 540,000 tonnes of cast iron and 1,600 tonnes of steel; in 1900 the figures were 1,590,000 tonnes of cast iron and 590,000 tonnes of steel. From then on the iron and steel industry moved eastward.

The textile industries were affected by the depression. Cotton spinning was concentrated in the Vosges, the northern region, the department of

Nord, Lille, Roubaix and Tourcoing. After the loss of Alsace the industrialists of Mulhouse moved their activities to the Vosges, the north and
Normandy. Economic difficulties were to hasten the progress of mechanization. Weaving was more dispersed and mechanization in the industry
less advanced. Resistance to mechanization lasted a long time. The
department of Nord, Roubaix, Tourcoing and Fourmies dominated the
woollen industry.

The trend towards concentration remained slow; small enterprises,
workshops and craftsmen coexisted with advanced forms of integration.
The building trade, the ready-made clothing industry and small-scale
metallurgy never became concentrated. The census of industries made in
1896 shows that 1.3 per cent of industrial establishments had more than
fifty employees; 13.57 per cent had between five and fifty; and 83.93 per
cent had one to four. Even if we take account of the fact that companies
employing more than fifty people comprised 44.75 per cent of the workers,
it remains true that more than 55 per cent of the workers were employed by
companies with less than fifty wage-earners.

The working class

The size of the working class in the French population grew slowly; below 5
million in the 1870s, it was to reach 6 million at the end of the century.
Apart from the north (62.1 per cent of employers in the working population
in 1896), the Parisian region and the south-east, there were no real
concentrations of workers but isolated groups in a largely rural France. The
part played by small enterprises, the contrast between the workers in big
industries and the craftsmen or people who worked at home, and the
differences in qualifications provide only a brief indication of the complexity of the working-class world. Geographical situation and historical
traditions were just as important. In the big cities like Paris or Lyon the
worker enjoyed a fairly free atmosphere; he could change his job without
too much difficulty and he rubbed shoulders with craftsmen, tradesmen
and small employers. In the industrial agglomerations the workers were
crushed by the power of a dominant industry which gave the town its
prosperity; such was the case at Le Creusot, Montceau-les-Mines and
Roubaix. In these places there were scarcely any urban traditions ante-
dating industrialization. Workers and managers confronted each other
undistracted by intermediary points of view. Workers who inherited the traditions of the early nineteenth century, peasants who had
recently arrived in the factory or the mine, with a crude mentality, divided
between passivity and rebellion, miners, metallurgical workers conscious
of forming part of a working-class aristocracy, textile workers, people who
worked at home – the diversities are myriad.

One of the most original workers' corporations, and also one of the best known today precisely because of its originality and specific characteristics, was that of the miners (R. Trempé and M. Gillet, Biblio. nos. 128 and 116). From the departments of Nord and Pas-de-Calais to Saône-et-Loire and Gard, the mining world displayed common features: black country landscapes, monotonous lines of workers' dwellings, and garden cities belonging to the employer. Carmaux is one of the rare exceptions to this rule of tutelage by the mining companies. From the cradle to the grave these companies enclosed the miner and his family in a network of welfare institutions; they gave considerable aid to the Church, building churches and denominational schools. One can understand why in the miners' view the struggle against clericalism and the struggle against the employers went hand in hand.

The National Federation of French Miners was founded in 1892. The miners' trade unionism rapidly became mass trade unionism. The conflicts, such as that at Decazeville in 1886, sometimes look like brutal revolts followed by collapses; this is partly explained by the recruitment of peasants. However, the most remarkable feature of the miners' trade unionism was the corporative egotism which indubitably expressed the 'workers' bloc mentality'. The 'reformism' of the miners,[7] who restricted trade union action solely to making protests, who had confidence in the arbitration of the State and in legislation, and who sought to obtain collective contracts, was due to a number of converging reasons: corporatism played a part in it. Moreover, the law of 1810 on mining concessions permitted the State – and members of parliament were able to remind the government of this – to exert pressure on the companies; and finally the paternalism of the companies had an influence that should not be underestimated. But surely the essential reason was the fact that this kind of trade unionism was not in a minority.

The world of metallurgy did not possess the unity of the mines. What was there in common between the specialist Parisian worker, with his florid complexion, described in Denis Poulot's novel *Le Sublime*, and the metal worker of Le Creusot, whose miserable condition was described by Jules Huret in his *Enquête sur la question sociale*? The specialized metallurgical worker, a waggish individualist proud of his skill and well paid, embodied a sort of aristocracy in the French working-class world – and he may well have been a militant. On the other hand, the iron and steel workers of Le Creusot were subject to the tutelage of Schneider – schools for apprentices, a hospital, pension funds, the policy of enabling people to own property. In the closed world of the small town the voters steadily voted conservative and chose their boss. Yet confronted with the working conditions of 'these thousands of beings throbbing in the jaws of furnaces ... foreheads wet with sweat, eyelids reddened, eyelashes burnt', journalists were amazed at the absence of revolt.

This same question, really a fundamental one, is raised by a recent study of the conditions of the textile workers in Lille at the end of the century (see F. Codaccioni, Biblio. no. 113). These workers were not combative: 37–8 per cent of the workforce consisted of women and children. Observers of the period describe situations which recall the big enquiries into working conditions held in the early nineteenth century. The same Jules Huret went to the rue des Longues-Haies in the centre of Roubaix; he describes the little red-brick houses, the wretched hovels, the unhealthy drains, the weavers' families waiting for help from the relief committee. In the south-east – Loire, Isère, Rhône, Ardèche – the female factory workers were accommodated in dormitories near the workshops. They arrived on Monday mornings from the country with their food and, supervised by nuns, did not leave this boarding school the whole week.

This enables us to understand the success of Jules Guesde and his messianic revolutionary ideas in the textile industry of the department of Nord and at Roanne. But the number of women in the workforce and the absence of a working-class élite in this industry resulted in producing only a small number of militants in comparison with the total number of employees. Among the militants whose names have passed into history textile workers are few and far between. This makes it all the more significant that it was a screw-thread worker, Delory, who became mayor of Lille in 1896.

It may be possible to sketch a few types in the world of the workers in large-scale industry, but the task becomes infinitely more difficult when we come to the workers in small firms, the craftsmen, and the people who worked at home. The building trade, the importance of which remained considerable – the sign of a still traditional economy – was still dominated by the very small firm; in 1891 an employer had, on average, fewer than three workmen.[8] Consequently the wage-earning mason could count on becoming a small employer one day, if he could get a bit of capital together; the building trade allowed a certain rise in the social scale.

Textiles remained the privileged domain of work at home. Home weavers were disappearing in Flanders and the west, but in the big cities the dressmaker, 'the lady with the needle' who worked for the ready-made clothing trade, lived a wretched life. The studies of a philanthropist like the comte d'Haussonville (*Misères et Remèdes*) tell the same story as Jules Simon in his book on the female worker at the end of the Second Empire: poor wages, a long working day with no time limit, unhealthy living conditions.

The workmen employed in a small craft enterprise or working as craftsmen on their own account – the shoemaker, the cabinet-maker, the tailor – did not have the minimum of economic independence on which membership of the middle classes was based. However, they often formed an élite. It is true that not all of them – far from it – attained the enviable

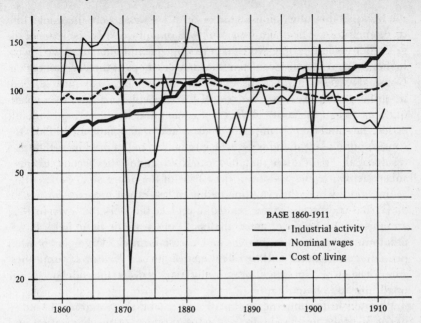

BASE 1860-1911
Industrial activity
Nominal wages
Cost of living

Wages in Paris

Source: J. Rougerie, 'Remarques sur l'histoire des salaires à Paris au XIXe siècle', *Le Mouvement social*, April–June 1968, p. 107.

position of the cabinet-maker from the faubourg Saint-Antoine described in a monograph of 1891, who earned nearly eight francs a day and went to cabarets and theatres, but they shared a tradition of working-class culture. It was they who called vociferously for compulsory lay education, and they also aimed at the development of vocational training, which had been so much neglected in spite of a few efforts due in particular to the initiative of the city of Paris. Whether he was a shoemaker, a tailor, a cabinet-maker or a printer, the small craftsman liked to be a revolutionary. He had been an internationalist, a communard, and he was tempted by anarchism, but as a small independent producer he did not like the idea of collectivism; without even being familiar with them, he hit upon the libertarian intuitions of Proudhon. A son of the *sans-culottes*, he was attached to the tradition of the French Revolution and to the Republic. In his hostility to priests and the 'big-wigs' he had the same attitude as the Jacobin lower middle class. Anarcho-syndicalism, radicalism, 'independent', 'French' socialism, and also a certain degree of nationalism all found a favourable response in these circles.

There is an undeniable diversity in the working class but the unifying features are also clear. Insecurity, a day-to-day life, the absence of savings, the impossibility of gaining access to culture – those were the things that distinguished it. The major insecurity was that of work. In the years of the great depression people were haunted by unemployment. Wages were higher for men than for women in the big workshops of the Parisian region. Nominal wages went on rising – a process that had begun about 1850 – but irregularly. It is true that the cost of living was falling, but, as a consequence of the uncertainty of the employment and the recurring economic crises, the standard of living too was either stagnant or falling.[9] In Paris the consumption of meat and wine, which remained high until about 1880 as a result of the revolution that had occurred under the Second Empire, subsequently declined – one of the effects of the depression.

In regions where the evolution had been less rapid, progress continued. At Carmaux, butcher's meat tended to replace salt pork; but even in 1892 an emissary of *Le Temps* noted that salt pork was the basic food. Pasta, potatoes, sugar, dried vegetables and cheese formed a large part of what people ate. Furniture followed new models, urban instead of rural ones. The chest and the bench were being replaced by the sideboard, the wardrobe and chairs.

We know little about the rhythm of work in workshops and small firms,[10] but it is probable that in big firms the progress of mechanization and stricter organization of the work resulted in a fuller, heavier working day for the workers. After all, for the employer that was a way of fighting against the drop in profits due to the depression.

The process of evolution which turned the miner-peasant of the middle of the nineteenth century into a mining worker has been traced in connection with the miners of Carmaux (R. Trempé Biblio. no. 128). It took some forty years for the farm labourers recruited by the mines to become professionally miners, socially workers and politically malcontents. The miner-peasants practised absenteeism, found it difficult to submit to the general discipline of the firm and did not enjoy obeying the foremen and managers. Between 1870 and 1890 the Carmaux Mining Company worked on these points and succeeded in obliging the miners to work regularly and industriously. Industrial wages overtook agricultural wages; the mode of life became an urban one; the miners became dissatisfied consumers and they had the feeling that the cost of living had increased, whereas prices had been falling for some years; and they turned to buying on credit, which permits immediate enjoyment. This proletarianization of peasants, who became wage-earners and gradually conformed to different rhythms, is typical. It may well be that it was in the last third of the nineteenth century that a real proletariat came into existence in France.

Social legislation remained extremely cautious. All in all, the Second Empire – and the Bonapartists did not fail to note the point – had been less timid. The law of 19 May 1874, the work of the paternal Moral Order government which wished to put a stop to the worst abuses of the liberal régime, forbade the employment of children less than twelve years old. They were not to be in the workshop for more than twelve hours; and night work was forbidden for girls not yet of age and for boys of less than sixteen.[11] A twelve-hour day was normal at that time. It was nearly twenty years before the law of 2 November 1892 finally triumphing over the long resistance of the Senate – that bastion of liberalism – forbade the employment of a child before the age of thirteen, or twelve if he possessed the school leaving certificate. Night work was forbidden and the length of the working day was limited to ten hours before the age of sixteen and eleven hours before the age of eighteen. Women were not to work more than eleven hours a day. These directives were the only ones with a general application issued in the field of labour legislation during the period up to 1898. It would be impossible to find better evidence of the republicans' attachment to economic liberalism. What is more, until 1890, the date of its abolition, the worker's identity card established a juridical inequality between employers and workers. So far as protection of work and social insurance were concerned, there was no legislation at all, whereas from 1883 to 1889 Bismarck's Germany introduced illness, accident, disability and old age insurance. It was only on 9 April 1898 that a law established the principle of the employer's responsibility in the case of an accident at work; in case of incapacity the employer was obliged to pay the worker a lump sum in compensation. One body, the miners, benefited, thanks to the pressure and skill in negotiation of its trade unions, from a statute which offered guarantees: the law of 8 July 1890, which created representatives to supervise the safety of miners, elected for three years by the workers. The law of 29 June 1894 established retirement pensions for miners. It is not surprising that it was in the mines that the first collective agreement between employers and strikers appeared, with the signature in 1891 of the convention of Arras.[12] All in all, the gains were slender. The Republic did not worry much about 'labour questions'; after all, it was based on an alliance between the rural world and the bourgeoisie.

Rural France

As the demographic analysis has already suggested, the France of the end of the nineteenth century remained largely rural. The rural population was 67.5 per cent of the total in 1876 and 61 per cent in 1896. The population living on agriculture fell from 51 per cent in 1876 to 45.5 per cent in 1891. At the same date the working male agricultural population was 45 per cent. The pleasure which republican orators found in extolling the conquests of the small landowners has been described, but in fact big aristocratic and bourgeois property owners maintained their position; in 1882 estates of

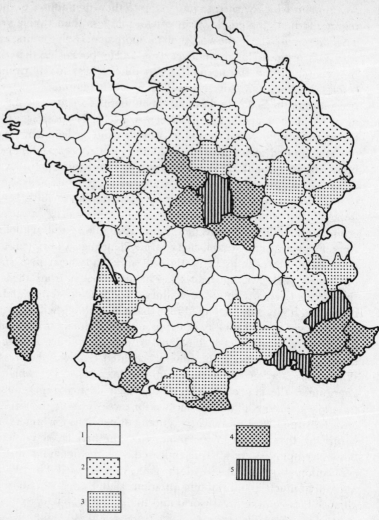

Population occupied in agriculture: the big estate in 1884

Proportion of areas occupied by estates of more than a hundred hectares:
1. Less than 20% 2. From 20% to 29% 3. From 30% to 39% 4. From 40% to 49% 5. More than 50%

Source: Map drawn by G. Dupeux, based on *Documents statistiques sur les cotes foncières* (Imprimerie nationale, 1889). Taken from the *Atlas historique de la France contemporaine 1800–1965*, edited by René Rémond (Paris, A. Colin, 1966).

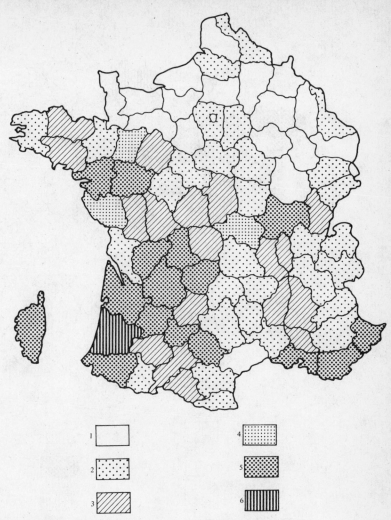

Population occupied in agriculture: share-cropping (métayage) in 1882

Proportion of share-croppers in relation to total cultivators:
1. Less than 1% 2. From 1% to 4% 3. From 5% to 9% 4. From 10% to 18% 5. 23% 6. 46%

Source: Map drawn by G. Dupeux on the basis of the agricultural enquiry of 1882. Taken from the *Atlas historique*.

more than 40 hectares, only 4 per cent in number, covered 45 per cent of the agricultural land. In the west – Vendée, Maine, Anjou, central Brittany, in Sologne, Berry, the Bourbonnais – the big aristocratic estates remained considerable, even though they were affected by the agricultural crisis.

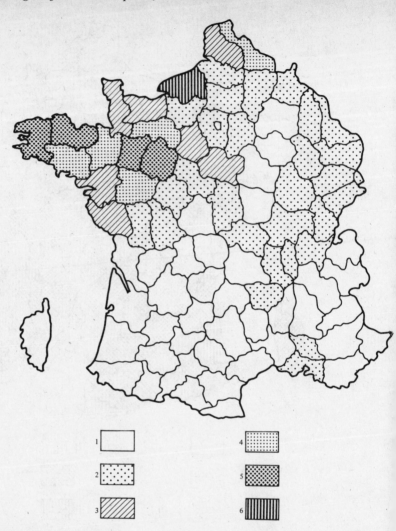

Population occupied in agriculture: tenant farming (*fermage*) in 1882

Proportion of tenant farmers in relation to total cultivators:
1. Less than 10% 2. From 10% to 19% 3. From 20% to 29% 4. From 30% to 39% 5. From 40% to 49% 6. More than 50%

Source: Map drawn by G. Depeux on the basis of the agricultural enquiry of 1882. Taken from the *Atlas historique*.

After 1880, at Mazières-en-Gâtine, M. de Tusseau, the squire, sold part of his land to a bourgeois, the son of a saddler of Melle, deputy for Deux-Sèvres. This is just one example among others of the defeat of the landed aristocracy by the republican bourgeoisie.

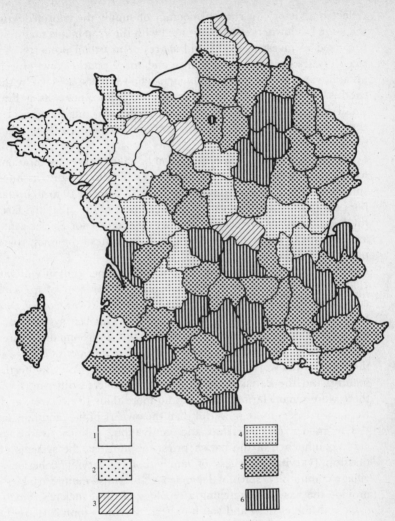

Population occupied in agriculture: direct farming in 1882

Proportion of owner cultivators in relation to total cultivators:
1. Less than 50% 2. From 50% to 59% 3. From 60% to 69% 4. From 70% to
79% 5. From 80% to 89% 6. 90% and more

Source: Map drawn by G. Dupeux on the basis of the agricultural enquiry of
1882. Taken from the *Atlas historique.*

There were many large bourgeois estates near to urban centres; the
industrialists of the department of Nord had properties in Flanders and
those of Rouen in the region of Caux. Nevertheless, the relative proportion
of large properties was falling. But it is difficult to know if this shrinkage

reflected a victory for rural democracy or simply the informed wisdom of the large landowners who, confronted with the drop in incomes from land, preferred to invest in stocks and shares or in urban property. Average-sized estates kept their importance and small estates grew, especially in area; it was the very small landowners who were first affected by the rural exodus. Eastern, south-eastern and southern France was a France of small and average-sized estates. The changes affecting the very large and the very small estates led to a certain 'democratization' of landed property.

The system of cultivation must also be taken into consideration. Here too it is important to rectify conclusions which too readily assumed that small cultivators were predominant. In 1892 farms of 10 to 40 hectares, 20 per cent in number, accounted for 30 per cent of the area; and farms of 1 to 10 hectares, 76 per cent in number, accounted for 23 per cent of the area. Farms of more than 40 hectares, 4 per cent of the total, covered 47 per cent of the cultivated ground.

Although direct farming was prevalent – 80 per cent of cultivators in 1882, 75 per cent in 1892 – in fact only 53 per cent of the land was cultivated directly by owner-occupiers; 36 per cent was worked by tenant farmers and 11 per cent by share-croppers. This last system was wide-spread in the west, the south-west and the Bourbonnais, where land-owners and general farmers relieved the share-cropper of a large part of the fruits of his work. Tenant farming was dominant in the north, Normandy, and the Parisian region. The term covered differing situations; there were tenant farmers working no more than 10 hectares, and there were big farmers more powerful than the owners of the land they farmed.

The modes of ownership and cultivation, political traditions, the varying influence of the parish priest or minister, the systems of rela-tionship (varying closeness of family bonds, varying cohesion of the village community, spirit of dependence[13]) form so many variables which provide the basis for sketching a typology of rural societies. Small land-owners in the eastern and south-eastern provinces founded a republican democracy, as hostile to reaction and the traditional notables as it was to the social revolution. These peasants – in Lorraine, in Savoy – were practising Catholics, or at any rate respectful towards the Church, but they did not follow the clergy on the political level and distrusted the Church's intervention in this field.

On the other hand, hostility to the Catholic Church and loyalty to the Republic were inseparable in the old lands of the Montagne of 1849 – in the Limousin, for example, where de-Christianization was of long stand-ing and went deep. In the Charentes, in Saône-et-Loire and in Yonne, a similar anti-clericalism was to be found and it led very quickly to rad-icalism. In the Cévennes or Drôme, the Protestant small landowners also voted for the advanced republicans out of denominational opposition and loyalty to the critical spirit of Calvinism.

But small properties were not linked solely to leftist political tempera-ments. Alongside republican or anti-clerical democracies there were also quite a few 'clerical' democracies, in which the influence of the Church was decisive. The vote for the established order in Béarn, the Basque country and Aveyron is to be explained by the desire to defend religion not by the influence of the notables whose authority could, on occasion, be success-fully challenged. The most remarkable case in this respect was that of Léon to the north of Brest, where in 1897 a 'democratic' priest, abbé Gayraud, as a result of an alliance between the village 'rectors' and the peasants, trium-phed over a monarchist supported by the châteaux, the comte de Blois. The success of abbé Lemire at Hazebrouck in 1893 was due to the same assertion of Christian democracy, hostile both to the secular spirit of the French Revolution and to the conservative notables.

As against these rural democracies, which in certain cases – in Nor-mandy for example – were more interested in business and the satisfaction of material interests than in politics, there were regions where the system of property and cultivation created durable hierarchies: accepted in the west, for example, in the interior of Brittany, Maine-et-Loire and Vendée. André Siegfried, in his *Tableau politique de la France de l'Ouest* (Biblio. no. 73), has provided the classical description of the interdependence of squires and share-croppers and of the patronage exercised by the nobles. However, in his explanations, he was led to overestimate the influence of the large landowners on the peasants. Unable to imagine, by and large, that the 'people' have other than a leftist bias, he concluded that the combined weight of the aristocrat and the priest distorted the results of universal suffrage. The whole question can be summed up as the acceptance by a whole peasantry of the tutelary authorities. And in the woodland areas people still remembered the terrible republican columns, the cult of the *chouans* and the martyrs of the counter-revolution.

Elsewhere, on the other hand, social superiors were challenged, in spite of their economic power, and the peasants refused to accept the traditional hierarchy. In the Allier, as described in Emile Guillaumin's novel, *La Vie d'un simple*, or Daniel Halévy's *Visite aux paysans du Centre*, small share-croppers were dependent on non-resident large landowners represented by despised farmers-general. Not very amenable to the influence of the Church, the peasants of the Bourbonnais were republicans out of hostility to the conservative large landowners. By the end of the century socialist ideas had met with success in the rural world. Cher and Indre underwent a comparable development. In the south-west, a region of share-cropping and small farms, and one that was not very religious, democratic Bonap-artism had taken solid root and had networks of adherents. It was only at the end of the century that the people, by-passing the stage of opportunist republicanism, were to become radicals.

Finally, the capitalist development of the big farms of northern France and the Parisian Basin produced many of the features of a very modern agriculture, with rich farmers on one side and agricultural labourers on the other. These not very excitable regions, favourable to established authority, gradually moved from the Empire to the moderate Republic; it was the same in Loir-et-Cher, where victory went to the 'satisfied' people hostile both to 'reaction' and 'revolution', attached to 1789 and the Civil Code (see G. Dupeux, Biblio. no. 71).

At the end of the century agriculture experienced serious difficulties, faced as it was with competition from foreign products. The phenomenon particularly affected producers of cereals, but also those of wool, hemp and silk, and contemporary observers were keen to seek the reasons for this agricultural 'crisis'. The fall in selling-prices was considerable: the hundredweight of corn, which fetched over 30 francs under the Empire, fell below 25 francs after 1882 and to 18.20 francs in 1895. And corn was the most commercialized product. Agricultural incomes, rising until the 1880s, were depressed until after 1895. Income from land diminished; landowners struggled in vain, trying to replace rents fixed in kind with rents fixed in money. The agricultural wage-earner resisted; as E. Labrousse has put it, 'The lord of the soil triumphed.' The fact remains that the increase in needs gave rise to a feeling of frustration, which was increased by the more perceptible rise in the income of the owner farmer. In fact, all round, the profit of the independent farmer withstood the depression better than the day-labourer's wages or the absentee landlord's income. Thus the movement in incomes consolidated a peasant middle class.

The 'great depression' involved a big fall in the value of rural property; from 1882 to 1892, the dates of the decennial enquiries, it was 18 per cent for arable land and 20 per cent for meadow and grassland. The fall was greater in the regions affected by the rural exodus – the south-west and the eastern part of the Parisian Basin. It was less marked in the north, the Ile-de-France and Brittany, where strong demographic pressure increased the value of the land. The fall in income from land and in the value of land led the landowner who did not cultivate his land to change his investments, to prefer stocks, bonds and urban property to landed property. But small and medium farmers, whether they owned their land or not, stabilized and improved their situation. The protective measures introduced in 1885 and reinforced in 1892 and 1897 were particularly advantageous to big farmers; but they also put a brake on the exodus from the countryside and provided support for the small and medium peasantry.

A real crisis struck wine-growing – the disease of phylloxera, an insect whose larvae caused the vine to die. From 1876 onwards the disease spread

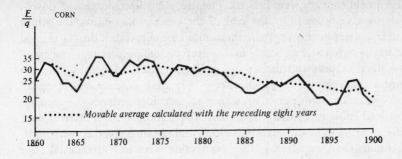

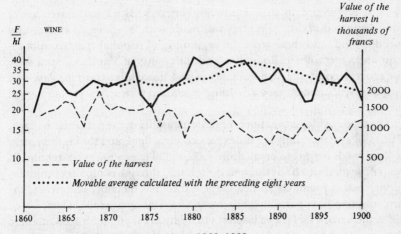

The movement of agricultural prices, 1860–1900

Note: as a consequence of the reduction of production owing to phylloxera, the significant curve is that showing the value of the harvest.

Source: P. Barral, *Les Agrariens français, de Méline à Pisani* (Paris, A. Colin, 1968), p. 70.

very rapidly. It produced a profound change in the geography of the vine, hitherto grown in most parts of the country. The crisis accelerated the exodus from the countryside, greatly reduced the purchase price of small vineyards and resulted in the concentration of viticulture in large estates. Some old vineyards disappeared – the back hills of Burgundy, the Yonne, the Aube, the Haute-Marne – and the vineyards of the Jura, of Lorraine and of the Charentes were severely affected. The only remedy was to graft French slips on to more vigorous American roots. The vines spread to the low plains of Languedoc, for it was thought for some time that flooding the plants enabled them to avoid the disease. In Bas-Languedoc the large estate tightened its hold. After some years of mediocre harvests, in the last few years of the century the threat of over-production appeared.

Technical changes were limited. The use of fertilizers increased slowly. Tools were improved. By the end of the nineteenth century the wheel plough was used everywhere; made completely of metal, it throws the soil alternately to left and right and makes deep ploughing possible. The use of harvesters, reapers and threshing-machines spread. In Loir-et-Cher the clearest progress was made between 1873 and 1882. As G. Dupeux observes, in stagnant periods recourse to machines reduces the employment – which is expensive – of human labour. Progress was often slower; many harvests were still cut with scythes and the corn threshed with flails. All round, changes affecting the countryside were less substantial than under the Second Empire.

Corn production increased through better yields while the area under corn decreased slightly. Progress was made with forage crops and natural meadowland, and there were the beginnings of regional specializations – fruit and vegetables in Roussillon and the county of Vaucluse. Such were the general trends; the predominance of traditional mixed farming gave way only slowly to modern mixed farming organized with a view to commercial profit.

The mode of life, the manners and the mentality of the peasants changed. The railways, especially the little cross-country lines, and the improvement of local roads helped to break down isolation. The town was nearer and its way of life made itself felt through the schools, through compulsory military service and through cheap newspapers. People's diets became richer; the consumption of sugar, butcher's meat and wine increased. When, about 1880, the hero of *La Vie d'un simple* is visited by his nephew, an accountant in Paris, wine and steaks are put on the table instead of grilled bacon. When the guests depart, the cowherd says to the maid, 'I should have liked the Parisians to stay longer; we ate better.' The poor dwellings improved in regions which were growing richer – in the Ambert area, for example, where cattle-rearing brought in a good deal of money. Lucien Gachon notes that fine farms with 'tiled roofs' were replacing the wretched 'straw hovels'.[14] Local costumes began to disappear; mail-order catalogues from the big stores imposed urban styles on the country people.

Another change affected the rural world – the development, in a limited way, of the spirit of association. The representation of professional interests had long been in the hands of the conservative or republican notables. The former, meeting in the Société des Agriculteurs de France, established at the end of the Second Empire, consisted mainly of large landowners who spent the winter in their Parisian drawing-rooms. The Société Nationale d'Encouragement à l'Agriculture, set up on the initiative of the republicans, also consisted of landowners. After the law of 1884 had been passed, agricultural trade unions were created in the wake of the two above-mentioned organizations. The Union Centrale des Syndicats Agricoles de

France (with offices in the rue d'Athènes in the building belonging to the Société des Agriculteurs de France) vegetated until 1900. It embraced most of the trade unions and is said to have had 600,000 members at the end of the century, a substantial figure when compared with that of the members of the workers' unions. However, it is not a very significant figure, for many of the members regarded the trade union primarily as a body which made possible the group purchase of agricultural tools, fertilizers and seed.

The most active organization was the Union du Sud-Est des Syndicats Agricoles. Founded in 1888, by 1900 it embraced 150 trade unions and counted 60,000 members. It preached the reconciliation and union of classes on the lines of the social Catholicism and corporatism of the marquis de la Tour du Pin. It was headed by Emile Duport, a landowner from the Beaujolais, and Hyacinthe de Gailhard-Bancel, a landowner from Allex in the Drôme, a former member of the Oeuvre des Cercles and later 'White' deputy for Ardèche. Before the end of the century priests in the north, in Franche-Comté, in Béarn and at Tarbes created agricultural unions motivated by a concern for pastoral and social action.

The unions attached to the republicans developed more slowly. Prefects and sub-prefects, schoolmasters and local professors of agriculture favoured these creations – Garola, for example, in Eure-et-Loir, who was secretary of the Chartres union for thirty years. Among its members were the big republican tenant farmers who elected the moderate republican Paul Deschanel.[15] Unlike the workers' organizations, these associations were 'mixed' and theoretically open to all. They aimed at promoting 'the union of the classes and social peace' according to their leaders, who were all 'notables who did not belong to the rural masses: sometimes large landowners, sometimes parish priests, sometimes trained republican activists' (P. Barral).

Trade unions of agricultural wage-earners which presented the claims of a particular class remained few and far between. In 1892 the agricultural proletariat, much affected by the exodus from the countryside, numbered 1,800,000 farm employees and 621,000 day-labourers who did not own land. In spite of the rise in wages their situation remained extremely poor. But isolated and dependent as they were, they were in no position to attack their employers. Only the case of the woodcutters of the centre, of Cher and of Nièvre was different; from 1881 to 1895 they formed unions which forced concessions out of the wood merchants.[16]

Bourgeois France

At the top of the social ladder reigned the upper middle class. The aristocracy still had a prestige in 'society' which should not be under-estimated, but it retained social power only to the extent that it had merged with the upper middle class. Matrimonial alliances and the acceptance of directorships made this merger possible. It was through the banks and industry, the liberal professions and the service of the State that the power of the upper middle class was established. Reference is often made to the 'kings' of the economy, heirs to the 'bourgeois dynasties' that managed to maintain their influence through all the nineteenth century's changes of government. Léon Say, a big shareholder in the Northern Railway Company and Minister of Finance at the beginning of the Republic, was the grandson of the liberal economist of that name. Casimir-Périer, who in 1894 acceded to the supreme magistracy, was a big shareholder in the Anzin Company, one of the descendants of le Périer de Vizille. There was a tremendous gap between the fortunes of the ruling classes and those of the other social classes. And it does not look as if this gap grew any smaller during this period. A study of Lille society at this time notes the concentration of wealth from 1873 to 1891, the years of economic difficulty; 10 per cent of those who died possessed 92.08 per cent of the total wealth (see F. Codaccioni, Biblio. no. 113). In the pyramid of fortunes the base was extremely wide while the summit looked more like a slender needle.[17]

This business middle class had a fringe of people from the liberal professions – well-known surgeons, highly respected lawyers, successful barristers. Waldeck-Rousseau, a much sought-after commercial lawyer, a scion of the Nantes bourgeoisie, found a niche for himself in the upper middle class of Paris. This upper middle class did not turn up its nose at the idea of serving the State or working in the civil service. This was much more out of a sense of tradition than from any wish to make a profit out of the State; heir to the jurists and civil servants of the monarchy, the French bourgeoisie regarded public service as a very honourable profession. The purge carried out by the republicans after their victory did not put an end to the dominance of the upper middle class in the senior posts of the civil service, and even after the purge of the Council of State in 1879 the great majority of the magistrates and half the appeal judges belonged to the aristocracy or the upper middle class, although the proportion falls to a quarter for the councillors among whom representatives of the 'new strata (of society)' figured prominently.[18] The recruitment competitions for the top services – the Inspection of Finances, the Council of State, the Court of Auditors – ensured the power of the bourgeoisie. These competitions were to some extent a process of co-option. Preparation for them was undertaken by the Free School of Political Sciences founded by Emile Boutmy, under the patronage of Taine, immediately after the defeat 'in order to create the élite which step by step will set the tone for the whole nation'. A bastion of liberal thought, the School of Political Sciences numbered among its very first subscribers Jacques and Jules Siegfried, P. Hély d'Oissel, Adolphe d'Eichtal, Henri Germain and Casimir-Périer – a business and finance 'cabal'. Léon Say, the economists Emile Levasseur and Paul Leroy-Beaulieu, the historian Albert Sorel and senior civil servants such as René Stourm all taught at the establishment, which took up residence in 1881 at 27 rue Saint-Guillaume.

Can one speak, in spite of the attraction of Paris, of a provincial 'grande bourgeoisie'? Henri Germain, the founder of the Crédit Lyonnais, pursued the second half of his career in Paris. Another native of Lyon, Bonnardel,[19] the founder of the Compagnie Générale de Navigation Le Havre–Paris–Lyon–Marseille (*HPLM*), also settled in Paris at 44 avenue des Champs-Elysées. On the other hand, Edouard Aynard, governor of the Bank of France, president of the Lyon Chamber of Commerce, a man who was both solemn and fond of good living, was a typical product of his native city. He was attached to economic liberalism and to the principle of free exchange so dear to the silk fraternity. At the Collège d'Oullins, on which Lacordaire had left his mark, he learned to be a liberal Catholic. Convinced of the value of private enterprise for resolving 'la question sociale', he called upon employers 'to practise the social duties. Self-interest itself can benefit from so doing.' A republican and a Catholic, he became a deputy in 1889 and opposed both the radicals and the intransigent Catholic right. The latter was represented by another bourgeois figure, Joseph Rambaud. A director of the Mining Company of Roche-la-Molière and of the Foundry and Forge Company of Terrenoire, La Voulte and Bessèges, he was also an important landed proprietor. He busied himself with re-afforestation at Yzeron, followed the fortunes of his vines at Lantignié and farmed at Vaugneray, where he was vice-president of the agricultural committee for thirty-one years and mayor from 1882 to 1892 (see L. de Vaucelles, Biblio. no. 136). The father of twelve children, he questions himself in his *Livre de famille* on the responsibilities and duties of property owners. In his view, a fortune honestly won, wisely managed and augmented by daily work is one of God's ways of calling its owner to fresh duties; the divine approbation consecrates the successful man to the service of the Church and to good works. Although he does not question economic liberalism he denounces the spirit of the Revolution and political liberalism; in this he is opposed to a man like Aynard.

In the north the employers reached the zenith of their success around 1880. This curious world, whose caste feeling was asserted at the end of the century, was characterized by a completely dynastic conception of the firm, the identification of family interests with those of the company and an austere mode of life. 'Business, religion, family' formed an 'indissoluble trinity'.[20] Just as it has been found possible to trace a link between puritanism and capitalism, so the same link – the example from the north confirms that from Lyon – exists between a certain kind of Catholicism and capitalism. Success in business is a sign of divine protection and it imposes its own duties – to be self-financing in order to ensure the independence and the expansion of the firm, and to behave magnificently towards the workers in order to correct the excesses of liberalism. The Descamps, the Delesalles, the Tiberghiens, the Mottes, the Prouvosts and the Dansettes formed a secret world shut in on itself. Here again there was no uniformity of behaviour in political matters. A man like Eugène Motte, the successful rival of Guesde at Roubaix in 1898, was a republican; Ribot and Waldeck-Rousseau supported his campaign. Much more than a mere difference in emphasis separated him from people like Plichon or Dansette who were attached to the Orleanist tradition but were themselves very far from the intransigent Catholics who, inspired by the Jesuits of the house of retreat at Mouvaux, founded the Catholic Association of Northern Employers.[21]

Further analyses would confirm these examples. It is true that the upper middle class displays some common characteristics: the size of their fortunes – but not their activities; their mode of life – but not their tastes; their concern for order in business, in the streets and in the State, their anxiety to keep their distance from the people, a moral attitude based on the certainty of individual success. But there were ideological divisions which involved two opposing conceptions of the world and of man. Some continued to believe in the Enlightenment, in progress, and professed an optimistic view of the evolution of society. Therefore they did not separate themselves entirely from the third estate in its confrontation with traditional élites, and they were loyal to the spirit of the French Revolution. Others were more conservative than liberal, more attached to order in society than to the freedom of the individual, and they professed a pessimistic view of history supported by the teaching of the Church and by experience. Where the Orleanist formula – order and freedom – and the positivist motto – order and progress – were concerned, they were keener on the first term in each phrase than on the second. And this lies at the root of that division between the centre parties which is certainly one of the keys to the history of the Third Republic.

It is relatively easy to trace the frontier which separated the upper middle class from the ordinary middle class. The scale of incomes establishes a primary distinction.[22] About 1880 it is reckoned that some 700 to 800 persons enjoyed an income of at least 250,000 francs (see G. P. Palmade, Biblio. no. 124, p. 253); among them were some large landowners. It is said that in the 1890s 3,000 persons had incomes over 100,000 francs, while there were 185,000 with between 10,000 and 100,000 francs. It can be seen that the upper fringe of this second category (9,800 persons seem to have had an income over 50,000 francs) would have formed part of the upper middle class if it had also acquired social influence and important responsibilities in government service or business.

The ordinary middle class did not really extend below the limit of an income of 100,000 francs, although some members of the lower fringe can be said to belong to it by their mode of life and by their scale of values, if not by their income. It comprised bankers in small towns, industrialists with average-sized enterprises, merchants; but it consisted above all either of the 'independent' bourgeoisie – unemployed 'landlords', members of liberal professions – or of the bourgeoisie which lived, at least partly, on salaries – magistrates, officers, engineers, teachers. The 'independent' bourgeoisie might be connected with industrial or commercial enterprises, but the income from these did not provide either the main part of its fortune or its authority. It remained alien to large-scale capitalism, did not like borrowing and regarded the soil as the real source of respect. Most towns had their 'landlords', who lived 'nobly', retired from active life, looking after a fortune which combined land, shares in real estate, state bonds or railway debentures and often urban property. They might play an important part in local life as members of learned societies or academies, of conservative committees and Catholic benevolent societies, of masonic lodges and republican committees.

The number of lawyers remained stable and quite a few barristers did not plead, resting content with the title; on the other hand, the medical profession made considerable progress. The abolition in 1892 of the diploma of 'Health Officer' was to put an end to second-class medicine. With exceptions, the doctor did not amass a large fortune but, like the chemist, he enjoyed great consideration. Both men of science, they had faith in progress and they were frequently to be found in the republican, or even radical, ranks. Emile Combes, a doctor in the Charentes, gained the sympathy of the electors by dispensing free medicine. He was thus enabled to defeat the Bonapartist, first in the general council and later in the Senate.

The numbers of the salaried bourgeoisie increased with the development of the civil service and the economy. Magistrates were poorly remunerated – to defend the social order it was fitting to have some money of one's own. Magistrates were long tied to the conservative world. Senior civil servants and departmental heads of services, some of the secondary school teachers, officers – even though 'military society' had its own ideals and aristocratic code of values – and engineers also formed part of this bourgeoisie.

Between this 'ordinary bourgeoisie' and the people came the immense 'bourgeoisie in embryo' of the lower middle classes. These were characterized by their desire to become part of the bourgeoisie but because of an inadequate income, the mediocrity of their education or their proximity to somewhat lowly origins they were only on the fringe of the bourgeoisie. It was the absence of manual work which distinguished them, in the full sense of the term, from the popular strata. The small building contractors, the small employers, the independent craftsmen, the retail shopkeepers rarely had the minimum of education which makes the bourgeois, but they had the economic independence which the worker lacked. They were the enemies of the Treasury, of the civil servants and also of the 'big' people – big stores, big industrial enterprises. They seem to have been particularly affected by the big depression. Their sympathies were with radicalism, less willingly with socialism, which is hostile to free enterprise. Xenophobic nationalism and anti-semitism, which protected small businesses, were to find a favourable response in this social group.

The category of wage-earners – average clerks and civil servants – increased as the proportion of independent lower middle class people tended to diminish. Clerks in banks, insurance companies and big business houses, and accountants differed in dress – the 'white collar' – and style of dwelling from the workers, who were sometimes better paid. Junior civil servants, post office employees, primary school teachers and tax-collectors were paid little, but they had stable employment, 'acquired rights' and a pension.[23] A modest education, that provided by the primary or sometimes the 'senior' primary school, enabled the son of a peasant, a small trader or a craftsman to become a civil servant. It was the good fortune of the Republic, and one of the reasons why it took root, to have thus offered numerous jobs to a social stratum anxious to rise in the world.

It was via the lower middle classes, who came much more from the peasantry than from the world of the workers, that the 'people' turned into the bourgeoisie. We should perhaps mention the rôle of the *bourg* or the small town, an intermediate stage in the exodus from the countryside, and that of the school, better attended by the peasant's son, who had no obligation to take over a farm that was too small, than by the worker's son, whose additional wage was indispensable. The peasant's son was a school-teacher or a clerk; his grandson could become a doctor or a graduate of a technical college and thus join the bourgeoisie proper. The lower middle classes were a half-way stage between the rural population and the élites. Birth control made possible a certain renewal of the latter. The success of some was the basis of the persistent desire for self-improvement which was felt by all.

Thus in spite of the enormous differences in incomes the bourgeois shared the same scale of values. They kept away from anything 'popular'. The man was attentive to his dress; the starched collar and the hat were indications of respectability. The bourgeois made plans, lived in the future, made calculations and kept accounts. The family budget was managed with scrupulous attention. Every day the mistress of the house noted her expenditure, which was checked at the end of the month by her husband, who gave her a monthly allowance (see M. Perrot, Biblio. no. 125). An uncle would give his niece an account book as a wedding-present. The account book reflects the preoccupations of people who have reserves. As André Siegfried has noted, it is the psychological key to the bourgeois universe. The servants' wages, modest though they were, represented an appreciable proportion of the budget. Here we surely touch not only on one of the most substantial – and least well known – social realities of the age, but also on an external sign that one belonged to the bourgeoisie. It was the same with houses; contrary to current opinion, the rent took a considerable part of income, almost as much as food; in a third of the sample budgets studied it exceeded 15 per cent of expenditure. A third burdensome section of the budget was the education of the children. Secondary education had to be paid for; a day boy at a Parisian *lycée* had to pay annual fees of 300 francs in 1873, 450 francs at the end of the century, and 720 francs in a good private establishment.

Taxes were low: a middle-class man in a liberal profession with an annual income of 20,000 francs paid 2 per cent of it in taxes. The tax on land hit rural fortunes fairly hard, but the urban bourgeoisie was protected by a fiscal system which did not include a tax on income. If the bourgeois could count, he saved money. The stability of the currency invited him to do so, as did the absence in those days of a system of pensions for educated people. A doctor or an engineer would retire in his fifties without his standard of living suffering. The France of that period contained several hundred thousand people living on unearned incomes; many were small investors who had emerged from the lower middle classes.

A certain concept of family life, and the place it gave to women, was also typical of bourgeois society. Conservatives of the time liked to assert that the individualism bred by the Revolution had undermined the family, but in fact family feeling had changed rather than weakened. The bourgeois family looked inward, concentrating on the child and his future. It was a family of limited births, anxious to rise in the world through birth control and saving. It was more oppressive for the child than the working-class family and it was hateful to those who rebelled against it. 'The whole energy of the couple is directed towards furthering a voluntarily reduced posterity' (Philippe Ariès). The concern for family honour and for the dignity of life was considerable; Jules Siegfried deplored Gambetta's celibacy and urged him to marry before coming into power. The middle-class woman did not work; to do so would be a sign that she had come down in the world or that she wished to subvert her own class.

All in all, from the early days of the Third Republic to the end of the century, French society only changed in a limited way; the inequalities between different social groups remained unchanged. The small and medium peasantry and the 'new strata' who made possible the republican victory did not expect the régime to effect a profound transformation of social relations, but to put an end to the political influence of the traditional hierarchies and to provide the possibility of rising in the social scale. Did the opportunist Republic correspond to their expectations?

3

The period of Jules Ferry, 1879–1885

In the Waddington ministry, formed on 4 February 1879, Jules Ferry became Minister of Education; on 30 March 1885 the second Ferry cabinet was overthrown by the news of the Lang Son disaster. During those six years Ferry was Minister of Education for five years and Prime Minister for three years, two months and twenty-five days. Even if we take into account that Ferry was Prime Minister on two separate occasions, first from September 1880 to November 1881 and then from February 1883 to 30 March 1885, this stability was remarkable; it recurs only in the time of Méline and in those of the Republican Defence and of the left Bloc. Bothered little by the opposition of the extreme left and the right, the governing republicans, in spite of their divisions, founded the lay, democratic Republic, maintained the liberal State and took decisive initiatives in the colonial field. The deputy for the Vosges was one of the main architects of this policy. After Gambetta's failure and death, it was certainly Ferry who was the visible embodiment of the regime.

The political forces

The extreme left

Once victorious, the republicans were to split up. The radicals went over to the opposition. It is true that in the 1876 elections, at Marseille, Naquet, considering Gambetta too moderate, had already suggested forming 'a group to form the advance guard in the fight for democracy' which would agitate for the revision of the constitution and the Belleville programme. But the struggles of 16 May and then the anxiety to conquer the Senate muted these disagreements. Naquet himself proclaimed 'the complete and absolute union of the republicans until the senatorial elections'. Henceforth, on the other hand, the radicals marked their hostility to the governments which were to succeed each other. Freycinet alone briefly found favour with the most moderate of them in 1880 and 1882. These formed the parliamentary group of the radical left, founded after the 1881 elections with Floquet and Allain-Targé. This paradoxical name in fact covered a group on the right of radicalism. A range of shades led from the intransigents (there were some twenty of these, headed by Clemenceau) to the radical left, even to those radicals who supported both the extreme left group and Gambetta's Republican Union. Part of the radical family retained some affinities with Gambetta and his supporters, but on the other hand all the radicals were unanimous in detesting Ferry, who in their view embodied reaction.

As for their number, Jacques Kayser, who has studied the voting in great detail, reckons that in 1879 (Biblio. no. 57) there were about a hundred of them. They consisted of deputies for Paris, the Rhône valley and the Mediterranean Midi – Saône-et-Loire, Rhône, Drôme – plus one or two isolated deputies and about ten for the 'red' departments of the western and northern edge of the Massif Central. The big cities and the country districts which secured the success of the socialist democrats in 1849 were the radical bastions in the early days of the Third Republic. The links with the socialist democrats were all the stronger in that the men were sometimes the same; it would be wrong to think that the radicals were younger than the rest of the republicans. A recent study shows that in Haute-Loire the republican leaders made their début under the Second Republic.[1] Jules Maigne, who was elected deputy for Brioude in 1866, had been deported after 13 June 1849. Barodet, who was so typical of the group, had been a schoolmaster at Louhanc in the Ain; he was dismissed in 1849. Madier de Montjau, one of the spokesmen in the Chamber, was one of the *montagnards* of 1848.

Like the *montagnards* of the Second Republic, the radicals wanted a 'democratic and social' Republic. They demanded the revision of the constitution and the abolition of institutions emanating from monarchical parliamentarianism – the Senate and the presidency of the Republic. Like Gambetta at Belleville, they demanded administrative decentralization, the election of judges and the separation of the Church and State. They demanded the ratification of the constitution by the people (as Clemenceau did in the *XVIIIe arrondissement* in 1881) the responsibility of the elected deputy to his electors and a binding mandate. It was Barodet who in 1881 secured the adoption in principle of the publication of a profession of faith by successful candidates. Thus the radicals preserved something of the ideal of direct democracy dear to the *sans-culottes*. They wanted to found social democracy by a progressive tax on incomes. In the face of business interests they accepted a certain amount of intervention by the State in the economy through the 'revision of contracts that had alienated public property – mines, canals, railways'. They preached limited social reforms – reduction of the legal duration of work, 'pension funds for the old and for those disabled at work' – but they wanted recognition of the legal standing of workers' trade unions. They thus hoped to retain the sympathy of the workers and to respond to the challenge of the socialists; significantly, the republican committee which supported Clemenceau in 1881 added the adjective 'socialist' to the word 'radical'.

For many years socialism was non-existent on the parliamentary level, but it gradually re-acquired a modest importance in the country. However, at a time when the German Empire had a powerful social Democratic Party, France had only small groups whose history is confused and whose influence was minimal. The suppression of the Commune was partly responsible for this situation. Those convicted were not pardoned until 1879 and the amnesty was only voted, at Gambetta's insistence 'to avoid the loss of Paris', on the eve of the first *fête nationale*, officially celebrated on 14 July 1880.[2]

Two points should be emphasized: the slow introduction of Marxism; and the persistence of divisions. The first series of Jules Guesde's newspaper, from November 1877 to July 1878, had as its subtitle *Socialist Republican Newspaper*; the second series, which started in January 1880, proclaimed itself a 'revolutionary collectivist organ'.[3] Between the two series the Socialist Workers' Congress of France was held at Marseille in October 1879. It brought together delegates from the trade unions and by 73 votes to 27 adopted a Marxist programme, declaring its support for collectivism. The congress denounced the illusion of co-operation, of the alliance of capital and labour. *L'Egalité* attacked the radicals. In 1880 the congress of Le Havre adopted a programme that can be ascribed to Marx and Guesde. The actual texts of Marx were scarcely known: it was only in 1885 that the weekly journal of the Workers' Party (*Parti ouvrier*) published a complete translation of the *Manifesto*. It was reproduced the following year in *La France socialiste*, a book by the journalist Mermeix, who was soon to become a Boulangist. Guesde and his companion Lafargue, a more original thinker, tirelessly popularized the main themes of Marxism – capitalist exploitation, the class struggle, the ineluctable march towards collectivism. The conviction that the revolution was near was the basis of the messianic intransigence of the Guesdists. In the textile industry at Roanne, Reims, Troyes and Roubaix, among the iron and steel workers and the miners at Montluçon or Commentry the impact of Guesdism can still be seen.

The defeat of the party's candidates in the elections of 1881 caused a split. The conflict concerned the organization of the party – was it to be unitary or federal? – and tactics – were they to be revolutionary or reformist? At Saint-Etienne in 1882 the minority broke with the 'possibilists' who wanted to split up their aims 'to the point of making them possible' and to practise 'the politics of the possible'. The Guesdists formed the *Parti ouvrier*, while Doctor Brousse and his friends set up in 1883 the Federation of Socialist Workers (*Fédération des travailleurs socialistes – FTS*).

They were not very far from the advanced radicals; for them the struggle for the Republic took priority over the class struggle. They preserved good relations with the trade union world. The groups embraced by the regional federations of the *FTS* were study circles or trade union associations. Their influence was considerable among Parisian artisans and in the small industrial centres close to the rural world.

It was in this same world, in which the tradition of the secret societies and of the revolutionary days was still alive, that the disciples of Blanqui, Granger, Edouard Vaillant and Eudes founded in 1881 – after the amnesty – the Central Revolutionary Committee, a closed group which only later became a political formation. Often confused by outsiders with the socialists, the anarchist 'companions' differed profoundly from them in their rejection of politics. Via Bakunin and the Jura Federation, and also through Kropotkin, anarchist ideas circulated particularly in the south-east, inside little groups opposed to the socialists, whose membership at that time was not much bigger. Anarchism could break out in direct action with spectacular attacks, as for example at Montceau-les-Mines in 1886. Thus personal enmities, the diversity of professional backgrounds and above all the influence of historical traditions explain lasting divisions. Perhaps these were all the more animated in so far as they implicated small groups,[4] sects in which internal conflicts were aggravated. At that date, apart from the conquest of a few town halls, the various brands of socialism scarcely counted on the political level. The workers and progressive peasants remained loyal to the radicals.

The governing republicans

Once the republicans had gained their victory the centre left played a smaller rôle than it had previously. It was still dominant in the Waddington ministry of 1879 but subsequently held a secondary place in governments. In the Chamber of Deputies it was now no more than a weak group which returned in 1881 with thirty-nine deputies. On the other hand, in the Senate it maintained an appreciable hearing, although the renewal of January 1882 which confirmed the republican successes made its support no longer indispensable. The big division in the governing republicans was the one between the republican left of Grévy and Ferry and the Republican Union of Gambetta. It has been suggested that the opposition reflected that of two different kinds of people, the established bourgeois of the republican left and the political newcomers of the Republican Union. But this analysis does not always hold good: Waldeck-Rousseau, who was to move over to the Republican Union, came from the Nantes middle class; and Paul Bert belonged to a family of country notables who had made money. The Bert family lived at Auxerre in a former Dominican priory. Beyond the personal conflicts or the social contrasts between two sets of people it is essential –

more so than is sometimes realized – to note a slightly different emphasis and tone. Of course, the gap was a small one; all these men felt the same concern, connoted by the very term 'opportunism', to make a list of priorities, to carry out only those reforms which were really possible; they all recognized the necessity for order 'in the budget as in the streets', to use the phrase of André Siegfried, the son of one of the outstanding personalities of the régime. Nevertheless, Gambetta's followers, unlike the republican left, wished the State to affirm its authority over the business world. Gambetta was to try in vain to revise the railway contracts. On 14 July 1882 Waldeck-Rousseau denounced at Rennes the 'oligarchy of the big monopolies, which still receive the title of commerce and industry, an oligarchy of high finance bold enough to have leased out credit' (quoted by Joseph Reinach, Biblio. no. 135, p. 129). In that way the Republican Union, which embraced a certain number of radicals, kept in contact with the progressive republicans. For Gambetta and his supporters, it was in any case less a question of ending an injustice than of affirming the authority of the State. Gambetta had attained a very clear vision of the need for authority in a democracy. It was the basis of his initiatives in favour of the *scrutin de liste* (voting for several members on a list), which would put an end to the *petit scrutin*, to the tyranny of electors and committees over the successful candidate; it asserted the independence of the administration. The circular issued on 24 November 1882 by Waldeck-Rousseau, Minister of the Interior in Gambetta's Great Ministry', expressed opposition to interference by members of parliament. Gambetta wanted a 'strong power' based on organized parties in the English fashion, with the prime minister's job going to the leader of the majority. Neither the radicals nor probably all the members of the Republican Union, and certainly not Grévy's supporters, would have accepted such a political system. To be convinced of this one has only to read the memoirs of Bernard Lavergne, a doctor at Montredon in the Tarn, the confidant of Grévy, who was dominated by fear of the tyranny of a man who plays disturbingly on his popularity, by fear of personal power.

There was something else as well – the underlying conflict on foreign policy. The former leader of the Tours Delegation wanted a policy of 'national pride'. Gambetta was enthusiastically interested in military affairs; he travelled in Europe and he gave foreign policy a very high place, calling it 'the true, the only policy which can and must interest a great and noble nation that has been defeated and discouraged'.[5] On 9 August 1880, watching the review of the fleet at Cherbourg by the side of the President of the Republic, Gambetta, President of the Chamber of Deputies, spoke of the lost provinces. 'Great redress', he asserted, 'can overstep the law', and invoked 'immanent justice'. These remarks were in fact moderate and indicated the rejection of a 'bellicose spirit'. Nonetheless, Gambetta was regarded as the man of revenge. In fact he wished to guide France towards expansion overseas. Already in 1872, at Angers, he predicted that France could regain her position if she turned towards expansion in the world. He pushed Ferry to appropriate Tunisia. At the time of the Great Ministry he adopted a vigorous attitude on Egyptian affairs which, according to Freycinet, provoked the cry, 'Gambetta wants war.' Here he came up against the advocates of a policy of self-communion, like Grévy, as well as the radicals, who were hostile to colonial enterprises. It is clear that the main lines of foreign policy were an appreciable element in a conflict which provides the key to the political evolution of the first few years of the Republic of the republicans, the direction of which can seem difficult to grasp. It also explains why, after Gambetta's death, many of his friends gave their support to Ferry, in whom they recognized a statesman.

The right

The opposition of the right had little vigour. In parliamentary debates it fought only lost battles. The most it could achieve was, with the support of the centre left in the Senate, to prevent the passing of Article 7, which was aimed at non-authorized religious communities. But Ferry and Freycinet by-passed this obstacle by issuing the decrees of 29 March 1880. Neither the resignation of numerous magistrates nor the legitimists' attempt at resistance by force could stop the dissolution of establishments run by the communities affected. Ranc and the bishops, conscious of the way in which opinion was running, wanted moderation. Except in a few departments the Catholic right did not succeed in mobilizing the crowds against the policy of laicization.

The elections of 1881 took place in an atmosphere of apathy; abstentions increased considerably and reached 31.4 per cent. The indifference mainly affected the conservatives, who returned less than a hundred deputies, half of them Bonapartists. In many departments won for the republicans, such as the Côte d'Or, the right did not even bother to campaign. In eastern and south-eastern France where republican ideas were firmly in favour, the voters of the right often considered it a waste of time to go to the poll. In 1883 the elections for the general councils left the right with a majority in only nine departments. The death in the same year of the comte de Chambord did not end the divisions among the royalists. All the legitimists did not transfer their support to the Orleanist claimant, the comte de Paris. As for the Bonapartists, since the death of the Prince Imperial in 1879 they were divided between Prince Jérôme, who was an anti-clerical, and his eldest son, Victor, designated in the will of the Prince Imperial.

Yet although the right had lost political power it retained social influence through its wealth, its prestige in society, its place in the great state services – only the prefects and the procurators-general had undergone a thorough purge – and its links with the world of business. So long as business interests were not at stake – and this attitude angered the intransigent extreme right – the conservatives confined themselves to parliamentary opposition. However, the governing republicans hardly thought of questioning the social order.

The Church was not a political force but was a powerful social one, and under the Moral Order government and in the time of 16 May, leaned towards the conservative right. It is therefore important here to analyse its influence. It could not fail to worry the republicans, even if the supposed peril was much greater than the real danger. The annual budget for religion exceeded fifty million francs.[6] The supervision of religion, attached sometimes to the Ministry of the Interior, sometimes to the Ministry of Education, was, in the numbers of people dependent on it, one of the principal civil ministries; in 1876 there were 55,369 secular priests, the great majority of whom were paid. The republicans still hoped, by a vigilant application of the Concordat, to control the secular clergy, whom they thought they could wean from ultramontane and counter-revolutionary ideas. Such was the attitude of Flourens, a councillor of State of a Gallican turn of mind, who was to head the supervision of religion from 1877 to 1885, except during the Great Ministry of Gambetta. On the other hand, the religious orders were the object of considerable mistrust and in certain cases, in particular that of the Society of Jesus, of lively hostility. In 1876 there were 30,287 men and 127,753 women in the religious orders. These figures illustrate the size of the Catholic restoration, which had been accompanied all through the nineteenth century by the development of the female orders. Nuns were three times more numerous than on the eve of the Revolution. The unauthorized orders of women were the small minority; they had 14,000 members. On the other hand, a quarter of the men (7,444) belonged to unauthorized orders and were more or less tolerated. Such was the case with the Jesuits, who in their twenty-nine colleges taught 11,000 pupils – a quarter of all the pupils in colleges run by religious orders. The rôle of the religious orders in education was accordingly denounced with considerable vigour by the republicans, who claimed that the 'ultramontane militia' provided an education contrary to the 'principles of modern society' and inimical to the Republic. The extension of mortmain, 'a scandal', according to Gambetta, 'in this land of the Gauls, consisting as it does of peasants and landowners', was no less of a peril. An enquiry into the wealth of the religious orders had revealed that it amounted to 40,520 hectares of land, with a market value of 712,538,980 francs.

The budget allowed by the government for religion, the resources of the religious orders and the donations of the faithful gave credence to the idea that the Church had an immense fortune. It did in fact occupy a fairly important place in social life. In 1880 the hospitals and hospices run by the religious orders dealt with 114,199 persons in need of assistance. Over

60,000 children were received in orphanages and workrooms, to which must be added the apprenticeship schools, the Church clubs, the rest homes and the lunatic asylums.

At the time when the republicans came to power the place occupied by the Church in education was large. Since the Falloux law of 1850 the colleges had continued to grow; in 1876 they had 46,816 pupils. If account is taken of the pupils in the junior seminaries, we almost reach the number of pupils in *lycées* and local *collèges*, which was 72,250. These colleges were run either by secular priests or by religious orders. The Church was present even in the universities; bishops sat on the Conseil Supérieur and priests sat on the academic boards. Religious instruction, given by chaplains, formed part of the timetables of *lycées*.

In primary education the Church was almost mistress in her own house. Members of the religious orders were responsible for the teaching in more than two-fifths of the public primary schools. Even when the headmaster was a layman the school was denominational. The headmaster taught the catechism and biblical history.[7] Classes began and finished with prayers. The schoolmaster sang at the lectern and took the children to the church services; according to the official instructions he had to 'show them by his own example the value of quiet contemplation'. The younger generation of teachers found it difficult to put up with the tutelage of the parish priest, which varied in degree from one district to another, and they were to regard the secularization of education as a liberation. In 1880, 39,000 nuns taught more than half the girls attending primary schools.

The law of 1875 on the freedom of higher education was to increase the Church's influence still further; it allowed the opening of Catholic free universities, and allotted the award of degrees to mixed boards of examiners consisting of professors from State faculties and from the free universities. These claims of the Church were opposed by the very spirit of the University, attached as it was from its origins to the formation of minds. It was a public service determined to regain its rights.

The opportunist ministries, 1879–1885

As soon as he took office Grévy used the right of the president of the Republic to designate the prime minister; he did not call on Gambetta but on Waddington, the former Minister of Foreign Affairs, who formed a government consisting of men of the centre left and the republican left, including Ferry. Faced with the hostility of the Republican Union, the government resigned on 12 December. Grévy called on Freycinet, the friend of Gambetta, who encouraged him to accept. Gambetta himself preferred to wait for the elections of 1881 and to use his influence as president of the Chamber of Deputies. The centre left broke away from the government and was succeeded by the Republican Union. By the decrees of 29 March Freycinet notified the unauthorized orders that they must ask for state authorization. He gave instructions for the dissolution and expulsion of the Society of Jesus. At the same time he started negotiations with Ranc, wishing to deal with the other orders by recourse to a law on associations. But the Republican Union ministers, advised by Gambetta, requested the execution of the decrees. Freycinet resigned. Grévy, once again, did not turn to the man responsible for the government's fall but to Ferry, who retained Education and enlisted only three new ministers. He proceeded to disperse the unauthorized orders, except for the Carthusians and Trappists.

Thus for nearly three years Grévy, playing skilfully on the fact that there was no real majority, just a coalition of groups, had been able to keep Gambetta at bay. Time was working against Gambetta; his influence irritated people and the hostility of the radicals was growing sharper. He hoped for the *scrutin de liste*; the Chamber of Deputies accepted it by a small majority but the Senate rejected it. It was a setback for him. The elections passed off without much enthusiasm and – unlike those of 1877 – without national slogans. The rôle of the committees and the local notabilities was decisive. It would long remain so, preventing the formation of real parties. Gambetta was not, as he had been at the time of the victory over MacMahon, the leader of an organized majority. It is true that the Republican Union, with 204 members, beat the republican left, which had 168 successful candidates, but the differences among Gambetta's followers were considerable, much greater than they had been four years earlier. They were united more by the 'attraction of a leader than by a convergence of opinions'.[8]

After the elections, the resignation of Ferry who was worn out by the Tunisian affair finally opened the way to power for Gambetta. He, too, was tired. Did he believe in success? Freycinet and Léon Say refused to co-operate with him. The former would have carried with him a small proportion of the radicals and the latter would have won over business circles, who were worried about the plans attributed to Gambetta to buy up the railway companies. Gambetta did in fact wish to revise the contracts. As soon as the government was formed the 3 per cent stock fell on the Bourse. The Great Ministry consisted of young (thirty to forty-five years of age), little-known members of the Republican Union. Gambetta's tone and his appointments – General de Miribel was made Chief of Staff – annoyed the deputies. Gambetta staked his all: he put down a motion for revision concerning both the Senate and the *scrutin de liste* which would be inserted in the constitution. Defeated by a coalition of the moderate republicans, the extreme left and the right, Gambetta resigned on 26 January after sixty-seven days. With no illusions left, he retained only one fragile hope –

dissolution and elections with *scrutin de liste* which would force the country to choose 'between debasement and national pride'.[9] But in the last few days of 1882 he succumbed to a minor infection. From the Palais-Bourbon to the Père Lachaise cemetery the funeral procession 'wound through Paris like a mourner's sash' (G. Hanotaux). The death at forty-four years of age of the leader of the Ministry of National Defence and of the republican party marked the end of the 'heroic age' of the Republic.

Yet the legacy of the Great Ministry and of Gambetta's ideas remained. Gambetta had separated the Ministry of Agriculture, which thus attained its full dignity, from that of Commerce. He had created an under-secretaryship at the Ministry for the Colonies. He had given ministerial responsibility to men whose rôle in the history of the Republic was to be considerable. Félix Faure, Under-Secretary of State for the Colonies, was one day to be prime minister. Rouvier inaugurated a long career in politics and business and Waldeck-Rousseau, Gambetta's young Minister of the Interior, was to become, after the Dreyfus affair, prime minister at the time of the 'republican defence'. Above all, on Gambetta's death, his political friends avoided splitting up. United by political comradeship and common struggles, they were, to use Freycinet's phrase, 'the Republic's motive power'.

And so in February 1883, after ephemeral cabinets led by Freycinet and Duclerc, Ferry found a centre majority which was to support him for over two years against the extremes. It was based on an understanding between the Republican Union and the republican left. Ferry wanted 'a solid base secure against the incessant crises' and 'the government to be left with the initiative which belongs to it by right'. Several members of the Great Ministry formed part of the government, including Waldeck-Rousseau at the Ministry of the Interior. The reconciliation of the opportunists allowed the Republic, in Ferry's words, 'to be a government' for a short but decisive period.

The achievements of the opportunists

The republicans were united in their intention to carry out their pro-gramme of democratic liberties and to laicize the State and the schools. That is undoubtedly the most original aspect of their achievements and the one which was to leave the deepest mark on contemporary France. We must therefore devote our attention to it first of all.

Democratic liberties

The republicans abolished the repressive measures from which they had just suffered in the days of Moral Order and of 16 May. One law made it possible to open or move a drinking shop simply by making a declaration at the town hall. This was an essential step; the tavern, that republican 'church', was no longer subject to the arbitrary functioning of administrative authorization. Similarly, a law of 1880 established the freedom to peddle. The law of 29 July 1881, a reply to the repression of Moral Order, laid down an extremely liberal set of rules for the press. All preventive obstacles were removed but the possibility of the right to reply was retained. Press offences were to be tried by jury. These new rules resulted in an unparalleled expansion of journals dealing in the expression of opinion. The republicans in the government, unlike the conservatives, knew the press well enough to see no very considerable risk in this step. They realized that the press 'was so diversified in its tendencies that its redoubtable influence could no longer constitute a real power' (P. Albert, Biblio. no. 137).

The law of 30 June 1881 made it permissible to hold public meetings without authorization. It required simply a prior declaration,[10] and the formation of a committee. On the other hand, plans concerning freedom of association were not put into effect, since this seemed to be leaving the field open for the activities of the religious orders. More generally, the individualism of the age distrusted groups and associations. However, the republicans agreed to grant trade union freedom by the Waldeck-Rousseau law of 1884.

The law of 4 March 1882 gave all municipal councils the right to elect their mayors. It ended the arrangements inherited from the monarchy, with its qualified franchise, which prescribed that in communes with an income of less than 100,000 francs those who paid the most taxes should be co-opted to the municipal council for votes on exceptional loans and rates of taxation. The law of 5 April 1884 on municipal organization confirmed the election of mayors and their deputies, and the public nature of council meetings. Paris retained a different system – an indication of the provinces' mistrust of the revolutionary capital. The prefect of the Seine exercised the powers of mayor and the prefect of police kept an eye on the 'municipal' police. Elsewhere the mayor 'was responsible, under the supervision of the higher administration, for the municipal police, the country police and the execution of the relevant acts of the higher authority' (Art. 91). The town halls were centres of life and political education, especially in the country. The activities of the municipal councils, especially in religious affairs (subsidies for buildings, payment of curates, vetoes on processions) and educational matters (creation of schools, laicization of the staff) were the occasions of important debates. On the other hand, the maintenance of the prefect's administrative guidance, denounced by Ferry in 1865 at the time of the Nancy programme, limited the financial autonomy of the municipalities.

In power, the republicans also abandoned their plans for decentralization; the experience of governing led them back to the Jacobin ideal of centralization which Gambetta himself asserted that he had always defended. In 1886 the vote on the Colfavru amendment abolishing sub-prefects came to nothing. The republicans preserved the administrative structure bequeathed to nineteenth-century France by Bonaparte. The Council of State, detested in 1870 for its rôle under the Empire and threatened by the National Assembly, was remodelled in 1879 by the law of 13 July. The government appointed its own nominees to vacant seats and created a republican membership.[11] The Council of State kept its essential rôle of high administrative tribunal, the sole judge of the administration's actions. When in 1880 the expelled members of the religious orders lodged complaints against the prefects in the civil courts for illegal entry the courts were instructed not to proceed and the question was referred to the tribunal des conflits. Half the members of this court were members of the Council of State: it pronounced the complaints inadmissible. Nothing was changed either in the other big state services for which recruitment was by competitions which were a kind of co-option. On the other hand, the posts of prefect and sub-prefect could go to members of the political class – journalists, members of parliament. That is how Arthur Huc, before heading the *Dépêche de Toulouse*, came to be a sub-prefect.

The opportunists did not interfere very much with the magistrature any more than with the administration. The radicals wanted judges to be elected, as during the French Revolution and in the United States, and to end the security of tenure that the bench enjoyed, 'a monarchical principle'. The law of 1883, which reduced the number of judges' posts, made possible a purge through the retirement or transfer of conservative officials who had just begun to defend the religious orders. Security of tenure was suspended for three months. In addition, courts of summary jurisdiction were given juries again. The reforms stopped there.

The Congress, meeting in August 1884, voted for a limited revision of the constitution: it abolished public prayers at the opening of the parliamentary session, thus confirming the laicization of the State. 'The republican form of government' could not be subjected to revision – a measure which made royalist propaganda into an act against the constitution. Above all, the mode of election of the Senate was no longer inscribed in the constitution. The principle of life senators was abolished and the life seats were allotted to the most densely populated departments as vacancies arose. Communes had from one to thirty senatorial electors, according to the number of municipal councillors. None the less, the electoral law maintained the dominance of rural France. The extreme left did not succeed in securing election by universal suffrage and even less the abolition of the upper chamber.

The work of laicization and educational policy

The real cement which kept the republican party together, was as we have already emphasized, the common desire to secularize the State and social life. In that it was faithful to the French Revolution, whose 'great passion' was 'to have established this lay state ... to have finally made society's institutions exclusively lay ... to have stripped the clergy of its political organization, its rôle as a State institution' (Ferry to the Chamber of Deputies on 3 June 1876). The wish to take away from the clergy its influence in society and its political authority was at the root of republican anti-clericalism, which had been exasperated by the attitude of the Church alongside the conservatives under the Empire and the reign of Moral Order. The appearance of the word 'anti-clerical' in the supplement to Littré in 1877 revealed how public opinion was evolving. From the end of the Empire to about 1885 there was a big wave of anti-clericalism, which was followed for some fifteen years by a period of calm. It is true that this anti-clericalism took various different forms. It could be rooted in the tradition of the Revolution, with its de-Christianizing tendencies; it could be based on adherence to a materialist philosophy – such was often the attitude of the radicals, and it was also that of a man like Paul Bert among Gambetta's followers. It could be grounded on devotion to the positivism of Auguste Comte, either through direct acquaintance with it – such was the case with men like Ferry or Challemel-Lacour – or through a knowledge of it acquired at second hand. In any case, its main themes inspired the opportunists. Anti-clericalism found in this philosophy, and also in liberal Protestantism and Kantian philosophy, the idea that the revealed religions of the theological age were required to withdraw, that it was possible to come to terms with them if they agreed to confine their influence to the private domain. On this last point the republicans received the assent of all those who repudiated clericalism, including those moderate, 'universal suffrage'[12] Catholics who continued to vote republican so long as the Republic did not attack religion. The governing republicans accordingly displayed in practice a certain moderation. Although Ferry wished, in his famous words to Jaurès, 'to establish humanity without a God and without a King', he also knew that he was, as he wrote to his wife, 'the elected representative of a people that makes wayside altars, that is fond of the Republic but is just as fond of its processions'.

The annulment in 1880 of the law of 1814 forbidding Sunday work, the abolition by the law of 28 July 1881 of the denominational character of cemeteries, the law of 15 November 1887 on the freedom of funerals, which favoured the activities of societies supporting civil funerals, the laicization of the hospitals, the removal of crucifixes from courtrooms, and the passing in 1884 of the law on divorce tabled by the radical Naquet (the divorce by mutual consent authorized by the articles of the Civil Code but annulled in

1816 was not reintroduced; here too Ferry showed prudence) all combined to complete the French Revolution's work of secularization.

However, the opportunists did not attack government financial aid to religion, or the Concordat which the radicals wanted to abolish. This attitude is explained not only by a cautious attitude to the electorate but also by the wish not to renounce a valuable weapon for controlling the influence of the secular clergy. The possibility of suspending or abolishing ecclesiastical salaries, authorized by a judgement of the Council of State of April 1883, the appointment of bishops by the president of the Republic and of parish priests by the Direction des Cultes (Board of Management for Religion) were means of applying pressure not to be disregarded. Relations with the nuncios in Paris, especially with Mgr Czacki, appointed in 1879, remained courteous. Leo XIII was not hostile to a régime which protected the overseas missions and, was, all round, less hostile to the Church than Bismarck's German Empire or unified Italy. The Pope accordingly advised French Catholics to practise moderation when the government attacked the unauthorized orders, basing itself on texts to which many previous régimes had had recourse. The Pope did not abandon this attitude when confronted with the government's educational policy.

This was certainly the keystone of the work of laicization. It also provoked the clearest expression of what Ferdinand Buisson, Ferry's associate, called 'lay faith'. It is essential to define the components of this policy before outlining its main features. In the *Revue pédagogique* of 1882 Ferry described the policy of laicization as

> the greatest and most serious of social reforms and the most lasting of political reforms ... when the whole of French youth has developed, grown up under this triple aegis of free, compulsory, secular education we shall have nothing more to fear from returns to the past, for we shall have the means of defending ourselves ... the spirit of all these new generations, of these countless young reserves of republican democracy, trained in the school of science and reason, who will block retrograde attitudes with the insurmountable obstacle of free minds and liberated consciences.

To provide a foundation for social progress, to give the Republic roots and to liberate consciences – such was the triple aim of the founders of the republican educational system.

Apart from a minority among the socialists, the republicans, whatever their divisions, had no doubts that education was a powerful factor in social advancement, in bringing about equality and in putting an end to traditional social hierarchies. They shared the nineteenth century's optimism on this point and thought, as Allain-Targé had written under the Empire, that 'the spread of enlightenment' would end 'inequality in social relations'.[13] At any rate, faithful to Condorcet's ideas, they regarded the institution of scholarships granted on merit as an adequate remedy for 'the social inequality resulting from the inequality of fortunes'. In so doing they gave satisfaction not only to the 'new strata' but also to a whole section of the population keen to rise in the social scale. Founded in 1866 by Jean Macé, a boarding-school headmaster of Beblenheim in the department of Haut-Rhin, the Ligue de l'Enseignement, which acted as a pressure group for laicization, grew between 1870 and 1877 from 18,000 to 60,000 members. It touched a chord not only with the middle classes but also with a working-class élite that associated education with progress.

To establish lay schools was also to establish the Republic and – for the two notions were at that time inseparable – to strengthen 'la patrie'. It was a question not only of winning over the new generations to the régime but also of affirming a single, united conception of the national community. The school benches were intended to make pupils forget class divisions and regional differences and to develop a feeling of national unity. In other words, in the days of the republicans' Republic the idea of secularism was identical with patriotic feeling: the Prussian schoolteacher had produced his country's victory; the schoolteacher of the Republic was to prepare the revenge. Ferry ordered for distribution in the schools 20,000 copies of Déroulède's *Chants du soldat*. In a speech to Gymnastic Societies at Reims in 1882 he extolled physical training as the foundation of military training. Pre-military education was one of the teacher's tasks. The Ligue de l'Enseignement took as its motto, 'For the fatherland, by book and sword'. Ferdinand Buisson was on the managing committee of the League of Patriots.

To establish secular education was also to liberate consciences from the 'retrograde spirit'. Ferry and his associates, in spite of their sincere declaration of respect for people's beliefs, thought that the Church was an obscurantist force doomed to disappear. The secular idea embraced a precise ideological orientation and was inseparable from a system of thought. Here we come up against the double face of secularization; was it the acceptance of a mere fact, the neutrality of the State and its refusal to profess a religion or philosophy, or was it rather an independent philosophy inspired by rationalist or even anti-religious ideas? The 'secular credo', disseminated in particular by the manuals of morality, was nourished first by Kantian morality – such was the case with the manual published in 1883 by Louis Liard, then rector of Caen University, for primary schools – and second by liberal Protestantism. Ferdinand Buisson, who in 1866 founded the paper *Le Christianisme libéral* at Neuchâtel, and Steeg and Pécaut, both former pastors, shared a spirituality which rejected dogmas and a religiosity related to the profession of faith of the 'vicaire savoyard'. Félix Pécaut, director of studies from September 1880 at the *Ecole normale supérieure* of Fontenay-aux-Roses, gave the future mistresses and heads of teachers' training colleges a lecture on morality every morning, followed by a secular hymn. According to Buisson, he wanted to be the 'lay Saint-Cyran, a philosopher and a republican', of a new Port-Royal. At Steeg's funeral Buisson recalled their ideal: 'to draw from traditional Christianity viewed as a whole a sort of gospel, a secular religion of moral ideas without dogmas, without a morality and without priests'.

Republican spirituality did not always attain these heights. The secular ideology was very often reduced to a somewhat short-winded moralism which sometimes ended in a defence of *petit-bourgeois* life, in a practical wisdom which praised saving and economy, preached hygiene and sobriety, rejected any mystery and paid as little attention to fairies as to the Virgin Mary. It was Franklin's utilitarianism, Le Bonhomme Richard's wisdom all over again. A book that was very typical of this state of mind was a reader that moulded generations of children, *Le Tour de la France par deux enfants*, published in 1877, with the subtitle *Devoir et patrie*, by G. Bruno. The pseudonym, which paid homage to the free-thinker Giordano Bruno, concealed Mme Guyau – whose second husband was the philosopher Fouillée – the mother of Jean-Marie Guyau, the author of *L'Irréligion de l'avenir*.

Ferry, without introducing the comprehensive law that Paul Bert would have liked, adopted a method that tackled the different questions one by one. However, this empirical approach was backed by a coherent plan: all levels of education were reorganized. The bill for a reform of the Conseil Supérieur de l'Instruction Publique was tabled by Ferry as soon as he took over the ministry in the Freycinet government. Adopted in February 1880, the law excluded from the Conseil people not involved in education and in particular ministers of religion. It was the end of the system that had been created by the Falloux law. Now the Conseil only comprised those who worked in education and who were appointed or elected by their colleagues, an arrangement which reinstated the University as an autonomous body. This reform was of enormous significance. The Conseil Supérieur and its permanent committee played an essential part in producing the legislation and the regulations which gave a new look to French education. The quality of the discussions and of the members of the first Conseil Supérieur bears witness to the wide scope of the educational thinking which accompanied the educational work of the republicans. Specialized associations such as the Society for the Study of Questions of Secondary Education and the Society of Higher Education acted as sounding boards for the work of the Conseil Supérieur and started discussions which were continued in the Conseil.

Ferry, opening the first meeting of the Conseil Supérieur, exclaimed, 'For thirty years the University has only been an administration; from this day, which must be described as a memorable one, it is a living, free, organized body.' Henceforth the University had to perform 'by itself and on itself the reform of studies ... so often attempted, so long awaited and which, at the present time, it is no longer permissible or possible to postpone.' The academic work of the republicans affected every level of education, but it was primarily the university staffs who carried it through. A decisive rôle was played by personalities such as Michel Bréal, Henri Marion, Charles Zévort, Octave Gréard, Lavisse and many others. Under Ferry, a number of them had the satisfaction of restarting the great movement of renewal of studies for which Victor Duruy, under the liberal Empire, had provided the stimulus. Besides, Napoleon III's former minister was soon sitting on the Conseil Supérieur and meeting former associates among the senior civil servants of the rue de Grenelle.

The law of 18 March 1880 ended the conferment of university degrees by mixed boards of examiners that had been established by the law of 12 July 1875. 'The examinations and practical tests which determine the award of degrees can only be taken before State faculties.' Moreover, the free institutes of higher education could not 'take the title of universities'. This measure was aimed at the 'Catholic universities' created after the law of 1875 in Angers, Lille, Toulouse, Lyon and Paris, which offered considerable competition to the State universities, had substantial means at their disposal and at the start attracted staffs comparable to those of the State.

Ferry, and his successors, worked to give higher education, which had been stagnating, the means worthy of the dignity of its task. Chairs and lectureships were created, new faculties were built, a start was made in 1889 on the reconstruction of the Sorbonne, and a plan was drawn up – to be finally implemented by the law of 10 July 1896 – for the creation of autonomous universities uniting the faculties and schools of individual towns. Higher education was not to advance again at such a rate until much later on.

Secondary education did not undergo such sweeping changes. However, the reform of the timetable carried out in 1880 by Charles Zévort was important. It marked 'a perceptible retreat from the old pedagogy' (A. Prost) based on memory. The rules, the compositions, the Latin or French speeches and the pedagogical methods inherited from the Jesuits were all challenged. Thus Ferry had the feeling that he was 'fighting two battles at the same time; an external one against certain parties and an internal one against routine' (quoted by M. Reclus, Biblio. no. 81). On this level, too, ulterior motives of a political kind were not absent. However, although modern languages and science were given a bigger rôle, the classical humanities retained their primacy. The novelty was the expansion of a philosophy of teaching which was long accepted without question; it was based on the experimental method. 'The observation of things is the basis of everything', said Ferry, speaking about the dissertation, the translation and the explication of texts.

The most revolutionary innovation in secondary education was the creation of *lycées* and *collèges* for girls. Victor Duruy had encouraged the creation of secondary courses for girls where the teaching was provided by masters from boys' *lycées*. This initiative had encountered the hostility of the Church and the conservative world. As early as 1878 Camille Sée, a young deputy in Ferry's party, tabled a bill which finally became the law of 21 December 1880. (Ferry once again showed how prudent he was by not retaining the compulsory creation of boarding schools provided for by Sée.) The secondary education of girls included two original features. It was to be provided by women and this reform necessitated the creation of a teachers' training college for girls. It was also secular. The teaching of morals was compulsory but that of religion was optional. The project was also intended to end 'intellectual and moral divorce in marriage', to provide 'republican companions for republican men'. Ferry was delighted with a movement which carried women 'towards the light, towards knowledge, towards secular science'; he saw in it a 'guarantee of the unity of the French family'.[14] The Camille Sée law was certainly intended to end the Church's influence over middle-class girls.

The republicans devoted their keenest attention to primary education. The three points – that it should be compulsory, free and secular – were in their view an inseparable whole. Making it free made it possible to make it compulsory and this, in a country divided in its beliefs, involved making it secular. As usual, Ferry acted cautiously and methodically. He began by introducing the law of 9 August 1879 which obliged departments to create a teachers' training college for schoolmistresses within four years; sixty-seven departments did not possess one. Then Ferry tabled two separate bills; one made primary education free (this was the law of 16 June 1881), the other made it compulsory. Ferry declined to envisage the laicization of teaching staffs in the immediate future; there was no point in upsetting people and it was essential to train the necessary teachers. On the other hand, Ferry, like the parliamentary commission, wanted the content of the school timetable to be neutral. Disagreement between the Chamber of Deputies and the Senate, where moderate republicans like Jules Simon joined the right in defending the teaching of religion and of 'duties to God and one's country', resulted in the adjournment of the vote on the law, which was not passed until 28 March 1882. It made education compulsory from six to thirteen years and religious instruction no longer figured in the timetable; it could only be given 'outside school premises'. However, in the syllabus of 'moral and civil instruction' the Conseil Supérieur inserted a paragraph on duties to God. The teacher, according to Ferdinand Buisson, 'confines himself to inculcating in his pupils the fundamental ideas which recur in all religious denominations and even outside them'. It was necessary to wait more than four years before the Senate, henceforth secured for the left, would accept the laicization of the teaching staff. This was established by the comprehensive law of 30 October 1886 on primary education, promulgated when Goblet was Minister of Education. In boys' schools the substitution of lay teachers for members of the religious orders had to be completed within five years. On the other hand, in girls' schools secularization was to be achieved by the progressive disappearance of the members of religious orders then at work. So this was done slowly, especially when local councils did not want to upset people. Local studies show how different the situation could be (see Bernard Ménager, Biblio. no. 150). In the north the law was applied energetically and laicization took place more quickly than in the rest of France. Nevertheless, in 1889 11 per cent of communal girls' schools were still run by members of the religious orders.

In their educational policy, which formed part of the series of basic laws, the republicans responded to the aspirations of society – to the 'new strata', and also to those in the working class who shared the current faith in the value of education. Their policy was only possible because it was supported by majority opinion. In this respect the cautious realism displayed by Ferry, who refused to rush things as the radicals or Gambettists like Paul Bert would have liked, was extremely important.

Economic and financial policy

The economic and financial policy of the opportunist republicans or, as it was called in those days without any pejorative connotation, *la politique d'affaires*, was conducted, as we have said, in the context of the difficult days of the 1880s; however, although the economic situation affected this policy, it does not explain it. The essential point was certainly agreement on the basis of economic liberalism. No less remarkable was the poverty of the economic education of the vast majority of the persons concerned, who tended to put their trust in well-known experts such as Léon Say or Rouvier. The permanence of the ministers was remarkable. From December 1877 to 30 March 1882, apart from Allain-Targé's brief appearance under Gambetta, three men in turn ran the Ministry of Finance – Say, Magnin and Tirard.

Inside the government some men – Freycinet and Gambetta – did envisage limited intervention in the economy by the State. In 1878 Freycinet secured the adoption of a plan for capital expenditure which was intended to boost the economy immediately after the victory of the republicans. As soon as he came into power he presented to both chambers a huge public works programme which would permit the construction of ports, canals and 16,000 kilometres of railway. Industry needed the improvement of communications in order to reduce costs. Freycinet challenged the arguments of the conservatives, who thought that the planned rail network, which would also serve the poorer regions, would not pay. The State, he said, should not reason like a private individual. The 'wealth created by the railway'[15] counted as much as the profits made. 'The general objective', Freycinet said to the Senate, 'is to initiate a public works programme in France so as to retain capital which is otherwise dispersed in all directions – to Italy, Spain, Peru, Turkey. It is important to assist such an objective by improving facilities for the nation's commerce and industry.'[16]

The expenditure, reckoned at four milliards over ten years, was to be covered by a 3 per cent loan redeemable by an annual lottery. The modes of subscription were new; the Minister of Finance, Léon Say, who like Gambetta gave his endorsement to the project, had to take account of the pressure of opinion; for the first time the issue was sold directly by the State on the Bourse and at the Treasury. However, when the 1881 3 per cent loan was launched, Magnin, Say's successor, once again authorized the banks, who in any case had played a decisive part on the Bourse in the previous operation, to act as intermediaries between the State and the public. In the view of the radicals and of Gambetta the Freycinet plan was to lead to buying up the railway companies, or at any rate to a tighter control of them by the State. The State did buy out some bankrupt companies in the west and thus created a State network. But Léon Say considered that the new lines built by the State should be operated by the companies under a state guarantee.

Gambetta, at the time of the Great Ministry, thought of imposing new contracts which would strengthen State control over the railway companies, and his programme worried the world of high finance.[17] Léon Say, a director of the Northern Railway Company, declined the post of Minister of Finance in the Great Ministry. Hostile to the conversion of the stock and to the plans for contracts, the financial world indicated its mistrust; the stock fell. It was in this atmosphere that a few days before the fall of Gambetta the Union Générale went bankrupt. The Union Générale was a merchant bank founded by Bontoux in 1878; its capital came from the conservative world, mainly from the south-east. Although the crash consolidated republican high finance, it testifies to the listless state of the market and shows how depressed the economy was.

The State's receipts, largely based on indirect taxes, were affected. The remissions of fines gained by pressure from republican deputies on the administration (see Seignobos, Biblio. no. 41, p. 89), the increasing amount of fraud, the reductions in the taxes on drink and sugar made by the republicans when they came into power, reduced resources. The budget, until then in surplus, showed a deficit. The cost of the Freycinet plan was greater than had been foreseen; it rose to four milliards, then to six and finally to eight. A different policy seemed to be demanded.

The entry of Léon Say into Freycinet's cabinet after Gambetta's fall reassured business interests. The collective ministerial declaration read out in the Chamber of Deputies on 31 January outlined a very cautious policy in conformity with the rules of financial orthodoxy.

> Nations do not live solely on politics, they also live on business and material interests ... There is nothing in the situation to alarm us, but certain precautions must be taken ... There can be no question at the moment of conversion, of buying out railways or even of issuing redeemable stock. For some time we must restrict appeals to public funds and demand to a large extent the co-operation of private industry.

The financial world made use of the economic crisis and the financial difficulties to return to rigorous accounting. Léon Say introduced a budget of 'truth',[18] which showed a deficit. He explained that his predecessors had been putting ordinary expenses on the extraordinary budget, where they were covered by loans.

His successor, Tirard, followed the same policy in all essentials. However, to balance the ordinary budget, in 1884 he proposed the conversion of 5 per cent stocks into 4½ per cent, a measure of limited scope which lightened the charges on the State. Allain-Targé was unable to secure conversion to 3 per cent and the deputies for agricultural constituencies were able to obtain only the use of the proceeds of the conversion for a reduction of rates in favour of agriculture.[19] Strict financial orthodoxy won the day. The law was promulgated on 27 April. The moment seemed favourable for the operation; the 5 per cent quoted at 85.55 francs in 1874 was priced at 115 francs. The same concern for financial orthodoxy involved the modification of the Freycinet plan. In July 1883 the Chamber debated the agreements with the railway companies which Raynal, the Minister of Public Works, had negotiated in March. The State abandoned its right to buy up the lines already operated by the railway companies. It made over to them 2,823 kilometres of lines in operation which had been built on the basis of the Freycinet plan. It conceded to them 8,360 kilometres of lines still remaining to be built. The capital for construction and putting into service was obtained by issues of debentures by the companies. The State guaranteed the loans and guaranteed the dividends if receipts proved insufficient. This, according to an observer who nevertheless favoured the system, was the 'really dangerous side' of the agreements (*L'Année politique*, 1883, pp. 240–54). On the other hand, the companies completed the Freycinet plan. The radicals, including Pelletan and Clemenceau, and some of the Gambettists, including Allain-Targé, denounced the agreements as too favourable to private interests. Allain-Targé demanded the purchase of the Orléans Company alone; the State network would then be large enough to act as a model for the big companies. Rouvier, secretary of the committee on the bill and a former Gambettist like

Raynal, had moved a long way from the bold conceptions of the Great Ministry. He had close links with high finance and the companies, and he showed that in the prevailing financial climate the agreements alone made it possible to go on with the construction of the railway network.

Published on 20 November 1883, the agreements modified the Freycinet plan – which had been an attempt, contrary to prevailing ideas, at state intervention in the economic field – to the advantage of private interests. Nevertheless, the agreements involved for the companies a state super-vision the consequences of which were far from being advantageous to them. In fact state supervision transformed the railways into a public service, imposing heavy obligations and a rigid fares policy. 'Robbed of all freedom of action, the companies paid dear for their monopoly.'[20] The agreements were a victory for the railway companies in the short term, but not in the long term.

The companies had subsidized the press heavily to fight re-purchase; they had created a 'publicity service' and won over journalists and members of parliament to their cause. These methods, which were to come fully to light at the time of the Panama crisis, bore witness to a new relationship between politicians and business. Men like Pouyer-Quertier and Say were both politicians and big capitalists.[21] This fact inspired confidence in public opinion rather than the reverse. From now on business interests remained more and more in the background and had recourse to the good offices of professional politicians, who were often all the more accessible to pressure from business circles because they were of humble origin. In France, as Seignobos perceptively notes, collusion between politics and business was frowned upon, so the intervention of pressure groups, far from being public as it is in the United States, and hence subject to control, took place in secret. As a result, it was all the more likely to lead to scandal.

The pressure groups who favoured a return to protectionism achieved only limited success during the first few years of the republicans' Republic. The republicans in fact remained attached to free trade and a policy of commercial treaties. The first steps came from the industrialists, and Méline, who had connections with the weavers of the Vosges, was keen to protect their interests (see P. Barral, Biblio. no. 107, p. 84). As vice-president of the Customs Commission, he secured in 1881 a slight increase in duties on certain manufactured articles. As Minister of Agriculture in Ferry's second government, he adopted, though not until June 1884, the cause of protectionism in agricultural affairs 'so far as it was reasonable and possible'. It was just before the fall of Ferry, on 28 March 1885, that the laws putting duties on corn and cattle were promulgated. They were increased in 1887. The duty first of 3 francs, and later of 5 francs, on each hectolitre of imported corn put an end to the policy of cheap bread. The government, and Ferry in particular, had shown some hesitation in following the Minister of Agriculture; but the difficulties of farmers decided a majority of the deputies to vote for the duties in spite of the opposition of the radicals, who founded the People's League against Duties on Corn, and of advocates of free trade such as Henri Germain or Frédéric Passy. The Senate, less concerned about the reactions of urban populations, was itself largely converted to the cause of protectionism.

Favourable to the railway companies, to the agriculturalists and to protectionist industrialists, but hostile to the intervention of the State in the social field, Ferry's Republic alienated the sympathies of the workers. Its colonial policy was to rob it of support in the countryside.

Colonial expansion

In the days of Moral Order and the Republic of the dukes colonial expansion had come to a halt, first as a result of France's international position, and second because of the conservative right's lack of interest in overseas enterprises. With the advent of the republicans' Republic some decisive initiatives evidence a resumption of the expansion interrupted at the end of the Second Empire. What were the reasons for it and what were its principal manifestations? The rôle of a few men – Gambetta, Ferry – was decisive. They were motivated primarily by the wish to assert France's right to colonize like the other powers and to pursue an active policy so as not to lose prestige. After the signature of the treaty of Bardo, Gambetta congratulated Ferry: 'People who are distressed will just have to make the best of it, everywhere. France is taking her place as a great power again.' Colonization was intended to give a boost to national feelings after the humiliation of defeat. That was unquestionably the main reason for the initiatives taken by the opportunists. In this, as in other things, patriotism and the desire to assert national greatness were the basis of their policy; they were not affected in the beginning by economic considerations. Subsequently, to justify their policy, they showed that it served French economic interests. After he had finally given up power, in July 1885 and above all in 1890 in *Le Tonkin et la Mère Patrie*, Ferry justified colonization by the need to find outlets for French industry in the face of mounting protectionism. But people have too often taken as an accepted fact what was primarily an argument intended to convince industry, which was not in fact enthusiastic.

The colonial policy of the opportunists found very few supporters. Among them were the members of the geographical societies which developed after 1871. They had nearly 10,000 members in 1881 out of 30,000 in the world (Brunschwig, Biblio. no. 44, p. 23). Often linked, as in Lyon, to local chambers of commerce, they instigated voyages of exploration, stimulated in things overseas and developed themes which led to

expansion: a great nation must colonize; colonization is the task of civilization and so on. In 1874 Paul Leroy-Beaulieu, the son-in-law of the
economist and Saint-Simonian Michel Chevalier, published *De la colonis-
ation chez les peuples modernes*; he was thirty-one at the time. He argued that
colonization promotes material progress and trade, extends the domain of
industrial civilization and opens markets. For a people, it was the condition
of 'its greatness'.[22] These arguments provoked only a limited response. The
book, which was to become the bible of the defenders of colonization, was
not reprinted until 1882. 'The national consciousness', the author wrote in
the preface to the second edition, 'is beginning to realize the importance of
the colonies.' Apart from the soldiers and sailors, the missionaries, the
Gambettist journalists of *La République française*, the merchants in the big
ports and the colonies, no one felt very much enthusiasm for colonization.
Commercial interests thought that the operation would not pay. Members
of parliament distrusted costly and adventurous steps that turned France's
eyes away from 'the blue line of the Vosges'. In the name of 'continental'
patriotism the radicals and the conservative right denounced Ferry's
policy. The right and the radicals also rebelled against conquests which
were contrary to France's humanitarian traditions and which assisted
'speculators' overseas. Consequently Ferry, who in any case acted without
any preconceived plan, confronted Parliament with the *fait accompli*,
defying hostile opinion.

It was at the Congress of Berlin in 1878 that England gave France to
understand that she could have a free hand in Tunisia. This was because
England had just obtained a controlling influence in the Anglo-French
condominion in Egypt which demanded some compensation. Bismarck
was equally in favour of French intervention. In his view it could only help
to make France forget 1871. It was also bound to contribute towards
embroiling France with Italy and to maintaining her diplomatic isolation.
The French government, confronted with the progress of Italian influence
in Tunisia, contemplated intervention. However, the President of the
Republic, Grévy, was hostile to the idea[23] and Ferry himself was for a long
time far from enthusiastic. What was decisive was the attitude of Gambetta, whose influence on the conduct of affairs is well known. It was
baron de Courcel, director of political affairs at the Quai d'Orsay, who had
persuaded the president of the Chamber of Deputies. At that point Ferry
made up his mind. Claiming that the Kroumirs were making incursions
into Algeria, on 7 April 1881 he secured the voting of military credits. On 12
May, the Bey, in his palace of Bardo, at Ksar-Saïd, signed the treaty which
marked the beginning of the protectorate. The Chamber passed the treaty
on 24 May. Even those on the right and the extreme left, who criticized the
intervention, did not go further than abstention. But Ferry's success was
clouded by an insurrection at the end of June. After the elections, when

Parliament met, Clemenceau questioned Ferry sharply and accused him of deceiving the Chamber. He denounced the involvement of Roustan, the French Consul in Tunis, with certain business circles. At the end of a very difficult debate Gambetta's authority was required to impose a vote on the affair which, by 355 votes to 68 against and 124 abstentions, called for 'the execution in full of the treaty signed by the French nation'. The intervention in Tunisia is noteworthy not only because it inaugurated a new policy. The way in which it was carried out is typical; Parliament was ill informed and had to ratify retrospectively what had already been done. The military means were inadequate; the government did not want to worry people at the start. It was a policy of 'bits and pieces'. Certain groups of speculators, without playing a decisive rôle, may have precipitated the intervention, which assumed a murky look to the general public.

The dissatisfaction of members of parliament with the Tunisian enterprise explains why France let England act alone in Egypt. The fear aroused by the possibility of Gambetta's intervention had something to do with the fall of the Great Ministry, and it explains Freycinet's fall on 29 July 1882. The Gambettists, who reproached the government with timidity, were joined by the opponents of any intervention. The English troops alone crushed the Egyptian nationalist movement and occupied Egypt on a provisional basis. The French government could only subsequently indicate its dissatisfaction. For many years the dispute over Egypt was to put France and England at loggerheads.

When Ferry returned to power in February 1883 the expansion was to be resumed with the conquest of Tonkin. Ten years earlier, at the request of a trader called Dupuis, Francis Garnier, a naval officer who had links with Gambetta's circle, supported by merchants interested in trade with China, and by officers and missionaries, had seized Hanoi and then been killed in an ambush.[24] The treaty signed between the Emperor of Annam and Lieutenant-Commander Philastre had recognized France's possession of Cochin-China and granted France a protectorate in all but name over the Empire of Annam. The treaty was applied literally until the advent of the republicans. Admiral Jauréguiberry, who was several times Navy Minister, was by 1879 thinking of intervening.[25] In September 1881 the first Ferry government instructed the governor of Cochin-China to 'raise the prestige of French authority' without for all that 'embarking on the adventure of a military conquest'. In fact the Emperor of Annam had once more recognized the suzerainty of China and the 'Black Flags' were making navigation on the Red River impossible. Despatched to Tonkin with a few hundred men, Commander Rivière, egged on by the missionaries, the traders in Hanoi and Haiphong and his military colleagues, went beyond his instructions. On 25 April 1882 he seized the citadel of Hanoi. What was at the start only an incident, and one all the easier to settle since the court of

Hue favoured conciliation, was to lead to the conquest of Tonkin and war with China. At the end of 1882 a cautious policy was still in the ascendant in conformity with the wish of the President of the Republic, Grévy, and of the Minister of Foreign Affairs, who distrusted the Navy. Bourée, the minister in Peking, seemed to have obtained agreement with China on the basis of the opening up of Yunnan and a double protectorate over Tonkin.

With the start of Ferry's second ministry French policy suddenly changed direction; the Navy Minister telegraphed to the governor of Cochin-China, 'The occupation of Tonkin has been decided upon in principle.' Bourée was repudiated. Rivière, on his own account, embarked on the conquest of the delta. In China the war party won the day, whereas the French government had believed that China would do nothing. The court of Hue was in disarray, but a 'national resistance movement' made its presence felt in Tonkin. On 19 May Rivière, who then had 1,400 men under his command, was killed in a sortie. The Chamber had just voted money, on 10 May, for the despatch of troops to Tonkin. When the bill was read for the second time, after the news of Rivière's death, the vote was unanimous. This vote on 20 May had decisive consequences. France was caught in a double, large-scale conflict, with the Annamese Empire and the Chinese Empire. An expeditionary force of 20,000 men and a squadron of four battleships and twenty-five smaller ships were involved. The affair gradually assumed considerable proportions. On 25 August 1883 the Annamese Empire recognized France's protectorate over, and direct administration of, Tonkin, but the very difficult operations did not for that reason come to an end. The population carried on a war of ambushes which lasted until the end of the century. The Chinese army fought a war of the classical type. After several French successes China signed an agreement in 1884. An incident provoked the resumption of the conflict, which took the form of a naval war; the French fleet destroyed the arsenal of Foochow and blockaded the rice trade. By the second treaty of Tientsin on 9 June 1885 China promised to withdraw its troops from Upper Tonkin and gave French trade access to the southern provinces. The terms of the treaty were settled by the last few days of March, but it was Brisson, Ferry's successor, who signed the treaty. Ferry was swept from office on 30 March by the Lang Son affair. On 24 December, by a very small majority – 274 votes to 270[26] – the Chamber voted money for Tonkin, rejecting the idea of evacuation.

There were various different reasons for the conquest of Tonkin and it is important to appreciate the respective importance of each. The influence of the missionaries certainly played a part, as did that of groups of speculators who went so far as to arrange for the distribution in the Chamber, in May 1883, of rough maps on which 'big nuggets of gold' were marked. In 1883–5 the chambers of commerce were worried about the difficulty of exporting and wanted expansion in the Far East to provide outlets. The Lyon silk dealers were in favour of acquiring Tonkin,[27] which would ensure for Lyon 'the monopoly in silks for Europe'. Yet the administration distrusted the missionaries and although it may be true that economic interests influenced the process of decision, the interests of the 'Tonkinese' do not seem to have played a decisive rôle (see Dieter Brötel, Biblio. no. 129).

In fact, economic reasons and political motives were closely intertwined. The opportunist republicans did not distinguish between the national interest and commercial and industrial interests, but that is not to say that purely political reasons and the concern for national greatness were not essential. The legacy of the treaty of 1874 and the desire 'to assert the power of France' in the Far East were reason enough for involvement in Tonkin. After all, Tonkin was the road into the Chinese world, over which the European powers were just in the process of extending their influence. The personal initiatives of the 'sailors' and Ferry's own wishes also had their importance. The enterprise encountered opposition which continued to increase until it caused Ferry's downfall. Ferry deceived Parliament, so it was said, sacrificed 'the gold and blood of France' in foreign adventures and pursued a policy contrary to the rights of man. Although the radical extreme left was the only party to develop this last argument, the other themes of anti-colonialism were common to left and right, who joined forces to denounce the odour of speculation that permeated the affair.

The defenders of 'continental' nationalism – men like Clemenceau and Déroulède – vehemently attacked a policy which led France to renounce her essential interests. By involving France outside Europe, Ferry came up against England and Italy. He was led to envisage at the very least 'occasional collaboration' with Germany. 'It is useful', he wrote to his wife, 'to have an understanding with her in fields of common interest.' For all that, he did not respond to the advances of Bismarck, who in 1884 went so far as to let Ferry glimpse the possibility of an alliance. Ferry distrusted the manoeuvres of Bismarck, who wanted mainly to worry Great Britain while maintaining the isolation of France. Above all, public opinion and the political world would not accept an understanding with Germany at the cost of renouncing Alsace-Lorraine and Ferry himself could not forget 'the touching lament of the conquered'.[28] Even so, under Ferry Franco-German relations were 'better than they had ever been since 1871' and colonial expansion was the cause of this. Ferry was therefore treated as a Prussian, a Bismarck. On 1 January 1885 Clemenceau's paper *La Justice* branded 'reconciliations which wound the most sacred aspects of the country's dignity and hopes'. We shall never understand the unpopularity of Ferry's colonial policy and the evolution of French nationalism after 1885 if we disregard the effect of overseas imperialism on Franco-German relations.

It is difficult today to imagine the vehemence and the extraordinary passion which characterized the arguments for and against colonization in

the 1880s. 'We do not know you any longer, we do not wish to know you ...
These are no longer ministers that I see before me; they are men accused of
high treason.' These words of Clemenceau during the session of 30 March
1885 give some idea of the tone of the attacks on Ferry and his policy at the
height of his unpopularity. There is an amazing contrast between the scope
of Ferry's achievement (and we have not mentioned the maintenance of
French influence in Madagascar and the support given to Brazza's enterprises in the Congo) and the fragility of a policy which found limited
support. Of the politicians, only the opportunists supported him, and not
without reservations that occasionally reached the point of hostility. The
memoirs of Bernard Lavergne, Grévy's confidant, show clearly that the
President of the Republic and his political friends were not very enthusiastic. It was among the followers of Gambetta that Ferry found his supporters. In the country as a whole, Ferry the 'Tonkinese' was extremely
unpopular and this allowed the combined oppositions of the right and the
extreme left to bring him down. His majority, which had been shaky for
several months, disappeared on 29 March at the news of the evacuation of
Lang Son, which was presented as a disaster. Ribot, one of the leaders of the
centre left, rose at Clemenceau's side. 306 deputies voted against Ferry and
149 for him. This vote demands an explanation. It reflected the antagonism
of the urban population towards Ferry, who was held responsible for the
economic difficulties and for dear bread. The intransigent radicals, constant opponents of Ferry, perceived this dissatisfaction, and they were
followed by the radical left, a section of Gambettists upset by the absence of
reforms. The hostility of the right to the author of the laws on laicization
was long-standing. But for them Tonkin was not a mere pretext. The
decisive reason for the vote was certainly the rejection of colonial expeditions that were costly in men and money. Rural France had had enough of
these adventures, of which the business world also disapproved. In this
respect the attitude of the centre left is characteristic and would suffice to
destroy the simplistic view of colonial imperialism based on the requirements of business interests. The fall of Ferry illustrates the interaction
between home policy and foreign policy; it was a case, exceptional in these
early days of the Republic, of a ministerial crisis provoked by a question of
foreign policy.

After his defeat Ferry defined retrospectively (more clearly than he had
in 1882 in the preface to the *Affaires de Tunisie* of his associate, Alfred
Rambaud) the basis of his policy. The first argument is an economic one:
'colonial policy is an offshoot of industrial policy'[29] – colonies provide
outlets. The second argument is 'humanitarian'; the 'superior races' have a
'duty to civilize the inferior races'. The work of colonization aims at
emancipating, at bringing enlightenment and progress; in this sense there
is a link between the policy of laicization and colonial policy. Finally,

colonization is necessary for political reasons. 'The policy of contemplation or abstention', Ferry exclaimed again to the Chamber on 28 July 1885, 'is simply the road to decadence.' This statement bears witness to the haunting worry about national decline, to the obsession with 'status' which was at the heart of French nationalism of both the left and the right after the defeat of 1871. In this line of thought, which was subsequently adopted again by the defenders of the colonial idea, it would be just as incorrect to consider 'the patriotic argument ... as an alibi for economic demands' (R. Girardet) as to assert the opposite. In fact, the necessity of industrial and commercial expansion was subordinated to the need to maintain national greatness. In this sense, neo-mercantilism and nationalism are inseparable.

Colonization was of a piece with patriotism and the wish to regenerate France – and it is essential to realise this to understand the founders of the Republic. Whether he was sending Admiral Courbet's squadron into the Gulf of Tonkin or addressing the schoolmasters of the Republic, Ferry was pursuing the same policy, that of forging a new France, of giving back to the country defeated in 1871 its place in the world. To him or to a man like Paul Bert, the 'patron saint' of the teacher training colleges who ended his life as governor of Indo-China, there was no contradiction between the idea of laicization and the colonial idea. On the contrary, the first justified the second. After all, laicization taught the end of traditional beliefs and civilizations and the victory of a progress based on science and reason. The Alliance Française, founded in 1884, aimed at disseminating this ideal beyond the seas. Once again we can see that there is unity in the opportunist republicans' conception of the world and their political philosophy. Once again, we can see that the patriotic and obstinate son of Lorraine who established the non-denominational school and the colonial empire embodied their aspirations.

4

Beliefs and cultures

The first decades of the Third Republic saw only limited economic and social change. As we have already said, the growth of the economy was much more rapid on either side of the period which runs from Thiers to Méline. The relative importance of the various social groups hardly altered. But what about modes of belief, of thinking, of feeling? What about levels of education and cultural ideals? The reply to this series of questions is all the more difficult to provide if we want it to apply not only to the culture of the élites but also to that of the various social groups. However, the effort is worth making, since after all the ambition of the founders of the Republic was, by the secularization of society and the development of education, to finish with traditional beliefs and systems of values and to develop the ideas of enlightenment and progress. In this sense the republicans, even if they did not think of changing the relations between the social classes, wanted to transform the appearance of French society. To outline the successes and failures of their ambitions is to spotlight the areas of resistance, the confrontations and the challenges. Whether we describe the forms and evolution of religious feeling, the systems of education, the penetration of popular circles by the dominant cultural patterns, or the literary and artistic creations, we shall discover permanence, innovation and anticipation. The delays and the time-lags between social and mental attitudes, the diversity of the social groups which do not always coincide with any particular mentality, and finally regional differences all demand a description that must be all the more cautious in that it rests on analyses that are still relatively few and far between.

Beliefs and unbelief

The religious attitudes of the French demand a very fine analysis. Does France remain 'catholic France', the 'eldest daughter of the Church' because the vast majority of the population is baptized? The defenders of the Church thought she did, and they attributed the misfortunes of the times to the plots of a minority of freemasons, Jews and Protestants.

Certainly attachment to the major rites of Catholicism which form the landmarks of life was incontestable. And Christianity was deeply rooted in the nation; after all, the dominant morality, the very morality disseminated by the non-denominational school, was the laicized form of the morality taught by the Church since the beginning of the modern age. These substantial facts, too often forgotten, explain the illusion of those who held the 'plot' theory. Nevertheless, these people forgot the fundamental fact which numerous contemporary observers – Taine,[1] for example – perceived: the differing intensity of practice and fervour.

In the first few decades of the Third Republic practice appears to have been conscientious in the west of France, in the north, in the east from the Vosges to the Basses-Alpes, via Franche-Comté and the Savoys, and in a final block running from the Basque country and Béarn to the highlands of the east and south-east of the Massif Central – Ardèche, Aveyron, Cantal, Haute-Loire. In addition, a certain number of dioceses of the south-west had not yet been affected by a laxity in attitude. This feature is sufficient to distinguish this map from the map of religious practice in rural France drawn up by Canon Boulard just after the Second World War. In the rest of the country practice was average; it became indifferent in the Parisian Basin, the western fringes of the Massif Central, the Charentes and the Midi.

It is true that the de-Christianization of the rural world had begun way back before the Revolution. Nevertheless, it accelerated in many regions between 1860 and 1880 – in the Parisian Basin, for example. The increasing numbers of civil marriages and burials, and then the growing abstention from baptism reflect the progress of detachment. Renan, in Seine-et-Marne, noted the phenomenon; 'we are witnessing a curious about-turn', he wrote to Berthelot, 'the Catholicism so long supported by the peasant has lost his support, after that of the urban populations'. The enquiry ordered by Mgr Goux in the diocese of Versailles in 1880 revealed that in Seine-et-Oise attendance at mass varied from 5 per cent to 30 per cent of those liable and performance of Easter duties from 3 per cent to 14 per cent.[2] Loyalty to the big acts of seasonal conformism remained, but church attendance by men was very poor and that of married women indifferent; the questions of confessors about contraceptive practices seem to have had something to do with this attitude. In Champagne and Burgundy, Touraine and the Orléanais the experience was similar. It seemed as if the republican victory was unsettling one kind of conformity (see C. Marcilhacy, Biblio. no. 148) to replace it perhaps with another. In this sense political developments may have had some influence. In addition, the frequent collusion between the clergy and the conservatives under Moral Order contributed to the growing indifference. On the other hand, mere chronology shows that the policy of laicization cannot have had any

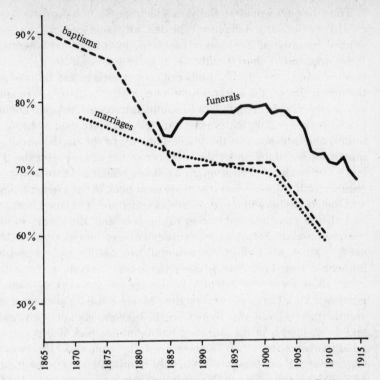

Evolution of the rates of Catholic baptisms, marriages and burials in Paris

Source: Fernand Boulard, *Archives de sociologie des religions*, 31, January–June 1971, p. 80.

influence in the period with which we are concerned and far from it being responsible for de-Christianization, as the priests asserted, it was much rather the consequence of it. In fact, the meeting between the modern world and religious conformism had decisive consequences. The press and military service opened wider horizons; the progress of education in itself, the improvement in living conditions and the acquisition of wealth gradually established new systems of values alien to the Church.

Rural emigration also contributed to its de-Christianization. The author of a monograph on a little commune between Aubusson and Guéret says, 'There is much indifference for all that concerns religion. The services are poorly attended. The men in particular rarely go to church.' The Church's blessing was requested only on the occasions of birth, marriage and death. The emigrants returned from Paris, where they had abandoned all contact with religion, with advanced ideas and in winter employed the dead season indoors to carry on republican and anti-religious propaganda.[3]

Thus the city, a modern Babylon which the Church distrusted, was the citadel of religious indifference. The de-Christianization of Paris has been studied recently on the basis of baptisms, marriages and funerals.[4] The trend accelerated sharply after 1875; there was a fall in the number of baptisms and a rise in the number of civil marriages and burials. Among the urban classes, the workers were particularly indifferent to religion. Of course, there were exceptions and subtle differences. At Saint-Etienne the working-class population practised its religion more than at Lyon; in the mines, and still more in the textile industry of the north, working-class minorities remained under the influence of the Church. But the massive fact of the workers' abstention from religion remains. There were complex reasons for it. Anti-clerical traditions went back to the French Revolution and sometimes beyond it to the world of craftsmen. That the Church which had always preached resignation to the poor and almsgiving to the rich compromised itself with the 'authorities' counted for just as much. We still need to know what effect this 'scandal' had on the workers and how it influenced their behaviour where religion was concerned. No doubt one must allow for the indifferent knowledge of the working-class world possessed by a clergy of rural origins. Moreover, the parishes were huge and the priests badly distributed. In 1877 the parishes of Saint-Ambroise and Saint-Joseph in the faubourg Saint-Antoine had 66,000 and 54,000 inhabitants respectively.[5] The rigidity of the framework laid down in the Concordat and the passivity of the public authorities made the creation of new parishes very difficult. Not only was the organization poorly adapted to meet the needs of the situation; so was the language of the priests. They lived the life, spoke the language and often adopted the moral code and system of values of the bourgeoisie of notables who had attended church more regularly since the middle of the century.

The religious evolution of the bourgeoisie was complex. While the old bourgeoisie, once disciples of Voltaire, had partly returned to the Church, especially in the provinces, the 'new strata' of the bourgeoisie were indifferent if not hostile to a Church which, since the *Syllabus* and the Council, seemed ever more profoundly alien to the spirit of the century. It needed the new atmosphere that became apparent after 1885 to produce a change. Some of the élites began to have doubts about science and progress, while in Rome Leo XIII adopted a different tone when he spoke about the modern world. There were resounding conversions in the intellectual world, Catholicism began to enjoy growing prestige among young people and the notion of Christian democracy had considerable success – as we shall have occasion to repeat – among the working population. These aspects of the situation at the end of the century cannot be omitted from the picture.

Church attendance is only one sign of religious vitality. It is the forms of

Qualitative data:
estimate of
religious practice by
bishops and prefects

Boundaries

[IIIIII] Good

[////] Good, but with
political independence
vis-à-vis the clergy

————— of the ecclesiastical provinces

[IIIIII] Average

————— of the dioceses

[   ] Indifferent

- - - - - of the departments

[×] Unknown

Scale 0   100 km

Religious vitality in French dioceses in 1877

Source: J. Gadille, *La Pensée et l'Action politiques des évêques français au début de la IIIe République* (vol. I, Paris, Hachette, 1967), p. 152.

devotion and spirituality that define the religious climate of an age. We have already mentioned devotion to the Sacred Heart and indicated its political dimension. This devotion assumed exceptional importance. It was the incarnation of the intransigent, ultramontane spirituality which triumphed in the 1870s. Its religious significance was fundamental. A cult of sorrow and expiation, devotion to the Sacred Heart was also the re-discovery of a personal, incarnate God in line with the spirituality of the nineteenth century. The reservations of some of the élites should not be allowed to hide the success of this devotion in the popular Catholicism preached by the religious orders and the young clergy. The cult of the Virgin Mary and of the saints and belief in miracles developed in an extraordinary way. Pilgrimages to Lourdes and the multiplication of devotions to Saint Michael, Saint Joseph and Saint Antony were all part of the same challenge by popular religiosity to the world and liberal values. Whatever the reservations of 'enlightened' Catholics, bourgeois or aris-tocratic heirs to the liberal or Gallican Catholic tradition, this was certainly the dominant pattern of Catholicism. Of course, all the faithful did not follow it to the same degree, and there was a big gap between mere churchgoers and the pious. But it was certainly this brand of Catholicism that was preached to pilgrims, people making a retreat, members of third orders and the audiences of missions.

The importance of this religious revival, which began in the 1860s, should not be underestimated. It explains how French Catholicism passed through the anti-clerical storm. What is more, it made possible re-conquests which historians, primarily sensitive to the one-way movement of de-Christianization, have sometimes failed to recognize. In Arras, Mgr Lequette, Bishop from 1876 to 1882 and successor to Mgr Parisis, favoured the growth of pilgrimages and pious associations and organized missions in the parishes.[6] The limits to these attempts at reconversion are obvious. Nevertheless, they slowed down, if they did not stop, the process of de-Christianization in the regions where practice was indifferent. Above all, in regions where people did practise their religion they maintained and even increased its vitality. The religious background and enthusiasm for religion seemed stronger in Flandre Intérieure, Haute-Loire or Morbihan around 1890 than they had been twenty years earlier. The temporary ebb of the tide of anti-clericalism and the tolerant application of the legislation on laicization by the 'progressives' favoured this efflorescence, which is attested by, among other things, the increase in the number of vocations.[7] This phenomenon heightened the contrast between the Christian areas and the regions where people were indifferent.

There was thus some sort of victory for 'intransigent' Catholicism, which was able to confront the liberalism it condemned with a kind of 'alternative society'. But this challenge contained its own contradictions; did it take account of the intermediate mass of people with a Christian tradition who rejected both militant Catholicism and militant secularism? Were these strongholds of faith not going to turn out to be geographical and social ghettos? This brand of religion which made a special appeal to sensibility and sentiment was largely a women's affair. It did not worry much about responding to the questions posed by the development of the religious sciences. Finally, this brand of religion was becoming more and more profoundly clerical. It insisted on the virtues of authority and the merits of obedience; it drew a vertical picture of religious society in which laymen were on the lower level. 'Parish men', members of the building committees or Catholic committees, most of them the ex-magistrates, retired officers or 'men of property' so typical of the Catholic élite of that time, acted as assistants to the clergy.

The place occupied by the Protestant minority, which numbered 580,000 at the census of 1872, was substantial. Its geographical distribution discloses the existence of a number of bastions – Drôme, Ardèche, Gard, Lozère, Tarn, Tarn-et-Garonne, Charente and Deux-Sèvres. There were also islands of Protestantism – the Montbéliard district, the Parisian region, Seine-Inférieure. Apart from Nîmes, Bordeaux, Le Havre and Paris, the Protestant communities were established in small towns or villages. But this rural Protestantism was not necessarily peasant Protestantism; the rural Protestants could be craftsmen, tradesmen, 'men of property', as they were in Gard. André Siegfried, whose mother was the daughter of Pastor Puaux, from the Ardèche, has shown very clearly that the Protestants of the Cévennes[8] were part of the ordinary people, but a 'relatively aristocratic' part. In many communes they dominated the Catholics, who were day-labourers or tenant farmers who had arrived more recently. In parallel to these rural Protestants the Protestant bourgeoisie formed a powerful group in the economy, the senior ranks of the civil service and the universities.

After the annexation of Alsace by Germany the Lutheran community numbered '80,000 persons at the most' (D. Robert, Biblio, no. 156, p. 319). The Lutherans were less troubled by disagreements than the Reformed Church, in which the 'orthodox' and 'liberals' confronted each other. After the synod of 1872 the liberals refused to accept an orthodox declaration of faith. Gradually 'a *de facto* organization that confirmed the division of the Reformed Churches into two' was adopted. The liberals were numerically in the minority but their intellectual influence was considerable. Liberal Protestantism rejected dogma; it reduced religion to morality and led to theism or even free thought. It is impossible to exaggerate the influence of liberal Protestantism on the republicans' Republic. Buisson, Pécaut, Steeg and Elie Rabier played a decisive rôle in Ferry's education work. Protestantism awoke considerable sympathy in élite circles, including that of Jules Favre, whose wife, *née* Charlotte Velten, was the first head of the *Ecole normale supérieure* at Sèvres, and that of Taine, who wanted a pastor to preside at his funeral. The philosopher Renouvier called on republicans to become Protestants. The Reformed religion, without dogma or mystery, accessible to reason, seemed the best adapted to give modern society the spiritual reinforcement it needed. It was the period of what E.G. Léonard called the great insight 'Protestant positivism'. Thus liberal Protestant-ism was one of the components of the secular, republican idea. While Catholicism, the religion of authority, seemed doomed to the decadence affecting the Latin peoples, the Reformed religion appeared to have the future on its side. In addition the democratic structure of the Reformed Churches developed the civic sense, and the practice of free enquiry developed the sense of responsibility. That is what explains the affinities between French Protestants and the Republic, even if all Protestants did not think alike. Even when he has given up religion the Protestant continues to be guided by a rigidly moral attitude, by the will to resist all power and by concern to assert the rights of the individual conscience. If need be, he can adopt a sermonizing tone which was to leave its mark on the republican spirit.

Another minority was the Jewish one (see M. Marrus, Biblio. no. 149). It did not exceed 80,000 at the end of the century, 50,000 of whom lived in Paris. The southern Jews who had been settled in France for a very long time were practically submerged in the mass of the population; similarly, the Jews of Alsatian origin were perfectly assimilated, or in the process of being assimilated. In contrast with this often moneyed bourgeoisie there were the immigrants who had come from Eastern Europe as a result of the persecution of their communities. Isolated by their language, Yiddish, they lived modest lives; round the Bastille and in the Marais they were tailors, shoemakers and furriers. As well as differences of language, social status and culture, there were differences in religious attitudes. Liberalism had affected western Judaism as it had the other denominations. Religion no longer played the part of special bond between the members of the Jewish community. The historian Jules Isaac, the son of an artillery officer, reports that only his mother practised her religion. On the other hand, the Jews from Poland or Russia were surprised by the surrounding scepticism and remained very much attached to their traditions. Assimilation by French society and culture seemed to involve the loss of Jewish religious originality. Although they were divided in their political attitudes, French Jews were attached to the legacy of the French Revolution which had liberated them by granting them citizenship. That was why they were attached to the secular, emancipating Republic.

In a picture of the spiritual attitudes of the French space must be found to delineate the forces hostile to the Churches and particularly to the Catholic Church, though it was not the only target. We have mentioned the anti-clericalism of the republicans and described its significance and its various facets. Anti-clericalism could be first and foremost a political reaction against the political and social influence of the Church. It could also disseminate its own ideology, one hostile to all religion. No proper history of this militant irreligion, of this French non-conformism, has ever been written. It would be necessary to note the figures for militant anti-clericalism – the numbers of refusals to allow baptism, of civil marriages and burials,[9] of anti-religious meetings, of demonstrations at sermons, processions and pilgrimages. One would have to look at the question from a sociological point of view. This would show that militant anti-clericalism affected various different circles: workers and craftsmen in Paris and Lyon, who saw in Blanquism the de-Christianizing tradition of the *sans-culottes*; peasants of Creuse, Yonne, Charente; bourgeois, especially in the small and middle-sized towns of the areas where on the whole people were practising Catholics. These towns, as Gabriel Le Bras noted, were hotbeds of insubordination.

Militant anti-clericalism gave rise to various organizations. At Le Mans a society known as the Free Thought was founded in 1883. It kept an eye on the conduct of civil burials, to which it sent delegations of ten members, who threw a spray of everlasting flowers into the grave. Every Good Friday the society held a carousal.[10] Recruitment to the Free Thought societies was more democratic than recruitment to freemasonry. Crétois, a former schoolmaster and prefecture employee, who was the tireless promoter of the Free Thought society in Le Mans, was never a freemason. The subscription kept the working classes out of the lodges, where the members of the middle classes were to be found. The lodges were the cement that kept the 'republican party' together. This is not the place to describe their political rôle, but for tens of thousands of members they were also a sort of 'alternative Church'. A better acquaintance with this 'Church' is indispensable if we are to understand the spiritual side of the France at this period.

Education and teaching

One of the most remarkable characteristics of the school system was the place occupied by secondary education. It was, in Lucien Febvre's penetrating phrase, 'on the pedagogical map, our all-powerful empire of the Middle'. The phrase says a great deal: it indicates simultaneously the important position of secondary education between primary education and higher education, the strength of its traditions and the rôle that it played in the formation of the élites. That is the essential point; there were two school systems with practically no communication between them. The primary school was the school of the people; the *lycées* and *collèges*, with their fee-paying elementary classes, were the schools of the bourgeoisie. The children of the lower middle classes, even the most brilliant pupils of the primary school, could gain entrance to it if they had a scholarship. This fact was reckoned to give the system a democratic character. During the period which concerns us the number of pupils who passed the *baccalauréat* did not increase any more than did the numbers of children attending the *lycées*; the figure varied between 6,000 and 7,000 per year from 1873 onwards. This total was not exceeded until 1891 with the creation of the modern *baccalauréat*. It was, then, an extremely restricted élite that took the *baccalauréat* and many dropped out during the course, partly owing to the high cost of the fees.

The *baccalauréat* formed a certificate of entry to the bourgeoisie; it became, as the liberal economist Courcelle-Seneuil observed as early as 1872, a sort of 'mandarin's diploma'. This criticism sums up a whole body of opinion which, together with Hippolyte Taine and the linguist Michel Bréal, denounced this authoritarian kind of education cut off from life. The failure, in the reform of secondary eduation, of the 'moderns' and the admirers of Anglo-Saxon models was extremely significant. The conclusion this suggests – that secondary education was the preserve of the bourgeoisie – may be obvious, but in saying this one in no way exhausts its importance, and one says nothing about its originality. It is noteworthy that the ruling classes were not unanimously in favour of the classical humanities, and that the scholarship boys' parents and the 'new strata' of the bourgeoisie were no less attached to the classical pattern. In any case, in neighbouring countries the ruling classes managed to maintain their primacy without the selective barrier of Latin. In fact, secondary education, the heir to the Jesuit and Oratorian colleges of the Ancien Régime, revealed an aristocratic conception of culture dear to the hearts of a good part of the French bourgeoisie. Readers of Virgil, Horace or Cicero, as well as of Jules Grévy who was so typical of the provincial bourgeoisie, they respected disinterested study for the very reason that it did not prepare pupils for the real world of technology and economics. Secondary education, a remarkable example of the time-lag between mental attitudes and social needs, reflected the aspirations of a bourgeoisie faithful to the eighteenth-century bourgeois ideal of living 'nobly' and devoted to a Latin civilization of 'lawyers' not 'producers'.

In these circumstances it will be readily understood that discussions of the content of education aroused sharp controversies, for the very foundations of a society seemed to be at stake. The reform of 1880 reduced the importance of the dead languages, but they still occupied a third of the timetable in secondary classes proper. What is more, the reforms of 1884 and 1890 reduced the subjects favoured in 1880 – science, modern languages, history, French. Alongside this literary education, terminating in the *baccalauréat ès lettres*, there were 'preparatory' classes for the 'higher schools'; pupils entered them after the third or second form and they led to the *baccalauréat ès sciences*. It was not until 1890 that the distinction between the two *baccalauréats* disappeared.

In the same period the special instruction instituted by Victor Duruy to prepare pupils for careers in commerce and industry was gradually integrated in secondary education. In 1881 a committee chaired by Duruy remodelled the course of study; it was expanded from four to five years, divided into two cycles of three and two years, and was crowned by the *baccalauréat* in special secondary education. In 1891 Léon Bourgeois changed special secondary education into modern education and created a 'modern' *baccalauréat*. This *baccalauréat* remained a second-class qualification; certain careers – law or medicine – were closed to those who held it, and teachers and pupils on the classical side despised the 'French' or 'cattle', as they called them – another sign of the strength of traditions.

The private secondary schools or colleges had as many pupils at the end of the century as the *lycées* and state *collèges*. They do not seem to have been distinguished by any particularly original feature, apart from being denominational. Boarding, the primacy of the humanities and concern for the *baccalauréat* were common to both kinds of schools. The education given to the daughters of the bourgeoisie reflected a particular conception of woman. Destined for marriage and to look after the home, she had to learn how to keep house, rule the servants and bring up her children. Her virtue had to be guaranteed by a solid moral training. She had to do her husband honour, know something about literature, and possess some artistic accomplishment such as playing the piano, painting or, most often, doing needlework.

Early education took place, as far as possible and as for boys, at home. Then the girl could spend a few years at a boarding school, either run by nuns or not; she often remained a boarder until her first communion. At about fifteen her education was generally regarded as complete; at the most she might attend a few classes. In Paris at any rate the fashion was for examinations; young society girls and those belonging to the rich bourgeoisie regarded the elementary certificate as the finishing touch to their studies. The higher certificate was exceptional and the *baccalauréat* even more so, since girls were not brought up on the humanities. Generally, everything seems to confirm the following statement by a teaching nun, Mère Marie du Sacré-Coeur, speaking of the teaching in convents. 'In education we seem to have had only one dream, to possess pious, obedient pupils and to keep them, when it is not too late, in the innocence founded only on ignorance' (*Les Religieuses enseignantes*, Paris, 1898). When a girl married, her ignorance of life was great; a moralizing education concealed the realities of the flesh, as they say. Opinion was severe on a woman who 'fell by the wayside'. In spite of the light tone of the vaudeville theatres, a woman who committed adultery was a ruined woman.

The republicans introduced innovations in the field of secondary education for girls. We have mentioned the intentions of the Camille Sée law.

Its implementation was difficult and proceeded cautiously. Members of parliament and journalists belonging to the right grew very excited. There was talk of 'barracks for girls' and it was argued that the system of scholarships would certainly produce a reservoir of future nihilists, of *déclassées* – women who had 'come down in the world'. The law was denounced as a work of immorality and apostasy. The republicans had no more intention than the conservatives of opening professional careers to girls; their education, crowned by an internal certificate without any real validity, was to remain a domestic adornment. On the advice of the cautious Conseil Supérieur – there was no wish to upset parents – it was decided that the school timetable for girls should be shorter than that for boys and much less heavily laden; the new *lycée* pupils did not do Greek, Latin or philosophy. Instead they were given courses in morals, needle-work and music. The patronage of the State may have been new, but the content of feminine education was not.

The secondary education of girls was not conceived with the intention of revolutionizing society. However, it did have one important social conse-quence: it created a reliable and honourable career for single women without any money of their own at a time when the practice of a profession – apart from risky artistic careers – was a downward step for a woman belonging to the bourgeoisie. At first women teachers were regarded with suspicion; they were isolated, doomed by public opinion to celibacy or to a late and indifferent marriage. But they acquired citizenship as much by the dignity of their lives as by the material independence of their position. Their pupils, who belonged for the most part to the middle ranks of the bourgeoisie, had the choice of either becoming mothers of families as the legislators wished, or teachers. In the period with which we are concerned any other career was excluded, for the girls did not take the *baccalauréat* and higher education was thus closed to them. The situation does not seem to have created any real problem before 1910, judging by the growing success of the new institution.

For in fact although the beginnings were extremely modest – the girls' *lycées* opened with thirty or forty pupils – growth was regular without any recession up to 1914, at the very time when people were talking of a 'crisis' in the recruitment to boys' *lycées*. In November 1891 there were 11,645 girls enjoying secondary education in 29 *lycées*, 26 *collèges* and 61 secondary courses. Twelve years later the feminine school population was 28,207, with an annual increase that rose from 700 to 4,000 pupils. It is almost certain that few inroads had been made on the traditional clientèle of the convents; the success is explained, at this time, rather by the entry into secondary education of girls for whom twenty years earlier primary education would have been judged sufficient.

In the first few decades of the Third Republic the face of higher education changed and acquired the characteristics which it was to retain until our own day. Although the schools of law and medicine, which trained people for specific professions, had students, the faculties of letters and science had always been essentially the scene of fashionable lectures. Their principal reason for existing was to confer degrees, in particular the *baccalauréat*. At the end of the Second Empire a desire for change arose. This is seen in Victor Duruy's creation in 1868 of the *Ecole pratique des Hautes Etudes*, which was to train people within a very flexible framework for critical research. University staffs, who belonged to the Society for the Study of Questions of Higher Education, were able to express their views from 1881 onwards in the *Revue internationale de l'enseignement*,[11] and to exert pressure for thorough-going changes. This group – in which we find men then at the beginning of their careers who were to be among the ornaments of university life; historians, for example, such as Lavisse, Seignobos and Georges Weill – provoked a sympathetic response in ministers like the Hellenist Waddington, Ferry and Goblet. The Directors of Higher Education – Albert Dumont from 1879 to 1884 and Louis Liard from 1884 to 1902 – formed part of this university community. The work of a man like Albert Dumont – the first director of the French School in Rome and subsequently its rector before he was forty – as Director of Higher Education was decisive.[12] The creation of scholarships for the *licence* in 1877 and subsequently for the *agrégation* in 1880, the employment of lecturers with the task of looking after the students, who were obliged to apply themselves to their work, the organization of the *licence* and the creation of the *diplôme d'études supérieures* as an introduction to private research were all lasting innovations. The number of students increased, especially in literature and science. It doubled between 1875 (9,963) and 1891 (19,821). The expenditure involved was considerable. Posts of professor and lecturer were created, university 'palaces' were built and the Sorbonne was reconstructed; there was to be no comparable achievement until the time of the Fifth Republic. The promoters of the Society for Higher Education wanted a certain amount of administrative and financial autonomy. The Goblet decrees of 25 July 1885 (drafted by Liard) gave faculties a legal status and authorized them to receive subsidies from local bodies. Another decree, on 28 December, gave the faculties councils and assemblies. Liard and Goblet saw these as the first beginnings of universities – centres of regional life and of the dissemination of scientific knowledge – whose creation had been one of the major concerns of the Society for Higher Education since 1879. Lavisse wanted in this way to establish 'all the desirable links between the teaching of the sciences and that of medicine, between the teaching of law and that of literature'. He also hoped to do away with 'the isolation of the faculties, each of which has its own little administration and its own little private institutes'. But many people feared that the existing system was going to be dismantled. Local interests did not want just five or six big regional universities. But by beginning with the organization of the faculties, it made it difficult for them to federate themselves into a university.

The law of 10 July 1896, however, created universities, one per academy, which replaced the 'faculty bodies', assemblies of the faculties of the same academic discipline, endowed with financial powers since 1893. The law did not have the scope expected. This setback should not lead us to underestimate the major fact, which was the establishment of high-level scientific teaching, a step prompted by two concerns, the need to take up the challenge represented by German science, and the foundation in 1875 of the Catholic universities.

The latter were badly hit by the re-establishment of the awarding of degrees. Unlike private secondary education, 'free' higher education was a failure. When the state faculties had nearly 30,000 pupils there were at the most 1,400 in the 'free' faculties, 'one in ten of the young men whom we have brought up', as was observed in 1900 by the general secretary of the Catholic faculties of Lille. In fact, if an appreciable fraction of the élite avoided the university it was via the special schools – the *Polytechnique*, the *Ponts*, the *Mines*, the *Centrale*, the *grandes écoles*. Those were the aristocratic channels, while the faculties trained the 'proletariat of bachelors of arts' who vainly applied for teaching posts, like Racadot and Mouchefrin in the *Déracinés*.

We have mentioned the importance the republicans attached to the primary school and the passing of the laws which founded the schools of the Republic. It remains to explain in detail how these laws were applied and to estimate their influence.

Teaching in the primary school was based on the concentric method; every year the knowledge inculcated in the previous year was studied more thoroughly. The subjects taught were French, arithmetic, history and geography, the natural sciences, civic affairs and morality. They were intended to provide sufficient intellectual equipment for the pupil's whole life; hence the encyclopaedic nature of the instruction, which led up to the *certificat d'études*. 'The elementary school remained dominated by the concern to train adults for a rural, commercial, thrifty society' (A. Prost).

The primary school began, before the compulsory school age, with the *école maternelle* (nursery school), a term which – significantly – replaced that of *salles d'asile* (refuge rooms) on the publication of the decree of 2 August 1881. The first timetables made the nursery schools a real preparation complete with 'lessons' for the primary school. But very soon the nursery schools were to introduce their own sort of teaching based on play, thanks in particular to Pauline Kergomard, the inspector-general, who had close links with highly placed republicans, but also to the influence of child psychology in which considerable progress was being made. In accordance with Pauline Kergomard's wishes, the nursery school became 'an educational establishment, not an instructional one'. Before 1900 about one child in four, from the age of two to that of six, went to nursery schools, which, unlike the elementary schools, were mixed.

Primary education was prolonged by higher primary education. Created on Guizot's initiative, this was in a somewhat stagnant state. When 'special' education became 'modern' education, the higher primary school was revitalized. The Goblet law of 1886 fixed its status as well as that of the 'the classes of higher primary education adjoined to the elementary schools and known as "complementary courses" '. Higher primary education developed rapidly. From 1889 to 1899 over 60,000 pupils – the children sometimes of peasants, but more often of tradesmen and craftsmen and even of workers and clerks – passed through the higher primary schools. All round, because of the training it gave in the general sections – the most numerous ones – and in the professional sections, higher primary education ensured that the members of the 'new strata' had some chance of rising in the world. After all, the certificate of elementary studies and the higher certificate made it possible to sit the administrative competitions for the post office and the railways and to enter the primary teacher training colleges.

What should our final evaluation of the Republic's educational work be? It has rightly been said that when compulsory schooling was introduced most children were already attending elementary schools. Ferry's compulsory schooling was 'essentially an extension of effective schooling' (A. Prost). Previously it was only between the ages of eight and ten that almost all children went to school. The progress of schooling was not complete; there were exemptions from compulsory attendance. Acquisition of the certificate of studies at eleven gave exemption from the school years remaining and children who had reached the age of apprenticeship – twelve years – and were employed in agriculture or industry were exempted from attendance. Above all, the education committees responsible for supervising the implementation of the law did not function very well. They were inclined to be swayed by the demand for workers in the fields, by the need for contributory wages and for domestic work – which explains why the number of girls who attended school was lower than the number of boys.[13]

As a result, the proportion of conscripts who were illiterate was still 5.2 per cent in 1896. The old contrast still remained, too, between an educated France to the north of a line running from Mont-Saint-Michel to Lake Geneva and a backward France – Brittany, the centre. And in the industrial departments of the north and north-west – Seine-Inférieure, Somme, Pas-de-Calais, Nord, Aisne – the level of literacy was below that of the departments of the north-east and east. As E. Levasseur observed,

'Industrial agglomerations are not always favourable ground for the development of primary education.'

The culture of the people, and the culture of the educated classes

We must now ask to what extent the primary school helped to modify systems of values and to change popular ways of thinking. The question is vital, for the republicans and their opponents were both convinced that elementary education exerted a decisive influence on the formation of people's minds. Yet the answer is not easy to formulate, for it looks as if the changes in the way people thought often preceded the advent of the republican school. The idea of laicization, faith in progress and religious indifference came before the school established by Jules Ferry and Ferdinand Buisson. Conversely, the influence of the school did not make itself felt immediately, but the fact remains that in this domain schoolteachers were able to shape attitudes and to reinforce developments. The textbooks of history, geography, reading and morality developed national feeling and crystallized the legendary symbols of patriotism from the Grand Ferré to Jeanne d'Arc, from the chevalier d'Assas to the drummer-boy Bara. The image of France projected by books like *Le Tour de la France par deux enfants* is that of a country with well-balanced resources and climate dominated by a rural, craft economy. Good housekeeping and thrift are the virtues praised above all others. This has been described as the subjection of the primary school to the dominant morality of the bourgeoisie, a summing-up undoubtedly inadequate and hardly more convincing than the Catholic pamphlets explaining 'de-christianization' as a plot by the freemasons and the scheming of schoolmasters. In fact, a whole people – in Michelet's sense of the word – were deeply devoted to the values disseminated by the republican school and did not question the faith and morality of the secular school. It believed in learning, in education and in the opportunity for betterment offered by the liberal, democratic society. The schoolmaster's influence was only so great because his audience was ready to listen to him.

In addition, other sources of information helped to lead people in the same direction. The newspaper became an article of daily consumption: the penny press experienced growing success. It accounted for nearly half the number of papers printed in 1870 and three-quarters in 1880 (P. Albert, Biblio. no. 137), thanks to technical discoveries (the rotary press), to distribution by railway in bundles, post-free, and to the mass appeal of advertising. *Le Petit Journal* and after 1890 *Le Petit Parisien* reached the countryside. *Le Petit Journal*, a republican, socially conservative paper, printed 220,000 copies in 1872 and 700,000 in 1882. No other paper of small format (44 cm x 30 cm) succeeded at that time in imitating it. It published the serials of Xavier de Montépin and Jules Verne and, on the front page, perhaps a simple political commentary, perhaps a moralizing tale. It was 'in these little papers that the people learnt to read and, thanks to them, were prevented from forgetting the lessons they had learnt at school' (P. Albert).

Nevertheless, the local press retained a considerable readership. There were the papers published in the *chefs-lieux*, the *arrondissements*, or even the cantons – often the only ones read by the peasants; they were weeklies or bi-weeklies, soothing in tone, gently polemical except during election periods. There was the departmental press, daily papers often subsidized by a politician and printing several thousand copies. One editor working with scissors was sufficient to run these papers. A novelty was the appearance of big regional newspapers, all, except the conservative *Nouvelliste* of Lyon, supporting the republican cause. There was *Le Progrès* in Lyon, *La Petite Gironde* in Bordeaux and, above all, *La Dépêche* in Toulouse. At that period these papers gave relatively little space to local news and helped rather to make Paris more familiar to the public and to make French life more uniform, encouraging centralization.

The big papers strove to win readers by printing illustrated supplements, by giving space to small news items and by including serials, the typical kind of literature aimed at a popular readership. The serials were subsequently published in cheap bound volumes. This kind of literature liked to picture the aristocratic world in the time of the monarchy, but it also adopted a 'populist' tone, dealing with the little people, shop-girls and even workers. The heroine of *La Porteuse de pain* by Xavier de Montépin, published in 1884, is a workman's widow unjustly convicted of burning down a factory and of murder. The illustrated magazines, popular novels and catalogues from the big stores were the components of a new popular culture, successor to the traditional culture which had been undermined by the activities of the schools and the broadening of horizons resulting from better means of transport, movements of population and military service. The decline of the dialect was the clearest sign of this process. No doubt schoolmasters scolded children who spoke in dialect, but in so doing they were following the wishes of the children's parents, who were anxious to enable their children to rise in the social scale through a confident knowledge of the national language. (Local dialects continued to put up a vigorous resistance in the heathlands of the interior of Brittany and in the mountains of the Massif Central.) Schoolmasters and minor civil servants, who saw themselves as the nameless agents of progress, thought that rejection of the national language was equivalent to rejection of the Republic and the modern world.

We do not really know what was read by those French people, the huge majority, who had not been educated at the *lycées* and *collèges*. It is no doubt safe to assert the popularity of Victor Hugo, the 'national poet', who formed the link between the popular strata and cultivated public. The crowd that attended his funeral in 1885 bears witness to the wide influence of the author of *Les Misérables* and the *Châtiments*. Erckmann and Chatrian were more 'people's writers' than Hugo and were despised by bourgeois taste. Hostile to nobles and priests, democrats who distrusted socialism, hostile to personal power, patriots opposed to wars, the authors of the *Romans nationaux*, of the *Histoire d'un homme du peuple* and of the *Histoire d'un plébiscite* embodied the very essence of the republican spirit. Exiled, after 1871 they symbolized the Alsace-Lorraine myth. G. Bruno makes the heroes of the *Le Tour de la France par deux enfants* leave Phalsbourg by the legendary Porte de France, and this is certainly because the little fortress in the Vosges was known, thanks to Erckmann and Chatrian, to millions of Frenchmen and because its name awoke lasting echoes.

We suggest that such a culture was profoundly political (cf. P. Joutard in G. Duby, Biblio. no. 35). The 14 July, a republican and patriotic festival, was also a secular feast. Schoolchildren had to take part in it so as to 'rescue the younger generations from superstitious practices' (municipal council of Paris, 22 June 1880). The civic religion was to replace 'old dogmas'. *Marianne*, wearing the Phrygian cap, crowned with laurels, holding the flag in one hand and leaning with the other on a sword, was the incarnation of the Republic:

> C'est une femme au corps brûlant
> Au sein gonflé d'indépendance ...
> Notre maîtresse à nous Français
> Répond au nom de Marianne.[14]

It would be very wrong to underestimate the popular fervour and enthusiasm on the occasion of the first festivals of the 14 July and to fail to recognize the emotional power of the myth of the Republic. In Paris the lower-class quarters were the ones most bedecked with flags. André Siegfried describes his father, the mayor of Le Havre, going round 'the popular quarters in an open carriage, moving from post to post, shaking innumerable hands, encouraging the militants, leaving here and there gifts and subsidies. The city disappeared under a mass of tricolour flags, streamers and slogans.' The popular festival with its balls in the squares and fireworks was a sort of political liturgy. With the end of the century and the celebration of 1 May, the 14 July would lose the atmosphere of militant unanimity that was so characteristic of the early days of the Republic.

In the France of villages, *bourgs* and small towns in particular, the electoral struggles and the discussions in the bars at fairs were all part of this common culture that stretched from the middle classes to the peasantry. This is less true of the big agglomerations. There social integration was less strong; the cultural progress as a result of the development of reading and the rôle of the schoolmaster was less evident. There, new forms of leisure activity, such as the café-concert, came into being. Members of both the working classes and the bourgeoisie were to be found in such places, for social stratification and cultural stratification were by no means entirely identical.

Yet the bourgeois élite certainly had its own culture, expressed in the homage rendered to a certain number of institutions and in values consecrated by the canons of taste in art as well as literature. Here we can only report a few incontestable facts and ask a few questions, for a history of art or literature primarily sensitive to major works can provide only a partial idea of the reality. It is scarcely necessary to add that the cultural dominance of Paris, where fashions and reputations started, helps to falsify our picture of bourgeois culture.

Convinced that it was an élite privileged by its culture, did the bourgeoisie of the first few decades of the Third Republic understand the literary and artistic creations of the age? We know little about the relations between the creations of writers and artists and the society of their time; nor did the entire bourgeoisie react in precisely the same way. A Parisian banker, an enlightened amateur or experienced collector, such as Cernuschi, was more open to new ideas than an industralist of Lille or a lawyer of Mamers. What seems bold to one generation may be accepted by the next; Wagner, not understood by the public of the Second Empire, was – in spite of the nationalists – the 'god' of the 1890s. Nevertheless, the gulf between public taste and the real creative artists seems to have grown wider. 'I used to be taken every year', André Siegfried recalls, 'to the private view at the Salon, so that I could have the great painters of the day pointed out to me – Bonnat, Carolus Duran and Bouguereau; I vaguely knew that there were daubers called Monet or Renoir, but as for Cézanne or Van Gogh, I did not even know their names.' Public favour was in fact reserved for the portraits of Bonnat, a painstaking painter of illustrations of the budding Republic, for the battle pictures of Meissonnier, Detaille and Alphonse de Neuville, who flattered patriotic feeling, and for the academism of Bouguereau.

'The beginnings of Impressionism mark one of the fiercest points in the conflict which broke out at the end of the nineteenth century between bourgeois taste and artistic creation' (J. Cassou). The first exhibition of the Impressionist group at the Nadar photographic gallery on 15 April 1874 caused a scandal, as did succeeding exhibitions. It was to be years before Impressionist pictures ceased to provoke hostility. Renoir and Monet, Clemenceau's friend, found some understanding. Manet, who received a medal at the Salon of 1881, was decorated with the *Légion d'honneur*, thanks to his friend Antonin Proust, ephemeral Minister for the Arts in Gambetta's Great Ministry. But even in 1890 the State refused to accept *Olympia* as a gift for the Louvre. Pissarro and Sisley inspired mistrust and Cézanne remained uncomprehended.

Although in general the canons of the Academy of Fine Arts triumphed in the realms of painting and sculpture, the isolated genius of Rodin was in fact recognized. Architecture persisted in imitating classical models, taking a cool attitude to new materials and forms. Interior decoration was no less clearly marked by love of imitation; the republicans' Republic did not produce an original style of furnishing. The 1880s were the great days of the imitation Henri II style: the dining-room with a heavy carved sideboard, square chairs covered in Cordoba leather, walls papered in dark colours.

Bourgeois circles particularly enjoyed spectacles, social amusements to which one went to see and to be seen. The subsidized theatres – the Opéra, the Opéra-Comique and the Comédie-Française – were loyal to accepted values. Regular visitors to the Opéra gave an enthusiastic welcome to Verdi and applauded Gounod and Massenet. At the Opéra-Comique *Carmen* cause a scandal in 1875 through its realism. The classics triumphed at the Comédie-Française. Yet the public was also fond of lighter works. It was the golden age of operetta, with Lecocq's *Fille de Mme Angot*, Audran's *La Mascotte* and Messager's *Véronique*. The boulevard theatre, where vaudeville and the plays of Labiche, Meilhac and Halévy reigned supreme, also drew a large public. The theatre's good fortune was not confined to Paris; provincial towns, even quite small ones, attached great value to having an opera house or a theatre.

There was a flowering of music too; Colonne and Pasdeloup organized weekly symphony concerts to educate the public. However, César Franck, the organist of Sainte-Clotilde, was appreciated only by a small circle of people. Vincent d'Indy and the founders of the Schola Cantorum met more success.

Literary taste was dominated by the success of naturalism. It was the day of the Goncourts, Zola and Maupassant. The Rougon-Macquart series, *Histoire naturelle et sociale d'une famille sous le second Empire*, began to appear from 1871 onwards. It offended traditionalists but was successful, as Albert Thibaudet saw very clearly, with the 'new strata' of the bourgeoisie, whose positivism was satisfied by the determinism asserted by the novelist. Zola was popular enough to have his books published as serials in the newspapers. Not everyone, especially women, could appreciate this 'vulgar' and 'daring' literature. Writers like Octave Feuillet and Georges Ohnet provided books which satisfied their yearnings for an ideal world of dreams.

Poetic innovation went unnoticed puzzling people by its hermetic nature and Verlaine, Rimbaud and Mallarmé were more or less unknown. It was Symbolism – the manifesto of Moréas dates from 1886 – that made them known, but only within a restricted circle. The Parnassians, on the other hand, with Leconte de Lisle, seemed accessible; Sully Prudhomme and François Coppée in particular became famous. After all, the authors of *La Justice* and *Les Humbles* conformed to the dominant ideology of faith in knowledge and progress. Gaining an audience with the lower class through the schools, they were to figure as official poets of the Republic, like Victor Hugo.

Around 1885 the climate changed and the systems of values hitherto dominant seemed to be shaken. This *'fin-de-siècle* neurosis' cannot be separated from the general history of the period – the economic difficulties, the aggravation of the social situation, the willing audience for nationalism and socialism, these ideologies heralding the twentieth century, the return to a spiritual outlook on life, the 'new spirit'.

It was just when Zola was enjoying his greatest success[15] in October 1883, that Eugène Melchior de Vogüé, who was to become the mentor of a whole generation, began to publish his articles on the Russian novelists (they appeared in book form in 1886). In Tolstoy and Dostoyevsky, translated into French from 1884 to 1888, French readers discovered the suffering masses, the aspiration to the ideal, 'nihilism and pessimism ... the shadow of the infinite' (Vogüé). In 1889 Paul Bourget published *Le Disciple* which questioned the ideals of the scientific approach to life. In the same year Bergson wrote *L'Essai sur les données immédiates de la conscience* ... The deaths in 1892 and 1893 of Taine and Renan meant the disappearance of the men in whom, in spite of their moroseness in old age, the hopes pinned on science, progress and the positive method had been embodied. The changes in the *Revue des deux mondes*, that old citadel of liberal thought, are significant. On 1 January 1895 it published an article by its director, Brunetière, entitled 'After a visit to the Vatican', which proclaimed the 'partial bankruptcy' of science.[16] Brunetière himself, like Bourget, went back to the Church, the guarantor of social order.

The questioning of positivism was accompanied by the discovery of irrational forces. Edouard Schuré's book *Les Grands Initiés* dates from 1889. Buddhism, occultism and hypnotism all became fashionable. People enthused over Charcot's experiences with the hysterical inmates of La Salpêtrière; the explorations of the subconscious began. The pessimism of Schopenhauer, whom Challemel-Lacour had introduced to the French public as early as 1870 in the *Revue des deux mondes* and whose works had been translated by Burdeau, the Bouteiller of the *Déracinés*, met great success with the *décadents*. In 1886 the first number of the *Décadent* proclaimed that 'Religion, manners, justice are all in decline, or rather are undergoing an inevitable transformation.'

Here we can only note the most important aspects of this complex movement. It is essential, of course, to define its limits; it affected first the bourgeois and Parisian élite, relatively limited circles who gravitated round sometimes ephemeral reviews such as *La Conque, Le Banquet*, the *Revue blanche, Le Mercure de France* ... In 1889 the bestsellers of the year were Zola's *Bête humaine*, Maupassant's *Fort comme la mort* and Georges Ohnet's *Dr Rameau*.[17]

Yet many signs bear witness to the breadth of the reaction against positivism and naturalism. The Symbolist poets, together with Moréas, drew Rimbaud, Verlaine and Mallarmé out of obscurity. In 1891 the enquiry into the evolution of literature conducted by Jules Huret in *L'Echo de Paris* bore witness to the success of these poets. Whether they were Catholics or tempted by anarchism, the Symbolists rejected positivism and the poetry of plain statement. In 1893 Lugné-Poe staged Maeterlinck's *Pelléas et Mélisande*, which reveals so well the elusive and unfathomable *fin-de-siècle* spirit. At the Théâtre Libre Antoine acted Ibsen and Strindberg. Like the Russian novelists, the Scandinavian dramatists brought a 'new spirit'; the phrase was much employed at the time to indicate that change in sensibility which was marked by a return to idealism, to a spiritual attitude, to the irrational. In painting, Gauguin, Cézanne and Van Gogh, *peintres maudits*, went beyond Impressionism, which in their view remained attached to the 'fetters of verisimilitude'. A new aesthetic was coming into being, one breaking free from reality.

5

The Republic confronted by nationalism and socialism

With the fall of Jules Ferry on 30 March 1885 the period of the founders of the Republic comes to an end. A new period opens, marked by increasing ministerial instability and by the rise of brands of opposition hostile to the régime. In the years of economic and social difficulties the liberal, parliamentary Republic disappointed the masses, so they turned to ideologies that corresponded better to their aspirations. Nationalism changed character at the time of the Boulangist crisis and socialism became a political force. These were considerable changes and we need to measure their impact.

The elections of 1885

Ferry's opponents did not constitute a governing majority. Increasing divisions in the republican ranks opened a period of instability. Brisson, the president of the Chamber of Deputies, who was close to the radicals and 'imbued with the masonic spirit' (J. Kayser) formed a government of 'republican concentration', a formula which at that time denoted the union of all republicans, including the extreme left, against the conservatives.[1] It scarcely lasted beyond the elections. These were held with voting for several members from a list (*scrutin de liste*); Waldeck-Rousseau, Ferry's Minister of the Interior, had had this method accepted by both Chambers – neither Chamber saw the same inconvenience in it as when Gambetta was alive. Each department received a number of deputies in proportion to its population, one member for every 70,000 inhabitants. If there was no absolute majority a second round of voting took place. This system, unique in French electoral history, did not help the republicans. In thirty-four departments (according to Kayser, Biblio. no. 57, p. 141) they split up and presented two lists, one of moderate republicans, and the other of radicals on which socialists sometimes figured. In Paris the list of 'radical, progressive committees', which favoured the union of republicans, was opposed by the list of radical socialists, including Clemenceau. The parties of the right managed to agree on single list. They reproached the republicans with the financial deficit, the economic crisis, the policy of laicization, and 'the war undertaken, and continued, in Tunisia, Tonkin and Cambodia with criminal lack of foresight'.[2]

The poll was higher than in 1881, abstentions falling from 31.4 per cent to 22.4 per cent. The conservatives virtually regained their position of 1877. They won the votes of the abstainers of 1881 and of a certain number of republican electors. After the first round the conservatives held 176 seats against 127 republican ones. Nord and Pas-de-Calais went over to the conservatives. Almost half the seats hung in the balance; very often the republicans' divisions had prevented them from attaining an absolute majority. The resurgence of the conservatives bore witness to the permanence of the great political forces and to the discontent arising from the economic difficulties and the policies of the opportunists. This brought a return to 'republican discipline'. Agreement was reached on the candidates best placed in the first round. In most cases the list that had finished up on top was retained; sometimes new coalition lists were drawn up. The radicals of Bordeaux withdrew in favour of Raynal, the man who had made the agreements with the railways, and those of the Côte d'Or made way for Spuller. But the agreement often favoured the radicals who had headed the list in the first round. The electors followed this tactic. What is more, the sole republican list often gained votes in comparison with the total of republican votes in the first round. The right won only 25 seats against the left's 244. Altogether the new Chamber had 383 republicans, 223 of them members of the previous Chamber, and 201 conservatives, of whom 72 had sat in the old Chamber. The conservatives were twice as numerous as in 1881. The group known as the 'Appeal to Bonapartists', which had 65 members, and the royalist right, while retaining their autonomy, formed a 'Union of the Right'.

The main results of the election were the resurgence of the conservatives, who started to re-group, the renewal of the membership of the Chamber, 41 per cent being newly elected deputies, and the realignments in the republican ranks. The agreements to stand down had favoured the radicals, better placed after the first round than the opportunists, who absorbed the débris of the centre left. The radicals retained the same strongholds and gained a foothold in Seine-et-Oise and Haute-Garonne. The conquest of the south-west was just starting. Jacques Kayser (Biblio. no. 57, p. 146) basing his conclusions on a study of the electoral campaign, of the candidates' professions of faith and of the first polls, reckons the number of extreme left members elected at about a hundred; among them were a few socialists, who were outbidding the radicals. Moreover, some forty deputies of the radical left were close to this extreme left, whose success brought with it a rejuvenation of the Chamber. Thirty of the radicals elected were less than forty years old; among them was Millerand.

On their own, the governing republicans, mostly united in the 'Union of the Left', no longer had a majority; they were hardly more than 200 in number. The Chamber consisted of three more or less equal groups and was ungovernable. The only possibilities were coalitions, which were liable to be unstable, based as they had to be on the support of the radical left and the toleration of the extreme left. The only other conceivable solution was a government by the centre, allowed to exist by the toleration of the right, and this was a hypothesis unacceptable to the old republicans. Grévy, re-elected President of the Republic on 28 December 1885, opted to start with for the first of the two solutions described.

For the third time he called on Freycinet, whose skill in manoeuvring he admired, to form a government. Freycinet requested 'the support of all the groups in the republican majority'. For the first time radicals entered the government, as individuals, alongside the moderates. Freycinet secured the passage of the law of 30 October 1886 on the laicization of the state schools, but he did not really satisfy either the radicals, who wanted social reforms, or the moderate republicans. In a letter to Joseph Reinach, Ferry denounced Clemenceau as 'un premier ministre occulte'. Freycinet fell on the question of the estimates for sub-prefects, a victim of the radicals and the right, but his successor, Goblet, who was close to the radicals, formed a government that was practically similar. Above all, he retained his predecessor's Minister for War, General Boulanger – the radicals' choice – whose popularity soon reached phenomenal proportions. The Boulangist crisis had begun.

The Boulangist crisis and its consequences

In the Boulangist crisis, the régime's first trial of strength less than ten years after its inception, what matters is not so much the episodes of the story, which after all were quite brief, as a proper understanding of an intellectual phenomenon which contained various different components and has considerably more significance than the ephemeral hero who gave it its name.

The social problems consequent on the economic crisis of 1882, the rise of anti-parliamentarianism and the evolution of French nationalism are all factors which explain Boulangism. We have spoken of the economic difficulties. They created a difficult social climate, marked by strikes, some of which, such as the strike at Decazeville at the beginning of 1886, had nationwide repercussions. And in 1888 a very serious strike by building workers broke out. As well as discontent there was disappointment at the policies pursued by the republicans. The workers turned away from the parliamentary Republic which was socially conservative, and out of hostility to opportunism pinned their hopes elsewhere. This important fact did not escape the notice of the author of the *Histoire socialiste*.[3]

Anti-parliamentarianism affected not only the working people but also the middle classes, who, especially in the big towns, were influenced by the press and the main currents of opinion. The fall of Ferry, like the elections of October 1885, marked the beginning of a period of ministerial instability that made more impression on public opinion than the scarcely appreciated stability of the governmental personnel and the continuity of the main lines of policy. We must also take care not to adopt an anachronistic approach. Because the régime did in fact last we are liable to underestimate the discontent caused by the 'ministry waltz' and the consequent fears for the future of a régime which seemed, only a few years after its inception, so fragile. Paul Cambon, Ferry's friend, who had links with all the republicans and was at that time resident in Tunisia, wrote to his wife in autumn 1885, at the end of a visit to Paris: 'The general impression is that the Republic is at the end of its tether. Next year we shall have revolutionary excesses and then a violent reaction. What will emerge from all this? Some kind of dictatorship.' He added, to one of his associates, 'There is no government in France' (Biblio. no. 17, vol. I, p. 261).

The feeling that the Republic was powerless and in no condition to prepare the 'revenge' for the defeat of 1871 was particularly painful to the nationalists. We have spoken of the ardent patriotism of the republicans after the defeat and their desire to forge a new France through education and the army. In May 1882 the League of Patriots was founded.[4] Its first president was the historian Henri Martin. Among its vice-presidents was Félix Faure and his deputy was the poet Paul Déroulède, the author of the *Chants du soldat*. The League enjoyed the patronage of eminent people from the republican world and was established in the wake, so to speak, of Gambetta. Its foundation had no other political aim but that of 'developing the moral and physical forces of the nation' and of keeping alive the flame of revenge. Déroulède claimed to be a mere 'sounder of the bugle'. The League of Patriots was first conceived as part of the movement for civic and patriotic education so characteristic of the early days of the Third Republic. It swiftly attained a membership of 182,000, a considerable figure and one out of proportion to those for the political and trade union organizations of the time. However, the caution of the opportunists where Germany was concerned and the abandonment of revenge in favour of colonial enterprises led Déroulède to give the movement a different emphasis when he became president in March 1885. He was convinced that the absence of authority was putting the country in danger. This diagnosis led him to regard the 'revision of the parliamentary régime' as a prerequisite for the 'revision of the Treaty of Frankfurt'. Non-political at the start, the League was to venture, not without internal disturbances, into the political field. Social aspirations, rejection of the parliamentary Republic, assertion of popular sovereignty, exaltation of national feeling – such a programme, by its very confusion and vagueness, was of a kind to catch the imagination of those disappointed by the policies of the opportunists. It followed in the tradition of the men of 1793, whose descendants the radicals claimed they were, the radicals who thought they had found in Boulanger the 'booted Jacobin' of whom they dreamed.

When Freycinet appointed Boulanger, then commander of the troops in Tunisia, Minister for War, he was pleasing Clemenceau, who had close links with Boulanger, and Granet, another of Freycinet's radical ministers. Boulanger had in his favour a brilliant military career and was well-connected politically. He had a sense of theatre and knew how to secure full value from the initiatives he took. He had none of the discretion of the generals who preceded him at the Ministry of War. Rightaway he justified the extreme left's friendly feelings towards him. He attacked 'the coteries who parade their hostility' to the Republic. He struck the duc d'Aumale off the army list.[5] He justified the presence of the army at Decazeville: 'It is not acting in favour of the company against the miners any more than it would act tomorrow in favour of the miners against the company.' The left acclaimed him when he declared, 'Perhaps at this very moment each soldier is sharing his soup and bread ration with a miner.' At the ministry Boulanger took all kinds of initiatives. His technical achievements were by no means negligible. The Lebel automatic rifle replaced the Gras rifle, the lot of the troops was improved, the wearing of beards was authorized and the use of plates was made general. Boulanger tried to make the army popular; sentry boxes were painted in the colours of the tricolour and a review was held once again on 14 July. In 1886, at Longchamp, it was an exceptionally splendid one. The Parisian crowd acclaimed the Minister for War, and the variety singer Paulus à l'Alcazar wrote *En revenant de la revue*. Sensing what the public wanted, he asserted:

> Moi, j'faisais qu'admirer
> Not'brave général Boulanger.[6]

Boulangism was created by public opinion and nurtured by songs, pictures and the press, which gave wide publicity to the minister's statements and speeches. At this point republican politicians, apart from Ferry and his supporters who had been hostile from the start, remained favourable to Boulanger. After all, he was drawing up a plan for the reorganization of military service that conformed to democratic aspirations; service would be extended to three years, exemptions and volunteers would be abolished and priests would carry their packs on their backs like everyone else (the law was adopted in July 1889). On the other hand, the moderate republicans, but not the radicals, were seriously worried about Boulanger when a campaign in favour of revenge developed round him, supported by papers such as *La France militaire* and *La Revanche*. It looked as if the tone of Boulanger's initiatives might push Bismarck into a preventive war.

Did the German Chancellor really think that a conflict was imminent or did he simply want to take advantage of the situation to obtain an easier passage for a new military law after the dissolution of the Reichstag? However that may be, Bismarck took intimidatory measures and mobilized reservists near the frontier in the middle of winter. At the same time a period of reaction began in Alsace-Lorraine in contrast to the toleration exercised since 1879. From 31 December 1886 no one belonging to the French army could stay in the German Empire without obtaining prior administrative authorization, and on 29 March the measure was extended to all French people. The Attorney-General of the German Empire had the houses of members of the League of Patriots living in Alsace-Lorraine searched. A case to which great publicity was given was heard by the Supreme Court in Leipzig. But on 21 February 1887, at the elections following the dissolution of the Reichstag, in spite of intimidation by the government ('The elections in Alsace-Lorraine are not without significance for the question of war or peace.'), only 'protesters' were elected. The 'autonomists' who had sat in the previous Reichstag were beaten. The government dissolved any society with tendencies hostile to Germany. Two Alsatians accused of spying were tried by the Leipzig court. On 21 April 1887 Schnaebelé, the police superintendent at Pagny-sur-Moselle, summoned by his German colleague on official business, was arrested on suspicion of spying in Alsace. This was the height of the crisis; the excitement was extreme and nationalist circles in France thought there would be war. Boulanger, in cabinet, proposed sending an ultimatum to Germany. Grévy stopped him: 'An ultimatum means war and I do not want any war.'[7] Flourens, the Minister of Foreign Affairs, sent a request for an explanation to Berlin, alleging machinations by the German police. Bismarck had Schnaebelé released. Had peace been seriously threatened? It is not certain, but public opinion thought so and the German threat, which had seemed to have disappeared for some years, was suddenly once more present. It was indissolubly bound up with the unhappy state of the 'lost provinces'. As the Barrès of *L'Appel au soldat* wrote, 'a shudder went through the country'. This fever strengthened the popularity of Boulanger, to whose firmness Schnaebelé's release was attributed. But the opportunists, anxious to preserve a peace, wanted to get rid of a Minister for War who was leading France into adventures. On 17 May the Goblet cabinet fell by 275 votes to 257; confronted with Boulanger, the right and the moderate republicans found a common cause.

Was there going to be a realigned majority? The hypothesis was not altogether unlikely in so far as there were signs of two developments, on the right as well as in the ranks of the moderate republicans. On the right, some people were thinking of giving their support to a conservative Republic; in 1886 Raoul Duval, a Protestant and former Bonapartist, formed a group of the republican right. Above all, some conservatives, from fear of the radicals, were ready to tolerate a government dominated by the moderate republicans. The latter were prepared to accept a Republic 'open' to the conservatives provided that they did not try to destroy it. Rouvier, who had links with the business world, formed a government which relied on the 'Union of the Left', followers of Ferry and former followers of Gambetta, and the neutrality of the right; Boulanger was no longer a minister. The brevity of Rouvier's ministry should not lead us to underestimate the meaning of the experiment; it heralded the 'policy of appeasement' which was to be resumed some years later. All in all, it represented a return to the combination of centres with a view to a policy of social defence. It met the same difficulties as before. It is interesting that as soon as Rouvier came into power he declared that he would not preserve the government, even with a majority, if it did not have a republican majority;[8] so strong were suspicions of the right. The religious question was still the major problem; at the most the opportunists could only promise some form of compromise on the policy of laicization, a concession which the right – and particularly its electors – considered inadequate. The questions which were to crop up again at the time of the alliance were already visible on the horizon. Moreover, the right's support for Rouvier was all the more hesitant because the progress of Boulangism and anti-parliamentarianism led the men of the authoritarian right to think that it was possible to overthrow the régime by making use of Boulangism.

As soon as the Goblet government resigned Boulanger's friends did not miss any chances to stimulate demonstrations of public opinion in his favour. During the crisis itself the editor of *L'Intransigeant* and former communard, Rochefort, taking advantage of the Parisian by-election of 23 May, recommended adding Boulanger's name to the voting slip. More than 38,000 voters followed his advice. On 8 July 1887 Boulanger's supporters wanted to prevent his departure for Clermont, where he had been appointed to command the 13th Corps. There was an extraordinary demonstration in which the crowd sang the *Marseillaise* and refrains in honour of 'General Revenge'.

> Il reviendra quand le tambour battra,
> Quand l'étranger m'naç'ra notre frontière.
> Il reviendra et chacun le suivra
> Pour cortège il aura la France entière.[9]

The demonstration worried old republicans attached to the supremacy of the civil authority; men like Clemenceau parted from Boulanger at this point. Clemenceau feared caesarism and a soldier who was too popular.

Yet Boulanger's working-class supporters certainly came from the left, even from the extreme left. As a shrewd writer in the conservative *Correspondant* (25 July 1887) observed: 'The journalists of *La Lanterne* and *L'Intransigeant* who laud Boulanger are not particularly fond of the army; in fact Boulanger has let himself be acclaimed by the revolutionary party as one of its leaders.' Boulanger enjoyed the support of the men of the Commune: 'It is to be feared that, except for M. Déroulède and his friends of the League, revenge is the least of these bawlers' concerns... For them, revenge is revenge inside the country, revenge on the men of Versailles, on the bourgeois, on the opportunists, on Ferry and Rouvier.' The analysis is a penetrating one and well defines a Jacobin, plebeian, Parisian Boulangism.

Once Boulanger had left for the provinces the fever seemed to be abating when the honours scandal broke out. Wilson, Grévy's son-in-law, had been using his influence, even to obtain the *Légion d'honneur*. For the first time scandal struck the régime in the very entourage of the statesman who was its incarnation. Rouvier asked for the adjournment of a reply to an *interpellation* by Clemenceau; he was defeated by 317 votes to 228 on 19 November. The right abandoned Rouvier, 'out of fear of its electors', as Adrien Dansette justly writes – they would not allow the right to close its eyes to the affair. There was another reason for the vote: the parliamentary right, in the 'Union of the Right', had been overwhelmed by the authoritarian right. The latter, Bonapartist by tradition, found weighty support in the declarations made by the comte de Paris on 15 September. The claimant to the throne gave his support to the idea of a plebiscite; he thought above all that the country, 'disgusted with republican parliamentarianism', would want a strong government.

Grévy was the target behind Rouvier. None of the politicians who were sounded out would agree to form a government. Grévy, who had persisted in remaining president of the Republic, finally resigned on 2 December. It looked as if Ferry's time had come. Confident in the support of the majority of the Senate, he seemed to have a majority in the Congress, but found himself bitterly opposed by Clemenceau and the radicals. Whether they were for or against Boulanger, the latter joined the members of the League of Patriots and the Blanquists to attack Ferry. There were demonstrations in Paris against 'Famine Ferry' detested since the Commune, and 'Tonkin Ferry' who had forgotten about revenge. The worst was expected if he was elected president of the Republic. At the meeting of republicans in Versailles Ferry was just ahead of Freycinet. Clemenceau pushed the candidature of Sadi Carnot, whose name was dear to the Republic. However, he was not very well known, except for refusing recommendations of Wilson's when he was Minister of Finance. At the Congress, Carnot was ahead after the first round and at the second Ferry and Freycinet stepped down in his favour. As in 1879 the politicians preferred a relatively obscure man, who would not exert excessive authority in the supreme magistracy, to a strong personality. But the fear of disturbances if Ferry was elected cast a shadow over the deliberations at Versailles. By frightening the opportunists, the radicals, Boulangists and socialists had triumphed over Ferry. The man who had been defeated on 30 March 1885 was never to return to power.

The coalition was less heterogeneous than it seems at first sight; in reality it was none other than that of the 'national party' which was to shake the Republic in 1888 and 1889. It is true that a certain number of radicals were gradually going to move away from Boulanger. One of those who did so was Clemenceau, although he did not disdain Boulangist support against Ferry; another was the former pastor Frédéric Desmons (Daniel Ligou, Biblio. no. 147), a leading freemason and deputy for Gard, who parted from the movement rather later. The 'possibilist' socialists certainly made the defence of the Republic a first priority and the Guesdists kept away from the 'national party', although Lafargue regarded it as a 'popular movement' and Guesde, who had little sympathy for it, did not regard it as his greatest adversary. However, the reservations or hostility of some in the radical or socialist world, reservations and hostility which grew progressively stronger, should not be allowed to obscure the very important fact that right to the end the people round Boulanger, the general staff of the 'national party', were men who came from the radical or socialist extreme left – the polemicist Rochefort, editor of *L'Intransigeant*, Eugène Mayer, editor of *La Lanterne*, and the deputies Laguerre, Francis Laur, Laisant, Le Hérissé, Turigny, the old radical from the department of Nièvre, and Senator Naquet. The only men who did not come from the extreme left were Dillon, a businessman, the Bonapartist journalist Georges Thiébaut and Déroulède himself. The same sort of authoritarian temperament is possibly what most united these men. Radicalism, as Albert Thibaudet felt very strongly, carried in itself this proconsular, Jacobin seed. It combined authority and democracy. The desire for a strong régime that would sweep away the compromises and surrenders of principle of opportunism was inseparable from the wish to let the people speak again, to re-establish popular sovereignty which had been confiscated by parliamentarianism and the representative government inaugurated by the 'monarchist' constitution of 1875. The democracy desired by the revisionists would be 'social'; the Boulangists, who were in a majority in the parliamentary 'socialist' group formed on 16 December 1887, proposed a programme which was in the tradition of non-Marxist socialism or early radicalism – pension funds, participation of the workers in the rewards of capitalism, co-operation (see Z. Sternhell, Biblio. no. 163). The measures to protect the 'national workforce' from foreign competition formed the link between this kind of socialism and nationalism.

What united Boulanger's supporters was the longing for revenge, glorification of the nation betrayed by the opportunist bourgeoisie. The political parties were divisive; what offered unity was *la patrie*. Mingled with this nationalist fever was the feeling that France was sick and decadent; to save France, the parliamentary régime had to be revised. Finally, Boulangism was inseparable from a romantic protest against the established order, against a settled régime. The Republic no longer aroused, as it had twenty years earlier at the end of the Empire, the enthusiasm of the younger generation. Barrès gave admirable expression to this feeling of rejection of a country 'inhabited by civil servants thinking of their careers; by administrators dreaming of spending summer at the seaside, of a *baccalauréat* for their sons and dowries for their daughters; and by political committees which, for lack of a principle of national unity, suggest factional formulas' (*L'Appel au soldat*).

Adopting a theme which came straight from the radicals, 'dissolution, constituent assembly, revision,' the 'Committee of the National Party' undertook a campaign in which it was ready to accept help from any side. Among the members of this coalition of opponents of the régime were those conservatives who repudiated parliamentary Orleanism. Without his supporters' knowledge, Boulanger met the leader of the 'Union of the Right', baron de Mackau, and made him promises[10] which gained the author of the duc d'Aumale's expulsion support from the right.

Meanwhile the parliamentary régime seemed to be demonstrating its powerlessness. Carnot had formed a 'business cabinet'. On 14 March it relieved Boulanger of his post and then on 27 March put him on the retired list. Boulanger's friends had put his name down as a candidate in a by-election on 26 February. Since he was now retired, Boulanger was eligible. He stood in the department of Nord. On the day that his candidature was announced, 30 March, Laguerre called for a vote of urgency on a motion for revision tabled by the radicals. It obtained 286 votes against 237; the right and the radicals, whether they were Boulangists or not, overthrew the moderate administration. People returned to an alliance with the radicals. Carnot called on Floquet, the President of the Chamber of Deputies, who co-opted Goblet and Freycinet. The latter was the first civilian to become Minister for War; he was to remain in this post, under various governments, for nearly five years. The politicians who had launched Boulanger were going to try to fight him.

Boulanger was elected in the Dordogne on 8 April by the radical and Bonapartist votes and in Nord on 15 April with the support of the workers' votes. Wishing to measure his popularity, he resigned and had himself elected again on 19 August in Nord, Somme and Charente-Inférieure. Every time he gathered against his name the conservative votes, especially the Bonapartist and clerical ones – after all, he had spoken in favour of an 'open Republic' – and also the radical and socialist votes. He was assisted by American-type campaigns organized by Dillon, who had seen the American party machines at work. The brochures, photographs and portraits, songs, hired newsvendors and knick-knacks bearing the likeness of the 'brave général' were all novelties. Encouraged by these successes, Boulanger stood as a candidate on 27 January 1889 in Paris. The radicals had warned him against standing; the bastion of the left and of the Republic would give him a nasty surprise. It was a triumph; the General obtained 245,236 votes against the 162,875 cast for the moderate radical Jacques and 17,039 for the navvy Boulé, the candidate of the Guesdists and Blanquists. The people of Paris had voted for Boulanger, an important event which signified much more than a passing infatuation; revolutionary Paris was soon to be succeeded by nationalist Paris.

It was from the provinces that the Republic's salvation was to come. On the evening of 27 January Boulanger, haunted by the memory of 2 December 1851 and loyal to the rule of law, refused to march on the Elysée Palace. He hoped that the general elections of 1889 would give him success. But at the time of the by-elections he had not faced the republican fortresses of the east and south-east. The conservatives were unreliable allies; in Ardèche they preferred to abstain, causing his defeat in July. In the north, part of the Orleanist electorate abstained. Above all, the republican defence was being organized. At the Grand Orient lodge on 23 May Clemenceau chaired the inauguration, together with the Gambettist Ranc and the possibilist Joffrin, of the Society for the Rights of Man and of Citizens. Its aim was to defend the Republic against a Caesarian dictatorship. Freemasonry entered the fight and with it the network of active republican committees and societies that was so active in the *bourgs* and small towns. There seemed to be a possible remedy – a return to voting by *arrondissement* (i.e., by constituency), a breakwater against the plebiscitary wave. Nearly two-thirds of the general councils demanded it, while the radical leaders remained in favour of voting by lists. Boulanger's election in Paris led Floquet, although he himself was hostile to voting for a single member, to table a motion for the reintroduction of voting by *arrondissement* which was passed by a small majority, 268 votes to 222. The moderate republicans and some of the radicals voted in favour, while those against were the right, now converted to voting by list, about thirty radicals and the seventeen Boulangists. The Senate, which was representative of the republican countryside, passed the motion by a huge majority – 222 votes to 54. Thus Floquet secured the passage of the electoral law but the moderate republicans reckoned that the moment had come to abandon him as he did not seem capable of stopping Boulangism. In addition, he had just tabled a motion for a tax on income and a draft plan for a revision of the constitution which included a Senate elected by universal suffrage in two stages. Thanks to the votes of the right, the moderate republicans obtained the adjournment of the revision. Floquet resigned on 14 February. Carnot recalled Tirard, whose second administration had more character than his previous one. He relied on former Gambettists, Rouvier at the Ministry of Finance and Spuller at the Foreign Office. Above all, Constans, who had been Minister of the Interior in Ferry's first cabinet, returned to the place Beauvau. He announced his intention 'of ensuring the maintenance of legal order and of the respect due to the Republic' and a week after his arrival in office he dissolved the League of Patriots. The members of its committee were prosecuted for belonging to a secret society.

However, the Boulangist general staff made a supreme effort to win the elections; they sought to gain the Catholic vote. Previously the transactions with the conservatives had been kept secret; this time the alliance was signed and sealed in broad daylight. On 17 March Boulanger spoke in Tours at a banquet organized by the journalist Jules Delahaye.[11] Boulanger defined the limits of his relations with the conservatives: 'No one among the conservatives who follows me does me the insult of saying that I support the Republic in order to betray it.' The restoration of the monarchy was impossible and would leave the nation 'divided'. The hopes that certain royalists put in Boulanger, as the 'battering ram' to topple the Republic, could not have been more clearly dissipated. But Boulanger was addressing not only the monarchist leaders but also conservative Catholic electors, whom he invited to enter the Republic: 'By accepting the Republic they imply the wish that it should be liberal and tolerant . . . that a break should be made with this system of oppression . . . The Republic . . . must repudiate the Jacobin heritage of the present Republic; it must bring religious stability to the country.' The Tours speech annoyed the monarchist leaders, who were hoping to make use of Boulanger; as for the left, it could henceforth denounce Boulanger as the 'leader of the clericals'. Many Catholic electors had not waited for this speech to support Boulanger, in spite of his anti-clerical entourage and the fact that he was the man who had used the phrase 'priests with their packs on their backs'. The interesting point about the Tours speech, which was written by Naquet, is that it shows the Boulangists' desire to channel to their own advantage the longing of the Catholics for a Republic that would make religious peace.

Constans took the initiative. This law don, enriched by politics and not immune from criticism when he was governor of Indo-China, knew how to intimidate his adversary and handle the police. Boulanger, threatened with impeachment before the Senate for 'endangering the safety of the State' fled to Brussels on 1 April. He, Dillon and Rochefort were prosecuted for contempt of court. The country did not react. On 5 May, the anniversary of the meeting of the States General, the Universal Exhibition to commemorate the centenary of the French Revolution opened. As the

Exhibition of 1878 had done after 16 May, it usefully lowered the political temperature and strengthened the Republic. On 17 July a law was promulgated forbidding multiple candidatures and requiring a compulsory declaration of candidature in order to avoid a plebiscitary demonstration using Boulanger's name. Boulanger himself was condemned by the High Court to deportation for contempt of court on 14 August and thus became ineligible. The verdict caused little stir. A few days earlier the ashes of La Tour d'Auvergne, Lazare Carnot, Marceau and Baudin had been moved to the Panthéon – so many national, revolutionary and republican glories. On 18 August all the mayors of France attended a banquet to mark the exhibition; it was a gastronomic, republican feast for the provinces who were to save the régime.

Conservatives and Boulangists went their separate ways to the polling booths. Where the conservatives had no candidates they supported the revisionists. After all, the comte de Paris, like Prince Victor, the Bonapartist claimant, had adopted the theme of revision as his own. In the opposite case the Boulangists gave their support to the right. This was the situation which occurred most frequently, since in fact the electoral organization of the Boulangists was non-existent. Thus except in Paris Boulangism was 'dominated by the conservative Union' (A. Dansette, Biblio. no. 159, p. 235); with voting by lists the national committee could have given its backing to Boulangist lists, but voting by *arrondissement* forbade this. The 'national party' did not have sufficient members to put forward numerous candidates against the notables. The clergy intervened more openly in the elections than in previous ones, taking a stand against the republicans, who had just passed the law establishing three years' military service and obliging seminarists, like students and future members of the teaching profession, to serve for a year. The military law and the educational laws were from then on the Catholics' great subjects of protest.

Electoral participation on 22 September was comparable to that in the elections of 1885, which themselves had been a hard-fought struggle. The left obtained 4,333,239 votes and 366 seats, the right 2,914,985 votes and 168 seats, and the Boulangists 709,223 votes and 42 seats. The majority system and the withdrawals among republicans favoured the left,[12] though several of its leaders, including Goblet and Ferry, were beaten by revisionists. All round, the coalition of the right and the Boulangists gained hardly more than 100,000 votes in comparison with the conservative vote of 1885. In fact, the reality was more complex than the comparison of the overall figures would lead one to think; there is no doubt that an appreciable number of left-wing electors, particularly in Paris, voted Boulangist. Conversely, in the countryside the republican conquest marched on. The Boulangists' lack of success has often been emphasized; it was certainly undeniable in the rural world, where the revisionist candidates were in fact identified with the conservatives. On the other hand, the Boulangists had considerable success in Paris and lost very few votes in comparison with 27 January (as J. Néré astutely notes). Boulanger defeated the socialist Joffrin in the *XVIIIe arrondissement*,[13] Laguerre was elected in the *XVe arrondissement* and Laur at Saint-Denis. They also did well in Bordeaux, where they benefited locally from the support of the Guesdists. In Nancy young Maurice Barrès won and so did the former radical Le Hérissé in Rennes. The France of the big cities, the France of the age of the masses had not abandoned the 'national' and 'social' General. But the France of the *bourgs* and the countryside declined to support him; by July, Boulanger, whom his friends had put up as a candidate in eighty cantons in the general council elections, had won in only twelve. The parliamentary elections confirmed this first test. From then on Boulangism was finished; the conservatives closed ranks and the men of the 'national party', now divided, were to finish up as nationalists or socialists. Boulanger, vanquished, committed suicide soon afterwards on the grave of his mistress in Ixelles cemetery.

Although his political intelligence was greater than has sometimes been admitted, Boulanger, for lack of coolness, consistency and decisiveness, had been the mediocre leader of a movement whose scope was beyond him. Actually, the Boulangist crisis, which brought so much into the open, helped to modify the public attitude and the facts of political life. That Boulangism was the expression of popular disappointment with the opportunist Republic is quite clear. It is also clear that the popular electorate which turned away from the moderate republicans or the anti-Boulangist radicals was now unattached; it was to swell the ranks of the socialists, where, indeed, it met some of the leaders of the 'national party'. The Boulangist crisis not only produced favourable conditions for the rise of socialism; it also stimulated the development of nationalism across the spectrum from 'revenge' patriotism to anti-parliamentary, authoritarian nationalism. There is nothing more remarkable than the electoral changes in a Paris that before 1889 had been republican and radical. After 1889 the suburbs became socialist and the centre nationalist. The hotbed of the revolutions of the nineteenth century was no longer the heart of the Republic. In this sense Boulangism strengthened the influence of the provinces in French life. The reintroduction of voting by *arrondissement*, previously odious to the republicans, was to have the same consequence. The veto on multiple candidatures made the deputy the man of his constituency, and he espoused its interests very closely. There were other consequences: radicalism, until then urban and revisionist, took root in the countryside. What is more, it acquired a foothold in the Senate as well. As for revising the constitution, reforming the State, reinforcing authority in the democracy, these ideas now bore the brand of dishonour. It was no longer possible for the left to take up Boulanger's ideas again. The military were also victims of Boulangism. The army as such had not adopted a position in the crisis, but the fact that one of the leading actors in the crisis had been a general was going to linger in the republican memory.

Socialism and the workers' movement

'We were gliding down the revisionist current. Then came the severe storm of September which shattered our big hopes. Were we going to perish? Many people thought so, but we meet again on the fair, hospitable shore of socialism. Socialism is our Jersey.'[14] We have to keep returning to the famous words of Barrès, written when he was the young deputy for Nancy, only a few months after the elections of 1889. They reveal the new position of some of Boulanger's supporters, indicate the tone of the 1890s and provide their key word. The convergence of dates is significant. There was the agitation for the eight-hour day at the call of the Guesdists on 1 May 1891, which was marked by the volley of shots at Fourmies; there was the organization of the French Workers' Party, which became the first party of the modern type; in autumn 1890 the Allemanist party was founded at the congress of Châtellerault; May 1891 brought the encyclical *Rerum novarum* on the condition of the workers; in 1892 the Federation of Trade Unions adopted the notion of the general strike; there was the constituent congress, also in 1892, of the Fédération des Bourses du Travail; the socialists were successful in the municipal elections of 1892 and in the parliamentary elections of 1893; and there was the evolution towards socialism of politicians who came from the bourgeoisie, such as Millerand, or who had been followers of Ferry, like Jaurès. All these facts explain why the moment was right for socialism – until then a sect and an ideology – to become a great movement. As Ernest Labrousse put it, it was the moment when trade unionism really started to grow and when the ruling classes regarded it as indispensable to pursue a policy of defence of the social order.

Perhaps the best way to retain our sense of direction through the difficult landscape of the socialist groups and the trade union movement is to start from the solid mass of Guesdism.[15] The French Workers' Party (*Parti ouvrier français, POF*) of Jules Guesde was certainly the magnetic pole – both attracting and repelling – which decided the alignment of the socialist groups with trade union tendencies. We mentioned the beginnings of the Workers' Party. During the years 1890–8 it changed profoundly. The number of members increased considerably; there were 2,000 in 1889, 10,000 in 1893 and 16,000 in 1898, a modest figure compared with the population of France or socialism abroad, but appreciable in comparison with the other socialist groups. 'The sect became a party' (Claude Willard), and abandoned its early tone, which had been dominated by revolutionary messianism and faith in the imminence of the revolution.

The Workers' Party organized itself locally, regionally and nationally on the pattern of German social democracy and sought to gain power via the electoral path. The party, which attracted a derisory number of votes in 1889, had 160,000 electors in 1893 and 295,000 in 1898, that is, 40 per cent of the socialist votes and 2.7 per cent of the whole electorate.

The party was largely – 60 per cent of its members – a party of industrial workers. The textile workers, particularly the weavers, accounted for a quarter of the members – perhaps their very poor working conditions and the impossibility of escape is sufficient explanation for their liking for a dogmatically intransigent revolutionary party. The iron and steel workers came next; they represented one-seventh of the Guesdist workers. On the other hand, the building, leather and wood workers came last; Guesdism achieved its first successes with the workers in heavy industry, although the miners, both of the Loire and the north, did not have much time for it.

Then came the tradesmen, 17 per cent of the members of the party. Grocers, bar-keepers and commercial travellers, they modelled themselves on their working-class customers; some of them were former workers dismissed by their employers. Finally, the *POF* had some peasant supporters; 7 per cent of the members were small landowners, vine-growers in Champagne or Languedoc, market gardeners in the Midi.

A map of Guesdism would show the massive support of the north of France and particularly of the textile centres; the Northern Federation, which covered the departments of Nord and Pas-de-Calais, embraced half the party's supporters. In the Midi, in Aude, Hérault, Bouches-du-Rhône and Gard, the *POF* was the heir to the 'Reds' of 1849. It was less well organized than in the north but was regarded as the party furthest to the left and took over where radicalism left off. Finally, Guesdism was strong in one last zone which embraced the Allier, the Loire, the Rhône and the Isère, among the iron and steel workers of Montluçon, the textile workers of Roanne and Beaujolais and the paper-makers of Voiron.

Without analysing the character of the France of the end of the nineteenth century, it is fair to say that the Guesdists vulgarized Marxism. They created a class party with a centralized organization, they strove to subordinate the Federation of Trade Unions, of which they had held control since 1886, to the activities of the Workers' Party. These were all reasons for conflicts and divisions. The Marxist graft, especially in the academic form of a man like Guesde, did not take very readily, caused resistance and showed signs of rejection. The pattern of organization was repugnant to the French socialist tradition. The workers' movement, jealous of its autonomy and loyal to libertarian traditions, was to regain its independence of the Workers' Party.

Round about 1890 the two movements which had opposed the Guesdists for ten years, namely the Blanquists and the possibilists, seemed to be running out of steam. It was true that Vaillant, Blanqui's disciple and a former communard, retained exceptional personal influence, but the Boulangist crisis had deeply divided the Central Revolutionary Committee. Eudes, who died in summer 1888, after the navvies' strike, and Granger and Ernest Roche, elected deputies in 1889, were ardent Boulangists, loyal to the heritage of Blanquism – revolutionary and anti-parliamentary nationalism. Under the influence of Vaillant, whose knowledge of Marxism was real, the Revolutionary Committee evolved; in 1892 it recognized 'the struggle of the working class against the capitalist class as the characteristic of socialism', proclaimed itself internationalist and above all renounced clandestine activity. On 1 July 1898 it became the Revolutionary Socialist Party. In this 'non-doctrinaire' synthesis 'of Marxist teaching and the French revolutionary tradition',[16] Vaillant drew closer to the Guesdists; but he did not share in any way their conception of a trade union dependent on the party. Moreover, while the Guesdists regarded the anti-clerical struggle as secondary, the followers of Vaillant professed a rigorous atheism, in the tradition of the *sans-culottes*.

In 1890 Brousse's Federation of Socialist Workers (*Fédération des travailleurs socialistes, FTS*) was in decline. It certainly had strong positions in Paris – eight members of the municipal council, including Brousse, who was vice-president of the Council – but, apart from the Ardennes Federation, its provincial roots were restricted; there were nearly three times fewer member groups at the Châtellerault congress in October than at the congress held in Saint-Etienne in 1882.[17] The lax structure of the organization does not by itself explain this decline. In fact, the strategy of 'republican defence' pursued at the time of Boulangism had not always been understood. Brousse was the ally of the radicals and was regarded as a moderate. Jean Allemane, a typographical worker – untypically for the socialism of the period, whose leaders came from the bourgeois classes – and a former communard, had founded in 1888 the paper *Le Parti ouvrier*. In October 1890 Allemane and his friends, notably the poet J.-B. Clément, leader of the Ardennes Federation, were excluded from the Federation of Socialist Workers. They immediately founded – taking the subtitle of the Federation – the Revolutionary Socialist Workers' Party (*Parti ouvrier socialiste revolutionnaire, POSR*). It is true that the Allemanists, as they were called, while desiring the 'eradication of charismatic personalities' within the party, retained the legislative and municipal programme of the Federation of Socialist Workers, but they asserted their revolutionary faith in the class struggle, professing a vigorous anti-militarism and anti-parliamentarianism. For them, elections were just propaganda exercises. Their members of parliament were regarded as mere mandatories who had to hand over undated resignations into the party's keeping. They also paid most of their salary into the party funds. For the Allemanists, the real struggle took place in the economic domain; they accordingly attached tremendous importance to the trade unions, the proletariat's decisive weapon, the basis of the society of the future in which the trade unions would manage firms. The Allemanists adopted the idea of the general strike. The party was a working-class one in its ideology, though it did not reject intellectuals – the young Lucien Herr and Charles Andler were members of the *POSR*. One can see the importance of the *POSR*, which was a real platform for the working-class, socialist movement. Close to anarchism, anti-militarist, attached to direct democracy, it took over from Blanquism, quoted the Marxist manifesto and disputed Paris with the Vaillantists. The Allemanists, who were anti-parliamentary and put their hopes in the trade unions which some of them ran – Bourderon led the coopers' union and Faberot the hatters' union – heralded revolutionary trade unionism, playing a decisive rôle in its early beginnings. It is hardly necessary to add that Allemanism did not renounce 'municipal socialism' and could very well lead to practical reformism. Really, in its very complexity, Allemanism was very typical of the reality of those brands of socialism whose inevitably battle-scarred history should not close our eyes to their true character.

Apart from Guesdism, a powerful movement whose organization and dogmatism set it somewhat apart, it is not always very easy to distinguish between the different currents and the historian must take care not to exaggerate the differences. There is also the problem of little groups or sects whose minority nature increased their propensity for division and their inability to overcome conflicts in any other way than by splitting up. In addition to the clash of personalities and temperaments there was the atmosphere of suspicion based on the conviction, sometimes justified, of police plots. The conflicts took the form of ideological confrontations; no doubt they in fact expressed other things, and nothing is more striking at the end of the nineteenth century than the intensity of the ideological struggles and the actual poverty of French socialist thought. In any case it is by no means certain that the militants perceived all the shades of opinion that the historian listing the organizations takes pleasure in revealing. In his study of the working-class world in the Lyon region Y. Lequin notes the uncertainties of vocabulary and the confusion of language.[18] He cannot see 'any bodies of coherent doctrine. The same militant can perfectly well express simultaneously propositions which seem, by reference to their doctrinal construction and its logic, absolutely contradictory.' Action and repression, which do not bother about shades of difference, could produce a short-lived unity and determine realignments. It is also important not to underestimate the effect of militant personalities. A Blanquist could arrive in a district and found a group which then stagnated once he had departed. Vaillant gained for his party Cher, his home department, and the neighbouring departments. J.-B. Clément played a decisive rôle in the Ardennes. Yet the establishment of socialist groups other than Guesdist ones deserves an explanation which depends on history as much as on sociology. The craftsmen, clerks and workers of Paris or Lyon found Guesdist collectivism distasteful. Was it that small independent producers and wage-earners unfamiliar with large-scale industry do not get on well with collectivism? Perhaps, though it should not be forgotten that the miners of Pas-de-Calais or the Loire, devoted to their corporative traditions and convinced of the possiblity of negotiation, voted for reformist socialists.

In reality, two historical traditions give us the key to the resistance to Guesdism – the revolutionary tradition running from 1793 to the Commune and the republican tradition based on the union of the middle classes and the proletariat against reaction. Except in the Midi, Guesdism hardly shared in this double inheritance. The *Carmagnole* and the *Marseillaise* were long sung alongside the *Internationale*, which was slow in gaining acceptance. To the first of these traditions French socialism owed its distrust of organization, its taste for direct democracy, its cult of heroic minorities, its faith in the virtues of direct management by the producers, and finally its anti-clericalism which declined little in intensity. Was it not this anti-clericalism which caused many people, once they had accepted the principle of electoral battles, to support the strategy of defending the Republic? This strategy gained acceptance in the small towns in particular, where the masonic lodges assisted contacts between socialist and radicals.

One can thus understand the role in French socialism of the 'independents', who rebel against any kind of organization. The term can denote ordinary militants,[19] intellectuals, journalists or writers, or parliamentarians. It was the independents who founded the first socialist daily papers to have 'any staying power, any circulation, any influence'.[20] *La Bataille*, founded in 1882 by Lissagaray, the historian of the Commune, and *Le Cri du Peuple*, founded by Jules Vallès in 1883, appeared until 1887 and 1890 respectively and had much more influence than the weekly organs of the currents of thought mentioned previously. Like Benoît Malon, the former shepherd from Forez, who in 1885 founded the *Revue socialiste*, they tried to let the various different groups put across their ideas. Benoît Malon attempted to achieve a synthesis, 'integral socialism'. He questioned 'the struggle for material interests alone'. Socialism should lead to the renewal of social life as a whole: 'Family reform, educational reform, political and civil demands, the emancipation of women, philosophical elaboration, softening of manners; for the contemporary question is not only social, it is also moral.'[21] This assertion of the ethical dimension of socialism linked up with the utopian tradition of French socialism.

In Parliament, the figurehead of this independent socialism was Alexandre Millerand, soon to be followed by Jaurès. A scion of the well-to-do Parisian bourgeoisie, elected on 26 December 1885 at a by-election, a radical, a member of the workers' group in the Chamber, Millerand refused to choose between Ferry, the bourgeois reaction, and Boulanger, who was the Empire: 'We want a democratic, social Republic.' In the Chamber of 1889 he was close to the various members who professed socialism. In 1893 he took over the editorship of *La Petite République* which became the forum of the independent socialists. Condemnation of violent action, faith in universal suffrage, development of the property held by the public services – a programme of this sort could appeal to the members of the middle classes, the country people and the advanced radicals. At the elections of 20 August 1893 the other combined socialist groups had only sixteen candidates elected, but the independent socialists won twenty-one seats. They constituted a magnetic pole which was to attract a dozen or so members from radicalism or Boulangism.

Socialism, trade unionism – to people of our day the two terms denote two different things and a complex system of relations. At the time with which we are concerned the distinction was largely a formal one and the ties between socialism and trade unionism were close enough to justify studying them in parallel.

We have already mentioned the rebirth of the trade union chambers after the Commune and the efforts of Barberet and his friends to create a moderate trade unionism that would collaborate with the State. The aim of the Waldeck-Rousseau law of 1884 was to put the law in harmony with the facts and to promote the rise of professional trade unions 'whose exclusive object would be to study the defence of economic, industrial, commercial and agricultural interests'. The law called for the depositing of the statutes and the names of the administrators, a regulation with which a certain number of unions refused to comply. In the first few years the law did not have the expected consequences. There was mistrust of the procedure of declaration, repression by employers who denied their workers the right to form unions, refusal to negotiate and a poor economic situation. In 1891 the number of trade union members was still derisory.[22] In October 1886 at Lyon, the constituent congress of the National Federation of Workers' Trade Unions (*Fédération nationale des syndicats ouvriers*) drew hardly more than a hundred delegates. The Guesdists defeated the moderates and dominated the Federation until 1894; but its activities were very restricted. In the Guesdists' view trade union action made it possible above all to promote agitation and develop political awareness. We should not underestimate the influence of the Guesdist unions, particularly in the demonstrations of 1 May for the eight-hour day in 1890 and 1891. But the refusal to recognize that trade unions had their own value, Guesde's intransigence, the weakness of the Federation's organization and the workers' persistent fear of the party's policy explain the decline of Guesdist influence in the unions.

The *bourses du travail* were to help give the French working-class movement a character of its own. The idea of a 'labour exchange' came from the Belgian liberal economist Gustave de Molinari. Following the Belgian example, and also in response to the invitation included in the law of 1884, from 1887 onwards a number of municipalities put rooms at the disposal of trade unions. These labour exchanges were at the same time job centres, headquarters for the local trade union federation, meeting places and libraries. Far from being dependent on the party that controlled the municipality, the exchanges were to be bastions of trade union independence. The Blanquist, Allemanist and anarchist trade unionists were to use the *bourses du travail* against the Federation of Guesdist trade unions.

In February 1892 the constituent congress of the Fédération des Bourses du Travail took place at Saint-Etienne; ten *bourses* were represented. They developed rapidly; there were ten of them in 1895 and fifty-one in 1898. From 1895 the secretary of the Federation, a post previously held by a Blanquist, was Fernand Pelloutier. He was just twenty-seven. Until his death in 1901 he was to put his stamp on the working-class movement, whose deepest aspirations he thoroughly understood, although he himself had not emerged from it. The grandson of a *carbonaro* and the son of a postal employee stationed in Saint-Nazaire, Pelloutier, after failing the *baccalauréat*, became a journalist on the paper *La Démocratie de l'Ouest*. Like other socialists and trade unionists, he was by origin, if not a bourgeois, at any rate – as said himself – a hybrid. At that time he was following in the wake of a young lawyer called Aristide Briand who had stood as a candidate in the elections of 1889 as a revisionist radical. In 1892 Pelloutier became editor-in-chief of *La Démocratie de l'Ouest* and made it a socialist paper open to all leftist tendencies. With Briand he orchestrated the theme, already launched by the anarchists and Allemanists, of the general strike. At the congress of the Workers' Party in Marseille, Guesde opposed the idea of the general strike. Pelloutier broke away from the Guesdists. Coming to Paris, he turned to the Allemanists and anarchists. In 1894 he became assistant secretary and in the following year secretary of the Fédération des Bourses du Travail. Although he may not have been at all typical of working-class circles, at any rate Pelloutier pursued an interesting career, from radicalism to a socialism tinged with Guesdism, and from Guesdism to anarchism and trade unionism. And even these stages overlapped considerably.[23] His career testifies to the evolution of the most determined section of the working-class movement, and also to the importance of the anarchists; the *bourses du travail* were to contribute to their penetration of the trade unions.

The years 1892–4 saw the reappearance of 'propaganda through action' and the individual attempts on people's lives that had disappeared for several years. The anarchists themselves considered this activity ineffective; 'An edifice based on centuries of history', Kropotkin wrote in *La Révolte* in 1891, 'cannot be destroyed with a few pounds of explosive.' The infiltration of the masses by the 'anarchist idea' was more important than assassination attempts. The wave of terrorism in 1892–4 was responsible for the passage of repressive measures, christened the 'lois scélérates' ('wicked' laws). The trade unions, particularly favourable ground for anarchist propaganda, also became refugees from the rule of law. In *Les Temps nouveaux*, by Jean Grave, Pelloutier observes that 'many trade unions in Algiers, Toulouse, Paris, Beauvais and Toulon, penetrated by libertarian propaganda, are today studying doctrines which yesterday, under Marxist influence, they would not even hear of'. The masses thus learned 'the real significance of anarchism, a doctrine which – we must repeat – can perfectly well do without dynamite to gain a hearing'. Above all, the 'entry of the libertarians into the trade unions' gives trade unionists a proper idea of what a trade union is: 'a laboratory for economic experiment unconnected with electoral rivalries, favourable to the general strike with all its consequences, governing itself anarchically, the trade union is thus the only revolutionary and libertarian organization which can counterbalance and succeed in destroying the baneful influence of collectivist politicians'. A bastion of 'free men' against the 'authoritarians', when the revolution comes the trade union will smash 'any attempt to reconstitute a new power'; it will found the 'free association of free producers'. Words like these reflect much more than the solitary meditations of one individual; they reflect the diffuse feelings of a world of militants, anarchists, Allemanists and socialists disappointed by political struggles. Thus was born an anarchist trade unionism which rejected both collectivism and reformism. There were many reasons for its success. There was the refusal of the employers to recognize the trade unions and to negotiate with them, and the powerlessness of the politicians to achieve social reforms. Let us cite one example: the law on the responsibility of employers in the case of an accident at work did not reach the Senate until 1898. Contempt for politics and anti-parliamentarianism affected the parliamentary socialists, particularly after their entry in force into the Chamber of Deputies in 1893. These facts account for the faint but persistent echo of libertarian traditions older than the Marxist conquest, the importance of which had probably been overvalued. The fact that at this time the working-class world was not dominated by workers in large-scale industry was no less decisive. The highly qualified workmen – building workers, metal workers (founders and boiler-makers), men employed in the book trade and the artistic industries – discovered the main themes of anarcho-trade unionism in their own working lives, such themes as management by the producers, 'self-culture' (to use Pelloutier's phrase), education. In addition, the worst-off workers – navvies, dockers – furnished the movement with troops, attracted by the slogan of direct action and ready for violent struggles.

Although we are discussing a movement that remained a minority one – the number of trade unionists in 1895 was 450,000, and they were not all anarchists – its scope should not be underestimated; the French workers' movement, loyal to its autonomy and independence, was not going to take the English trade union path or the German path of an organization subordinated to social democracy. Nevertheless, possibilities other than revolutionary syndicalism still existed in the trade union movement: Guesdist unions, especially in the textile industry; and reformist unions in the mining industry and in the Book Federation dominated by the positivist Keufer. The radical municipalities, which could understand the socialists, and also some masonic lodges attempted to promote this practical reformism, which is not very well documented – history is primarily interested in heroes – but was probably more extensive than people say; otherwise it would be difficult to understand the subsequent extent of 'Millerandism'.

This divided working-class movement had aspirations towards unity. They were expressed in particular in a secret organization whose name, the Chevalerie du Travail (M. Dommanget, Biblio. no. 165), was inspired by precedents in the United States and Belgium. Founded in 1893, it was related to freemasonry, to which a number of *chevaliers du travail* belonged. They included anarchists like Pelloutier, Allemanists like Guérard, subsequently to become secretary-general of the *CGT*, Guesdists like Lafargue and socialists with some sympathy for anarchy like Briand. Although the Allemanists played a particularly important part in it, thanks to its varied recruitment the Chevalerie du Travail formed a prelude to trade union unity.

At Nantes in 1894 Briand induced a majority in the National Federation of Trade Unions to adopt the principle of the general strike. The idea of uniting the Federation, which embraced professional and industrial federations, with the Fédération des Bourses, which embraced the local unions, also gained acceptance. At Limoges in September 1895 the non-Guesdist majority of the Federation of Trade Unions formed the Confédération Générale du Travail (*CGT*). (The Guesdist organization survived until 1898.) Allemane, Guérard who was secretary of the railway union, and also Keufer played a decisive part in the foundation of the *CGT*. The organization still had to be consolidated. The Fédération des Bourses stuck to its independence of the Confederation, and Pelloutier also stood aside. Until the beginning of the twentieth century the existence of the *CGT* remained frail. It did not embrace all the trade union organizations. A few months after its foundation Keufer noted that only four organizations had paid their subscriptions – the Book Federation, the Railways, the Mechanics' Circle and the Federation of Porcelain-makers. The title of the congress – Congress of trade union chambers (*chambres syndicales*), corporate groups, trade federations, and trade union and *bourses de travail* – points clearly to the complexity of the existing organizations. The statutes recorded this situation; the *CGT* admitted trade unions, *bourses*, local combinations of trade unions, departmental or regional federations of unions, national trade federations and industrial federations. Allemanists, libertarians and reformists all agreed to put in the statutes: 'The elements forming the Confédération Générale du Travail must remain outside all political groupings'. That was the essential point, both for the present and the future; the advocates of trade union independence had won the day.

6

The moderate Republic, 1889–1898

The social question: Christian democracy and the Ralliement

The progress of socialism and the working-class movement made the 'social question' one of the main preoccupations of the 1890s. Insufficient attention has been devoted to the important fact that the Commune and its suppression did not unduly disturb the conservative ruling classes or the new republican strata then rising in society. Only the legitimist reactionaries, the aristocrats and priests interested in the Catholic Workers' Circles saw in the popular insurrection a sign of the failure of the liberal society that had emerged from the Revolution. The bourgeoisie, Orleanist or republican, did not see in the drama of May 1871 any reasons for doubting its certainties. The Commune seemed a tragic but aberrant parenthesis and it did not shake people's faith in the liberal social order and in individualism. The gloomy meditations of Renan or Taine found few echoes. All round, faith in the Republic, science and progress was hardly affected. Fear and defence of the social order counted for less than the hopes pinned on the new society 'without priest or King' which the republicans wished to found.

In the 1890s, on the contrary, the bourgeois classes were affected by 'social remorse'. The indifference of twenty years earlier was replaced by curiosity, interest, pity, and even the desire for reforms to prevent another revolution. A few examples will show how attitudes had changed. In *Le Figaro*, soon after the volleys of shots fired at Fourmies, the journalist Jules Huret published an 'Enquiry into the social question in Europe'.[1] Articles were written by the principal French and European socialist leaders and by well-known employers, who did not appear to much advantage. The enquiry also described the condition of the workers by means of precise examples, in accordance with the method employed at that time by statisticians, philanthropists and 'sociologists', especially the disciples of the school of Le Play's *Réforme sociale*. Enquiries and monographs multiplied. The Social Museum, founded in 1894, assembled a wealth of documentation. Zola's novel *Germinal* appeared in 1886; its heroes were the miners. The bourgeoisie and the employers were described in cutting terms. Artists painted pictures of strikes – an indication of the general interest.

What was the scope and what were the consequences of this process of evolution? The bourgeoisie took steps which were supposed to end the evils of the workers' condition. There was the campaign against alcoholism, against cohabitation, an improvement in hygiene and living conditions – the Society for Cheap Dwellings was founded in 1896 – and an appeal for the development of pension funds and mutual assistance societies. Moralism and paternalism were accepted without question and not the slightest doubt was expressed about the benefits of economic liberalism. Nevertheless, we must not overlook the importance of a movement which echoed the steps taken by employers and stimulated initiatives – in Nord, for example, and at Le Creusot. There were associations, as we shall have occasion to repeat, of Catholics hostile to state intervention and of moderate republicans such as Jules Siegfried, the mayor of Le Havre, who were concerned about social conditions. They thought that private initiative was sufficient to resolve society's ills and to end abuses. On the other hand, some of the middle classes came to doubt the virtues of liberalism and of economic individualism. They no longer believed that the inauguration of the republican régime sufficed to solve social questions. They adopted the socialist ideal alongside the republican and democratic ideals. The development of a man such as Jaurès, or that of the young Léon Blum, seems typical in this connection. It illustrates the gradual move of so many young intellectuals in search of justice towards socialism. They thought that it was necessary to develop fully the principles of liberty and equality born of the Revolution. Others, however, repudiated the ideals of political liberalism, democracy and reason. They professed an anti-capitalism that was sometimes accompanied by anti-semitism. They indicated their sympathy for anarchist ideas.

The progress of socialism and the rise of social democracy produced the climate for change in the French Catholic world and the upsurge of social Catholicism. The latter, just like socialism, swept over France and all the other countries that had experienced the industrial revolution. And, like socialism, social Catholicism had a later and more limited success in France than in the countries of central Europe. Nevertheless, it assumed considerable importance in the eyes of contemporaries and, like socialism, worried the proponents of economic liberalism. We have already mentioned the first kind of social Catholicism, that of Albert de Mun and the association of Catholic Workers' Circles, which was counter-revolutionary, anti-liberal, corporative and paternalist. There was also another school of thought and action whose rôle should not be underestimated, that of *La Réforme sociale*, founded by Frédéric Le Play. It is true that Le Play did not wish to carry out a denominational work of charity, but he referred to the

Ten Commandments and to a society ruled by the principles of the Gospel. By calling on the 'authorities' to fulfil their duties as patrons, the school of *La Réforme sociale* undoubtedly played a large part in the upsurge of activity by employers. But its real importance lay elsewhere: by recourse to enquiries and monographs it informed people of the realities of the social situation. In this respect the career of a priest like the abbé Lemire, who was an obscure teacher in a school at Hazebrouck before becoming one of the leading figures of Christian democracy, is typical; he was influenced first by the work of the Circles and then by *La Réforme sociale*. From the former he acquired a hostility to liberalism and the dream of a corporative society, and from the latter a taste for social studies. Like many militants, whether priests or laymen, of 'Christian democracy', he was always to retain in his heart something of the ideal of traditionalism – mistrust of industrialism, nostalgia for the eternal order of the fields, a hostility – not exempt from anti-semitism – to the world of gold and speculation and the dream of a society in which capital and labour would be reconciled.

But this heritage should not lead us to overlook the ruptures and innovations in the Christian democracy movement which took shape from 1892–3 onwards. The very word 'democracy' deserves a moment's attention; it denoted not only concern for the people's cause but also rejection of a hierarchical society and the aspiration towards a fraternal society. This social democracy, a middle way between liberalism and socialism – both rejected – was envisaged in much the same way by the Christian democrats as it was by the radicals: co-operation, participation in profits, solidarity – these were the remedies for the ills of society.

The step from the social to the political is a short one and it was soon taken, at any rate by the boldest wing of the movement, which adopted the ideals of political democracy: acceptance of the heritage of 1789 and the sovereignty of the people, autonomy of politics, distinction between the spiritual and the temporal. This was the liberal Catholic tradition again. The encyclical *Rerum novarum* of 15 May 1891 and the desire to respond to the socialist challenge launched a movement which was to demand attention for several years. Newspapers and reviews were founded, trade unions, co-operatives and rural banks were formed, and there were regional and national congresses that attracted hundreds of militants. The importance of the movement was far from being negligible and it worried the socialists. 'Very soon', wrote Gérault-Richard, 'the so-called Christian democrats will have caught us up.' Jaurès was no less sensitive to the extent of the phenomenon, as he showed in his articles in *La Dépêche*, and it also disturbed the opportunists. The prefects and special commissioners devoted great attention to the activities of what they called 'Christian socialism'. This Christian democracy was headed by priests, like those who met at Reims in 1896 at the request of abbé Lemire. They wanted to 'go to the people', to 'leave the sacristy' to which religious liberalism had confined them, and to 'remake Christian France', without clearly distinguishing whether the first necessity was to remake Christian institutions or to forge a Christian people. These priests were joined by clerks, often former members of Church clubs, by sons of the bourgeoisie, old pupils of Catholic schools, and also by workers. In the south-east at Lyon and Saint-Etienne, in the north at Lille, Charleville and Roubaix, in the east at Nancy and at Reims, in Brittany at Brest and Rennes, a lasting organization was established. But though it was active in the towns, Christian democracy was to have its only electoral successes in the country where the peasants, wishing to emancipate themselves from the tutelage of the notables, voted for priests – for abbé Lemire at Hazebrouck in 1893 and for abbé Gayraud in a by-election in Léon in 1896. However, the political aspect of the movement was only the tip of an intense agitation which was religious below the surface. The status of the clergy was questioned, the traditional style of authority was contested, there was a demand for democracy in the Church and a desire for new forms of mission; abbé Calippe, a priest from Amiens, in a novel about the future, created a 'worker monk'. These are just some of the facts that stand out in these very 'new' years which left their mark on a whole generation of priests and militants. Here, as elsewhere, the 1890s were decisive years.

They were also years of intellectual ferment among the educated clergy and in the educational institutions of the Church. The creation of the Catholic institutes bore fruit. The time-lag between traditional teaching and the religious sciences was to give birth to the modernist crisis. It did not emerge fully until ten years later, but the teaching of abbé Duchesne, the historian of Christian antiquity, and of abbé Loisy, the exegetical scholar, who in 1892 founded the review *Enseignement biblique*, was already arousing controversy and suspicion. In autumn 1893 Loisy had to leave the chair of Scripture at the Catholic Institute. These were the first signs of deeper troubles.

Wishing to apply remedies to the social question and eager to make converts, priests and militants also wanted to reconcile the Church and the Republic, and took up Leo XIII's invitation to rally to the Republic. But although the Christian democrats may have rallied to the Republic, all republican Catholics were not democrats and the Ralliement cannot be confused with Christian democracy. The reasons for the Ralliement were complex and must be explained before we describe the various stages of the movement and its scope. The personal rôle of Leo XIII was considerable. Since his accession in 1878 he had always displayed moderation in his relations with the Republic. He did not think it desirable to encourage violent protests against the policy of laicization. He had repeatedly let it be understood that French Catholics should accept the country's institutions.

After the elections of 1889 he thought it was essential to intervene. He was guided by a number of different aims; he wanted to assert the distinction between the spiritual authority and the temporal authority, to break the link between French Catholics and the monarchy, and to safeguard the Concordat and the state subsidy to religion – which was threatened by the radicals – by enabling the conservatives and the moderate republicans to come to an understanding. Ulterior diplomatic motives were also at work. The Holy See was the adversary of the young Kingdom of Italy and remained intransigent on the 'Roman question'; and its relations with Protestant Germany and the Josephist Austria–Hungary were not very good. In these circumstances good relations with the Republic, the protector of overseas missions, were desirable. In Ranc's eyes France remained 'the eldest daughter of the Church'.

These preoccupations struck a chord with a proportion of conservative politicians, who thought it pointless to go on swimming against the stream of public opinion. Acceptance of the régime seemed inevitable. In face of the progress of radicalism and socialism it seemed essential to come to an understanding with the governing republicans in order to establish a majority to defend the social order. All things considered, this would be a return to the combination of centres. In March 1890 the Orleanist Jacques Piou founded a parliamentary group of the 'constitutional right' which accepted the 'legally established' institutions in order to defend a society under threat. Some of the opportunists were not indifferent to such advances. But they could not envisage a rapprochement unless the conservatives agreed at the very least not to question the 'untouchable laws on laicization', the foundation of the Republic. In the republicans' view, these laws had to be the touchstone of the Ralliement.

After several fruitless attempts to find a member of the episcopate who would agree to take the initiative, Leo XIII chose Cardinal Lavigerie. Primate of Africa, Archbishop of Algiers and Carthage and founder of the White Fathers, the cardinal, after conversations with the Pope (see Xavier de Montclos, Biblio. no. 170), agreed to speak. In November 1890, welcoming the staff of the Mediterranean squadron, the cardinal, to the surprise of these monarchist naval officers, called on Catholics to accept the Republic in the following words:

> When the will of a people has been clearly asserted, when the form of a government contains in itself nothing contrary, as Leo XIII recently proclaimed, to the principles by which civilized Christian nations can live, when unreserved loyalty to this form of government becomes necessary in order to snatch one's country from the abysses which threaten it, then the moment has come ... to sacrifice all that conscience and honour permit, even command, each one of us to sacrifice for love of our country.

These few sentences outline all the themes of the Ralliement – recognition of the will expressed by universal suffrage and acceptance of the institutions thus established, rejection of the policy of expecting the worst, the will to fight, as the cardinal proclaimed later in his speech, against the 'social peril' and finally patriotism, before which old loyalties must bow.

The radicals saw in this toast only a trick by the Church; the opportunist press expressed its satisfaction; and the royalists protested. *L'Univers*, read by all those who saw themselves as 'first and foremost Catholics', was indifferent to the form of the régime but anxious to see the 'rights of the Church' respected, and was not at all scandalized by the idea of accepting the republican régime, but doubted whether the primate of Africa would accept in the same breath the 'laws against religion'. Let the Republic first grant Catholics the liberties due to them. All round, in the Catholic world, reserve, if not hostility, was the main reaction. In any case, the whole affair had been tackled badly. The nuncio in Paris knew nothing of the initiative taken by Leo XIII and the cardinal and gave it little support. Most of the bishops, possibly judging the cardinal's intervention unfortunate or inopportune, remained silent. Only four intervened publicly – two for and two against. Mgr Freppel, the Bishop of Angers, was contemptuous of Lavigerie's 'illusion', namely 'the belief that the Republic in France is a mere form of government as elsewhere, in Switzerland or the United States, for example, and not a doctrine fundamentally and radically contrary to Christian doctrine'. Were the republicans not unanimous in requiring Catholics to accept the educational laws and the military laws? Here the Bishop of Angers was simply developing the line of argument of the majority of militant Catholics.

A few months later the Archbishop of Paris, Cardinal Richard, whose entourage was monarchist, neatly deflected the intentions of Leo XIII. On 2 March 1891 he published a 'Reply to eminent Catholics who have consulted me about their social duty in the present circumstances'. He confirmed that the Church did not condemn any form of government, but he denounced the anti-Christian sects who wanted to make 'a series of anti-religious laws the essential constitution of the Republic'. He invited Catholics to unite to defend religion, laying aside for the time being their political preferences. This was a long way from rallying to the Republic. The monarchists and most of the Catholic papers were satisfied with the cardinal's letter. Sixty-two bishops wrote to him to express their approval. A few months later the Union of Christian France was founded. Its committee, which included all the principal conservative leaders, demanded the 'co-operation of Christians and all respectable people, whatever their political opinions, to defend and demand unanimously civil, social and religious liberties'. The Union did not mention the Republic. What is more, at Toulouse on 19 July 1891, the comte d'Haussonville – the representative of the comte de Paris – expressed the view that it was 'extremely probable' that at the next elections the candidates of the monarchist committees would identify themselves with those of the committees of the Union of Christian France.

Leo XIII was forced to forge ahead. He appointed a new nuncio in Paris, Mgr Ferrata, a former adviser in the Paris nunciature, a friend of Cardinal Lavigerie and an expert on French political life. His position was a delicate one; the slightest incident was exploited by the extremists – monarchist and radical – to secure the failure of the desired reconciliation. In February 1892, after a declaration by the French cardinals, published without the Pope's being consulted and condemning the 'government of the Republic' while calling for acceptance of the country's institutions, Leo XIII was compelled to speak clearly. On 14 February he received Ernest Judet, an editor of the *Petit Journal*, and made some important statements to him, which were printed on 17 February. The unusual procedure of appealing to public opinion indicated in itself the importance of the event. On 20 February the encyclical *Au Milieu des sollicitudes* was issued, dated 16 February and written in French. It said that the Church was not tied to any form of government, and that accepting the Republic did not mean accepting legislation hostile to religion: 'Good people must unite like one man to fight these progressive abuses of legislation by all legal and honest means.'

Thanking the cardinals on 3 May for their support for the encyclical, the Pope defined his ideas and rejected 'false interpretations'. He put them on their guard against those who 'would subordinate everything to the prior triumph of their respective parties, even on the pretext that it seemed to them the one best adapted to defend religion'. Such indeed was to be the main argument of the opponents of the Ralliement, the *réfractaires*.

The welcome given to the encyclical was moderate. About twenty bishops expressed their satisfaction. Most adopted a reserved attitude; the bishops, without being devoted to royalty, had often emerged from the ranks of the intransigent Catholics and had been appointed under Pius IX; consequently they were fundamentally hostile to the secular Republic. In the west and the Midi they had fears for the charitable works supported by the monarchists. A certain number of bishops did not publish the encyclical. Some gave a very restrictive interpretation of it: in the diocese of Cambrai (department of Nord), a brief communiqué simply indicated that the encyclical 'recalled the duties as well as the rights of the constituted powers and the obligations imposed on all Christians by the dangers which threaten religion'. The clergy could not express open opposition any more than the bishops. The avowed *réfractaires* were in a minority. But there were a great many different shades of opinion between reluctant agreement and whole-hearted agreement. Some people took the view that the infallible

Pope had spoken *ex cathedra*, others that he had merely given some advice. Above all, what did 'accepting the Republic' mean? Was it a 'baptized' Republic that had become Christian, as *La Croix* and the Assumptionists wanted, or the Republic of Jules Ferry? Such was the crux of the debate which was to produce extraordinary divisions inside the Catholic world. The Union of Christian France dissolved itself. Its leaders, Buffet, Chesnelong, Keller and Lucien Brut, withdrew from public life; they did not wish either to oppose the Pope's wishes or to abandon their loyalties. Part of the royalist right behind the comte d'Haussonville recognized the Pope's authority 'in matters of faith', but proclaimed their rights 'as citizens'. Loyal to the 'national tradition', they were the heirs to a political Gallicanism which rejected the legitimacy of the Holy See's intervention on the temporal level. One can thus see that the Ralliement did not divide Catholics along the line of cleavage between the intransigent and the liberals. Catholics belonging to the liberal tradition, Orleanists such as the comte d'Haussonville, figured in the front ranks of the *réfractaires* alongside counter-revolutionary legitimists from whom until then they had been separated by a wide gulf. On the other hand, intransigent Catholics, out of loyalty to ultramontanism, were to follow the instructions from Rome – and from *L'Univers*, or Albert de Mun at the regional congress of the *Association catholique de la jeunesse française* (Catholic Association of French Youth, *ACJF*) at Grenoble on 22 May 1892. De Mun expressed his determination to situate his political action 'on the constitutional level'. He was motivated not only by obedience to the Pope but also, like many legitimists – such as Henri Lorin – who followed the same course, by the wish to go to the people, the sole foundation of power since the disappearance of the legitimate dynasty. An enemy of Orleanism, he put his hopes in the people. For him and his friends the encyclical *Rerum novarum* and the encyclical on the Ralliement could not be separated.

The world of the *ralliés* was far from being homogeneous. *La Croix* said the Republic must be accepted but in fact called for the creation of a great party to defend religion: 'Let us attack these unfortunate laws and let us urge all Catholics – royalists, Bonapartists, republicans – to unite their efforts in order to try loyally to establish a Christian Republic in France.' *La Croix* accepted the tricolour but only on condition that the white part bore a picture of the Sacred Heart, the sign of the consecration of the Republic to Christ. Many Christian democrats thought along the same lines. They would have liked a Catholic and social party like the one whose programme was outlined by Albert de Mun at Saint-Etienne in December 1892 and they dreamed of a denominational State. They accepted democracy with more enthusiasm than they accepted the Republic. Others, on the contrary, accepted the secular State and would have been content with a non-sectarian application of the educational laws; they rejected the

Catholic party. This was also the point of view of Jacques Piou, who at the beginning of 1893 christened the group of the constitutional right the 'Republican Right'. He wanted to make preparations for 'the formation of a Tory party', conservative in the English style, which would unite 'all men of good will'. He called on 'all those who mean to resist the apostles of socialist neo-radicalism and the sectaries of freemasonry' to unite for 'an open, tolerant, honest Republic'. Without any doubt Leo XIII wanted the creation of a big conservative party uniting the Catholics and the 'honourable men', but he wished this party to be aware of social problems. But in fact the politicians who followed Piou were often connected, like the prince d'Arenberg or the baron Hély d'Oissel, with the business world and were anxious above all to defend the social order. Here we touch on the main difficulties of the Ralliement; those who agreed to enter the Republic were not doing so for the same reason. Some wanted to save society, others to turn to the people; some wanted to put an end to impious legislation, others were prepared to accept this provisionally; some had in mind the German centre party or the Belgian Catholic party, others the English Conservative party.

We shall indicate the repercussions of the Ralliement when we come to describe the political history of the years 1893–8. Here it is enough to note its ambiguities; they account for the mistrust of the Republican politicians, who feared Christian socialism as much as clericalism and in whose eyes interventions by Rome were suspect. The fact remains that by putting an end to the solidarity between the Church and the monarchists Leo XIII had made possible realignments which explain, as much as the consequences of Boulangism and the rise of socialism, the political evolution of France from the 1890s.

Protectionism and Panama. The elections of 1893

Immediately after the Boulangist crisis the parliamentary world relapsed into its usual apathy. 'After the General's death', the Barrès of *Leurs figures* was to write, 'everything turned into a featureless marsh again.' After the elections of 1889 the 'republican concentration' which had overcome Boulangism was maintained; the opportunists, their numbers increased by the moderate radicals, formed the majority. When Tirard resigned in March 1890 after a hostile vote by a protectionist Senate, refusing to ratify the Franco-Turkish trade treaty, Freycinet became head of a government which was hardly reshuffled and which lasted nearly two years. This stability is explained by the memory of the Boulangist threat and by the appearance of the socialist menace. Thus Constans at the Ministry of the Interior and Rouvier at Finance remained in office for nearly three years.

It was under the moderate republican government that the evolution towards protectionism begun in 1881 and 1885 accelerated. Méline, president of the Customs Commission, headed the movement in the Chamber. The textile manufacturers, the iron and steel makers and agricultural circles conducted an active campaign. They adopted the ideas of P. Cauwès, a professor of political economy and a disciple of Frédéric List, whose lectures on political economy advocated the idea of the national economy. The Chamber elected in 1889 by *arrondissement* was particularly sensitive to the grievances of agriculture and favourable to protectionism.

Trade treaties were not renewed.[2] The law of 11 January 1892 subjected foreign products to two tariffs: a general maximum tariff in the absence of any particular agreement and a minimum tariff applied to countries with whom an agreement had been signed. In both cases duties were decidedly higher than before. Having lost the support of the wine-growing regions since the phylloxera crisis, the only advocates of free trade left were the Lyon silk manufacturers and the shipowners of the big ports. Neither Léon Say nor Aynard, neither the Marseille man Charles-Roux nor the radicals, the defenders of the urban consumers, could shake the majority. Ferry, president of the Customs Commission in the Senate, gave the reason for the conversion of the republicans to protectionism: 'The present protectionist movement has its roots in the democracy which cultivates the vine and corn. That is why it has succeeded' (P. Barral, Biblio. no. 107; and Augé-Laribe, no. 106, pp. 242–4). In installing this protective system, which also applied to the colonies, France was only following the general trend. But 'the defence of the country's toil', as Méline put it, was scarcely utilized, as it was in Germany or the United States, for the development of industry. It simply constituted an opportune income for the industrialists and the agriculturists.

Opportunism had managed to defeat its opponents and pursue a business policy. The radicals, unhappy at the absence of social reforms and with Freycinet's kindly tone in dealing with the clergy, deserted him on 18 February 1892, the day after Leo XIII's interview with Judet. The colourless Loubet succeeded him at a time when, with the Panama scandal (J. Bouvier, Biblio. no. 165), nationalists, anti-semites and Boulangists were attempting to strike a blow at the régime.

The scandal was exposed in autumn 1892, at the beginning of an election year. In 1888 the Panama Canal Company, already in difficulties, had wanted to issue debentures by lottery. A law had to be passed. The goodwill of members of parliament had been obtained more easily by the distribution of cheques. The issue of the loan did not suffice to prevent the bankruptcy in January 1889 of a ruinous enterprise. An investigation into the activities of the Panama directors opened in May 1891.

La Libre Parole of Edouard Drumont and the Boulangist paper *La Cocarde* denounced the compromised parliamentarians. In the night of 19 to 20

November the baron de Reinach, the company's financial agent, the uncle and father-in-law of the Gambettist Joseph Reinach, editor of *La République française*, died suddenly. On 21 November Jules Delahaye, who had been behind Boulanger's speech at Tours, branded 'a whole political syndicate which bears the shame of venality'. With the approval of the extreme left and of the right he obtained a parliamentary commission of enquiry chaired by the radical Brisson, and at the commission's request the Chamber demanded an autopsy on Reinach against the advice of the government, which resigned. Ribot, a former magistrate from the centre left formed a government on 6 December; it was shaken after a week by the resignation of the Minister of Finance, Rouvier, who was implicated, as was Clemenceau. Ribot succeeded with great difficulty in avoiding the passage of a proposed law which would have given the commission of enquiry judicial powers. To demonstrate his firmness, on 16 December he had two directors of the Panama Company, Ferdinand de Lesseps and a former deputy, arrested. He demanded the removal of parliamentary immunity from five deputies, including Rouvier. The latter defended himself in the Chamber: he had accepted help from Reinach to pay back to the managing director of the Crédit Mobilier a loan contracted when he was prime minister in order to fight Boulangism. At the commission of enquiry Floquet had to admit that, to combat Boulanger's candidature in the department of Nord in April 1888, he had 'followed as closely as possible the allocation of the Company's advertising fund (300,000 francs), not from the commercial point of view but from the political point of view, which concerned the State'. On 20 December Déroulède had denounced Clemenceau's relations with the adventurer Cornélius Herz, 'a foreign agent', who had taken refuge in England after the death of Reinach whom he was blackmailing. Clemenceau had to agree that he had accepted Herz's financial support for his paper, *La Justice*. Like Floquet and Rouvier, he was implicated in the scandal.

The outcome of the Court of Appeal trial of the Panama Company's directors for 'fraud' was a light sentence which was set aside by the Supreme Court. The Assize Court trial of the parliamentarians for corruption ended on 21 March 1893 in the conviction of Baïhaut, Minister of Public Works in 1886, who had accepted 375,000 francs. The other members of parliament were acquitted; the prosecution was unable to establish proof of corruption. Baïhaut was the only one who had confessed. All round then, the campaign against the '*chéquards*' – the word was coined in November 1892 – had not shaken the régime as much as Delahaye, Drumont and Déroulède had hoped. Barrès, at the end of *Leurs figures*, well expresses the disappointment of the opponents of opportunism: 'As formerly after the Boulangist fever, when the Panama fit passed people returned to the most immoral kind of "everyone for himself" attitude.'

Nevertheless, the scandal left deep marks; the great public had had revealed to it the collusion that went on between the business world, the press and politicians. What is more, Floquet and Rouvier had justified it as politically necessary. The extent of the scandal, which brought a change of political personnel, shows that public opinion, as Seignobos notes, was 'very suspicious where money was concerned'. Yet the parliamentary scandal was relatively slight; a few members of parliament corrupted, rather more incautious ones discredited – it was enough to satisfy the Boulangists' desire for revenge. The other financial scandal, which was scarcely mentioned, consisted in the exceptional size of the commissions taken by the banks in dealing with Panama business. Finally, the revelation of the venality of the press, which was supposed to have received 'twelve to thirteen million of the twenty-two devoted by the Panama Company to publicizing itself' (P. Albert), made less impression on public opinion than the corruption of the members of parliament – on which the press concentrated.

A ministerial crisis once more played its cathartic rôle; Ribot, who had already reshuffled his government in January – abandoning Freycinet, Loubet and Burdeau, who had been accused of wanting to hush up the affair – resigned on 30 March 1893 on a minor issue. A new man, in the person of Charles Dupuy, a former Ministry of Education inspector and deputy for Haute-Loire, became Premier – an example of the renewal of political personnel brought about by the Panama scandal. The Minister of Education, Raymond Poincaré, was only thirty-three. A new generation assumed ministerial responsibilities and at the same time there was a movement towards the realignment of the political forces. The opportunists looked towards the right and the Ralliement; they pondered deserting 'concentration majorities' with the radicals for a majority based on the centres. This is the meaning of Charles Dupuy's statement at Toulouse in the spring of 1893. 'The advice given by Rome with a noble idea of appeasement ... must affect any thinking man.' He did not propose any concession in the domain of laicization, which irritated the Catholics, but he did envisage a law on associations 'to regulate the relations of the civil and religious societies in a generous spirit of tolerance'. Jonnart, the member for Pas-de-Calais and son-in-law of Edouard Aynard, a republican and a Catholic, an important banker and member for Rhône, 'saluted joyfully the movement taking place in public opinion, for it can contribute powerfully to social peace'. He added, 'The Republic is beyond discussion; this means the end of the policy of concentration.'[3] Constans, too, asserted that the Republic must now be tolerant. Everyone was pleased with the Ralliement, which would permit a majority for the defence of social order. Dupuy did not hesitate to act firmly in face of the workers' movement; on 1 May 1893 he closed the *bourse du travail* in Paris and two months later, on 7

July, he put troops into it, since the trade unions had been unwilling to make the declaration required by the law of 1884. The occupation of the *bourse* followed a week of street demonstrations arising out of student agitation that at the start had no political motive. The original cause of the agitation was the conviction of a student of the Beaux-Arts for immorality; then workers had joined in – the first sign of the troubled period that was to precede the elections.[4]

Millerand proclaimed in his profession of faith to the electors of the *XIIe arrondissement*:

> The social question is the great question of the elections of 1893. The Panama affair has shown all the social forces of this country to be in the service of and under orders from high finance. It is against high finance that we must concentrate our efforts. The nation must recapture from the barons of this new cosmopolitan feudal system the fortresses which they have stolen from it in order to dominate it – the Bank of France, the railways, the mines.

With this proposition, which he had defended in the Chamber as early as February, Millerand, who in July became editor of *La Petite République*, strove to unite the 'militants of all the socialist groups', the radicals and former Boulangists. He received the support of men like Goblet or Pelletan, who no longer wished to collaborate with the moderate republicans; on the left as well, the time for 'concentration' seemed to have passed. Moreover, the aim of the 'republican concentration' had been to defend the régime, and the régime was no longer called into question. The elections of 1893 were not fought for or against the Republic, or for or against clericalism, but on the 'social question'.

The elections of 1893 deserve analysis. The number of abstentions is striking. It amounted to 28.8 per cent of registered voters; between 1876 and 1914 this figure was exceeded only in 1881, when 31.4 per cent of the electorate abstained. It is fair to think that as in 1881, the electors of the right, thanks to the absence of their candidates in a number of solidly left constituencies, were mainly responsible for this rise in absentionism – in Mediterranean France, for example, and in central France. One must not overlook either the disturbance brought about by the Ralliement, which explains why there were over 35 per cent of abstentions in Finistère and Loire-Inférieure, and between 30 per cent and 34.9 per cent in Morbihan, Maine-et-Loire and Côtes-du-Nord. But the increase in the number of abstentions – 500,000 more than in 1889 – does not in itself account for the collapse of the right; it gained less than a million and a half votes against nearly three million in 1889.[5] In fact, several hundred thousand conservative electors seem to have voted for the republicans. One can now understand the progress made by the latter: moderate republicans, radicals, and radical-socialists obtained over 4,800,000 votes, that is, 500,000 more than in 1889. The socialists won 600,000 votes. Some complex transfers took place; revisionists of 1889 and radicals sometimes voted socialist, moderate republican electors moved over to mild radicalism, which in the south-west also attracted part of the Bonapartist electorate – conservatives who had come to accept the moderate Republic.

Thus socialism reaped the fruits of Boulangism, and opportunism those of the Ralliement. About fifty socialists were elected. They included only sixteen members of the four organized socialist groups: five Guesdists, five Allemanists, four Blanquists and two Broussists. The independent socialists were some twenty in number, nine of them elected in the department of Seine. They were to be joined by a few radical socialists, such as Thierry Cazes, elected at Lectoure, and Mirman, elected at Reims, and by certain revisionists such as Ernest Roche, elected in Seine. All these members formed a parliamentary group to which only the Allemanists did not belong; it was dominated by the personalities of Millerand, Jaurès and Viviani.

The radicals were rather more numerous than in the previous Chamber; the ministry statistics gave them 122 seats, but in fact, as the first votes in the legislature showed, they could also count on some fifty deputies elected as republicans. But radicalism was changing character. While in Paris and the big cities it was being replaced by socialism, it was taking root in the countryside, in particular in the south-west. It lost two of its leaders, Floquet and Clemenceau, although the latter had taken refuge in the constituency of Draguignan. Both were victims of Panama.

The governing republicans were over 300 in number and had a majority, but their lack of cohesion explains the instability of the early days of the legislature. In fact, only about 250 of them had a common attitude. Some of them remained attached to the republican, secular alliance with the radicals. Others thought of turning to the right and the *ralliés*. There were thirty-two of these. The main figures of the Ralliement had been defeated: Piou at Saint-Gauders; Albert de Mun in Morbihan, where the royalists were responsible for his defeat and, to overthrow him, voted radical (he returned to Parliament, elected at a by-election at Morlaix at the beginning of 1894); and Etienne Lamy in the Jura. The *ralliés* were dominated by former Orleanists and Bonapartists. The conservative Right – few of its members still called themselves monarchists, but they all kept silence on the Republic – had fifty-six members. All in all, the atmosphere of appeasement and the Ralliement caused the right to lose nearly half its seats. In this sense Leo XIII's initiative was a very real success: the monarchist parties were smitten once and for all. Henceforth the conservatives would try to fight on the 'religious defence' ticket. Moreover, the Ralliement had permitted a fringe of the conservative electorate to vote for moderate republicans as the lesser evil. However, the slide towards the extreme left pushed the moderate republicans towards the right. The Barrès of *Leurs figures* clearly perceived the phenomenon: Suret-Lefort was re-elected in Meuse with the secret complaisance of the conservatives.

The elections of 1889 and 1893 produced profound changes in the ranks of the politicians (cf. P. Sorlin, Biblio. no. 80, pp. 354–5). The victims of Boulangism were joined by those of Panama. The men who had dominated political life since the advent of the Republic disappeared, whether opportunists or radicals. One hundred and ninety members were newcomers. No doubt some members defeated in 1889 were re-elected in 1893, but apart from Goblet and Jaurès they were not people of any importance. The men who counted had entered political life recently: Léon Bourgeois among the radicals; Paul Deschanel, Jonnart, Georges Leygues and Poincaré among the moderates. André Siegfried, who used to be present at the parliamentary dinners organized by his father, saw them as 'a different generation, distinct from their republican ancestors; born under the régime, they had not had to suffer in order to found it'. These men were to dominate the political scene until about 1930. They were to impart a new style to discredited opportunism by imposing the term 'progressivist'. Deschanel, in a speech which he made outlining a programme when Parliament reassembled, asserted the necessity for a 'progressivist' policy to spare France the perils of revolutionary socialism.

The time of the progressivists

Contrary to what one might have expected from the results, the first few years of the Parliament inaugurated by the elections of 1893 were marked by extreme ministerial instability; four governments succeeded each other between November 1893 and April 1896. On the other hand, Méline's administration, which lasted from April 1896 to June 1898, beat all records for length achieved until then. The fact is that the moderate majority produced by the elections did not really emerge until the middle of the legislature's life; similarly, it was only in 1883, under Ferry, that the majority produced by the elections of 1881 had defined itself clearly. Without following all the ups and downs of a complex political story, it is essential to indicate the main stages in the period before drawing up the balance sheet of the progressivist Republic.

As soon as Parliament reassembled Charles Dupuy resigned, deserted by the ministers close to the radicals. On 1 December Casimir-Périer formed a centre government. He immediately started to combat the anarchists. He secured the passage of laws on the press and on the 'associations of evil-doers'; the opponents of these laws feared that they would be used against the socialists. In addition, without making any concessions to the right, the government announced a policy of appeasement in religious questions. Spuller, Gambetta's former associate, who had become Minister of Education, Arts and Religious Affairs, asserted in a very important debate on 3 March 1894 that it was time 'to make a real spirit of tolerance prevail in religious matters'. He called for a 'new spirit', defined as 'the spirit which in a society as deeply disturbed as ours tends to bring back all Frenchman to the ideas of good sense, justice and charity necessary to any society that wishes to survive'. The vagueness of the appeal did not conceal the wish 'to reconcile all citizens' in the face of the socialist threat. But did this not mean deserting the 'republican' tradition? Accordingly the government, which declined to accept votes from either the right or the left, tabled a motion of confidence in the will of the government to 'maintain republican laws and to defend the rights of the secular State'. It obtained 280 votes against 120. The right and the *ralliés* were divided.[6] Some voted against, sixteen intransigents joining the extreme left; some abstained, this course being chosen by forty-five conservatives; and some voted for, this attitude being adopted by eighteen deputies – a few former Bonapartists and some ten *ralliés*. About fifty radicals voted with the socialists against the government; the rest abstained.

Thus the centre majority dear to Casimir-Périer's heart was very slender. It was threatened by the 'coalition of extreme parties' denounced by Paul Deschanel and by the way these parties tried to outbid the groups close to them. On 22 May 1894, Millerand and a monarchist called de Ramel demanded in opposition to Jonnart, the Minister of Public Works, that the law of 1884 'should be applied to the workers and employees of state enterprises'. The government had 251 votes against it and 217 for it. Although thirty-seven deputies of the right (including twenty-two *ralliés*) had voted for Casimir-Périer, of whose social conservatism they approved, the rest abstained or voted against him. Most important, the government was abandoned by some of the moderate republicans. What displeased them was not so much the government's attitude to trade union affairs as its religious policy; they were somewhat dubious about the 'new spirit'.

Yet Charles Dupuy, who returned to power, was to rely on the same centre majority. This majority, after President Carnot's assassination at Lyon by the anarchist Caserio, elected Casimir-Périer to the supreme magistracy. Dupuy brought in a new law against 'anarchist theories' which transferred to the *tribunaux correctionnels* (county courts) 'anarchist propaganda via the press'. The socialists, most of the radicals and the extreme right opposed these 'wicked' measures in some stormy debates. The government was harried by the socialists and the radicals, who made repeated interruptions and asked innumerable questions. Through fear of losing left-wing voters a certain number of moderate republicans voted against the government and tried not to lose contact with the radicals. The Dupuy government succumbed in its turn on 14 January 1895 to Millerand's attacks on the application of the agreements with the railway companies. The ministerial crisis ran in parallel with a presidential crisis, for on 5 January Casimir-Périer had sent a message announcing his resignation. Sharply attacked by the socialists in whose view, as a shareholder in the Anzin Company and the grandson of Louis-Philippe's minister, he was capitalism incarnate, the President of the Republic found it difficult to stand up to this 'campaign of defamation and insults'. He had seen in Charles Dupuy's setback the sign of a division in the majority which had elected him to the Elysée Palace. Above all, he could not get used to the rôle that devolved in practice on the president of the Republic: 'I cannot resign myself to comparing the burden of the moral responsibilities that weigh on me with the powerlessness to which I am condemned.' The third presidential crisis in the history of the Republic was ended by calling on a second-rank personality, in accordance with an already established tradition. In the first round Brisson received the votes of the radicals and the socialists; the moderate votes were divided between two former Gambettists, Waldeck-Rousseau, recently elected to the Senate after several years of retirement from politics (cf. P. Sorlin, Biblio. no. 80), and Félix Faure, the Navy Minister. Waldeck-Rousseau, not very well known to the new progressivist deputies and suspected of authoritarianism, was outstripped by Félix Faure, whose elegance inspired confidence. In the second round of voting Faure was elected by 430 votes to Brisson's 361, with the support of some of the conservatives. A new majority appeared on the horizon.

However, two more cabinets were to be needed before a government supported by the right was formed. The first of these two cabinets tried a return to the 'concentration', the second tried the possibility of a radical administration. Ribot attempted concentration with a 'cabinet of republican union'. He broke with Dupuy's policy and passed amnesty laws. The passing of a fiscal law taxing religious orders – a law known as the 'subscription law' – an affair apparently of little importance, assumed extraordinary proportions. *La Croix*, the mouthpiece of the Assumptionists, conducted a campaign calling for resistance. the *réfractaires* exploited this 'persecution' to demonstrate the uselessness of the Ralliement. Attacked from the right, Ribot did not succeed in controlling the left. He was overthrown on 28 October for refusing to publish a report on a scandal involving a railway company. Once again collusion between business and politics brought about a ministerial crisis.

Léon Bourgeois, having failed to gain the co-operation of the moderates, formed a government consisting solely of radicals. He could only secure a majority in the Chamber through the toleration of a section of the republicans. In the Senate he was in a clear minority. The government included some new figures – Paul Doumer at the Ministry of Finance, Emile Combes at Education and Religious Affairs, and Mesureur at Trade. Eight members of the government were freemasons (J. Kayser, Biblio. no. 57, 229). Although Bourgeois postponed the prospect of separation and simply announced a law on associations as a prelude to the regulation of relations between Church and State, he encountered the resolute hostility of the Catholic right. They, apart from the few Christian Democrats, were no less opposed – like the moderate republicans – to a tax on income, the only point in the radical programme retained by Léon Bourgeois. By means of tax reform he wanted to correct social inequalities and to put into effect a policy of solidarity, the bases of which he outlined in an article in *La Nouvelle Revue*,[7] causing a considerable stir. This article developed the theory of the social quasi-contract, in order to show the debt owed by the privileged to the disinherited. Progressive taxation, laws governing social insurance and the protection of the workers and compulsory arbitration were the claims flowing from this doctrine. Mesureur announced 'a judicious, practical socialism'. The plans for fiscal reform calling for the declaration of income seemed to open the way to inquisitions and collectivism. The government simply asked the Chamber to vote on the principle of a tax on income. Even then an opposition amendment rejecting 'universal declaration and taxation' was only defeated thanks to the votes of the ministers. At their spring meeting fifty-five general councils indicated their dislike of the plan; and at that point a number of hesitant deputies deserted the government. Without a real majority in the Chamber and confronted with the opposition of the Senate, the government had to resign. The conflict lasted three months and posed a considerable constitutional problem: did the Senate possess the right to overthrow a government? Tirard's resignation in 1890 after an unfavourable vote by the Senate had seemed a mere pretext and had not created a precedent. In 1896 Léon Bourgeois was actually compelled by the upper chamber to resign. Since Bourgeois did not pay any attention to adverse votes by the Senate, the latter postponed voting the money required to bring back the expeditionary force from Madagascar. The leaders of the majority groups in the Senate made the following statement: 'Three times the Senate has refused the government its confidence, by substantial majorities. Nevertheless, in violation of the constitutional law, this government has remained in office . . . We do not refuse the money, but we cannot grant it to the present government.' Léon Bourgeois resigned; doubtless he did not have a majority in the Chamber, but by his gesture he gave the Senate a power which it would not fail to use in the subsequent history of the Third Republic, especially after 1919.

Méline, Ferry's former minister, the protectionist, formed a homogeneous moderate government. Two former associates of Ferry figured in the government: Alfred Rambaud at the Ministry of Education and

Gabriel Hanotaux at the Foreign Office, where he had already served as minister under Charles Dupuy. Barthou was Minister of the Interior. The Prime Minister retained the Agriculture portfolio. The government would have the support of rural France. It received the support of the Senate and in the Chamber a slender but very stable majority which grew stronger during the twenty-six months of the administration's life. The reason for this exceptional stability was simple: the governing republicans, except for the Progressist Union which had drawn closer to the radicals, accepted the break with the left; what is more, they were content to have the support, or favourable abstention, of the right, even that part of it which had not rallied openly to the Republic. Thus on 12 March 1898, for example, when the government's general policy was challenged, all the deputies of the right, except for about ten abstentionists, voted for the government, which obtained 295 votes against 215. Méline had also rejected 'anti-clericalism, which he saw as a tactic by the radicals to make the electors forget their hunger', and pursued appeasement. It is true that he did not refrain from asserting the rights of the State against the Church with which he had some minor conflicts. He regarded the question of the laicization laws as closed, but he did not hurry to secularize the state schools and shut his eyes to the return of the religious orders. The *rallié* Jacques Piou was able to write subsequently: 'New foundations were laid and ecclesiastical property assumed hitherto unknown proportions.'[8]

Supported as it was by the advocates of defence of the social order, the government could not even carry through a plan for the reform of direct taxation which was to have been applied to stocks and shares, including the income from government stock. The most it could do was to pass several social laws in conformity with the programme of the progressivists, including the law of 1898 on responsibility for accidents at work.

The evolution of the political forces

Confronted with the majority of moderates, the opposition of the radical and socialist left grew stronger. A realignment of the parties began to take place which was to have important consequences. Socialism strengthened its roots by winning over the town halls. The municipal elections of 1896 were a success; Lille, Roubaix, Denain, Limoges, Montluçon, Commentry, Roanne, Firminy, Marseilles, Toulon, Sète, Carmaux and Dijon all remained or became socialist. This was the hour of municipal socialism; Guesdists, Vaillantists, Broussists and independents all carried out practical reforms, striving to develop the public services and to employ a democratic system of taxation. On the initiative of the socialist republicans of the *XIIe arrondissement* in Millerand's constituency a banquet for the socialist municipalities brought together all the leaders of socialism except the Allemanists – Brousse, Guesde, Vaillant and the three independent socialists who had won an important place for themselves in the Chamber, Jaurès, Millerand and Viviani. Millerand tried to set up the bases for a common programme. He defined socialism as 'the necessary and progressive substitution of social property for capitalist property' – he visualized a stage-by-stage transition to socialism. The sugar refineries seemed to him an example of an industry sufficiently concentrated and 'ripe, now, for appropriation by the State'. On the other hand, he reassured small property owners. The 'takeover of the administration' would be achieved by universal suffrage; 'revolutionary means' were ruled out. Just as he merged the democratic current with the socialist current, so he did not separate the affirmation of internationalism from attachment to '*la patrie française*, an incomparable instrument of material and moral progress'. The Saint-Mandé speech caused a considerable stir and should not be misinterpreted; in spite of its reassuring tone it caused extreme anxiety among the bourgeoisie (P. Sorlin, Biblio. no. 80, p. 358). Although reformist in tone, it did not for the moment encounter any opposition from the Guesdists. After all, at that time the Guesdists were taking a parliamentary, reformist line (C. Willard, Biblio. no. 164). A first step had been taken towards socialist unity; twenty-eight socialist deputies approved a declaration along the lines of the Saint-Mandé speech. The Allemanists stood aside.

Millerand's remarks were addressed to the radical-socialists and the radicals (both indispensable allies) as much as to the socialists. Shaken by the Boulangist crisis and the Panama scandal, radicalism was at that time acquiring a new look. In Daniel Halévy's words, 'Modern radicalism was coming to birth.' As the elections of 1893 had shown, although it was losing the big towns it was increasing its support in rural France. Another sign was that the radicals were entering the Senate. On the initiative of Combes, the senator for Charente, in 1891 they formed the 'democratic left' group, which united about forty senators belonging to the radical family. This group was destined to have a long history. As for the radicals as a whole, they remained divided between a wing calling itself 'radical-socialist' and a moderate wing, but they were all agreed on militant anti-clericalism and the rejection of the 'open' Republic, of any concession to the right or the *ralliés*. Confronted with the moderates, who seemed to be betraying the Republic, the radicals were to make an effort to reorganize themselves, re-grouping the departmental federations and committees. In November 1894 some very young radicals – René Renoult, Floquet's associate, and Klotz, an editor on the *Voltaire*, neither of whom was yet thirty – founded the Central Committee for Republican Action. With the main parliamentarians – Floquet, Brisson and Bourgeois – as patrons, the Committee set itself a task of propaganda and organization. It wanted to maintain a link between the radical committees in the country, the masonic lodges and the local radical press. The Committee was much more dynamic than the Association for Republican Reforms, which united members of parliament on the initiative of Mesureur, the deputy for Seine. The two organizations merged in November 1895 into an Action Committee for Republican Reforms which embraced seventy committees, fifty-three masonic lodges and sixty-two newspapers. We have here the origins of the radical party's constitution.

Divided on economic and social questions, the radicals were to attack Méline on his religious policy. 'The Church is infiltrating everywhere', exclaimed Léon Bourgeois at Château-Thierry in 1897; 'At the next elections the lists intended to produce a right majority in the Chamber will be drawn up in Rome.' The struggle against clericalism, the 'black International', was the slogan tirelessly repeated by radical orators. The lodges supported this effort; masonry slid from opportunism to radicalism and the convent (general assembly) of September 1897 demanded the end of a 'reactionary and clerical government'. Brisson described the thousand forms of the clerical hydra:

> These electoral committees that have spread everywhere and obey the orders of the Assumptionist fathers; the paper *La Croix* producing more and more local editions, enrolling under its banner, together with the parish clergy, all the religious orders of men and women and the thousand confraternities created by the Church's fertile imagination; junior civil servants watched, spied on, terrorized or recruited; senior civil servants uncertain and worried.[9]

In short, the 'new spirit' was leading to the return of the League... It was a speech that clearly revealed the deep fears aroused by the Catholic Church and the fear of the renewed influence of the notables defeated after 16 May. Thus anti-clericalism, as well as being a political strategy which made possible the union of the left and gave it a philosophical basis, was also the expression of radicalism's social ideal; it established the emancipation of small people from the traditional notables, from 'society', in which, especially in the provinces, the social influence of Catholicism was so considerable. Anti-clericalism was democratic and made people equal. Confronted with the reaction embodied by Méline, the radicals were keener on a return to the lay, militant Republic than on a tax on income; only half the radical deputies demanded this in 1898.

Confronted with radical and socialist dynamism, the progressivists were ill at ease. Although they had a majority in the Chamber their organization in the country was almost non-existent. The National Republican Committee for Commerce and Industry (P. Sorlin, Biblio. no. 80, pp. 363 and 381), founded in April 1897 with Deschanel, Siegfried, Poincaré and Waldeck as its patrons, pushed the evolution of the moderates towards protectionism and arranged for brochures and meetings to defend the

Méline government. But it was mainly a pressure group in the service of a policy. Another organization was to be created on the initiative of the *Revue politique et parlementaire* founded in 1894 by Marcel Fournier, a former professor of law, to provide a doctrine for 'resolute advocates of private initiative'. The review very soon became the mouthpiece of the moderate Republic. In 1898 Fournier, after securing Waldeck-Rousseau's support, founded the Grand Cercle Républicain as a meeting-place and secretariat which aimed to attract the commercial and industrial bourgeoisie. The Cercle had scarcely a thousand members. The provincial bourgeoisie was cool towards this realignment except in the east and the north where the industrialist Eugene Motte, who was one day to defeat Guesde at Roubaix, gave it his support. At the opening of the Cercle on 22 March 1898 Waldeck extolled the principles of the French Revolution as opposed to socialism. He called on his audience 'not to conceive of progress without freedom'. But the Grand Cercle Républicain did not fulfil, either in the elaboration of a programme or in the establishment of an organization, the hopes of Waldeck, who wanted 'a big, compact homogeneous party with superior and consistent principles'. The centre was unable to build up the solid governing majority desired by Waldeck, faithful to the supreme idea of Gambettism. While we must take account of this political family's lack of interest in organization, it is also fair to note that in their constituencies many moderate republicans, a prey to the attacks of reactionaries, did not want to cut themselves off from the left, the party that was on the move. Méline used to say 'neither revolution nor reaction'. The support of the right made some of his political friends, susceptible to the campaigns of the radicals, think that Méline ran a real risk of favouring 'reaction'.

The attitude of the intransigent right could only strengthen this view. In the Chamber the conservative right and the *ralliés* supported Méline. But intransigent Catholics saw this as a fool's bargain; the administration, they said indignantly, remains sectarian and the laicization laws are still inviolate. The government was not satisfying Catholic interests, nor was it making any effort to carry out the social reforms desired by the Christian democrats and by socially minded Catholics. Thus the Ralliement, though effective in the Chamber, was much less evident in the country. There were the *réfractaires*, coerced *ralliés* who grudgingly accepted the constitutional base without uttering the word Republic; there were the advocates of a Christian Republic, who dreamed of abolishing the educational and military laws as soon as possible; there were the Christian democrats, who accepted the Republic but regarded the régime as socially retrograde; and there were Catholic republicans who accepted the laicization laws as a possibility. Amid these various currents dividing French Catholics the strongest was without doubt the one represented by those who accepted the constitution without any further question but wanted to change the legislation and to unite all Catholics on the basis of the defence of religion. This was the attitude of the important section of the press backed by the Assumptionist fathers. The network of distributors for *La Croix* and *Le Pèlerin* (a popular weekly with a big circulation) was utilized to create an organization directed towards the elections, namely the 'Justice and Equality' committees. Nothing could have worried the republicans – moderate or radical – more. The vehement anti-secular polemics of *La Croix*, its anti-capitalist social demagoguery marked by an anti-semitism that was both economic and religious in its bases, convinced them that the Church, 'to regain its domination was calling itself republican and even socialist'.[10]

With a view to the elections of 1898, Rome tried to co-ordinate the action of Catholics. Piou was not helped by his timidity in the social field and by his monarchist past. Leo XIII turned to Etienne Lamy, who had always been a republican. At his request a certain number of Catholic groups, Christian democrats and friends of Lamy on the Justice and Equality committees formed an electoral federation. The programme was a compromise: 'Loyal acceptance of the constitutional basis; reform of the laws against Catholics in so far as they are contrary to common law and liberty; an understanding with those who want a régime of peace, in liberty and justice'. Lamy had had to come to terms with his most powerful allies, the Justice and Equality committees. He even started fruitless negotiations with Méline on the education laws. The electoral federation was a heterogeneous coalition and soon broke up. The episode confirmed two important facts: the exceptional divisions among the Catholics; and the hostility of the majority of militant Catholics (it was different with mere practising Catholics or traditional Catholics) to the laicization laws. The moment that the Republic identified itself with laicization the Ralliement could only be a failure; the elections of 1898 were to confirm this. In fact, the main result of Leo XIII's initiatives had been to put an end to monarchical loyalties. The defence of Catholicism from then on became one of the major themes of the right.

Thus while there was a combination of centres in Parliament, in the country the Ralliement came up against the conflict between blocs and the hostility of the right and left on the religious question.

Foreign ambitions

The moderate Republic continued the task of strengthening the army and put an end to France's international isolation. In doing this, as Jacques Bainville saw very clearly,[11] it calmed the anxiety that had given birth to Boulangism – Boulanger had forced the men who governed to take an increased interest in national defence. For nearly five years, from March

1888 to January 1893, this undertaking was the responsibility of the same Minister for War, Freycinet, Gambetta's former deputy at the War Office. The Lebel rifle was put into service, the 75 field gun came into use in 1897, and the High Command and the reserves were organized in a more efficient way. These were just some of a continuing series of improvements which Freycinet commended on 9 September 1891 at the end of manoeuvres in Champagne. In his view these improvements showed 'that the government of the Republic, in spite of surface changes, is capable of taking long views in the accomplishment of national tasks'. Freycinet made these remarks a few days after a 'new situation' had been created on the diplomatic plane by the Franco-Russian agreement of 27 August.

After Bismarck's resignation in March 1890 the German government decided not to maintain the treaty of 'reinsurance' with Russia, which had been 'an essential feature of Bismarck's policy' (P. Renouvin). It was at this juncture that the Tsar's government began to turn somewhat slowly and hesitantly towards the French Republic, whose régime it did not very much care for, even though it was glad to see Russian loans taken up on the French market after November 1888 when Bismarck closed the German financial market to Russian loans. For years the French banks and in particular the Crédit Lyonnais (J. Bouvier, no. 109, and R. Girault, no. 168) had taken an interest in Russian 'big business'. The initiatives taken by the credit establishments served the policy of the French government, which resorted to the financial weapon. To put an end to Russian shilly-shallying, in May 1891, the French government put pressure on the Rothschild bank to turn down a request for a loan.[12] The renewal in May 1891 of the Triple Alliance between Germany, Austria–Hungary and Italy, and the announcement by the Italian government of the existence since 1887 of a 'Mediterranean agreement' associating England, Italy and Austria–Hungary decided the Russian government to move from a mere understanding to a precise agreement. The French government wanted to obtain a military convention involving an automatic undertaking to mobilize in the event of any mobilization by the Triple Alliance. The exchange of letters of 27 August 1891 only provided that the two governments should act in concert in the case of a threat to peace. The Russian government did not wish to enter into any precise military commitment, but the Tsar finally agreed to negotiations.

On 18 August 1892 General de Boisdeffre signed a military agreement, which was kept secret, with the Russian chief of staff. France obtained 'simultaneous and automatic' mobilization without 'prior concertation'. But she agreed to mobilize even if Austria–Hungary alone mobilized against Russia. Although entry into war was foreseen only in the case of an attack from Germany, the fact remains that to obtain the signature of the agreement the French government was taking a risk in the case of an

Austro-Russian conflict. Yet the Tsar, who was worried by the fresh German initiatives, still hesitated. He finally accepted the agreement on 27 December 1893. In October a Russian squadron had visited Toulon as public testimony to the reality of the alliance. The evolution of German policy had enabled the French government to obtain the Russian alliance of which Gambetta had dreamed. The scope of Russian borrowing on the French market had considerably assisted French diplomacy.[13] France abandoned the isolation in which she had lived since 1871 and found a reverse alliance. At the same time as the Franco-Russian alliance was concluded Franco-German relations seemed to improve after the phase of tension corresponding with the Boulangist crisis. The idea of 'revenge' receded. There were various reasons for this development, but in general the memory of defeat was fading. In 1890 the generation born after the disaster came of age. In Alsace-Lorraine, from the elections of 1893 onwards, the concept of autonomy was in the ascendant. In 1898 twelve of the fifteen members elected to the Reichstag expressed their 'loyalty' to the German Empire. The 'lost provinces' no longer provided a picture of protest, even if the emotional attachment to the mother country remained. The acceptance of the facts prevailed both in Alsace-Lorraine and in France. Nevertheless, the Alsace-Lorraine question had not disappeared; it remained present in the collective subconscious. No government could explicitly renounce Alsace-Lorraine and this remained the obstacle to a Franco-German rapprochement.

Yet in the years of the moderate Republic politicians did not feel any repugnance towards such a possibility and it would have given France freedom of action overseas, where she was encountering in particular the hostility of Great Britain.[14] Gabriel Hanotaux, who was Minister for Foreign Affairs from 1894 to 1898, recognized 'the necessity of collaborating with Germany' (P. Renouvin) without being able to say precisely whether he saw this as just 'going round in circles' or the start of longer-ranging developments. In any case, Hanotaux interpreted the Franco-Russian alliance strictly and did not allow himself to give Russia any but diplomatic support in Balkan questions. Meanwhile the refusal of the French government to recognize the *fait accompli* of 1871 prevented a policy of rapprochement from taking shape. The reactions of public opinion are significant: when the French government sent some warships in June 1895 to the opening of the Kiel canal it had to defend its action against attacks from nationalists and radicals, even from a socialist like Millerand. The latter spoke of 'immanent justice', while Goblet denounced the 'violation of international law in the annexation of Alsace-Lorraine' (19 June 1895).

In the years following Ferry's fall from power, during the Boulangist crisis, colonial expansion came to a temporary halt. The Franco-German tension of 1887 also marked the return of continental preoccupations. After 1890 the climate changed and it was in the years of the moderate Republic that the 'colonial party' was born. This term, which was employed at the time, denoted the various groups interested in the development of colonization. November 1890 saw the creation of the Committee for French Africa, which brought together politicians, intellectuals and officers 'to develop French influence and commerce'. In 1895 the Colonial Union was founded; it embraced businessmen and 'those involved in economic life in the colonies'. And in 1892 a 'colonial group' was established in the Chamber. It was chaired by Eugène Etienne, an officer's son, deputy for Oran, and a former Gambettist, the very incarnation of the policy of expansion.[15] One of the vice-presidents of the group was the prince d'Arenberg, the president of the Committee for French Africa and of the Board of Directors of the Suez Canal. Another vice-president was Charles-Roux, the Marseille deputy and businessman. The group numbered at this time ninety-one deputies, two-thirds of them from centre groups (cf. Henri Brunschwig, Biblio. no. 44, pp. 111–37). It concerned itself with colonial questions in the Chamber and formed a real pressure group. Its numbers were to grow and its influence with ministers for the Colonies was to be decisive. The Committee for French Africa organized conferences and subsidized scientific and exploratory expeditions to Africa. It propounded the patriotic reasons for expansion. The Colonial Union devoted itself at first to the defence of economic interests. Mercet, its first president, a director of the Comptoir d'Escompte, addressing Delcassé, the Minister for the Colonies, deplored the fact that up to then merchants and industrialists in the Colonies had not been 'encouraged'. He rejoiced that this 'deplorable error' was being corrected, one indication among others of the good relations of the 'colonial party' with the members of the government.

These groups were not the only ones to act on public opinion: the geographical societies were developing strongly; the Exhibition of 1889 gave much space to the colonies; exotic subjects were becoming more and more popular in literature. In fact public opinion on colonization was changing. Colonization no longer aroused the hostility it had encountered ten years earlier. The creation of the colonial army in 1893 avoided the necessity of sending conscripts on overseas campaigns. The end of isolation since the Russian alliance meant it was no longer vital to keep watching the 'blue line of the Vosges'. Nationalism no longer restricted its gaze to the continental horizon. The conservative right, which had been hostile to colonization, began to favour overseas enterprises. This development was of a piece with the slide of the right towards nationalism and with its progressive acceptance of the Republic. The prince d'Arenberg was one of the principal *ralliés*. The Catholics, whether they accepted the Republic or not, were won over to the cause of French expansion overseas. It helped the missions; and at the end of the nineteenth century two-thirds of all the missionaries in the world were French.[16] To support the work of France overseas was a way of asserting one's patriotism while still condemning secularization in the metropolis.

The activity of the colonial party, particularly that of Etienne, who was Under-Secretary for the Colonies from February 1889 to February 1892, of Gabriel Hanotaux, who stayed four years at the Quai d'Orsay, and of Delcassé, who had once worked on *La République Française* and was Minister for the Colonies in 1894, resulted in renewed expansion, the stages in which – without recounting their history – we should recall. The years 1890–3 were decisive ones for the creation of French West Africa (see the restatements of J. Ganiage, Biblio. no. 45). The rôle of Etienne, who had an imperial vision of French Africa, was determinative. The Sudan was conquered after the campaigns against Ahmadou (1890–3) and Samory (1891–8), then Togo and Dahomey between the Gold Coast and Nigeria, which were British. In Madagascar a costly campaign in 1895 substituted a genuine treaty for the semi-protectorate of 1885. The revolts of 1896 led to annexation. Galliéni pacified the big island, combining flexibility with firmness. In this process of expansion France came into conflict with the ambitions of England. When Hanotaux was Minister of Foreign Affairs the Marchand expedition was sent, at the risk of a conflict, in the direction of the Nile basin.[17]

In a few years a vast empire was built up, the work of a small number of colonials – missionaries, merchants, soldiers anxious to avoid the dull life of the metropolitan garrisons. Metropolitan France let the process go ahead in the mood of relative indifference tinged with curiosity that had succeeded the impassioned hostility of the 1880s. Clear-sighted observers noted that the enterprise was not profitable and that the colonies bought more abroad than from the mother country. Their place in French life remained a slender one. No doubt the colonialists' trump card was to have diverted to their cause a whole sector of the nationalist stream.

Summary of the period 1871–1898

The first chapter was entitled 'the end of the notables', and it was doubtless necessary to point to the transformation that was represented by the victory of the republicans over the traditional social hierarchies. Yet the limits of this transformation are evident; social élites do not change much. The political personnel itself grew more democratic only very slowly; even in 1900 there were only about thirty deputies of fairly humble origin. Before 1898 less than a third of deputies came from the middle or lower ranks of the bourgeoisie. Between 1871 and 1898 more than two-thirds of the parliamentarians had benefited from higher education, the qualification for membership of the bourgeoisie.[1] It was only with the elections of 1902 and the victory of the radicals that the ranks of politicians were to extend to include the lower section of the bourgeoisie and the 'middle' classes. This transformation took place alongside the birth of political parties in the modern sense, with the entry into the age of the masses and of big organizations, and the rise of socialism and nationalism.

The realities of the first third of the twentieth century were just a glimmer on the horizon of later nineteenth-century France, the France of Gambetta, Ferry and Méline. The parliamentary, bourgeois Republic overcame its crises because it knew it enjoyed wide approval, primarily from the rural sector. Did the stability of the régime – beyond the instability of administrations – reflect, as has been suggested, the stagnation of the economy and society? Even if this diagnosis was accurate, we should still have to prove the link between socio-economic and political life. But perhaps this kind of explanation, which certainly has some truth in it, overlooks the essential point. The success of a political system depends in the first instance on political reasons. The parliamentary Republic, mistrustful of authority, attentive to the rights and liberties of the individual, was an acceptable embodiment of the dominant ideal. For a long time it did not worry much about social questions, but was reproached only by minorities on the extreme left or right.

In *L'Orme du mail*, written by Anatole France in the last few years of opportunism, the university teacher Bergeret confesses the reason for his attachment to the Republic: 'It does not govern very much, and I'm tempted to praise it for this more than for anything else.' This liberal France was keen to emancipate herself from the tutelage of the traditional social authorities and from the Church. In that she was the daughter of the Revolution, which was no more distant to her than Gambetta is to us. Other memories left their mark, those of 2 December and 16 May, which established hostility to 'personal power' and fear of authority. Authority and democracy were henceforth antagonistic notions. That had serious implications for the future, but contemporaries were mainly oblivious to them. Until the end of the century the Republic did not meet any problems so grave as to be insoluble, and the Republic's fundamental values – education, progress, parliamentary government, liberalism and finally patriotism – remained objects of widespread devotion.

PART II

A radical Republic? 1898–1914

7

The Dreyfus affair

The closing years of the nineteenth century in France mean primarily the Dreyfus affair. Anyone who leafs through the famous annual volumes produced almost on the spot by André Daniel – *L'Année politique*, 1898, 1899, and so on – can see at a glance that the workers' movement did not abandon its natural objectives (there was a strike of navvies in Paris in 1898), that colonial conquests went on, not without some rough encounters (the Anglo-French confrontation at Fashoda ended in November 1898 – a month after the capture of Samory – in the withdrawal of France), and that the difficult division of the African cake was started with England, while in the context of the long period of office which Delcassé was beginning at the Ministry of Foreign Affairs the Franco-Russian alliance was reaffirmed with new connotations. In spite of these areas of interest which seem external to the Dreyfus affair, in spite of the hushed-up financial scandals – that of the big loans, for example – of which André Daniel says nothing, it was certainly 'the Affair', with a capital letter and without any other qualification, that formed the centre of a debate of exceptional intensity and length, and also seriously jeopardized the political future of the Republic. What is more, at that time the whole of French society revealed in various degrees its tastes, its fantasies, its passions; one 'incident' demonstrated the impossibility of achieving a national consensus, the contradictions in the patriotic tradition, and made known the wishes of the silent majority as well as the militants and agitators. The Affair bears comparison with the greatest crises that French society has experienced. By studying it we shall not only be able to explain a great event; we shall also have the chance to take a cross-section of political life and of the machinery of French society at the moment when France was about to totter into the twentieth century.

The affair before the Affair, 1894–1897

We have to go back a few years to find the factual origins of something that was long seen only as a spy story, some of the details of which still puzzle us today.

The arrest of Dreyfus, 15 October 1894

It was at the end of September 1894 that the French Intelligence Service, discreetly called at that time the 'Statistical Section' and run by Colonel Sandherr, was shown a missive informing the German military attaché, Lieutenant-Colonel Maximilian von Schwartzkoppen, stationed in Paris from 1892 to 1897, of the despatch of confidential French military documents. This unsigned letter, soon known as the '*bordereau*' (memorandum), implied a long-standing relationship. The information sheets to which it referred have never been found, and it is difficult to judge the importance of the information which they are supposed to have contained. The precise origin of the *bordereau* is still discussed today; it was very probably the work of Major Esterhazy, as Dreyfus's supporters thought at the time and as Esterhazy himself admitted later. This is also what is asserted today by both Marcel Thomas and Henri Guillemin,[1] on the basis of a very careful examination of the file. But did it really arrive in the offices of the French Intelligence Service by the 'normal channel', that is, the military attaché's wastepaper basket carefully emptied by a charwoman devoted to French counter-espionage, or was it a piece of paper forged elsewhere and, if so, where and to what end? Indirectly connected with this question is the question whether Esterhazy was 'working' only for himself.

These questions were only raised later, in some cases very recently.[2] At the time the official suspicions of the army and subsequently of the politicians centred very quickly (by 6 October), at the suggestion of Lieutenant-Colonel d'Aboville and because of the tenor of the memorandum, on the artillery officers serving on the General Staff – there were not many of them – and in particular, because of certain similarities in the writing, on Captain Alfred Dreyfus, a brilliant officer, but he was a Jew working on the inner General Staff where Jews were extremely rare. Appointed to act as detective in the enquiry, Major du Paty de Clam, an expert in identifying handwriting by the Bertillon method (but weak in Gobert's method), organized the arrest of Dreyfus on 15 October in a scene subsequently immortalized in popular colour prints and long celebrated in caricatures and ballads. The machinery had been set in motion. The guilt of Dreyfus and the urgency of convicting him in an exemplary fashion had become articles of faith for de Boisdeffre, the Chief of Staff, General Mercier, the Minister of War, and the progressivist Charles Dupuy, the Prime Minister.

His conviction, 22 December 1894

The trial of Captain Dreyfus by the senior Paris court martial opened on 19 December and took place behind closed doors. There was still no firm proof to support the circumstantial evidence. They were still based solely on the writing in the memorandum. Alfred Dreyfus had denied everything right from the start. In any case it was difficult to imagine what possible motives there could be for his treason. He belonged to a family of industrialists from Mulhouse and in 1872 his father had chosen French nationality; it could not be alleged that his patriotism was suspect or that he needed money. His relations with women, *demi-mondaines*, had not put him in contact with any dubious circles. Would the military judges convict him in the circumstances? They might be pushed into doing so by the press, which since 31 October had announced the captain's arrest and demanded the rapid punishment of the traitor. However, the result was by no means certain. It was necessary for Major Henry, speaking semi-officially in the name of Colonel Sandherr, to throw into the scales all the weight of the Intelligence Service, and for the Minister of War to send to the president of the court, under totally illegal conditions, a 'secret file' which neither the accused nor his defender, maître Demange, had ever set eyes upon; it consisted of a few documents cobbled together by Henry and Sandherr. At least two of these documents had been forged by the Intelligence Service; the abuse of power was thus added to the abuse of the rule of law.

On 22 December the court martial unanimously pronounced Dreyfus guilty and sentenced him to deportation for life to a fortress prison. On 5 January 1895 he had to submit to the painful ceremony of cashiering. On 21 February he embarked for Devil's Island.

The 'admirable brother'

However, neither Dreyfus nor his family had lost confidence. But for family 'Dreyfusism' there would have been no Dreyfus affair; and the family meant Lucie Dreyfus, who wrote off in all directions, including a letter in Latin to the Pope; it meant Lucie's family, the Hadamards; and it meant above all the captain's elder brother, Mathieu, who was a French citizen and managed the family mill in Mulhouse. 'All his relations were still overwhelmed by the catastrophe, crushed beneath what seemed an inexorable fate, when he set to work, that is he began to search in the darkness' (J. Reinach). He appealed in vain to journalists, to the President of the Republic, Félix Faure – both personally and via intermediaries – and to the Vice-president of the Senate, Scheurer-Kestner. He interrogated provincial clairvoyants and made contact with English detectives. He did everything he could to prevent the affair from being forgotten. Almost everyone remained hostile. Not even the Jewish community stirred itself; the chief rabbi of France, Zadock Kahn, certainly promised 'the support of his great moral authority', but that was all, or almost all; the vast majority of the comfortable Jewish bourgeoisie had only one aim – the peaceful enjoyment of its rights. It feared disorder and was pleased to present the French army as an admirable school of toleration. Since the death of Captain Mayer, killed in a duel in 1892 by the marquis de Morès, a notorious anti-semite, this tendency had grown even stronger; the Consistory, convoked by its president, Alphonse de Rothschild, had decided that it was essential to do nothing. In these circumstances how derisory the accusation of the nationalist deputy Castelin looks; on 18 November 1896 Castelin denounced in parliament the machinations of a 'Dreyfus syndicate'. Those close to Dreyfus had obviously collected money for his defence, the rest was pure imagination.

The socialists were traditionally quick to denounce the acts of the authorities, but these were circles that Dreyfus hardly frequented. Some of the deputies on the extreme left applauded Castelin. Jaurès himself, the day after the conviction of Dreyfus, had denounced the court martial's indulgence and had compared it with the capital punishment frequently meted out to private soldiers guilty of a momentary act of insubordination. In underlining what he called the caste spirit of the higher ranks of the army, he had expressed the general feeling of the militant proletariat. Why, if no new element was introduced, did the situation change?

The affair becomes the Affair

The intervention of the printed word

Those who believe in the absolute power of the press have written that it was 'the first and almost the only factor responsible for the evolution of opinion' during the Dreyfus affair. We do not go so far as to think that the press creates history, but it certainly makes a contribution to it and the first triggers which were to make the name of Dreyfus the object of debate were in fact released in the world of the printed word – a somewhat wider world than that of just the newspapers. There were three different important moments. In autumn 1896 two papers with a large circulation, *L'Eclair* and then *Le Matin*, drew attention to the proofs which had caused Dreyfus's conviction. *L'Eclair* indicated for the first time – falsifying it into the bargain – the existence of one of the documents in the 'secret file' of December 1894; in it Schwartzkoppen, speaking to his friend the Italian military attaché, Panizzardi, mentioned 'that scum D'. Almost at the same time a Jewish critic and publicist, Bernard Lazare, convinced by Mathieu, sent to all the French political and literary notabilities and also to the best-known journalists a solidly argued pamphlet in favour of Dreyfus. There were few repercussions. A year later Mathieu had discovered at last the name of the author of the memorandum, one Major Esterhazy, a bold and vicious adventurer who nevertheless enjoyed the protection of those in high places in the army, and he disclosed his certainty to the press; *Le Figaro* published his letter on 16 November in a prominent position. Immediately there were replies from the anti-semitic press, and huge illustrated posters in honour of Esterhazy, 'the victim of the Jews', were distributed on the boulevards. Within a few days numerous newspapers had abandoned their mute stance. The great majority of politicians, the militants and the intelligentsia still kept silent. On 13 January 1898 came the third episode, this time a decisive one. Two days after the acquittal of Esterhazy, who had asked to be charged, *L'Aurore* published in an edition of 300,000 copies a 'Letter to the President of the Republic' signed by Emile Zola and topped by Georges Clemenceau with a withering title, 'J' accuse'. The intervention of Clemenceau, a redoubtable controversialist, and above all that of Zola, resulted in the Affair having extraordinary repercussions. The author of the Rougon-Macquart novels was known not to like committing himself politically, and it was in fact first as a novelist that he had recognized in the Affair a 'poignant drama' with 'superb characters'; especially important, his reputation extended far beyond literary circles, for *Germinal* had been published as a serial by numerous socialist journals both in France and abroad. His provocative action put the Affair before the masses by forcing the authorities to take legal action against the most popular of the great French writers. One can understand why Jules Guesde called his pamphlet 'the greatest revolutionary act of the century'.

Minority and marginal figures

Let us return to those people, whose obstinacy had ensured the elevation of Dreyfus's conviction to the status of a national affair. It will be objected that they were only individuals. This is true, but they were representative individuals. Representative of what? Almost without exception, of circles that were to some extent marginal or in any case in the minority on some important points.

Let us take Bernard Lazare. What had his young writer published? Not novels, but a poem and a collection of philosophical tales. As a journalist, what side had he taken? At the beginning of the 1890s, at the time of the anarchist outrages, he had been among those who supported 'the Idea', as is shown by the little review which he ran until 1893, *Les Entretiens politiques et littéraires*. At the 'trial of the Thirty' in 1894 he gave evidence for Jean Grave and in 1895 he was among the first to work on *Les Temps nouveaux*. Finally, he was a Jew, but of what kind? Léon Blum was to say 'of the great race', of the race of 'just men'. In any case, he was different from any others; a decided unbeliever, he professed universal contempt for all religions, including Judaism. Quite independent of the Consistory, he did not feel in the least bound by its passive attitude and while hoping for the total assimilation of French Jews into French society he began to think, with the rise of anti-semitism, that this would not be so easy. 'Captain Dreyfus', he wrote in his brochure of 1896, 'belongs to a class of pariahs.' Lazare, then, was a Jew, but one whose behaviour in comparison with the rest made him a marginal figure.

But, the reader may ask, what about Scheurer-Kestner? By his title – he belonged to the disappearing category of life senators – by his business activities – he ran a factory that made chemical products – and by his function – the vice-presidency of the Senate – did he not belong, unlike Lazare, to good society? He certainly did, but he was a Protestant, and although the Huguenot bourgeoisie found it easy to make a career in the republican administration, to which it was often called by the long-standing nature of its republican sympathies, Protestantism remained in France not only a religion but a minority group whose members were reckoned to be more disputatious than other people, with more confidence in the human conscience capable of being illumined by God than in hierarchical decisions trailing a faint odour of popery. It should also be noted that by his side, among the very first 'Dreyfusards', there were other Protestants, such men as Gabriel Monod, founder of the *Revue historique*, the lawyer Louis Leblois, who was to be suspended by his colleagues of the Paris bar for his sympathy for Dreyfus, and soon a well-known journalist from *Les Temps* and the *Revue politique et parlementaire*, Francis de Pressensé.

Other Frenchmen were quickly sensitive to Dreyfus's misfortune. Yet their regional or national origins, without making them strangers in France, put them outside the common run. Such was the case with those who came from the lost provinces. Scheurer-Kestner regarded himself as the protector of all the Alsatians in France. Leblois was an Alsatian, and so was his trusted friend, Major Picquart, who headed the Intelligence Service after Sandherr's death and was the first to discover proof of Esterhazy's guilt through the 'Petit Bleu' (express letter), a discovery which immediately earned him disgrace and a posting overseas. This solidarity seems to have extended beyond the Alsatians; Bernard Lazare has told of the warm welcome which he received at the end of 1896 from Garibaldi's companion, Amilcar Cipriani. Cipriani was exiled from his own country, a defender of all just causes. A member of the 'Free Cuba' committee, he was to set out in 1896 with the Greeks against Turkey; and he was doubtless the first socialist to be convinced.

Marginal figures in the intelligentsia, too, at the start

The first intellectuals to be won over to the cause of a revision of the verdict on Dreyfus also came – apart from Zola, of course – from slightly outside the main stream. They did not come from the accepted intellectual institutions, but from the young; not from the organized groups of socialist youth – Alexandre Zévaès, the main leader of the collectivist students, accused Bernard Lazare in *La Petite République*, November 1896, of being 'one of the most faithful admirers of His Majesty Rothschild' – but from the politically vaguer atmosphere of the *Ecole normale supérieure* in the rue d'Ulm. Some senior members of the *Ecole* were certainly involved – the vice-principal, Paul Dupuy, and above all the librarian, Lucien Herr. However, Herr, who was a philosopher and another Alsatian, an expert on Hegel, a socialist and an active member of Allemane's Revolutionary Socialist Workers' Party, did not go in for systematic proselytism. But, once convinced, from summer 1897 onwards he abandoned his reserved attitude to support the cause of Dreyfus. The literary generation of 1894, that of Charles Péguy, Albert Mathiez, Félicien Challaye, Paul Mantoux, Georges Weulersse and Mario Roques, was by 1897 almost entirely enthusiastically in favour of Dreyfus. Several pupils proclaimed themselves socialists as soon as they entered the *Ecole*, among them those who shared Péguy's room, the 'utopian digs'. For them Dreyfusism was the incarnation of the socialism of their dreams – a vast educational movement aiming to strengthen minds, to give individuals the means of resisting the pressure of society and the unacceptable deceptions and compromises it imposes. Their ardour and their youth undoubtedly helped in a decisive fashion to persuade Jaurès to enter the Affair actively. What he said at the time coincides with what Péguy said a little later. 'This very moment', Jaurès wrote in *La Lanterne* two days after 'J'accuse', 'we respectfully salute all those young men, outstanding in ideas and courage, who fearlessly protest in public against the growing despotism of the military élite, against the secrecy in which they shroud their parody of justice. I am almost tempted to ask pardon of these young men for our equivocation and prevarication.'

The story of two years

Events did not come to a halt the day after Zola's bombshell. Without going into all the extraordinary ups and downs we should summarize the principal stages; each crux in the crisis tore away a strip of the social organism. And the whole nation, men and women, not just the far-away Alfred Dreyfus – the worst informed of all – lived these events passionately; they found their opinions confirmed or changed; they grew angry, were filled with pity or rejoiced; in short, they lived.

From January 1898 to the end of 1899 each big moment in the Affair produced consequences that were the opposite to what those involved expected. The irony of history has perhaps never been revealed in such a lively fashion. Thus 'J'accuse', which Zola expected to result in a trial – a civil trial – which would enable him to make the truth obvious, ended on 23 February after an action for libel, skilfully limited by the efforts of General Billot, the Minister for War, in Zola's being sentenced to a year in prison. This was confirmed on appeal on 18 July. The declaration of General de Pellieux, who spoke of a 'secret' but in his view authentic document in which Dreyfus was explicitly named – the document later known as 'le faux Henry' – had obtained a decision undoubtedly in harmony with public expectations. A few months later a new Minister for War, Cavaignac, the son of the veteran of republican struggles at the time of the Restoration, decided on 7 July to abandon the silence his predecessors had observed; he read out the three documents, which in his view provided overwhelming proof of Dreyfus's guilt, from the voluminous file put together by the General Staff. The revisionists seemed to be crushed. But in fact this incautious utterance triggered off the process which was to end in the honest examination of the file by an officer who had had nothing to do with its compilation, and in the arrest and suicide on 31 August of Colonel Henry, who had been compelled to admit his forgery. Was revision of the original verdict on Dreyfus now at last certain? Many people thought so,[3] but they were wrong. During the winter and spring the resignation one after another of Ministers for War opposed to it and the attitude of the most senior judges of the Supreme Court of Appeal conspired to prevent it. It was only on 3 June 1899 that the Court set aside the judgement of 1894 and ordered that Dreyfus should appear before a new court martial in Rennes. This time the revisionists were full of confidence, but again they were wrong. After a month's deliberations the court martial found Dreyfus guilty a second time, but only, to tell the truth, by a majority; and they also surprisingly qualified the verdict with a number of mitigating circum-stances. It looked like the collapse of the revisionists' struggle. But no: on 19 September 1899 Loubet, the President of the Republic, signed the pardon of Alfred Dreyfus, who accepted it without renouncing action to secure the public recognition of his innocence. On 2 June 1900 the Senate voted an amnesty. Nevertheless, it was not until 12 July 1906 that the Supreme Court of Appeal set aside definitively the Rennes verdict and thus cleared Captain Dreyfus of any accusation. He was to die in 1935.

The State apparatus

Government and Parliament

People had to wait for the summer of 1899 – really for the for-mation of the Waldeck-Rousseau ministry on 22 June – before the government made up its mind to adopt a position in conformity with the minimum requirements of the republican tradition in the Dreyfus affair. The least that can be said of Waldeck's predecessors is that they displayed either remarkable obstinacy or remarkable laxity. The obstinacy was first shown by the Méline cabinet, whose long parliamentary reign is striking; it lasted from 29 April 1896 to 15 June 1898. It was during these two years, at the time when the governing republicans broke with the radicals and discarded the policy of 'republican concentration', resting satisfied with the sympathetic abstention or even the support of the right whether or not it accepted the Republic, that the Affair reached national dimensions. This period saw the start of that close collusion between the Prime Minister and the Minister for War which, even though it was subsequently to weaken, never completely disappeared. When, in response to Castelin's *interpellation* in parliament on 18 November 1896, General Billot sheltered behind the authority of a closed case, Méline echoed his words; when Méline declared on 4 December 1897, 'There is no Dreyfus affair', Billot supported him. Viewed from outside, the agreement seemed unbreakable, even though the Prime Minister may have hesitated for a time. After the elections of 1898 the situation might have changed; the person in power from 28 June was Henri Brisson, a man known for his uprightness, ex-president of the commission of enquiry into the Panama scandal, a well-known freemason and a good radical. He was probably not enchanted by the outbursts of his Minister for War, Cavaignac, but after all it was he who had appointed Cavaignac and it was he who, after Henry's confession, appointed two other ministers equally hostile to any revision – Zurlinden, who three days after his resignation was appointed governor of Paris, and then Chanoine. It is true that Brisson seemed to react fairly firmly on 25 October when Chanoine resigned amid a good deal of publicity, but only to withdraw without really fighting. His successor, Charles Dupuy, and the new Minister for War, Freycinet – a civilian this time, and one of the old guard – were to have Picquart summoned before a court martial. Whether the cabinet was composed entirely of moderates, predominantly radical or predominantly moderate, the political authority testified either to having decided against revision or to being so powerless that one might well think that it had deliberately chosen to be powerless.

There were in fact political reasons for this attitude, though they are not very obvious. It is particularly difficult to understand why the elections of April 1898 and the return to power of a cabinet headed by a radical did so little to change the situation. It would have been normal for Brisson to take the opposite course from such a mediocre 'republican' predecessor. He did in fact do so on a large scale, but in other domains. Called on to specify his programme, Brisson declared on 30 June 1898 that it was designed essentially 'to remove from any sphere of influence anyone who was opposed to the kind of régime desired by the nation as a whole'. Changes of prefects affected more than a third of all the departments in France and ten prefects had to leave the corps.[4] Although he was intransigent on this point, elsewhere Brisson had to cut his losses. It must be recognized that the situation in parliament was not easy. Almost all the parties emerged disappointed, even duped, from the elections of 1898. The socialists, who had hoped, if not for final victory, at any rate for a decisive surge forward,[5] found themselves only a little stronger, and this slight numerical advance was almost nullified in everyone's view by the spectacular defeats of Guesde at Roubaix and of Jaurès at Carmaux. The Catholic *ralliés*, led by Leo XIII's man, Etienne Lamy, had tried to form an electoral federation open to all centre groups, and had seen this federation split asunder at the first hurdle thanks to the pressure of opinion. The radicals themselves, whose moderate wing emerged from the polls perceptibly weakened, reckoned themselves more changed than helped by the progress of their left wing. All round, the Chamber did not differ much from the previous one except in the disappointments it had to swallow. In any case, the electoral campaign had not been fought on the Dreyfus affair. The politicians, interested but not excited, had not wanted to adopt any particular position on it; the Affair lay outside their traditional spheres of intervention and at the grass roots the election committees had preserved silence. There were at least two exceptions, both unfavourable to the Dreyfusards; the radical-socialist Hubbard was beaten at Fontainebleau and the marquis de Solages won his seat back from Jaurès. No doubt Brisson held other trumps in his hand, but a politician as clever as he was had little incentive to be too intransigent.

The army and the judges

It is worth asking what rôle was played in the political choices of the government by those two trump cards in the State apparatus, the army and the judges. Obviously we do not mean to imply that their attitudes and responsibilities were identical. They were two very different bodies. The conscripts, the constantly renewed masses of foot-sloggers, did not form the army, which existed only in its cadres of officers and non-commissioned officers – who were very considerable in number. They lived on the margin, so to speak, of civil society; the military schools were cut off from the universities; the frequent changes of garrison prevented contacts with the outside world; and progress in the cadres was made only by promotion, in which the civil authority, the ministry, never interfered. The army possessed its own rules and its own jurisdiction. In this strictly hierarchical environment, with the General Staff at the summit, a service enjoyed special rights which emerged into the light of day in the Affair: the Chief of Staff and his deputy controlled the all-powerful Intelligence Service. To interfere with the General Staff or Intelligence was to attack the very highest ranks of the army. How insignificant the civil authority on which it officially depended looked alongside it! The ministers for War were themselves aware of the ephemeral nature of their position and through them the whole political authority could feel quite fragile. In case of conflict the ministers chose to identify themselves with those who were regarded as the army establishment, for those men, in the name of the army, had the power to cause governments to fall.

Does this mean that the French army constituted a faction? The currents of opinion that swept through it, and the social ideological origins of the officer corps certainly suggest that this might have been the case. We do not possess for the end of the century information as reliable as that provided twenty years earlier by Gambetta's papers;[6] at that time nine-tenths of the divisional generals and three-quarters of the senior officers were royalists or Bonapartists. But when the republicans conquered the Republic nothing happened to disturb the conservative dust in the military cadres. The percentage of cadets at Saint-Cyr, at the Naval College and even at the *Polytechnique* who had had a Church education had noticeably increased – in 1896 nearly a quarter of the first-year cadets at Saint-Cyr and more than a third of these at the Naval College had been educated by priests – and although Boulanger had eliminated the duc d'Aumale from the army list the Rohan-Chabots and the Clermont-Tonnerres had reappeared in the Saint-Cyr directory. For the members of these old families who thought it possible to serve the State without serving the Republic ideologically the army was a last resort. 'With the departure and replacement of the leaders of the old army, who had had much more varied social origins, the links between the upper echelons of the army and the ruling circles of the conservative world grew continually stronger and more numerous' (R. Girardet, Biblio. no. 174, p. 198).

A world apart, a closed society that was mostly reactionary and even anti-republican, the army – that 'dumb giant' whose members did not have the right to vote – did not intervene as a dictatorial force. It did not take sides during the Boulangist crisis. During the Affair it took care not to attempt, or to yield to any temptation to mount, a *coup d'état*. At the funeral of Félix Faure, the President of the Republic, on 23 February 1899, General Roget, who was very much of an anti-Dreyfusard, refused to follow Déroulède, who tried to drag him to the Elysée Palace. It is true that on the General Staff and in the Ministry of War, the very places where the conviction of Dreyfus had been fabricated and upheld, the republicans had long been very much in the majority; real 'Jesuit generals' like de Boisdeffre were relatively few in number in spite of their influence. Thus the upper ranks of the army did not rise in protest against the Republic; it was just not the sort of army to try an open *coup d'état*. But how are we to describe its practice, the effective bludgeoning that it employed all the more vigorously because the civil authority could not bring itself either to enquire into its activities or to impose its authority on it? Soldiers of all ranks did not hesitate to make their feelings known publicly by sending their contribution and often their name to the fund opened in December 1898 by Drumont's paper, *La Libre Parole*, to enable Colonel Henry's widow to prosecute Joseph Reinach.[7] All round, during the Affair the army played the part of a pressure group that had long been invincible.

The case of the judges was quite different. The most violent anti-Dreyfusards were not mistaken when, before any decision of the civil courts, they launched all kinds of insults at the 'petticoats', while praising to the skies the decisions of the courts martial. The composition of the magistracy is not very well known, but the rules of recruitment and promotion, fixed in all essentials in 1810, made them in the absence of any competition and any grading committee almost totally dependent on the justice ministry. It is not surprising that only retired judges put their names to the subscription for Henry and that a close symbiosis developed between the choices of the Minister of Justice and the decisions of the judges most in the public eye. At Zola's trial the partiality of the President of the Court, Delagorgue, bordered on servility. During the winter of 1898–9, when the Criminal Chamber of the Court of Appeal was conducting an impartial enquiry into the possible revision of the Dreyfus verdict, Lebret, the Minister of Justice, Quesnay de Beaurepaire, the President of the Civil Chamber, and Mazeau, a senior judge, worked together to remove the case from the Criminal Chamber and to give it to the combined Chambers. However, the transfer law, passed on 1 March 1899, was not to prevent the Court from setting aside the verdict of the first court martial, the government having decided to support this course. The magistracy behaved not so much as a pressure group but rather – in spite of its official independence – as an official agent of the government.

Repressive function

The truth is that there was permanent collaboration between the government, the army and the judges. All three in fact shared the same task; the generals, whether they had been educated by the Jesuits or not, the docile magistrates and the ruling republicans were closely united in the defence of the social order. The strikes in the iron and steel industry and the miners' strikes were the proof of this. Aubin, La Ricamarie, Decazeville, Fourmies, Carmaux – there was no decisive stage in the workers' movement in which the troops were not called in to reinforce the gendarmerie. It is true that it became more and more difficult to employ them 'preventively', and that when the armed forces occupied a pit head or surrounded a big factory it was more and more a question of repression, to re-establish order disturbed by some demonstration with red flags blowing in the wind. It is also true that the troops did not always fire, that the cavalry was not always very enthusiastic about making police charges and that the infantry were always liable to fraternize with the workers. But the prefects showed little hesitation in deploying the military apparatus to intimidate the strikers and to bring them to heel. The government relied just as much, if not more, on the fear inspired in struggling workers by the threat of legal sanctions; the apparatus of justice, as under the Ancien Régime, was vaguely, undefinably threatening; accusation and arrest isolated the victim, humiliated him, robbed him of what gave him strength – membership of a group. Finally, the notion of what constituted an offence varied from one strike to another, on the minister's orders, and the application of the law varied in accordance with the agreements reached at the lowest level by prefects and prosecutors and at the highest by the Ministries of the Interior and of Justice. A common concern, the application of which could vary slightly, motivated the repressive elements of the State apparatus. It helped to produce good co-operation between them and it operated in the direction of anti-Dreyfusism.

The two Frances

Demonstrations and organizations

The violence of the passions unleashed by the Affair in France surprised the world. It is true that the press sometimes exaggerated these passions; for example, police reports indicate that the day after Dreyfus's second conviction no surge of savage anger followed the very lively reactions of the newspapers. Yet the behaviour of the press was itself one of the factors in the bitterness of the confrontations; for months the Affair occupied the number-one position in numerous papers and banner headlines multiplied, following the example of *Le Matin*, which at the start was strongly anti-Dreyfusard, or of *La Petite République*, in which Jaurès published 'the proofs' in August–September 1898. In the streets the agitation was at first and for a long time organized by the anti-Dreyfusards. They had in their favour numbers, passion, and a model in the events in Algiers, where colonial anti-semitism joined a growing autonomist feeling to unleash in the second fortnight of January 1898 what Ch. R. Ageron called 'a near-revolution' (Biblio. no. 211, vol. I, book 3). In Marseille, where Jews were numerous, the demonstrations which followed 'J'accuse' were accompanied by attacks on their shops. The larger the population of a provincial town, the earlier and longer-lasting were the demonstrations.

As for the meetings, they were organized by both sides, especially in Paris, where there were plenty of rooms capable of holding audiences of between 4,000 and 10,000. There was the Salle Cheynes at the rond-point de la Villette, the Saint-Paul riding-school in the heart of old Paris, the Guyanet riding-school in the avenue de la Grande Armée, where the anti-Dreyfusards gathered after the suicide of Henry, and the Tivoli Vauxhall, the fortress of Dreyfusism. The police occupied the approaches to these halls early on the evenings of meetings and their violence was proverbial. New social strata, mixing with the workers and students, thus had their first experience of a workers' meeting.

In the university cities – Bordeaux, Aix, Lyon, Rennes, Nancy – the students were in an awkward position; their social origin often gained them a certain indulgence from the police. Most of the Latin quarter remained on the right and people booed Dreyfusard professors in the street. But the response was not long in coming. In homage to Péguy, Daniel Halévy has left a memorable description of those times: 'A voice would shout, "Durkheim is under attack! Seignobos has been overcome!" "Fall in!" replied Péguy, who always liked military expressions. Everyone sprang to attention and marched with him to the Sorbonne' (D. Halévy, Biblio. no. 21). Songs clashed everywhere; the *Ça ira* and the *Internationale*, the vocal weapons of the Dreyfusards, were countered by the nationalist hymn built on a pun in honour of Déroulède.

Even families were divided. It is hardly necessary to recall the drawing, the most famous of them all, by Caran d'Ache which appeared in *Le Figaro* on 13 February 1898. The drawing, entitled 'A family dinner', showed ten comfortable bourgeois at table. 'Above all, don't talk about the Dreyfus affair', says the master of the house as a servant brings in the soup tureen. A bit later table and chairs go over and the diners start fighting. 'They did talk about it.'

Just individuals to start with, Dreyfusards and anti-Dreyfusards soon organized themselves. New structures arose in French society and others, old ones, were reactivated. The time of the leagues had arrived. One of the very first was the League for the Defence of the Rights of Man, conceived by the senator, Ludovic Trarieux, a former Minister of Justice, in February 1898, in the middle of the Zola trial. Its first general meeting took place on 4 June and its manifesto was published a month later. Taking its cue from its somewhat muted origins and the personality of its founder, a politically very moderate republican who did not mean to go further than the defence of the Rights of Man defined in 1789, the League equipped itself with a central committee on which sat respected intellectuals, and a few politicians chosen for their moderation – the old radical Ranc was the furthest to the left. It refrained from taking any political initiative. It is true that circumstances pushed it into action and prevented it from resting content with the study of individual cases. It collected large sums – 168,000 francs in a year – to publicize the truth about the Affair, its local sections organized numerous meetings and above all it provided chairmen and a deposit for public meetings. But its recruitment remained limited; at the end of 1898 it had 4,580 members and a year later 8,580. The League acquired a mass audience, but it was not a mass movement; it was more of a reception committee and working party. On the other side the League of Patriots was reborn, a Gambettist organization at the time of its foundation in 1882 and blessed at that time by Hugo and ... Joseph Reinach. Déroulède and his faithful lieutenant Marcel Habert put it back on the rails in September 1898. The times were different and so were the rails; it was no longer a question of grouping together all republican patriots but of organizing, in face of the parliamentary, semi-Dreyfusard Republic, a régime of 'mandarins and thugs', the supporters of the army and of a plebiscitary régime. A sister organization appeared on the scene, possibly a rival. This was La Ligue de la Patrie Française. It completed its organization in January 1899, just when the government was beginning to turn timidly towards revision; the movements of the government pendulum were matched at one moment by the defence, if need be against the government, of the 'Rights of Man' and at the next by that of the 'Patrie'. Jules Lemaître, a fashionable literary critic, and François Coppée, a popular poet and dramatist, held the new league over the baptismal font. Barrès joined its committee. Short on dogma and aiming to make itself a mass movement, it avoided appealing, like Déroulède, to the 'sacred bayonets of France' and after two months was able to announce that it had some 100,000 members. The League of Patriots was to be almost a religious order; the Ligue de la Patrie Française was a movement which was inflated by the wind of opinion and was to collapse again almost as quickly. And finally there was the Anti-semitic League, the bastion of the extreme anti-republican right, founded in 1890 by Drumont and run since 1896 by a fairly shady character, Jules Guérin.

From February 1899 anti-Dreyfusard demonstrations started attacking the Republic and those who represented it, in particular the new President of the Republic, Emile Loubet, a moderate senator but one elected by the votes of the left. On 4 June at Auteuil race course someone even hit him. On 11 June the forces of the extreme left met at Longchamp for the Grand Prix; this was a powerful demonstration. The streets were on the move and the Republic seemed to be in danger.

Two modes of discourse

'Two tragic choruses insulting each other'; it was Emile Duclaux, Director of the Pasteur Institute and Vice-president of the League for the Rights of Man, who hit upon this phrase to indicate the existence of the 'two Frances'. And each camp was convinced that it alone was France. On 6 January 1898, Zola in his 'Letter to France' called on 'those who love you, those who want your honour and your greatness'. The same terms were used by a teacher, formerly a soldier, who, at his parents' repeated cry of 'Vive la France', sent 1.50 francs to the Henry fund. The slogans shouted in street clashes, at meetings or in university scuffles translated into the language of the masses opposing ideas that had been long maturing elsewhere; the symbols reflected two opposing systems of values.

The anti-Dreyfusards asserted that they were fighting 'for the army', which could not be wrong and which even if it were wrong had to be defended against the world since it embodied eternal France, its continuity and also its unity beyond the political differences and social struggles that were tearing France apart. The authority of the *res judicata* was necessary for the maintenance of the State and the country. 'Truth or not, what did it matter?'. The theory of the 'patriotic falsity' legitimized by the need to assert the identity of France against the foreigner was not peculiar to Drumont, Déroulède or Maurras; Maurice Barrès expressed it in almost the same terms. An ideology of this sort is obviously impervious to fact; its strength lies elsewhere. Facing these people were the Dreyfusards, their proclaimed objectives Justice and Truth. The France they claimed to defend was the one which, by promulgating the Rights of Man, had identified itself in the whole world's eyes with Right. No doubt many of them would have gladly admitted that the real France began in 1789, when reason and the critical spirit triumphed over the malevolent and obscure powers of the past and made way for the France of universal suffrage and parliamentary democracy, which would lead easily to social democracy. The republican régime had to affirm its true nature against the organized forces which, from inside or outside, strove to drag it backwards – the sabre, and the holy-water sprinkler which Clemenceau soon associated with it. The alliance of clericalism and the army was the theme which was to make it possible for the Affair to be woven into the context of French political life with all its problems.

Ideology and society

For a long time in fact the lines of division with regard to the Affair remained essentially ideological. Two different kinds of language – on which actions were moulded – faced each other. But they did not correspond to the organized political forces – it was to try to fill this gap that the Leagues were created – or to the social classes. The confusion in parliamentary debates well indicates the inability of the parties to see where they stood in the Affair. No doubt nationalists, monarchists and Bonapartists chose their camp right from the start, and with them the great majority of the army and the clergy, the traditional cadres of France. The amazement of the prince de Guermantes, when he discovered that, like him, his wife was secretly having masses said for Dreyfus, is as telling as the fall in the circulation of *Le Soleil* when the royalist paper was converted to Dreyfusism. On the Catholic side, let us remember the statement of Eugène Veuillot, who was nevertheless keen to absolve the Church as a body from any responsibility: 'Priests and faithful were almost all, as individuals, for the *res judicata* and the army' (*L'Univers–Le Monde*, 10 September 1898). Catholic Dreyfusism is not a myth: Paul Viollet, together with Trarieux, was in at the start of the League for the Rights of Man and he only left it in order to found the Catholic Committee for the Defence of Right, but this numbered hardly more than a hundred members and the big Catholic papers – *La Croix*, *Le Pèlerin* – remained unrelentingly hostile to it.

In traditionally republican circles and groups there were divisions not only among the progressivists – Poincaré, Barthou, Yves Guyot and *Le*

Siècle were in favour of revision, the first two of these late in the day and discreetly, while Méline and most of the notables were hostile to it – but also among the radicals. At Toulouse the powerful *Dépêche* remained anti-revisionist and anti-Dreyfusard up to and including the Rennes trial even though Jaurès and Clemenceau wrote for it. René Goblet, with the approval of the management of the paper, interpreted Dreyfus's attitude at his second trial as a sign, if not a proof, of guilt. Old comrades-in-arms like Ranc – who kept *Le Radical* revisionist – and Lockroy parted company. Although among the radicals time was on the side of revision, as is shown by the gradual change in attitude of Brisson, Bourgeois and even Pelletan, Clemenceau did not succeed in representing radicalism as a whole.

Jaurès was in the same position with his socialist colleagues; Millerand and Viviani, who 'were looking over their shoulders at their constituencies', awaited the discovery of 'le faux Henry' to make up their minds. The behaviour of the leaders of the French Workers' Party was even more surprising; after welcoming 'J'accuse', the Guesdists voted on 7 July 1898 for the display on posters of Cavaignac's speech, and the declaration of their national council on 24 July sounded like a brutal break with any tendency to Dreyfusism: 'The proletarians have nothing to do with this battle, which is not theirs – The party cannot suspend its own war; to do so would be indulging in deceit and treason.' Thus the most powerful of the socialist parties refused to politicize Dreyfusism just when Jaurès was emphasizing that Dreyfus, an innocent victim, was no longer 'an officer or a bourgeois' but 'humanity itself' and that it was in the interests of the proletariat to precipitate the discrediting and downfall of the most reactionary bodies in the State apparatus. Except for old France and the professions (the army) or the Cercles (the clergy) closely attached to it, the divisions began to cut across the social classes, or certainly across the organizations that represented them.

That is why they also cut so brutally across the 'intellectuals' as a class. It looks as if the use of this word as a noun began during the Affair; Clemenceau, always good at coining a phrase, is supposed to have hit upon the title 'Manifesto of the intellectuals' in January 1898 for the first petition in favour of revision. The word and the thing were in the air, particularly in socialist circles, but the suspicious, disdainful reactions of Barrès and his friends[8] were to confer on the concept, at the moment of its birth, a leftist connotation that it was to keep until our own day. This does not mean at all that all the intellectuals who took part in the Affair were in favour of revision; anti-Dreyfusism also had its devotees – Maurras was to speak of the 'party of intelligence' – and Gramsci's subsequent analyses of the 'organic intellectuals' have rarely been bettered. However, the first intellectuals to commit themselves grouped themselves behind Zola; all the avant-garde writers were there – except for Barrès, whom Blum had hoped to convince, and Paul Valéry, who was to send 20 francs ('not without reflection') to the Henry fund – whether or not they were connected with the Symbolist movement and the young reviews like the *Revue Blanche*. They included Fernand Gregh, André Gide, Mallarmé, Saint-Pol-Roux, Marcel Proust and the young Apollinaire. The Impressionist painters were there too: Bonnard and Vuillard as well as Pissarro and Signac, the last two more committed politically. But the big battalions came from the University and liked to meet at Stock the publishers or at the Bellais bookshop in the heart of the Latin quarter. They were also to be seen, mingling with the writers, in a few hospitable salons, that of Mme Ménard-Dorian – which was more of a 'University' salon – and that of Mme de Caillavet, where Anatole France held court. The students seem to have been fully committed at the *Ecole des hautes études*, at the *Ecole des chartes*, at the Collège de France where textual criticism held a place of honour, and at the Pasteur Institute where scientific observation was king. At the Sorbonne and the *Ecole normale supérieure* Zola's point of view was shared not only by numerous professors but also by the great majority of students of letters as well as by certain scientists – Paul Langevin and Jean Perrin, for example. But the schools of Law and Medicine were anti-Dreyfusard.

Law and Medicine were the biggest and oldest schools, and for a long time the only ones to accept genuine students. Anti-Dreyfusism, which found its troops and its salons more quickly than its theorists, on the whole recruited its intellectuals from successful people: writers with regular readers, often members of the Institute – Bourget, Brunetière, the marquis de Vogüé – literary critics whose reputations had been carried by the press into the salons, and best-selling authors too, from Jules Verne to Daudet and Gyp. But Zola and France, the driving forces of Dreyfusism, were also successful writers, and equally one would be wrong to imagine that the Sorbonne was mostly Dreyfusard. For example, on 18 July 1898 its assembly refused by 21 votes to 16 the authorization requested by Jaurès, a *docteur ès-lettres* and former lecturer, to give a public series of lectures in the old university building on the principles of socialism.[9]

The very tone of the debate, in that traditionally somewhat deadened atmosphere, underlined the almost total impossibility of neutrality in the intelligentsia. That is why the silence of Marcelin Berthelot was so surprising. The plan for union and reconciliation outlined in January 1899 by a few well-known writers and university teachers – Lavisse, the semi-official historian of the Republic, the philosopher Boutroux and Jean Aicard, whose poems were familiar to all schoolchildren – collapsed through indifference in spite of the patronage of Waldeck-Rousseau. Among the intellectuals there were certainly two Frances.

A third France?

Was the whole country involved? For some years historians have been questioning this idea;[10] it has been suggested that the agitation and even the interest in the problems raised were the concern only of active minorities, and remained so throughout the Affair. According to this view the vast majority of Frenchmen lived through the Affair in an attitude of indifference. The urban nature of the demonstrations is hardly in doubt. But what about interest in the Affair? The exhortations to keep calm uttered by so many politicians bear witness to a disquiet which needs explanation rather than to the indifference of those to whom appeals were made – often in vain. In any case, soothing entreaties or recriminations had a political function and served to strengthen respect for the *res judicata* and the opponents of revision. An analysis of the newspapers of the period allows us to draw more precise conclusions. Janine Ponty's study, which embraces fifty Parisian and provincial dailies, with a total readership of ten million, suggests that at the height of the affair a third of these papers at the most were mobilized.[11] Moreover, the vast majority were anti-Dreyfusard: 96 per cent in February 1898 and still 85 per cent at the time of the Rennes trial. Judet's *Petit Journal*, which printed a million copies and had solid provincial foundations, maintained its nationalist line right to the end without any deviation. The same is true of *La Croix*, which, together with *Le Pèlerin*, reached about half a million readers (to which must be added the very numerous readers of the local editions of *La Croix*) and was solidly rooted in the peasantry or in the new working class of rural origin. In Nord too it was the same (see R. Gautier, Biblio. no. 173). *Le Progrès* of Lyon was one of the few provincial papers which had favoured revision from the start. It looks then as if most of rural France was indifferent, but not all of it. There remains the proletariat. Here too it is difficult to judge. In Paris in January 1898 the demonstrations did not affect the working-class quarters of the north-eastern part of the city. But among the first 100,000 members of the Ligue de la Patrie Française there are supposed to have been 10,000 Parisian workers, mainly railwaymen. On the other hand, in February 1899, a department as Guesdist as Aube, the home ground of the poverty-stricken textile industry, gave a wildly enthusiastic welcome to Jaurès, the man with a 'heart of gold', who was totally committed to the Affair. The Affair may have been mainly a bourgeois interest, but it was certainly not exclusively so.

In any case, it is almost certainly necessary to distinguish a process of evolution. It was during the first six months of 1899 that the Affair took on a political hue; not in the wide revolutionary context that Jaurès hoped for – the disunited socialists were incapable of heading the movement and both the leaders of the *CGT* and the most important of the anarchist papers, *Les Temps nouveaux*, kept their distance – but by becoming integrated in the conceptual and political cadres of the nation. Was the Republic really threatened? It seemed to vacillate, a prey to the blows of the 'Jesuit' generals and the monks and their Ligue. Were people not attacking the President himself, whose lack of power enhanced his symbolical character? In January 1899 Guesdists and Vaillantists agreed to form a liaison committee with the independent socialists and the Revolutionary Socialist Workers' Party. In June there were signs of a rapprochement between the Dreyfusard socialists and anarchists, whose newspapers called on people to demonstrate at Longchamp, and the republicans, who also wanted to deliver a counterblow. The camp whose plan of campaign was outlined on 11 June was that of the majority which a fortnight later was to support the Waldeck-Rousseau ministry, or at any rate to abstain from voting against it. There was a hard parliamentary battle. The 'republican defence' that had slowly matured finally obtained a majority in the Chamber of only twenty-five votes. The appointment to the Ministry for War of Général le marquis de Gallifet, 'the butcher of the Commune', led Guesdists and Vaillantists to take refuge in abstention; the arrival at the Ministry of Commerce of the 'collectivist' Millerand – the first socialist to serve in a bourgeois government – was criticized by the revolutionary socialists, and denounced by the great majority of the progressivists as a decisive step towards socialism; but the advanced radicals did not regard Waldeck-Rousseau as a man of the left, and that was correct. Brisson, addressing the Chamber, had to make the masonic sign of distress to limit the republican 'defections'. On this point his agreement with Waldeck-Rousseau was complete; in the eyes of these men who belonged to the same generation the monarchists, the Bonapartists and the Church were the only source of the harm. Their conspiracy had to be broken; it could be done by a few immediate measures and by the revival of the anti-clerical policy. Those in the country who hesitated – the third France – found themselves once again on ground that they knew. The Affair was assuming a classical political dimension; in other words, it was drawing to a close.

The ideologies revealed by the Affair

We can now look in the mirror of the Dreyfus affair at the ideologies reflected there and examine their origins.

From spy fever to occultism and clericalism
The Affair was bathed in an atmosphere of spy fever and mystery. The breathless fear of spies in the service of a 'foreign power' which propriety forbade one to name was not peculiar to the Intelligence Service. It was widespread and partly explains the belief in the existence of a Dreyfus 'syndicate', suspected not only of paying to save the traitor but also

of working with him. A few years later Anatole France was to make it one of the successful themes of *L'Ile des pingouins*: in the system of writing employed by Pyrot (Dreyfus), 'these words, "three beers and twenty francs for Adèle" mean "I have delivered thirty thousand bundles of hay to a foreign power…" ' But cloak-and-dagger adventures cannot rest content with stories about charwomen. Esterhazy understood this very well. *Le Petit Journal* had a fine time with episodes as fantastic as that of 'Speranza', the 'veiled lady' supposed to have procured for the handsome major the 'document that freed him'. Jaurès, in *Les Preuves*, had to take the trouble to expose the construction of this romantic tale.

Rational analysis, the method of the palaeographers and scholars, came up against – in the country of free thought – the fashion for spiritualism, which was so widespread that some early Dreyfusards employed the services of a clairvoyant from Le Havre. It may be said that hypnotism, practised under medical control, makes possible scientific experiments on the phenomena of transmission of thought and seeing at a distance. That is true. But in the eyes of the public at large the difference between experiments of this sort and the blackest occultism was imperceptible. The last decade of the century in fact witnessed a growing interest in mysterious worlds; it was in 1889 that Schuré published *Les Grands Initiés*, and the taste of Huysmans or Gustave Moreau for the curious was paralleled in the sphere of design by nightmarish chandeliers and coat-hangers shaped like bats.[12] Credulity, the passion for mystery and the appetite for the sensational went beyond Catholic circles. The sensational press, serials with over-ingenious plots, and short stories and novellas had contributed in the preceding years to the creation of this atmosphere.

Contemporaries put the question in blunter terms. The Affair was a struggle to pierce the fog of the many episodes and false proofs involved and it rejuvenated the critical spirit and the scientific approach, which had been threatened by the recrudescence of religiosity in various circles. The mystical renaissance that had appeared a few years earlier among the intellectuals had in fact merged with the new forms taken by Catholic piety in popular circles – miracles and prophecies, relics and visions. The regular clergy had not been very scrupulous in their choice of arguments with which to combat freemasonry, which Pope Leo XIII had labelled 'the party of Satan' in the 1884 encyclical *Humanum genus*. Between 1895 and 1897 the wealthiest and most active section of the clergy had even taken at their face value the extravagant revelations about 'palladism'[13] organized by one Léo Taxil, a clever hoaxer who was a bit short of cash. These same Assumptionist fathers and their powerful newspapers (all called *La Croix*) played a militant anti-Dreyfusard rôle in 1898–9; the abbé Pichot, one of the few Dreyfusard priests, thought that if the publications of the pious press had not over-excited priests the clergy would have confined itself to asserting its confidence in the General Staff. All this helps us to understand why the denunciation of clericalism seemed not only to republican politicians but also to the strata of the population that supported them and to intellectual Dreyfusards to be a common denominator. By combating the sort of education dispensed by priests and by reducing their power one would enable Frenchmen to see society in its true light; they would give up old habits of thought and all become republicans. A new Dreyfus affair would henceforth be impossible.

Anti-semitism

Not all the anti-Dreyfusards were adherents of occultism. They were not all haunted to the same degree by the dangers of espionage. But many of them were affected by the ground-swell of anti-semitism and in most of them one can observe the integration of composite elements in a new ideology, nationalism.

Although it is certain that neither *Le Petit Parisien* nor even *Le Petit Journal* employed anti-semitic arguments during the affair and although openly anti-semitic demonstrations were rare (see J. Ponty, Biblio. no. 177), nevertheless the anti-Dreyfusard passion needs to be analysed in the light of the anti-semitic tendencies which had developed in France since the beginning of the 1880s. There were two currents at the root of it: the old Catholic anti-Judaism, and socio-economic anti-semitism, which asserted that it was anti-capitalist and claimed to be modern. The result of these two currents was nationalistic anti-semitism. Yet the French Jews were not very numerous; there were rather more than 71,000 in 1897, 45,000 of them in the Parisian region. It is true that this figure, established by the Consistory, did not take account of the Jewish proletariat recently driven out of Russia. Locally the Jews were often well integrated; such was the case in Bordeaux.[14] Nor were they organized in a solid community; the Jewish bourgeoisie did not show much enthusiasm for welcoming the poverty-stricken immigrants from the East. It had been affected as much as the Catholics by the erosion of faith.

Nevertheless, from the beginning of the 1880s the Catholic press never stopped reminding people that 'the question of Christ' and of a 'deicide' people was at the bottom of the Jewish problem: 'They are accursed if we are Christians' (Father Bailly, *La Croix*, 6 November 1894). The Assumptionists were more virulent than others and above all they controlled an influential press, but they were not alone. A certain number of *semaines religieuses* – a minority, it is true (see J. Verdès-Leroux, Biblio. no. 183) – also believed in the ritual murder, in the curse on Israel; and the Catholic hierarchy, whom Drumont nevertheless accused of being 'Jewified', hardly disavowed them, in spite of the caution prescribed by the Concordat. These influences were very apparent in the hymns, devotional books and textbooks used in the private schools. In short, Catholics were indoctrinated by anti-semitic propaganda.

The wave of anti-semitism was also reinforced by a feeling that gained currency during the second half of the century, a feeling with which the Catholics concurred, though they held no monopoly in it. It was in evidence, for example, in Marseille, where shopkeepers, even those who were not religious, detested the competitive sales techniques used by Jewish shops. Taking up the medieval condemnation of speculation, people now denounced the Jews as the 'kings of the age', in the phrase employed in 1845 by the Fourierist Toussenel; the stereotype Jew was the banker who produced nothing and grew fat on the labour of others – workers, industrialists and tradesmen. Among unbelievers the concept of 'Jewishness' could even be used, in the absence of any Jew, to denote behaviour regarded as scandalous. Jaurès himself sometimes utilized the concept in this sense on his return from Algeria in 1895,[15] and it was employed much more often by socialists, radicals and even a Catholic republican like the abbé Lemire. But it is not easy to escape the grip of one's vocabulary; the great majority of those who used this concept slid towards racism, all the more easily since the pseudo-scientific claptrap emanating from Darwinism, anthropology and linguistics provided some curious models. Following in Broca's footsteps, anthropo-sociology strove, with Vacher de Lapouge, to classify the races according to physical features, while linguistics provided the principle of division between Aryans and Semites.[16]

No doubt the racial analysis was often secondary. Sometimes the anti-semites even officially denied the essential component in their racism; the Catholic press did from time to time when it happened to remember that a Jew could be converted. But the new anti-semitism was characterized by a virulent synthesis of all these brands of anti-semitism. The first man to achieve it, to make it a global vision of the world, was Edouard Drumont (1844–1917), a republican converted to Catholicism, full of false science and obviously talented as a popular controversialist. *La France juive* (1886), a bestseller, has often been imitated. The daily paper which Drumont directed from 1892, *La Libre Parole*, used to print some 100,000 copies. Elected 'anti-Jewish' deputy for Algiers in 1898, he created the composite portrait of the Jew in which the physical characteristics are chosen as indications of moral characteristics: 'The main signs by which one can recognize the Jew remain therefore the famous hooked nose, blinking eyes, close-packed teeth, projecting ears, square instead of almond-shaped nails, an overlong torso, flat feet, round knees, exceptionally knobbly ankles and the soft, melting hand of the traitor.'

Nationalism

The hand of the traitor. It was with the French nation that the anti-semites contrasted the Jews *en masse*. It was alleged that they were foreigners in a France that was too kind to them, a France that they betrayed by their mere existence even before, like Dreyfus, betraying it by their actions. Anti-semitism was one of the key elements in the nationalist ideology in gestation since Boulangism; it was in the name of this nationalism that the anti-Dreyfusard battle was conducted.

Up to the end of the nineteenth century the religion of *la patrie* had remained a republican ideology, in the style of the Jacobins and Michelet. By putting in the foreground the search for a national pseudo-homogeneity it could have turned towards the exaltation of the State to the detriment of the universality of the Rights of Man. In Paris and in the south-west, radicalism tended very much to support this tendency. But after the days of Boulangism the men who claimed to belong to the 'national party', although coming from politically different horizons, shared more and more often the tendency to condemn the political framework of the bourgeois Republic and even its institutions, which they accused of weakening 'France', of dividing it and delivering it up to its enemies. The Affair enabled them to secure mass support by identifying themselves with the army. It is true that for ten years the army had had to endure some harsh criticisms, both in certain intellectual circles where people laughed at the coarseness of the military life and from the working class, by whom it was cursed in every strike. But recent studies have shown that in the republican *petite bourgeoisie*, which enjoyed reading leftist writers – Séverine, Octave Mirbeau, and so on – the cult of the army, of its discipline and of its authority had weakened little.[17] By posing as the defender of the national army, the instrument of unity and a rampart against the foreigner, and as the adversary of naturally treacherous Judaism, nationalism's objective was to get itself accepted as the doctrine of the national consensus.

Why?

Whether or not all the implications of all this had been thought through, it was a clever move. There was fear lest the bond which united Frenchmen of different opinions round the Strasbourg statue be broken. (The bond ensured a minimum of social peace by outlawing revolutionaries accused of breaking it – such had been the object of the 'wicked' laws of 1894.) This fear was felt not only by the militant anti-Dreyfusards but also for a long time by many of those regarded as passive, and this – not just the pressure of the State apparatus, ignorance or bad faith – was the reason for the long insistence on the painful slogan, 'There is no Dreyfus affair.' The authorities never stopped appealing to 'appeasement', that key word. Why this longing for internal peace, this profound desire for order which the Affair disturbed and which nationalism, which shattered it, tried to turn into a shield for itself? The mutilation experienced in 1871 had not been forgotten. Relations between France and the great powers were still fragile: the formation of the big diplomatic blocs had hardly begun, while the rulers of France were pursuing a policy of colonial expansion which ran the risk of endangering European relations and even peace. From 26 September 1898, when the English arrived at the ruined fort of Fashoda where since July Captain Marchand had had the French flag flying, until 4 November, when the French government ordered Marchand to evacuate the fort, the Anglophobia partly repressed since 1870 by the memory of the lost provinces raged unchecked. Today the Fashoda crisis looks like a survival from earlier days. At the time things were less clear. The possibility of a Franco-German rapprochement had not been ruled out by Gabriel Hanotaux, the Minister for Foreign Affairs before Delcassé entered the Brisson cabinet. Certainly Delcassé's diplomacy, the Russians' huge needs in the way of capital and the pressure of the French banks who wanted high, stable profits were to put things right. The sharing-out of Africa was settled with England by the note of 21 March 1899 and the agreements with Russia signed on the following 9 August modified the official form of the alliance. The alliance's object was no longer 'the maintenance of peace' but 'equilibrium between the European forces'. The scope of Franco-Russian financial relations was also modified; from then on negotiations were to be 'as much the concern of governments as of financiers' (R. Girault, Biblio. no. 226, ch. 7). But by this date the Affair was drawing to a close and it had run its course in a quite different context.

The international situation was not the only factor involved. The French bourgeoisie was stratified in innumerable rival layers; the multiplicity of divergent interests made even any parliamentary decision difficult except when agreement was reached, in favour of protectionism, for example, to defend French producers against foreigners. The rural world itself was not completely reliable; among the woodcutters of the east of the Massif Central or the barrel-makers of Limousin, the momentous events of the recent past had not been forgotten and ideological frontiers divided the peasantry. Finally, in spite of the economic recovery the authorities persisted in describing big strikes as a threat to national unity. When the construction workers deserted building sites in Paris in October 1898, the government sent for troops from the provinces to reinforce the garrison of the capital and the district town halls became headquarters for patrols sent out in all directions.

Are we to think, then, as Jean-Pierre Peter has suggested, that the desire for appeasement should be understood as 'the expansion of a collective instinct for self-preservation in a much divided society whose deep conflicts condemned the national organism to extreme fragility'? Possibly, but on condition that we know which social strata felt this desire for self-preservation most keenly, and why. It was basically a question of the *petite bourgeoisie*, the lower middle class, as is shown by the composition of the leagues and demonstrations. Close to the working classes, from which it was continually renewed and replenished, the mentality of this *petite bourgeoisie* separated it from the working classes as soon as in 'the people' the fact and ideology of class gained the upper hand. It did not command the modes of thought and action which were forming in the working classes. In spite of the official political influence with which it was endowed by universal suffrage, it did not always feel at ease in the traditional structures created by the old or new notables and it remained outside the trade union movement and socialism. Junior civil servants, clerks and craftsmen, and small tradesmen with cultural and material ambitions difficult to satisfy, retained numerous contacts with their working-class or peasant families, but they were worried by the forces that shook industrial society and by the changes which were forced on them. Claude Willard has shown, in connection with the bar-keepers and municipal employees of the towns in the department of Nord who were in the process of moving over to socialism, how the hardening of the bureaucratic arteries affected them. In the countryside the inhabitants of the *bourgs* were badly hit by the prolongation of the economic depression. Politically divided, whether Catholic or not, the *petite bourgeoisie* was worried by this new world the French were entering; numerous, hard-working and thrifty though it was, it did not feel capable of finding its place in it. Its evolution was the great question for France; what was to become of what Jaurès called 'the urban and rural democracy'?

The results

Apparent victory

The Dreyfusards were apparently the victors, at the end of a passionate and resolute campaign of explanation and propaganda and despite the press, which eventually moved towards revisionism, although at the time of the Rennes trial only 15 per cent of it was really Dreyfusard. The pardon and subsequently the rehabilitation of Dreyfus ended in his reinstatement in the army. Waldeck-Rousseau took a number of decisions affecting particularly compromised senior officers – General de Pellieux, Zurlinden – and anti-Dreyfusard leaders and schemers, including Déroulède. Two decrees bearing the name of General de Gallifet made promotion in the army in practice a matter for the minister, and by restricting the system of patronage helped to make the military emerge from their isolation. The authority of the civil power was strengthened. Some very good harvests and lively business consolidated things.

At a deeper level the Affair, which had united workers and intellectuals in their aims and even in action, convinced the latter that the consolidation of democracy required their active participation in social life and the education of the people. The primary school was no longer sufficient. It was time to expose the mechanism of tyranny. 'Socialism in education': this phrase so dear to Péguy could serve to describe numerous initatives. At least three new periodicals had this aim: Lagardelle's *Mouvement socialiste*, founded in January 1899, Péguy's *Cahiers de la quinzaine*, founded in January 1900, and *Pages libres*, founded in January 1901 by Charles Guieysse, an officer who had resigned from the army after the Zola trial. There were many teachers among the subscribers; they accounted for 600 of the 2,000 subscribers to *Pages libres* in 1902. The Affair also assisted the development of the free establishments of higher education into which the introduction of the humane sciences had brought a breath of fresh air. The study of workers' institutions, of socialist doctrines and of social and political subjects of current interest gradually grew (under the umbrella of sociology) into the Free College of Social Sciences, founded in 1895, and into the School of Higher Social Studies, which devolved from the College in 1900. The aim was to introduce an already educated public to the social sciences. As for the proletariat, it was being catered for – so it was thought – by the popular universities, still so little known today, that were appearing on all sides. This movement did not arise out of the Affair but out of two different currents: anarchist education, which was the driving force behind the first *UP* (*Université populaire*) founded in 1896, the 'Soirées de Montreuil'; and a positivist current, fairly close to the Co-operative School at Nîmes, which inspired G. Deherme to found the 'Co-operation of Ideas for the Higher Education of the People' in the faubourg Saint-Antoine in January 1898. However, it was the Affair which gave the movement its real impetus; from 1899 to 1901 *UP*s opened almost everywhere, first in Paris and its suburbs, then in the provinces. 'Together', Jaurès declared, 'we shall drive away the phantoms of the night.'

Victory there was, then, for the first aims of the Dreyfusard intelligentsia. Yet it was a thin victory. Can one say that the moral problem posed by the Affair had really been resolved? The pardoning of Dreyfus was an act of individual humanity and appeasement, which avoided calling on the Court of Appeal and starting up the Affair again, not one of justice. By accepting the pardon – and who could blame him for doing so – Dreyfus ceased to be a symbol. In agreeing that he should accept it, Jaurès himself, profoundly torn, knew that the Affair would cease to be 'a sharp protest against the social order', or – the two are not totally synonymous – against the moral order. Péguy was to write about ten years later, in a famous essay, 'Notre jeunesse': 'The Dreyfus affair was, like every affair, an essentially mystical affair. It lived on its mystique. It died when it was made political.'[18] 1900 was to be the great year of Dreyfusism, which was soon to be afflicted by a crisis. However, contrary to an opinion that is widespread today, neither Sorel nor Péguy, through failing to grasp the real dimensions of anti-Dreyfusism, displayed in their judgements a perception superior to that of Jaurès or even to that – political though it might be – of a man like Waldeck-Rousseau. With hindsight it is easy to be perceptive: the cult of the soil, the mystique of race, the power of the military, all in the name of national order – these words mean something to us, these images are outlined on the horizon behind us. Dreyfusism undoubtedly deserves to be an eternal ideal. As for anti-Dreyfusism, it was certainly a sign for the future, but no one fully recognized it.

Real victory

Nevertheless, in this battle there were indeed victors. The order which triumphed after so much 'disorder' was not the order dreamed of by the nationalists, nor that heralded by the Ralliement, nor even the old order.

The arrival in power of the Waldeck-Rousseau government signalled the defeat of the nationalists, a defeat confirmed by the municipal elections of May 1900, at any rate in the provinces, where the shifts of votes often favoured coalitions between radicals and socialists; such was the case at Lyon, Bourges and Reims. The spectacular shift of Paris from a socialistic radicalism to nationalism – forty-five seats out of eighty – isolated the capital just when the Exhibition was opening. The nationalist phenomenon here went through its normal ceremonial without following the traditional clerical line, but the general victory made this disquieting fact look very strange. In the country as a whole nationalism was certainly forced back. Part of the *petite bourgeoisie*, tempted for a moment, had moved away from it.

This success coincided with a fresh realignment of the parties. Concealed in the Waldeck-Rousseau combination by the presence of dazzling personalities, and by the slender nature of radical participation, this was more evident in the kind of support obtained by the cabinet in the country. Except in the north-east, Normandy and Brittany, the new coalition received the congratulations of the great majority of general councils, district councils, municipal councils, prefectures and sub-prefectures. What characterized this coalition? The answer is the political liquidation of the Ralliement and the complementary collapse of the progressivist republicans, who split into three groups. The right joined the conservatives, the centre maintained a much devalued parliamentary title, and the left, which liked power and could find its way back to it, founded, with Etienne and Rouvier, the Democratic Union. In depth, and even before the fight against the religious orders had started, it was anti-clericalism which reunited the 'good republicans' on the basis of the rejection of the Ralliement, whose fragile hold on public opinion had been revealed by the elections of 1898. On this terrain socialism could follow. The union of lefts was to ensure for a time the stability, born in the 1880s out of the policy of concentration.

The realignments that took shape were not merely temporary. A number of uncertainties in France had been settled once and for all. The possibility of a union against a Republic of politicians and rogues between part of the proletarian extreme left and part of the nationalist *petite bourgeoisie* had disappeared. The sort of attempted union symbolized by Barrès's paper *La Cocarde* in 1894–5 was no longer possible; Barrès had chosen his camp and so had the socialists. In the country the prestige of the parliamentary Republic had been strengthened, even among those who fought the bourgeois Republic. At a stroke, anti-semitism had been swept out of the political cadres of the left; no more suspect formulas were to be found in the radical or socialist provincial press; in 1912 the *SFIO* (*Section française de l'internationale ouvrière*), at its congress in Lyon, like the combined secretariat of the *CGT*, was to condemn unanimously and without discussion the efforts of the new extreme right to import anti-semitism into the working class. On the other hand, anti-militarism was to develop in the working class and also in the lower middle classes closest to the proletariat. The condemnation of the 'sabre' ceased to be the perquisite of a few extreme groups. The nation's rampart or a threat to the Republic? For the moment these two visions of the army coexisted.

Finally, the Affair effected in the history of French society a change not recognized at the time. It marked the entry into public life of new strata of the population expressing themselves by new means. The absolute reign of committees of notables and of elected intermediaries had come to an end. This was a transformation which had long been maturing; it was finally accomplished during the Affair. After 1900 the political ruling class consoled itself in vain with the hope that in this respect the Affair was over.[19] Although the big leagues, except the League for the Rights of Man, were moribund, smaller ones were gestating; we shall meet them later – first and foremost that of the Action Française. The trade unions, the co-operatives, the professional societies and the university associations all felt themselves to be active participants in public life; many of them took part in the big procession organized on 19 November 1899 for the inauguration of the statue by Dalou, the 'Triumph of the Republic'. Headquarters were permanently manned, posters were stuck up, handbills were distributed. The influence of the speculative societies started to spread further. Illustrations forcefully imprinted certain themes on the imagination of the crowds. The big newspapers emerged consolidated from the Affair, in which willy-nilly they had had to take sides; Jean Dupuy of *Le Petit*

Parisien joined the Waldeck-Rousseau ministry. Women, too, kept out of public life in every domain both by the republicans and by their traditional opponents, had sometimes taken a hand in the Affair. Breton nobles called on the 'women of Brittany' to mobilize themselves by 'turning their distaffs'; feminine tenderness for 'the poor orphan' of Colonel Henry merged with invective against the Jews. Conversely, Zola received numerous letters from women bewailing the misfortunes of Dreyfus and Picquart. The first group of women socialists was formed during the Affair and three women joined the central committee of the League for the Rights of Man. Marguerite Durand's *Fronde* was enthusiastically Dreyfusard. Even deputies intervened: on 30 June 1898 the Chamber liberally passed Viviani's motion granting women holding the required diplomas the right to follow the profession of barrister. These were small indications, but they reflected the general trend, and this was, after all, the society that was to be transformed by the organization of the radicals and socialists into nationwide parties and by the formation of the *CGT*. And in what form was nationalism, temporarily repressed, going to reappear? The twentieth century was beginning.

8

The France of the left-wing Bloc and the rise of radicalism

The organization and rise of radicalism from 1899 to 1905, a process contemporaneous with that by which the new socialist parties acquired political structures, would be incomprehensible without the emergence on the surface of the social fabric of a profound movement which enabled new strata of the population to find a place for themselves in public life. This movement provided a sort of common stock drawn on by the political forces which participated in the defence of the Republic and soon in the coalition of leftist groups.

The common stock

Its plentiful constituents came from various different groups, none of them the monopoly of one particular socio-professional category. There was a whole network of speculative societies embracing the good republicans who were to become the members, sympathizers or at any rate the electors of the parties in process of organizing themselves. They provided a means of entry into practical politics for men – and much more rarely women – who otherwise would often have remained isolated and out of contact with their fellows.

Freemasonry

At its assembly of September 1899 the Grand Orient divested itself of its anti-semitic lodges, in particular the Algerian ones. In April 1900 it also got rid of those freemasons who had developed an openly anti-semitic spirit. Other lodges immediately sprang up; in Gard, which, with Charente-Inférieure and Lot-et-Garonne, was to be one of the most masonic departments in France, two new lodges were formed; 'l'Aurore' at Uzès in 1900 and the 'Progrès–Humanité' at Saint-Ambroix in June 1903. The whole movement underwent a radical change. The rationalism of some freemasons induced them to simplify the ritual to the extreme. The 'Enfants de Gergovie' (Clermont-Ferrand) thought that it was time to open 'a general enquiry into the state of mind prevailing' in the army. The lodges supported enthusiastically the policy of 'republican defence'; 4,000 masons in their aprons marched past Dalou's monument on 19 November 1899, and the assembly of 1901 decided to set up republican committees to organize propaganda in favour of ministerial candidates in the elections of 1902. This single-minded enthusiasm did not exclude diversity of options; social questions were discussed during the assemblies and in the north the Guesdist masons who controlled the big republican paper, *Le Réveil du Nord*, played an important part in the splitting-up of the *POF* (French Workers' Party). Maurice Viollette chaired the Friendly Union of Socialist Free-masons formed at the assembly of 1901, but although – or because – they were not very susceptible to the notion of party the lodges regarded themselves as on the whole radical. And, certainly, since 1896 it had been radicals who had 'wielded the gavel' in the Grand Orient – the pastor Frédéric Desmons, deputy and subsequently senator for Gard; Louis Lucipia, the former outlaw of the Commune and for a time chairman of the Paris municipal council; then Desmons again and afterwards his disciples Delpech and Lafferre.

The radical option, facilitated since 1876 by the suppression in the constitution of the Grand Orient of any reference to the existence of God and the immortality of the soul, would correspond fairly well with what we know – very little, really – about recruitment to the lodges. In the strongly masonic departments it was dominated by the *petite bourgeoisie* – school-teachers, tax-collectors, municipal employers, shopkeepers, craftsmen – and in twenty years grew much more democratic. But in departments where there were only one or two lodges the cost of transport and the influence of the republican notables tended to put a brake on masonic enthusiasm among lesser folk and the membership of the lodges was basically recruited from professors, doctors and surgeons, barristers and notaries, businessmen and, in Protestant districts, pastors. The initiatory character of masonry also limited recruitment, more no doubt than the modest cost of the subscriptions, and in addition the Grand Orient refused to let women join, in spite of a favourable vote by more than a third of the masons.[1] With a few hundred lodges, each of which rarely had more than about thirty members, the Grand Orient, so closely connected with the Coalition, cannot be regarded as a mass movement.

The League for the Rights of Man

The rapid expansion of the League – it had about 25,000 members in 1901 and over 40,000 in 1906 – distinguished it clearly from masonry. Because of its origins intellectuals occupied a privileged position in it.[2] Its vocation to defend citizens against any injustice, its powerful legal section and the influence which it enjoyed at the Ministry of Justice gained it a high rate of recruitment among lawyers and barristers, and also in Protestant, *petit-bourgeois* and rural France; in Gard whole villages, headed by their pastor, belonged to the League. Radicals did not hold, and were never to hold, the presidency; Ludovic Trarieux kept it until 1903 and he was then succeeded by Francis de Pressensé, the new socialist deputy for Lyon, a Protestant like Desmons and hailing from the same political circles as Trarieux. With Allemane and Sébastien Faure, socialists and anarchists played an increasing part in it; quite a few heads of *bourses du travail* belonged to it and trade unionists, railwaymen in particular, joined its central committee. This committee was largely radical and the departmental federations sometimes acted as staging-posts on the way to radicalism; such was the case in Charente and at Lyon, where the sections of the League which had supported Victor Augagneur in his political career counted for a good deal in November 1905 when a radical university teacher with a brilliant future, Edouard Herriot, became mayor.

Free thought

Recruitment to the Free Thought societies, whence the radical-socialists, and more and more the socialists, drew a large part of their strength, was much more plebeian, even proletarian. Pure 'Waldeckists' often felt ill at ease in them. These groups which had few of the wealthy and few intellectuals – apart from teachers – were dominated by café-owners and junior civil servants, vine-growers and small farmers, clerks and workers; while the railwaymen and the building workers were the top dogs in the Côte-d'Or, factory workers supplied the main core of members in Nord and Pas-de-Calais, and as the century advanced women started to find their way into the Free Thought societies. Numbers grew rapidly; by the beginning of the century the Dijon society had some two hundred members, and communes of a few hundred inhabitants would have their own group, often a very active one. These grass-roots, mass organizations hesitated to federate, except in the north. Much effort was required from an unfrocked priest called Victor Charbonnel and from *La Raison*, the Franco-Belgian anti-clerical weekly which he had run since 1901, in order to obtain the creation in November 1902 of the National Association of Free Thinkers of France, whose executive committee united once again the Dreyfusards.

Secular ceremonies gave the free thinkers the feeling of belonging like other people to a community, the community of true republicans; there were baptisms, marriages, first communions, secular burials, counter-processions and demonstrations against the crosses in cemeteries. People ate rich meals on Good Friday to assert their freedom of conscience, just as calf's head was consumed on the anniversary of the death of Louis XVI to ridicule kings. However, France did not enjoy its secularization in the same way everywhere; while the lodges were particularly active in the Midi, Free

Thought recruited its largest numbers in the Allemanist east, in the valley of the Rhône, and in the departments of Nord and Pas-de-Calais. It was in these Free Thought societies that socialists and radicals had the most frequent opportunities of exchanging ideas. What is a radical? What is a socialist? These questions were first debated in these societies before being publicly aired on the great day of the local elections. By asserting that free thought had no limits and that property must submit to examination like the army and like religious beliefs, by linking 'the intellectual and moral emancipation of individuals' to the 'material and economic enfranchisement of the working class',[3] the free thinkers did not so much contribute to the unity of the parties of the left as make their differentiation unnecessary. Starting from Pioneer departments – Isère, Côte d'Or, Nord and Pas-de-Calais, where the Fédération formed in May 1901 spoke of 'propagating the principles of scientific materialism' – the conquest of Free Thought by the socialist ideology spread to the whole of France.

Lay organizations

Teachers were usually free thinkers, even if they had their children baptized. Coming very low in the social scale, these men and women, who after fourteen years of service earned 100 francs a month when board and lodging at an inn cost 75 francs, often prolonged their classes, in which the defence of secularization was all part of daily lessons, by running outside activities. They were to be seen in masonic lodges, at the League for the Rights of Man, in the Free Thought societies or in their local republican committee. The talks for adults arranged during the winter helped to educate a peasantry that was still often unsophisticated; the peasants were encouraged to distrust alcohol and routine, and taught hygiene and love of the Republic. These aims, which were common to almost all teachers, did not prevent them from differing on the subject of the army or the social question; on the whole, primary teachers were to favour radicalism rather than socialism when the divergences between the two currents grew wider. Militant secularity also inspired a review which began to appear in June 1902, the *Annales de la jeunesse laïque*. Founded by Georges Etbert,[4] its purpose at that time was to assemble all shades of republican opinion, from Colonel Picquart to Charles Malato, from Henry Bérenger to Jaurès: 'The lay are all those who have faith in human reason, who want it to be strong and emancipated.' And the editorial of the *Annales* added in October 1902: 'The young ... are all those who like youth, who are interested in its efforts.' This comforting definition did not prevent the first congress of the Federation of Lay Youth, which was held in Paris on 8 and 9 November 1902, from attracting only young people from the schools. The new Federation quickly asserted its anti-religious attitude – 'Christianity is the enemy of all life, of all progress.' It was also pacifist and internationalist, and in favour of the emancipation of women, the theme of its second congress. It soon became the scene of debates, even confrontations, between 'republicans' and 'socialists'.

The people's universities

A striking element in the intellectual turmoil of those years was the birth of the *UPs* (*Universités populaires*). We have already mentioned the first of these, the ones that pre-dated the Affair; the 'Soirées de Montreuil' started in 1896 and the 'co-opération des idées', run by G. Deherme in the faubourg Saint-Antoine, at the beginning of 1898. But from 1899 to 1902 they spread and flourished in the wake of Dreyfusism. Although enthusiasm declined in the capital after 1902, the vitality of the movement remained intact in the provinces. A plan of *UPs* represented at the congress of May 1904 shows which areas were keen on them and which were cool towards them. The data is difficult to interpret, but suggests that in the towns the old crafts benefited more from them than industrial workers, and that ideologically they tended to spring up in areas where there was lively confrontation between the 'forces of the past' and those of the present. This institutional network of lectures, talks and educational festivals was almost always based on the idea that 'the people', the vast foundation of the Republic, were liable to be led astray and that it was the duty of the intellectuals, by proper instruction, to save them from the snares of clericalism and militarism. Thus for many people the commitments of two exciting years continued. No doubt the movement which attracted intellectuals to the *UPs* was populist and paternalist, but in any case it was after the Affair that this desire for contact between manual workers and intellectuals arose. It seemed to have been absent in the first few years of the Republic.

The difficulties were great. The lectures were magisterial and usually unconnected with the workers' daily experience or their lives as militants; the workers were tired after a hard day and sometimes still illiterate – in 1901, 14 per cent of men and 21 per cent of women over fifteen years of age were illiterate. In short, teachers and pupils spoke two different languages. Nevertheless, the meeting between the two sides did take place and when the *UP* was supported by a *bourse du travail* it could be a durable relationship; such was the case at Bourges from April 1900 and at Laval from November 1901. At the start some moderate municipalities subsidized certain *UPs* and the school inspectors authorized teachers in *lycées* to speak to the workers. The phrases 'mutual education' and 'exchange of services' recur often. But one can follow, in connection with the revival of workers' struggles and local confrontations, the stiffening of attitudes that eventually made co-operation between workers and intellectuals difficult or even impossible. At Laval, in May 1902, two professors from teacher training colleges resigned from the *UP*; a barrister gave up 'lecturing' there; and its founder and president, Félicien Challaye, a young philosophy teacher, was in July removed from office. At Bourges after 1908 the workers were in a minority on the managing committee of the *UP* and social subjects were no longer tackled. These two developments were different, but the result was similar.

However for a few years all these speculative societies seem to have been closely intertwined and points of disagreement were masked by the need to fight the common enemy. As one of the chairmen at the congress of May 1904 said, when lecturers called themselves radicals, radical-socialists or socialists, these were only 'forenames'; the surname was 'republican'. In the towns, the same men often met in different committees. In the villages, the same nucleus sufficed for all purposes. It was like that in the department of Yonne, where a professor from Sens, Gustave Hervé, started to make the rounds. His anti-militarism made him popular and, as a likeable commercial traveller for Free Thought, he made anti-militarism popular. There could not be too many of all these 'advanced' forces to bring home to people the idea of this 'democracy' which yet did not have a settled ideology. Sometimes the socialists benefited, as in Yonne, but most often the radicals. In the eyes of practising Catholics and of the republican notables who were not too keen on enrolling in the brotherly army of human emancipation, the men concerned were mostly 'authoritarians' and a danger to the social order.

The organization of the republican parties

The publication in Paris in 1901 of M. Ostrogorski's pioneering book, *La Démocratie et l'organisation des partis politiques*, was contemporaneous with the birth of the national organizations which claimed to represent the policy of 'republican defence' adopted by Waldeck-Rousseau or at any rate supported it when there was a risk of its being endangered. The parties which came into being at that time – the Radical and Radical-Socialist Party, the Socialist Party of France, the French Socialist Party and even the Democratic Alliance – sought to organize themselves outside the parliamentary groups whose recent past had shown their inadequate correspondence with a changing public opinion. The realignments adopted by old and new campaigners in the political and social struggle were not just tactical moves; they were part of the battle of arguments and ideas developing in the country.

Radicalism pulls itself together

In the Waldeck-Rousseau government the radicals filled only secondary posts, in particular Public Works, with Pierre Baudin as minister. This weakness reflected first of all the decline of their strength in Paris under the onslaught of nationalism. It was the municipal elections of 1900, with the spectacular defeat of Lucipia, that sounded the knell of Parisian radicalism, and the provinces had not yet clearly assumed the succession. Above all this weakness reflected their incoherence. There was no accord between them on the new questions, no group discipline, no recognized leader; Goblet was coming to the end of his career, Clemenceau remained apart, and Pelletan was reckoned to be too hawkish. Who then was radical? Even in parliament the answer was shrouded in obscurity. At the Luxembourg Palace the term still retained its disquieting overtones: there were no radicals in the Senate, only a group of some sixty members known as the 'democratic left'. This group comprised numerous radicals, but not all of them, and they were not alone. In the Chamber, for some people, the term had ceased to inspire alarm. Since 1898 there had been about a hundred deputies who added the epithet 'socialist' to the term 'radical' and who had elected Pelletan as chairman of their group. But there were almost as many whose feelings were still shocked by this epithet: under the chairmanship of a former military painter, Henri Dujardin-Beaumetz (he eventually became Minister of Fine Arts), they belonged, as in the Senate, to the 'democratic left'. Finally, there there were some independent radicals, such as Léon Bourgeois, the father of 'solidarism', and others who were not independent enough; one of them belonged to no less than three parliamentary groups. After the exclusion in December 1898 of openly nationalist and anti-semitic deputies, the 'true radicals', those who voted left in most important divisions, amounted, according to J. Kayser, to about 150.

In the country as a whole, however, it still meant something to call yourself 'radical'. It is true that many of the articles of the old credo had fallen into disuse – revision of the constitution, suppression of the Senate, hostility to colonial conquests. But a good radical had distinctive marks; he stuck to local realities, he knew the corridors of power and he kept as close as possible to the administration. In his view, the Republic was neither a mere constitutional form to which one could pay lip service nor the mystical source of happiness that so many workers had believed in for so long; it was the régime illuminated by the sun of 1789, or even by that of 1793, and under constant attack from the 'unacceptable coalition' directed by the Roman Church. In face of this enemy the radical attitude was progress within the limits implied by attachment to private property and finally by respect for the social order.

In the days of 'Waldeckism' the radicals pulled themselves together fairly quickly. Relieved both of power and of the game of parliamentary opposition, they had the time to listen to 'democracy', especially in the provinces where a number of moderate members of parliament saw part of their vote gradually move over to radicalism. In this development the national press – *Le Radical*, *La Lanterne* and a new daily, *L'Action*, launched in March 1903 by a young writer called Henry Bérenger – played a certain part. A still greater part was played by the local or regional press: important long-established dailies then in the process of expansion, such as *La Dépêche* in the south-west or *Le Progrès* in the Lyon region, more modest papers like *Le Réveil social* in the department of Nord, or even *Le Petit Rouennais*, and district weeklies launched by a candidate's committee at the time of an election. Numerous were the papers that, from urban centres, radiated over the network of *bourgs* and big villages and lent their voices to the speculative societies and to the committees in which provincial vitality was becoming organized.

Birth of the Radical and Radical-Socialist Party

At the beginning of 1901 the initiatives came from the various radical party headquarters in the capital, not from the parliamentary groups which had long said little, nor from the provinces, although the radicals were making good progress there. The Action Committee for Republican Reforms had already, at the end of the previous parliament, assembled members of parliament, committees and lodges to collect the munitions necessary for the elections, and Gustave Mesureur, a long-standing radical, deputy for Paris since 1883, and a freemason lawyer, René Renoult, played a large rôle in this. They made contact with the League of Republican Action formed to organize the demonstrations of 14 July 1900 and the Republican Committee for Commerce and Industry, founded in March 1899. The president of the last-named committee was Alfred Mascuraud (1848–1926), a man of old Parisian stock who had been anti-Boulangist from 1887 and who directed the Chamber of Trade for jewellery, which he had founded in 1873. On 8 April 1901 the Action Committee made public an appeal for the holding in Paris of a 'congress of the republican-radical party', whose 'unity it was necessary to ensure' in order to 'combat clericalism, defend the Republic' and implement a programme of 'democratic reforms' with a view to the elections of 1902. There was no need to say more; their programme existed 'just as our fathers ... formulated it' (Mesureur, in *La Lanterne*, 10 June 1901).

Coming from the top, this initiative corresponded to the aspirations of numerous militants whose political ascent, because of lack of money and publicity, was only possible if there was at least a minimum of organization at the top and, at constituency level, committees capable of taking an interest in those elected and in their activities. The provinces accordingly responded with enthusiasm, even including the radicals of the Midi, though they were a little worried at the idea of a congress assembled on such a vague basis. Was it only a question of preparing for the elections, or of founding a party? If the second hypothesis was the correct one, did the party wish to be a part of the republican bloc or the political expression of the whole bloc? Finally, was it possible to evade the social question in the name of republican defence'? On all these points the Action Committee remained silent. And in the end this silence turned out to its advantage. At that point the elected representatives could hardly refuse to fall in with the lead that had been given. From 21 to 23 June 1901 the representatives of 155 lodges, 215 newspapers and 476 committees met in Paris. More than 1,100 elected representatives, including 201 deputies and 78 senators, were either present or had signified their agreement. Of the radical leaders only Clemenceau was missing. From these foundations emerged an ambivalent organism; the statutes were not adopted in any case until 1903. The Radical and Radical-Socialist Republican Party was composed of 'committees, leagues, unions, federations, publicity societies, Free Thought groups, lodges, newspapers and municipalities'[5] which accepted the 'programmes' adopted at the first two congresses. This diverse and dynamic base meant that the new organization created by certain sections of the bourgeoisie and *petite bourgeoisie* was quickly woven into the national fabric, but it excluded the workers' organizations proper, the trade unions and the *bourses du travail*. This was a choice of class which the use of the word 'socialist' did not suffice to contradict. The elected representatives' direct membership of the party and the authority which they officially possessed at the congresses, where their vote carried the same weight as that of a delegate, came down to giving the electors a privileged position compared with that of members. The elected representatives meant to protect this privilege from any tiresome control; thus they sometimes groaned about the tyranny of the radical newspapers[6] but more rarely about that of the departmental federations, late-comers whose existence often remained nominal. The system, which did not provide for a card or for an individual subscription, did not even prevent a grass-roots group from having itself represented by a non-radical, even, as was to happen in 1905, by a socialist. To permit the biggest gathering possible, the party's declaration at the Paris congress was characterized above all by the desire to act quickly: 'This is the end of the era of adjournments.' The tone of voice retained its value, and, if what was achieved fell short in some areas, the shortfall was slight enough to give confidence in others.

With wide support in the country, the radical party thus asserted its mission to unite all the votes of the republican bloc. Its strength was primarily electoral. The existence of an executive committee, elected by the annual congress but too big to be really effective, and that of the managing committee, nominated by the executive committee, which soon changed into a secretariat with president, secretaries and treasurer, should not create any illusions, in spite of the obstinate (Jean-Louis Bonnet, for example) or enthusiastic (Pelletan) character of this or that secretary or president of the party. The executive committee, often criticized and more often ignored, was only one of the cogs in the mechanism which in 1901 set out to achieve power. The real strength of radicalism is to be found at this date in its elected representatives, in its committees, and in the lively local and regional forces which the congresses assembled annually without being able to claim to control them or even to point them in any particular direction. Later its strength was to come from the State apparatus, which it worked hard to infiltrate, and from its links with certain business circles.

The Democratic Republican Alliance

The formation of the radical party forced the Waldeckists to define their positions. The task was not easy and it was not one that was looked for. Many members of parliament varied their vote according to the issue involved from abstention to support for the government. Such was the case with Louis Barthou and the Pyrenean deputies who followed him, or Raymond Poincaré, who, worried about the 'collectivist' support for 'republican defence', could hardly part company from Waldeck since at Commercy the Catholics continually denounced his only speech in favour of revision of the Dreyfus verdict. This was an uncomfortable position which necessitated in a pre-electoral period some effort at coherence from members elected as progressivists. Thus in October 1901 the Democratic Republican Alliance came into being. It was nothing like a party. It was a re-grouping rather than a grouping, very lax, scarcely a framework, a sort of 'alliance' of politicians deprived of any politically structured base but sensitive to the opinions of their electors and often very rich and with close links with the 'big interests'. The new movement appointed two chairmen, Adolphe Carnot, President of the General Council of Charente, a member of the Institute and the brother of the former president of the Republic, and J. Magnin, former governor of the Bank of France. Thus big business and the official intelligentsia presided over its destinies. Among its best-known members were Barthou, Poincaré, Rouvier, Etienne, Henri Chéron, Jules Siegfried and also two ministers, Joseph Caillaux and Jean Dupuy. This alliance, ministerial, it was true (which was a guarantee), but to the right of the ministerial coalition and closely connected with the world of business (which was reassuring), quickly obtained the support of the papers with a big circulation – *Le Petit Parisien*, *Le Matin*, *Le Journal*. The manifesto which it issued to the electors, skilfully balanced to please both right and left, was nevertheless aimed against 'candidates patronized or favoured by the clerico-nationalist coalition' and it was with the radical party that a friendly understanding was reached.

The socialist parties

The term 'party' applies better to the socialist forces which structured themselves between December 1899 and March 1902. Here the organization was not born of an electoral requirement, even if the prospect of the elections was never absent from the thoughts of those concerned. The aspiration towards unity was theoretically based on the unity of class of the proletariat, affirmed by the Guesdists, experienced by the Allemanists, and embedded in the philosophy of Jaurès. Other, more contingent considerations affected the desire for unity both in Jaurès and in Vaillant, the leader of the Revolutionary Socialist Party (*PSR*). For the defence of the Republic against militarist and clerical nationalism and to start the work of social transformation a pressure group of a large workers' movement seemed indispensable. But socialist unity came up against numerous obstacles: the loyalty of the oldest groups to their own organizations, especially Guesdism, and concern at the conversion to expanding socialism of new strata of the population and of leaders suspected of careerism, such as Alexandre Millerand after his somewhat equivocal entry into the Waldeck-Rousseau cabinet. However, the basic urge for unity was very strong immediately after the Dreyfus affair, and in spite of the formal condemnation of 'Millerandism' by the *POF* and the *PSR* the first general congress of the socialist organizations was held in Paris, in the Salle Japy, from 3–8 December 1899. The 'socialist party' which emerged from it was composed of the five earlier national organisations – the *POF*, and *PSR*, the *POSR*, the *FTS* and the Confederation of Independent Socialists. These organizations were simply juxtaposed; they did not merge. Moreover, the political conditions which had made 'Japy' possible changed rapidly; the dangers which had been thought to threaten the Republic retreated and working-class confidence in the policy of participation in the government declined even among the railwaymen, particularly sensitive though they were to the intervention of the State. The Allemanist federations of the east then suggested that autonomous departmental federations should be formed embracing all groups claiming to be socialist, including the trade unions and co-operatives, whatever the national organization to which they were attached. The movement then developed very rapidly. However, it met the absolute opposition of the *POF*, which saw a threat to its existence in this even in its own private territories in the departments of Nord and Pas-de-Calais. At the congress of Wagram (28–30 September 1900) its militants walked out. At the Lyon congress (26–28 May 1901), a month before the foundation of the radical party, the *PSR*, called on to choose, joined the Guesdists. The split was final.

As a result of all this, two socialist parties, very different from each other, came into existence. The Revolutionary-Socialist Unity, formed at Ivry in November 1901 between the *POF*, the *PSR* and the Communist Alliance, a group which had arisen in 1896 out of a mini-split in the Allemanists, led in September 1902 to the creation of the Socialist Party of France (*PS de F*). 'A party of revolution and consequently of opposition to the bourgeois State', it laid down as its principles the refusal to approve budgets, to participate in the government or to make alliances with bourgeois parties. It was a centralized party and its central council and especially its executive commission, elected by the annual congress, had fairly extensive powers. A party of militants rather than of elected representatives, it was impoverished by numerous departures, especially in the Midi. Based on organic unity, it found that this worked fairly well. At the opposite pole, the French Socialist Party (*PSF*) organized itself at the Lyon congress on the basis of departmental federations which the Allemanists and independents agreed to join. During the first few days of March 1902 it defined its programme at Tours. An organism for 'social transformation and republican defence', it wished to be part of the republican bloc. The 'interfederal' committee which was supposed to run it was composed only of delegates from the federations. It was a party of elected representatives more than of militants and it was the parliamentary group which laid down its political line, in spite of considerable tension between this group and the interfederal commitee. As an opinion group, its semi-official voice was *La Petite République*, a daily with a large readership. Thus there were two socialist parties, and at some distance from them remained eight fully autonomous federations, too revolutionary for the *PSF*, too unitary for the *PS de F* and the cadres of the *POSR* who left the interfederal committee in January 1902. But the truth is that even the revolutionary socialists voted for Waldeck-Rousseau, or at any rate abstained, as soon as the government was threatened. The two socialist parties, even when the Millerandist embarrassment put them at odds with each other, in the final analysis acted as 'republican parties'.

The victory of the Bloc

The parliamentary elections, 27 April – 11 May 1902

Few elections have been prepared at such length and so passionately disputed as those of 1902. The very small national percentage of absentions on 27 April – 20.8 per cent of the registered voters; 3.1 per cent less than in 1898 – is a reminder that it was 'the Republic' that seemed to be at stake; if not its existence, at any rate its nature, which for many Frenchmen was much the same thing as its existence. There were doubtless people on the right who called themselves republicans, but the only good republicans were those who supported the policy of 'republican defence'. In the country as a whole, there were two camps: left against right. Even in the first round, which was traditionally propitious for multiple candidatures, in most cases there were two opposing candidates and two only. At the second round the withdrawal system functioned almost without fail; on the right, between the candidates of the Ligue de la Patrie Française, the traditional conservatives, from whom it was often difficult to distinguish the men of the Action Libérale founded by Jacques Piou in July 1901, and the anti-Waldeckist progressivists like the Roubaix industrialist Eugène Motte; on the left, withdrawals extended to collectivists extremely hostile to Millerandism. In Lille, the executive committee of the radical party called on people to vote for an old-established Guesdist, Gustave Delory, whom Pelletan came in person to support. All round, out of 589 constituencies 415 were filled at the first round, and there were only nine constituencies with three candidates standing at the second round.

The violent polemic of electoral addresses in 1902, their moving tone and their vehement denunciation of the opponent reflects the strength of the passions to which the candidates appealed, but also their confusion. There were very few programmes and when there were any they were very close to each other on numerous points; on both the right and the left, to win over the hesitant fraction of the electorate, there were declarations in favour of the Republic and talk of a fairer distribution of taxes, the improvement of the lot of the unfortunate and even of two years' military service. On foreign policy not a word was said at a time when French diplomacy was entering a decisive period. There was silence, too, on the colonies at a time when Algeria and Indo-China were much talked about. The profession of faith of the radical Paul Doumer at Lyon was symbolical: 'I am too well known to need to develop a programme.' As Goblet was to write in 1902, what took the place of a programme were declarations of support for, or opposition to, the government. Ministerial, anti-ministerial – these terms were charged with passion. Behind them lurked references to what Waldeck had not completely achieved – settle the 'religious question', republicanize the State. But in the eyes of the 'true republicans' the formula which affirmed continuity, and turned the Bloc back to the application of the measures taken by Waldeck-Rousseau, constituted a commitment to social moderation, decisive in winning the votes of the moderates. Similarly, on the right, it made it possible to re-group all the adversaries – traditional enemies of the Republic, worried *ralliés*, bourgeois of every grade horrified by the alliance of the 'republicans' with the socialists.

The parliamentary coalition which had governed France since 1899 emerged from the elections strengthened. The Bloc had won; it had a majority of eighty to ninety seats in the Chamber. Yet at the first round only about 200,000 votes separated the two camps. Unlike militant France, electoral France had changed only modestly in twenty years. The distribution of the seats on each side is not without interest. On the right, the thrust of the nationalists was not very strong except in Paris, where, continuing their conquest of the capital, they swept radicals and socialists out of the central districts and the Latin quarter and defeated in particular Mesureur, Brisson (he got in at the second round in Marseille), Allemane, Groussier and Viviani. The intermingling of the anti-ministerial progressivists and the old conservative right went so far that it is difficult to believe in the electoral existence of the Action Libérale; in any case Piou himself was beaten in Haute-Garonne. The bastions of the right were still the north-east, the north and the west, especially Normandy; and the right also held on to some useful positions, even some quite strong ones, from the Landes to the Ardèche.

On the left, the electoral mechanism which put forward the moderates in the case of bi-polar elections came into full play, reinforced by the anti-clerical nature of a campaign which ignored the working class. The previous efforts of the militant socialists were partly cancelled out by this. It is true that the number of votes they collected continued to increase but not their parliamentary strength; they had fewer than fifty deputies elected. The principal victims were the revolutionary socialists, who won only about ten seats, in working-class Seine, Nord and Pas-de-Calais, Allier and Isère. Above all, the Guesdists lost more than a third of their electors and in the Mediterranean Midi their defeat bordered on a collapse. Within the 'socialist family', the decline of the *PS de F* assisted those who professed 'republican defence'. The radical-socialists themselves were in a minority compared with those who rejected the adjective. On their right were about a hundred deputies who professed to belong more or less to the Democratic Alliance, a certain number of whom, like Poincaré, had played almost openly a double game. All round, the left was strengthened or remained stable in all the heavily industrialized departments except Seine-Inférieure. It made clear progress in the lightly industrialized departments of the south-west (where, from the Pyrenees to the Dordogne, it gained twelve seats), the valley of the Saône, the Alps and the Massif Central. However, the victory of the Bloc was accompanied by internal tensions very much favouring the most anti-socialist currents, and the trend of the government cannot be inferred from the arithmetic of Parliament immediately after the elections.

The conditions of the Bloc's victory

To clarify the limits and component factors of the victory we must now look at the Bloc's financial support and also at the prevailing economic situation.

The activity of the Republican Committee for Commerce and Industry remains simply unknown rather than misunderstood. It enjoyed a rapid rise: after a few months it was acting as a semi-official collective 'personage' and its annual autumn banquet gave the Prime Minister the chance to deliver a speech outlining his programme for the new parliamentary session. By 1902 it had some 4,000 members. In July 1905 it was to have 12,000.[7] It gave fairly generous subsidies to candidates for ministerial appointments. But on what conditions? In return for promises? We simply do not know. In its early days the Committee recruited from the employers of the old-established industries, among the men of the wine trade and the retail dealers. From Paris it extended its activities to Lyon and Saint-Etienne, Amiens and Lille, Rouen and Nancy, but especially to the wine regions. Its influence certainly counted for something in the evasion of economic and social problems which characterized the republican campaign of 1902 and in particular in the ambiguity about forms of taxation. It probably exerted pressure for a privileged agreement between the men of the Democratic Alliance and radicalism from which it benefited; on 6 October 1902, Combes was to make the leading figures of the Committee shudder by speaking in their presence of the 'haughty claims of an exasperated socialism (Emile Combes, *Discours*, Paris, 1909, p. 88). The connection between the elections and the economic situation is more problematical. The wave of strikes in 1902 – nearly five million working days lost – was unparalleled in the previous decade, but the general strike of the miners came after the elections and although the defensive strikes of the spring no doubt contributed to the decline in Millerand's popularity it would be risky to draw conclusions about the elections from that. Above all, they have to be placed in a much larger context, that of the short stock-exchange and industrial crisis which shook the economy from 1901 to 1903. There was a brief upsurge of unemployment, reductions in wages, and a general anxiety exploited by opponents of the Bloc; this may help to explain some leanings to the right in the cities – at Rouen, for example, where several hundred dockers declared in favour of the outgoing radical deputy's opponent.[8] However, the crisis of 1901 must be seen in the general context of prosperity which doubtless helped to reduce the scope, if not the repercussions, of the Dreyfus affair; it did not interrupt this prosperity either in all sectors or in every sector at the same time. Finally, in a country remaining predominantly rural but affected less by peasant pressure on the working population, the small peasant had some reasons, in certain regions, for feeling reassured: for example, the railways, which created jobs and trade, had facilitated the development of market gardening along the Rhône and the sale of meat in the valley of the Saône. However, not only had the sudden increase in the amount of wine coming from Languedoc begun to cause anxiety – the price of a hectolitre dropped from 18 francs in 1900 to 14 francs in 1901 without the full effects of over-production yet making themselves felt – but the rise in incomes of tenant farmers or owner farmers was not yet clear or widespread.[9] In this short period of hesitations and contrasts, the small peasant could hardly agree with those who

emphasized the stagnation of business. The differences in regional situations made conditions ideal for the dissemination of ideologies, especially
the republican ideology. And its most persuasive agents in the countryside,
the radicals, were especially successful in the *bourgs*.

Regional radicalism

Radicals or radicalism? The electoral map of radicalism throws
into relief the diversity of the radicals. By and large, there were two
Frances: to the north of a line from the Gironde to Savoy were the departments where the radical deputies were radicals without any qualification;
these were also the departments where revolutionary socialism had best
maintained its strength. To the south of this line were the departments –
some twenty-four of them – in which the vast majority of the deputies
added the qualification 'socialist' to the term 'radical'. This was also the
area in which the Guesdist retreat, both in Languedoc and Provence, had
gone furthest. Various regional or local studies sometimes make it possible
to refine on the election results.[10]
In the north there were at least three different situations, without
counting the old Parisian radicalism in the Clemenceau tradition, which
broke up under pressure first from socialism, then from nationalism, which
left it in electoral tatters. There was one exception: the department of
Nord, where radicalism, born late and in the working class in the face of a
powerful Catholic bourgeoisie, soon found itself blocked by the rise of
socialism, from which it could not fully differentiate itself without running
the risk of perishing. Influenced by strong personalities such as that of
Charles Debierre, a professor of anatomy, Nord radicalism, organized in
active circles rather than in electoral committees, favoured a solid federation and displayed an exceptional fondness for party spirit. This attitude
cut across that of most of the departments of the Parisian Basin where
major industry rubbed shoulders with high culture. Here radicalism
attracted satisfied republicans, moderately inclined to mass militancy and
hostile to any advance of socialism. Out of hostility to the traditional
personalities these radicals were in temporary agreement with the Bloc,
but it was they who were to produce by 1904 the first 'dissidents' – in
Aisne, for example, around Paul Doumer – and a little later those who
preached a complete break with the socialists: Klotz in the department of
Somme, Léon Mougeot in Haute-Marne. The radical vote was also
predominant in a big intermediate zone running across France from the
west of the Massif Central to the valley of the Saône. This one consisted of
essentially rural departments with a stagnant or declining population: the
long-standing nature of their de-Christianization and of their intercourse
with the big towns had coincided there, as early as 1849, with numerous

'demo-socialist' votes. Radicalism was well established here – in the departments of Ain and Jura all the deputies were already radicals in 1898 – but was nevertheless expanding at the expense of the governmental republicans (in Corrèze) or of the right (Haute-Saône, Côte d'Or).

In contrast to these brands of radicalism there was that of the 'Red' Midi, from Aquitaine to Languedoc and Provence. It was a vigorous, dynamic stream – in 1902 it gave the party sixty-five deputies – with various shades of opinion, it is true, but united not only by anti-clericalism but also by a taste for politics and the practices bound up with long-standing 'socialization'. In Provence and Bas-Languedoc radical-socialism continued to make progress on ground long favourable to advanced ideas and propitious to transitions between radicalism and socialism. In Aquitaine it was a real conquest, one of the principal instruments of which was the paper *La Dépêche*, run by Arthur Huc and the Sarraut brothers. Haute-Garonne, its home ground, had never been and was never to be again so radical as in these early days of the century: 43 per cent of registered voters and 50 per cent of those who actually voted cast their votes for the radicals. Out of the seven seats, six were won by radicals or radical-socialists. Working out from the towns, radicalism had won over the rural backwaters as they were gradually opened up to modern life. The process was difficult in the areas of plateaux and mountains and in the regions where share-cropping, a system that made the peasant submissive, was predominant, but easier in the valleys, which were areas of direct development and the regions with a strong Protestant tradition. The highwater mark of 1902 was due to the continued confidence of the urban electors combined with the growing confidence of the rural population. In this land where, except for the vines and the big ports, economic life stagnated and, since to expect returns from the soil often seemed like a gamble, numerous groups were looking for security, and radicalism developed in a heated and quarrelsome atmosphere; it attracted support from those who were looking for a large number of small satisfactions. It did not yet feel really threatened by a socialism whose working-class foundations were localized and isolated.

The Combes ministry and the organization of the Bloc

Elected as 'the government', but unquestionably more to the left than in the previous parliament, the deputies of the Bloc were to link their policy to that of a new government which was to last only six months less than the long government of 'republican defence'.

The resignation of Waldeck-Rousseau, which took place officially on 3 June 1902, still looks somewhat mysterious. Did he resign because of illness? Or did he have a presentiment of difficulties with a new Chamber? Or the desire to keep himself in reserve? The radicals quickly organized – as their success entitled them to – the occupation of the public offices. On

1 June the progressivist Paul Deschanel was replaced as president of the Chamber by Léon Bourgeois; and on 6 June Loubet, on the advice of Waldeck-Rousseau, asked Emile Combes, a radical senator from Charente, to form a government. He was sixty-seven years old and, like Jaurès, he had been born in Tarn into a family of poor craftsmen. A doctor, and a republican under the Empire, married to a daughter of the well-to-do Charente bourgeoisie, he had pursued a provincial political career at Pons, his wife's home town. He had been a municipal councillor in 1869, mayor in 1874, a member of the general council in 1879 and a senator in 1885 – a typical *cursus honorum*. There was one peculiar detail: it was thanks to an uncle who was a parish priest that he had been able to enjoy a good secondary and higher education before leaving the seminary without ever taking holy orders. A long-standing freemason, he was a convinced spiritualist (in the philosophical sense), a fact which did not prevent his anti-clericalism from being inspired less by concern for the independence of the State than by a restless contempt for the empty life of religious houses. The four parliamentary groups which expressed their confidence in him on 12 June by 329 votes were to constitute his majority. These groups were the Democratic Union (the parliamentary face of the Democratic Alliance), the radical left, the radical-socialists and the socialists, who were joined on numerous occasions by the revolutionary socialists. They shared the Chamber secretariat, which Jaurès entered in January 1903, and ministerial responsibilities; but the socialists, who wanted to avoid a second Millerand affair and whose presence was not much appreciated by the moderate wing of the governmental majority, did not enter the cabinet. With two radical-socialists, one of whom was Pelletan, four radical ministers and four republican ministers, including Delcassé at Foreign Affairs and Rouvier at Finance to reassure the banks, it was a 'balanced' ministry that included only three members of the Waldeck cabinet. The former Délégation des Gauches (Delegation of Left Groups), which had come into existence at the end of 1900 to study the problem of the religious communities, was put on a durable basis as a link between the Chamber and the government. Permanently representing the political forces which constituted the Bloc, the Délégation des Gauches henceforth consisted of delegates elected by each parliamentary group on a proportional basis. It was the directing body of the coalition; it planned tactics, managed the sessions and ensured liaison with the government. It was an original and not very well-known body, chaired by Ferdinand Sarrien, a radical deputy from Saône-et-Loire. Jaurès ran it as a sort of privileged alliance between the socialists in the government and the radicals.

What was the basis of the authoritative position which Combes managed to establish by the summer of 1902? P. Sorlin has emphasized the part played by myth in the common vision of Waldeck as a sort of Pericles of the

Republic, able to dominate the two chambers by his mere utterances. There is no temptation with Combes to create any myth of this sort. The little provincial doctor was a clever politician but he lacked lustre and presence. His influence rested much more in Paris on the Délégation and in the country on the militant will of the left-wing of his majority. Elected bodies and societies of every sort were continually sending him congratulatory addresses and later exhortations. *La Dépêche* forbade the forty deputies and twenty senators from the south-west, whose electors were its faithful readers, to indulge in any light-hearted displays of independence, by giving them to understand that their re-election depended on their loyalty to the Bloc. The paper thus reasserted the keystone of 'Combism': the alliance between socialists and radicals. To keep quite clear of Marxism, a doctrine contrary to free thought, but not of the socialists, and not to exclude any new idea even in the realm of property: doubtless this was not the ideology of Combes, but gradually it became that of 'Combism' in its most durable areas. That is why anti-clericalism does not entirely suffice to define it. And that is also why the Bloc did less of a disservice to socialism than people usually think.

The work of the Bloc

From the law on associations (1 July 1901) to the separation of Church and State (9 December 1905)

More than four years separate these two laws, fundamental to the laicization of France; the road traversed between them was both direct and uneven. Long desired by the republican bourgeoisie and presented explicitly by the radicals as 'an indispensable preliminary to Separation',[11] the law on associations included in fact a chapter directed against religious communities (*congrégations*). Its implementation immediately after the elections opened the door to strict 'Combist' practice. The latent tension with the papacy was aggravated and the conflict of authority which broke out in 1904 between the Church and the State led ultimately to the end of the Concordat negotiated by Bonaparte. The 'Congrégation' – Brisson liked to employ this majestic singular – in effect lay at the heart of the laicization debate reopened by the radicals at the beginning of 1898, the many implications of which had been brought to light by the Dreyfus affair. As a legal man, Brisson drew attention to the vagueness of the laws which, lying outside the framework of the Concordat, governed the communities. He brought to light the influence of the Catholic press and the way in which it was financed by the rich Assumptionists. Exposing the lies of the General Staff, he opened fire on the religious colleges, 'Jesuit lairs', where the officer class was educated. The Commission of Enquiry on Secondary Education of 1899 had also revealed the development of teaching by the religious orders: ten new schools had been set up in Lyon since 1880, and with more than 40 per cent of secondary pupils the religious establishments recruited not only among the rich bourgeoisie but also among senior civil servants, including those in state education, and among tradesmen who wanted to please their customers. The wealth of the religious orders, the mainstay of their power, was subjected to serious examination. It was said that their holdings of land had more than doubled in fifty years and the fruitful industry of the Salesians and Carthusians was denounced. Finally, people who paid their taxes were worried about the procedures by which the orders defrauded the Treasury.

In the law of 1 July 1901 this hostility was evident. It had been less explicit in the draft prepared by Waldeck-Rousseau, but he had adopted the harsher measure without protest under pressure from the Chamber. Unlike other associations, whose freedom of formation was complete and for which a (simple) declaration was not obligatory unless they wanted civil status, religious communities could not be formed without legislative authority (Article 13). Members of unauthorized communities did not have the right to teach and prefects were authorized to carry out an annual check on the property of communities in their area. 'Republican defence' was turning into an offensive, at any rate in the text of the laws. In fact everything depended on the way in which they were applied. At the congress at which the radical party was founded Brisson called for a 'long-lasting struggle' necessitating 'a resolute government resting on an equally resolute and loyal majority', in other words a government run by the radicals. The anti-clericalism of the populace was in accord with this attitude. Moreover, it was distinguishing less and less between secular clergy and regular clergy; the municipal councils who were taking down the crosses in the cemeteries or refusing to accept legacies for the purchase of bells were also the ones that were turning down requests for authorization from the communities that ran the hospices, and the term 'black party' covered the whole Church militant, from monks to parish priests. The establishments of the communities that had continued to proliferate after the passage of the law, were the first victims of 'Combism': the decrees of 27 June 1902 ordered the closing of 120 of them and the decrees of 1 August shut all those in contradiction with the law. From March to July 1903 Parliament rejected requests for authorization from communities hitherto not officially authorized. After four months of discussion the law of 7 July 1904, which prohibited all teaching by religious orders, was passed; it was the result of the continuous pressure exerted on the government and members of parliament by the most advanced part of the radical press and by the committees. Combism was not essentially the work of the 'Petit Père' (Combes) himself.

The question now was whether the State should be given the monopoly of teaching. The debate, which soon began, divided the Bloc along lines which did not correspond either to parties or to speculative societies. It simultaneously questioned a certain conception of anti-clericalism and a certain conception of the State. Alongside traditional anti-clericalism there was a militantly atheist current of opinion which was against the dissemination of any religious thought through the schools. It was often expressed in a frankly Jacobin tone by certain radicals and by the socialists, particularly the Blanquists: Arthur Huc in *La Dépêche*, Henry Bérenger in *L'Action*, Viviani and Albert Bayet, Maurice Allard and Vaillant. On the opposite side were more liberal or less profoundly atheist thinkers, from Ferdinand Buisson, a professor at the Sorbonne, a convinced free thinker but in a minority on this point in the radical party, to Jaurès, and even Combes who regarded spirituality as a guarantee of morality. In their view the communities as institutions should be destroyed, but the ex-religious had the right to teach freely like every other citizen; the monk, deprived of his habit, would assimilate the spirit of the times; belief was less dangerous than the organization which supported it; and secularization meant neither neutrality nor monopoly but the possibility of diversity. Finally, the coercive tactics attempted by some radicals at the Marseille congress in October 1903 came to nothing; the atheist advance guard agreed to drop the question of monopoly for the time being.

On the other hand, it was going to devote itself to finally securing the separation of Church and State and it was going to succeed, for although it was alone in its view of the methods to be adopted it was not alone either in parliament or in the country on the substance of the matter. Separation had in fact long figured among the essential objectives of the republicans. High on the Belleville programme defended by Gambetta in 1869, it was taken up again by a large number of radical candidates in 1902 and the French Socialist Party put it on its programme as a fundamental element in 'the complete laicization of the State'. First of all, it is important to understand the factors which, according to the agenda of the parties of the left on 10 February 1905, made it 'inevitable'. The Combes ministry, which had been so keen to ban religious orders, did not in fact seem to be in a hurry to put into effect this great plan; it was not easy for the government to deprive itself deliberately of a means of control over the secular Church such as that created by the Concordat and the Organic Articles; numerous deputies of the Bloc hesitated and the general councils, as one was to see in spring 1905, showed no hurry to take a decision.[12] The pressure came from the militant supporters of Free Thought through their contacts with socialists of various brands. It also came from Jaurès, who was provided with an adequate sounding-board by the foundation of *L'Humanité* in April 1904. But the wishes of these people would probably have been insufficient if the campaigns against the religious communities had not brought to light some truths not until then very clearly perceived and thus attracted the support of much more moderate republicans.[13] It became clear in fact that the secularization of social life and the process of de-Christianization made the links established by the Concordat between the secular clergy and the government look somewhat exotic to many Frenchmen. It also became clear that the Republic, by striking some hard blows at the monks active in the League – and at the rest – had both proved and confirmed its solidity; the obedience of the notables no longer depended on a clergy more or less kept on the leash by the Concordat arrangements. The home situation thus made Separation acceptable to a big majority and to the government, but not yet at all necessary. It became necessary when, from spring 1904 onwards, Pope Pius X[14] and his Secretary of State, Mgr Merry del Val, took a series of steps indicating that they wished to follow 'une politique de prestige',[15] which looked like a challenge to national independence and was immediately denounced. On 30 July 1904 France broke off relations with the Vatican. On 4 September Combes declared Separation unavoidable and a month later the Toulouse congress of the radical party unanimously accepted Buisson's report which concluded that the matter was urgent.

The draft law was carefully prepared during the winter of 1904–5 by Léon Parsons, Paul Grunebaum-Ballin and Louis Méjan, a Protestant senior civil servant. On 21 March 1905 the Chamber started to discuss the report presented by the socialist Aristide Briand. Divisions reappeared rapidly. Was the Separation to be the last stage in the secularization of the republican State or a weapon in the struggle against the papacy, 'the last of the idols', and for the triumph of 'emancipated reason'? The Briand draft, which Jaurès supported in *L'Humanité*, chose the first course as against Combes, whose initial text had found favour with Free Thought. The debates on the new version of Article 4, which was devoted to the *associations cultuelles* (associations for worship) threw this choice into relief. For its supporters, it was a question of making other things possible – 'political and social peace' according to Briand, 'study of the financial questions' according to Poincaré, and social reforms and action for socialism in the view of Jaurès. These were different objectives, but their temporary convergence signified that none of the three leaders considered the 'religious question' absolutely fundamental. For the opponents of Article 4 the Separation was a chance to liquidate the ideological bases of the revealed religions.[16] Finally on 3 July, Briand's text was adopted by 341 deputies; the free-thinking left had given its support and for the moment the Bloc had rediscovered its unity. The opposition numbered 233 deputies: all the Catholic right, assembled by the abbé Lemire.

Promulgated on 11 December, the law declared that the French Republic 'assures liberty of conscience' and 'does not recognize, subsidize, or pay wages to, any creed'. In order to give believers the assurance that the

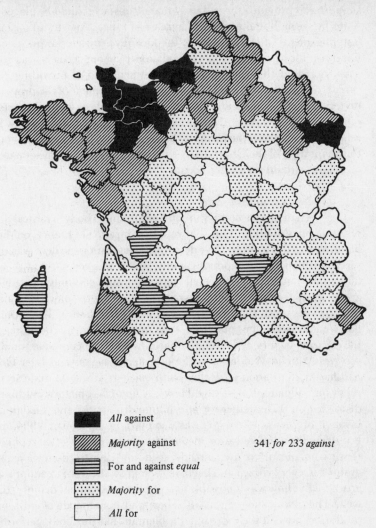

All against

Majority against   341 *for* 233 *against*

For and against *equal*

Majority for

All for

The voting for the law of Separation, 3 July 1905

Source: J.-M. Mayeur, 'Géographie de la résistance aux Inventaires', *Annales ESC*, November–December 1966, map no. 2, p. 1,267.

Note: The map does not take account of 14 abstentions or absences on leave.

associations cultuelles made responsible for Church property would not be an instrument of war against religions, Article 4, as modified, provided that they must conform to the rules for the general organization of worship. The law had a triple effect. From a disciplinary point of view it ended Gallican-ism, of which the Director-General of Worship, Dumay, had been a faithful supporter: it provided the certainty that no obstacle would be placed by the State between Rome and the Church of France. And by abolishing the 'establishment' of the Churches, the law gave priests the prospect of an uncertain life at a time when general anxiety about security was growing. This increased the difficulties of recruitment and of providing pastoral care. Finally, by involving laymen in the management of the property and material life of religions and their priests it gave them a new importance in relation to the hierarchy. It thus made possible in the future a new kind of relationship between the Church and civil society; it cleared the ground for the adaptation of the Church to the modern world, when the debate about clericalism would no longer occupy the foreground.

Republicanizing France

It had been necessary to convince the main body of radical deputies of the urgency of Separation. The republicanization of France, on the other hand, was at the heart of their demands. The main issue here was the civil service, which was expanding rapidly, and it was certain that there were numerous anti-republican civil servants, and certainly a number of aggressively reactionary ones, particularly among the older men and thus often among those carrying the greatest responsibilities. The republicans had some reason to be concerned about this situation, all the more so since the electoral victory of the Bloc had no automatic repercussions on the civil servive. As good Waldeckists, the ministers Leygues and later Chaumié had had no hesitation in dealing with teachers whose attitude seemed to them too 'advanced'. Gustave Hervé, a first-class history graduate, was dismissed on 8 December for anti-militarist remarks and Thalamas, 'the insulter of Jeanne d'Arc',[17] was removed in December 1904. Republicanizing the administration meant first of all protecting the 'republicans', those who meant to use, outside their job, the freedom of expression granted to every citizen and even, in their post, the right to adopt a critical attitude. But how was it possible to republicanize without democratizing as well? The case of the judges, with their traditional mode of entry into the profession, was all the more of a problem in that this body performed the major repressive function. Radicals and socialists reflected on the recruitment of judges with its long unpaid periods of training which restricted these posts to sons of rich families. Some pondered the idea of electing judges, others toyed with the idea of at any rate instituting a competition,[18] a method regarded as egalitarian.

Republican vigilance, heightened by the nationalist advance, did not confine itself to controlling the powerful or the 'petits chefs' – the expression appeared in December 1904 – and to devising new methods of recruitment. The radical party tended to confuse serving the State not only with serving the Republic but also with serving the radical government: 'When a civil servant does not feel in agreement with the government on which he depends, his honour and his dignity should bid him to retire.'[19] Should public posts be handed out in return for promises of loyalty to the government? In the provinces the hotheads denounced disloyal administrators. Several circulars from Combes – 20 June and 26 November 1902, 18 November 1904 – enjoined prefects to seek information about candidates for public service posts from republican deputies or from the 'delegate ... the prominent person in the commune entrusted with the confidence of the republicans and who on this basis represents them with the government when the mayor is a reactionary'. The *clientèle* system (the person elected establishes his popularity by placing his friends in secure jobs) was not far away. No doubt it was not new; after all, it is one of the classic rules of constituency voting when there is no institutional mechanism or other form of brake to check its use. We cannot be certain of its precise consequences, for there has not been enough research. Perhaps because of the lack of capable replacements, Combes does not seem to have systematically eliminated all the prefects whose departure was demanded by the lodges: the movement of prefects which followed the elections affected a quarter of all departments, whereas in 1898 it had touched a third of them, and those who left the corps were not sacked.[20] The fact remains that in office the radicals did not treat the civil service any differently from their predecessors; on the pretence of republicanizing it they placed their own men in it.

No part of the 'administration' was investigated more severely than the army. Its republicanization was the subject of numerous measures and much thought. Gallifet retired a few senior officers and busied himself with returning to the civil power, in this case the minister, supreme authority over the career of his subordinates.[21] The lodges discussed the reforms necessary and referred the question to General André, who succeeded Gallifet on 29 May 1900. The new minister took a few initiatives. He modified the regulations governing daily life – eating in the mess was no longer obligatory – and marriage – a dowry was no longer compulsory. Favours – or compensations for long injustices – were granted in the shape of promotion to republican officers on the basis of information collected by the Grand Orient; this was the point of departure for the affair known as that of the 'record cards', which blew up in the Chamber on 28 October 1904. Was it the deliberate leaking of information (Guyot de Villeneuve)? Republican duty (Lafferre)? An unimportant accident (Jaurès)? The affair caused the resignation of André a fortnight later and dealt a blow to the Combes government from which it was not to recover. However, other suggestions poured in from all sides: make public the reasons for the bad reports given by superior officers; close down the military schools where the non-commissioned officers were trained in a vacuum; abolish the *Légion d'honneur*, a 'bauble' which was a source of favouritism.[22] There was one concrete result: the military law of 1905 which reduced the period of service from three years to two and abolished the exemption enjoyed by students and ecclesiastics. The recruitment of the yearly intake would be more egalitarian, the soldier would spend less time shut up in barracks and the officer corps had been slightly republicanized. These were improvements but no structural reform. The vast majority of the bourgeoisie which had voted for the Bloc did not want any serious changes in the military force, guardian of the frontiers and of social order. The anti-clerical consensus could not be transferred to the army. The sabre had put up a better resistance than the holy-water sprinkler.

Modernizing France

The interesting modifications which appeared in 1902 in secondary education, after one of the first battles over the *baccalauréat* in French history, though enabling us today, thanks to the enquiry which preceded them, to perceive the elements of a long-lasting crisis, did not involve any structural changes and did not even help to democratize the recruitment to *lycées* and *collèges*.[23] The men concerned in the reform – Ribot, who had chaired the commission of enquiry in 1899, and the banker Aynard, president of the Lyon Chamber of Commerce, who vigorously supported Ribot in the Chamber in 1902 – were in any case moderates and notorious anti-Waldeckists. The explanation of the reasoning behind the commission's conclusions notes the rapid growth of industrial capitalism and stresses society's needs in the way of new cadres: 'The University can no longer rest content with preparing the young people entrusted to it for the liberal careers.' Ribot envisaged the modification of their training but without changing the recruitment, which was still to come from the bourgeoisie, the middle classes and scholarship winners 'emerging from democracy'. The timorous suggestions made by some radicals and socialists that higher education should be free immediately conjured up the spectre of legions of 'lawyers without briefs, of civil servants, social parasites'.[24] Jaurès alone perceived, in the inauguration of a 'first cycle' of secondary education, a step towards 'the education in common of all the children of the nation' (*La Petite République*, 4 February 1902). By opening the sacrosanct *baccalauréat* to modern subjects without Latin the reform certainly recognized in principle the legitimacy and the rights of a more 'utilitarian' education. But by continuing to accept a rhetorical conception of general culture in which modern languages were accepted as an inferior substitute for Latin and Greek,[25] by maintaining a watertight door between the primary and higher primary schools on the one hand and, on the other, the secondary schools whose pupils came from the primary forms of the *lycées*, and by rejecting the abolition of fees at *lycées* and *collèges*, the reform of

1902 confirmed the specific nature of secondary education as a class education. It put the finishing touch to the organization of the universities undertaken by the bourgeois Republic in the time of Jules Ferry, just as the law of 1905 on military service put the finishing touch to the work of 1889.

Social prospects and achievements: from Millerand to Trouillot

The republicanization of the country was thus reflected more in political vigilance and, to an extent still not very well known, in changes in State personnel than in institutional changes. However, in one area there was a coherent attempt to set up new structures: the working class was the object of this effort and the scene of it, from 1899 to 1902, the Ministry of Commerce, Industry and *PTT* (Post, Telegraph and Telephone). Contrary to the commonly held view, Millerandism cannot be reduced to the problems raised for French socialism by the participation in a bourgeois government of a socialist deputy without a mandate from his organization but popular with wage-earners as a result of his activity as a lawyer. Nor was it confined to playing a fresh variation on the old theme of reform versus revolution. The enterprise was one of much larger scope.[26] It was the prelude to the efforts led some years later by the true successor to Millerandism, if not to Millerand: Albert Thomas.

The enterprise in question was the first systematic attempt at the highest level to regularize industrial relations and to give the republican State, which had escaped from the claws of nationalism, a temporizing and inevitably integrating power over the classes whose relationship was regarded as 'barbarous' – the employers and the proletariat, with their strikes and lock-outs. Jaurès had unfailingly supported the glassblowers of Carmaux in their struggle of 1895 and he had discovered then not only the cost in suffering to the working class but also the extent to which the authorities could exert pressure on the final outcome. He was not the only one to think that this barbarity was intolerable and that it would be possible for the State to regulate labour struggles to the advantage of the workers. He supported the efforts of Millerand to first of all organize working-class action. French trade unionism, still so weak and in a minority, was encouraged to transform itself into mass trade unionism. Millerand worked towards this objective by proposing that the legal status of the unions should be improved,[27] and by organizing their representation on the Conseil Supérieur du Travail.[28] But he also worked towards another objective. He wanted to channel this increase in power towards negotiation, arbitration and the day-to-day cultivation of social harmony. This was the final purpose of the complex procedure of organizing and regulating the right to strike under discussion from March 1900 onwards.[29] State arbitration supposed a solid knowledge of industrial practices. Here Millerand was hardly making any innovations, either so far as institutions were concerned – the Conseil Supérieur du Travail and the Office du Travail dated from 1891 and the Inspection du Travail, which had led a somewhat spectral existence since its creation in 1874, had been reorganized in 1892 – or even so far as individual persons were concerned. He confined himself to making the best use possible, by means of energetic circulars or felicitous promotions, of what he found there already. For example, on 5 August 1899 he conferred high responsibilities on Arthur Fontaine, a graduate of the *Polytechnique* who had joined the Office du Travail in 1891. Fontaine became Director of Labour, a title he was to retain until he joined the International Labour Office in 1919. However, just Millerand's presence and activity as a minister who was a 'friend of the workers' restored and strengthened confidence in the virtues of the State. Moreover, by regulating the conditions of work for the execution of public works carried out for the State and by improving the material situation of the staff of the *PTT*, Millerand aimed to change the image of the State as an employer and to make it exemplary. 'The government of the Republic', he declared on 16 December 1900, 'must be the best, the fairest and the most humane of employers.'

The kind of socialism which was thus outlined against the background of participation in the government found much support, first of all in the professions linked to the civil service – the postal employees and teachers, and the railwaymen and the miners, who were well accustomed to seeking the support of Parliament through active pressure groups. Millerand's entry into the government assisted the formation of one or two trade unions, by the permanent employees of *PTT*, for example, but more often the formation of professional associations by civil servants. It gave rise to great hopes not only in small, local, isolated unions but also in the big federations. The railwaymen, after the failure of their attempt at a general strike in October 1898, fell back on a policy of negotiation, and all the pressure that the State could bring to bear on the companies was essential. As for the miners, whose federation formed in 1892 was not linked to the *CGT*, they had long relied on the State to arbitrate in their conflicts with the companies.[30] In fact Millerand had acted as lawyer for the miners of Carmaux in 1892. Finally, for some time socialist participation in the government created 'a triumphant attitude in the working classes',[31] who hoped to have found in the State a defender and protector. The decline of the Guesdists among wage-earners corresponded very largely with this current of thought. Yet Millerandism ended in a setback which was subsequently to weigh heavily on the history of the French workers' movement. The sole 'social law' of this long ministry, promulgated on 30 September 1900, resulted for the time being in extending by an hour the length of a child's working day: the advantages of the law of 2 November 1892 – extended, it is true, to the whole adult population of mixed workshops – were not to be regained, theoretically, until 1904. At the 1902 elections Millerand was re-elected as deputy for Paris only at the second round, and even then by a very small majority, and Combes replaced him with a sound radical, Georges Trouillot, a specialist in anti-clericalism. Trouillot made no difficulty about choosing a much more traditional policy and in March 1904 Millerand had the dubious pleasure of protesting against the abandonment of his social programme in favour of 'monk-hunting'.

The ruling classes had not allowed him much liberty of action. The prospect of the permanent intervention of the government under the guise of interpreter of the general interest did not suit them very well. The most powerful and best organized capitalists made no secret of their objections. This attitude was adopted, for example, by the central committee of the Coal Mines of France which after much procrastination finally refused on 28 September 1902 to discuss, in the name of the mining companies, the general claims presented by the miners. As was shown by Jules Huret's enquiry,[32] industrialists detected in Millerand's propositions a pretext for insisting on the disturbing presence of socialists in the government. From Schneider (Forges de Creusot) to Motte (Textiles du Nord), from the garment-trimmers of Saint-Etienne to the United Builders' Association, from the management of the Mines d'Anzin to the Chamber of Commerce of Lille, they all wanted to confine 'the modern State' to the rôle of 'assistant to private enterprise'; it was to let free enterprise have its head and exercise its rôle as boss. 'An idle tribune of the people would be less harmful' than this man Millerand, declared Eugène Motte. With a few exceptions – certain entrepreneurs of the port of Marseille, for whom any solution was preferable to 'the anarchy of a city in which there is a continuous threat of a strike', or a modern employer like Japy, the Vice-president of the Chamber of Commerce of Besançon – the doctrine laid down by Leroy-Beaulieu in 1898 in *L'Etat moderne et ses fonctions* received the unanimous support of the employers. Merchants and manufacturers preferred to settle their conflicts with their staff themselves, so long as they could call in the police or the military, if need be, to keep the order necessary for the creation of profits. Moderate republicans, whether they supported the Bloc des Gauches or not, endorsed this choice, and a good number of radicals, if not radical-socialists, were happy to take the same attitude.

Moreover, the plans for arbitration and for the organization of the right to strike were not the only ones to worry them. The problem of State expenditure and its financing lay beneath the surface of many attitudes. Although the French budget seemed to be on the right path, diminishing regularly from 1900 to 1904, few people wanted to risk reversing such a fortunate tendency by, for example, setting up a system of retirement pensions for workers that would be partly financed – and largely run – by the State. At the end of the long debate in the Chamber in June 1901 on the Guieysse proposal for workers' pensions, most of the deputies showed their uncertainty, and more probably their desire not to see the motion passed, by sending it back for consultation to the employers' and workers' professional associations (see H. Hatzfeld, Biblio. no. 296). In July 1905 the Chamber was to fall back on a motion making assistance by the State, the departments and the communes obligatory for men more than seventy years old. But there was something more worrying still in the eyes of the property-owning classes: behind the prospects of the reform of direct taxation loomed a 'fiscal inquisition' easy to denounce in the land of the Rights of Man. And so although a progressive tax on total income was an integral part of the old radical programme Combes warned deputies as early as 12 June 1902 that in this field it was necessary 'to act with discretion so as not to alarm the interested parties'. He was to repeat his warning opportunely at the annual banquet of the Mascuraud Committee at which he presided on the following 6 October: only reactionaries, he said, could preach measures of this sort, which were 'liable to upset business'. This attitude was reflected in the left-wing Bloc government by the presence at the Ministry of Finance of Rouvier, who was known to have links with the Rothschild bank. No member of parliament was to be really surprised by the failure of the botched bill on income tax which Rouvier was to introduce at the end of 1904.

However, the employers and the political forces linked to the property-owning classes as a whole were not the only ones to have finally rejected the Millerandist scheme. Attracted at first, the working class soon came up against hard reality. As early as November 1899 the railwaymen, who expected much from the Minister of Public Works, a radical called Baudin who was a member of the legal council of the railwaymen's national union, noted that the decrees which he was promulgating and which governed the regulation of work marked a clear retreat from the Berteaux law passed two years earlier by the Chamber but not yet, in fact, adopted by the Senate. Three months later, in February 1900, the savage repression of the demonstrators in Martinique and the strikers of Chalon-sur-Saône was a reminder of the traditional rôle of the State as gendarme. The governmental stick was too big and the carrots too few. The militant anarchists and numerous socialists – Guesdists, Blanquists and Allemanists – tried to find an explanation, on bases that were in any case heterogeneous. At the confederal committee at Lyon in September 1901 the *CGT* decided by a very small majority to continue to sit on the Conseil Supérieur du Travail, but the draft bill on the organization of strikes and the one which aimed to institute compulsory pensions for workers were rejected by a very large number of votes. The Confédération did not reject any social laws, but it refused to collaborate in drawing them up: 'it leaves to the legislators the task of finding the resources necessary for the introduction of workers' pensions' (*Documents de l'enquête parlementaire*, p. 604). Doubtless the railway union, in spite of its critics, continued to congratulate itself on the fact that for the first time the State had intervened officially between capital and labour (*Tribune de la voie ferrée*, 15 June 1902). And the miners' federation asked the Prime Minister on 9 October 1902, the very day on which it declared a general strike, to use his authority with the central committee of the Coal Mines of France to induce it to accept a discussion with the unions. In addition, on 25 June 1903, the 'miner deputies' of Pas-de-Calais introduced a draft bill for the return of the mines to the State. The attitude of these two unions, like the somewhat more hesitant one of workers in the book industry, needs to be underlined all the more in that they represented – especially the miners' union – large numbers of workers. Such was not the case either with the majority of the unions grouped together in the *CGT* or with the *bourses du travail*; J. Julliard admits that at the turn of the century only 1.25 per cent of the industrial population belonged. But the unorganized masses did not protest against the choice made by the national union organizations. And in fact, still more clearly than at the congress of the *CGT*, the union speech which won the day at the congress of the *bourses du travail* from 17 to 21 September 1901 sounded the death knell of Millerandism by demanding in particular the face-to-face confrontation in the Conseil Supérieur du Travail of employers and proletariat, and the elimination of the state representatives – in other words, class against class.

There was very little social legislation in the years that saw the rise of radicalism. Social reforms were not the strong point of the Third Republic at any point in its career. The Millerand episode was only a flash in the pan. Was the attempt doomed to failure? It does not look as if its failure can be attributed to purely contingent reasons. The forces on which Millerandism could rely were in the final analysis unsubstantial: the civil service was insufficiently numerous and not well enough organized, and the miners and railwaymen themselves were insufficiently attracted. On the level of the politicians who backed Waldeck-Rousseau, and even more those who backed Combism, there was little encouragement. In the ranks of the militant workers concerned there appeared an attitude of opposition or at best of sympathetic expectancy, whereas at the start their attitude had been very favourable. Millerandism, soon forgotten by the ruling classes, left very unpleasant memories in organized labour; these were disadvantageous to French socialism for a long time and, except for the interlude of the Union Sacrée, helped to keep Millerand out of any government for many years. (Millerand's reputation for careerism was another contributing factor.) Hostility to Millerand also helped to turn the most combative workers, if not the masses, towards revolutionary trade unionism. The social and political crisis which shook the radical Republic from 1904 to 1907 grew out of the experiment to which the name of Alexandre Millerand has stuck, and the failure of which had already been ratified by Combism.

9

Crisis and death of the Bloc, 1904–1907

Concealed in the glorious days of the Bloc by the popular enthusiasm for anti-clericalism, a crisis which threatened as early as 1904 subsequently grew more serious. It was a political and social crisis born of the contradictions in French society but also aggravated – this was something new – by the changes beginning to make themselves felt throughout the world. We are going to follow it, not as it developed chronologically, but by underlining its principal aspects during this period of four years. Although republican discipline was maintained when it came to voting, the Bloc des Gauches was certainly dead at the end of 1907. But of what did it die?

The agitation of Catholic France

The protests of French Catholics against Combes's policy and later against the implementation of the Separation were never widespread enough to weaken the republican camp. In any case, confronted by the enemy, the republicans would have re-forged a unity which was otherwise breaking up. However, in the crisis which shook the country, particularly in 1906, the resistance to the law of separation underlined the fact that some Catholics were living in a mood dictated by nostalgia for a past that had gone forever and that they could display their rejection of modern society with a sombre brilliance.

The closure of the schools run by the religious orders and the expulsion of famous orders like the Carthusians had certainly caused demonstrations, but without the organization of any real resistance to the enforcement of official decisions. In spite of the surprising campaign conducted on their behalf since November 1902 by the Radical paper *Le Petit Dauphinois*, the Carthusians were expelled on 29 April 1903 without the dragoons, sappers and gendarmes having to face anything more serious than the shouts and songs of a few thousand demonstrators. When Combes forbade secularized orders to preach, there were some brawls in the churches at Aubervilliers, Belleville and Plaisance, but on the whole there were few reactions and not even much fuss.

Things changed with the making of the inventories prescribed by the separation law. No doubt in the winter of 1906 nothing was usually to be seen but futile anger and passive forms of resistance: women praying in front of churches, parish officials and peasants listening bare-headed to the protests of their parish priest. But often too, by February 1906 and above all in the first fortnight of March, the assembled faithful showed their intention not to yield to legal force, at least not without fighting. The incidents began in Paris on 1 February at the church of Sainte-Clotilde. At the end of the month they spread to the provinces, not only to the departments of the Vendée, but also to the mountains of Velay and Flanders where there were deaths. The object was always to defend actively, or at any rate symbolically, the church, a sacred building, and to prevent an inventory of the objects which it contained. Before the occupation of factories came the occupation of churches. The church bells would ring and people would barricade themselves in the house of God, shoring up the heavy doors with piled-up chairs. Hymns were sung and the men armed themselves with sticks, stones and sometimes white-hot lances.[1] In the country the peasants, equipped with forks, iron-tipped sticks and iron bars, mounted guard by the side of the church; they went to confession and communion after dictating their last wishes. In the Pyrenees the Basques brought their bears. Facing them, the adversary: the tax-collector, the key person and the one particularly detested, the representatives of the public forces – policemen, gendarmes, sometimes troops – the sub-prefect and, in Paris, Lépine, the prefect of police, who was at the beginning of a long career. The doors were battered in with axes and the expulsion of those barricaded inside was carried out without mincing matters: comfortable middle-class people and poverty-stricken peasants experienced a violence previously reserved for the strikers in towns, for the workers.

Why?

There were several different reasons for this flare-up of violence. The first reasons were connected with decisions external to French Catholics. The prospect of an inventory of ecclesiastical property before its transfer to the *associations cultuelles* had not provoked any particular excitement during the parliamentary debates. But on 2 January 1906 the head office of the Registry department ordered its officials to ask priests to open the tabernacle, and this document was made public ten days later; from there it was only a short step to mutterings about 'profanation', and this step was soon taken by part of the Catholic press. It was the sacred order which was being interfered with; not just the church, but in the church the place of mystery.[2] Nevertheless, the very first inventories passed off calmly enough. The intervention of Rome was to change the atmosphere. On 11 February, after a long silence, the Pope published the encyclical *Vehementer nos.* Subjected to contradictory requests – the French clergy and French Catholics were very much divided on the attitude which it was proper for Rome to adopt with regard to the law – Pius X condemned the Separation as 'profoundly insulting to God, whom it officially denies by laying down the principle that the Republic does not recognize any creed' and as 'gravely offensive' to the dignity of the Apostolic See. The Pope certainly did not call on the faithful to undertake an armed struggle; he suggested on the contrary that the members of the clergy should respond 'to outrage with mildness'. However, the 'vehemence' of the language was taken as an encouragement to the most energetic resistance. Ultramontane Catholicism seized its chance: 'Roma locuta est', exclaimed the comte Albert de Mun and the Catholic press echoed his words.

On the whole, the clergy – bankrupt bishops, rich parish priests in Paris who found themselves 'jeered at in their own churches', country priests vainly appealing for calm – tried to put a brake on the zeal of the protesters. But the churchmen were overtaken. A minority of laymen deeply regretted these acts of violence – liberal Catholics who thought that the Church had 'everything to gain by showing that it was large-minded and modern', certain Christian democrats like abbé Lemire and centre-right intellectuals in the Orleanist tradition, like the academicians who on 26 March sent to the French bishops the missive known as 'the green cardinals' letter'. Nevertheless, it was laymen who had seized the initiative and organized the violent resistance. Former notables sought to maintain their social influence, and the new strata sought to assert their political influence. Such was the case with the Sillonist Young Guard which took part in the Parisian demonstrations with the approval of Marc Sangnier,[3] and especially with those who in other contexts were already sworn enemies of the Bloc, the neo-monarchists inspired by the Ligue d'Action Française. In the provinces it was the peasants who were in the forefront of the resistance, sometimes strictly officered by the notables, sometimes moved by more personal and inward feelings.

What were these feelings? Light is thrown on them by a 'map' of the serious incidents connected with the inventories. This does not align with the religious map of rural France drawn up by Canon Boulard, or with that of the French right, the section of the population that voted against the law of separation. Some mainly Catholic areas do not appear on it; for example, the two Savoys where all the deputies had voted for the law, or Seine-Inférieure where they had all opposed it. A certain kind of Catholicism was involved, that of the old Catholic counter-revolution, which intended to fight against 'all the forces of evil and of freemasonry'. It found its troops among peasants cut off in their mountains and woods, under-politicized people who were unwilling to be organized by anyone except those who had looked after their ancestors, namely their parish priests. The Inventory rioters were the people left out of the reckoning by the France of the railways and markets, by modern France. They only knew the State as an oppressor. This is the explanation of the steely hatred which they displayed not only against the forces of law and order, in particular the gendarmes, but also against the tax-collectors, the agents of the republican Treasury that had succeeded the royal Treasury.

The various stages

That is why at a time of rising prosperity they did not pose much of a threat to the established order. These killjoys did not really spoil the radical holiday. But they did cast a shadow on it. The death of Ghysel decided abbé Lemire, deputy for Ghysel's constituency, to put a question to the minister, and the parliamentary debate of 7 March 1906 bore witness to a good deal of confusion. The Bloc's majority in the Chamber voted in turn for the posting-up of the speeches of Briand, Ribot, the Minister of the Interior and abbé Lemire! The Rouvier government resigned and was replaced by a Sarrien cabinet in which Clemenceau made his grand return to politics as Minister of the Interior.[4] 'The law will remain a law of tolerance and equity', in the words of Briand, who had piloted the bill through the Chamber, and now became a minister himself for the first time. By 16 March Clemenceau had called on the prefects to halt the inventories if they had to be made by force. The elections were only a month and a half away and the maintenance of republican calm – if not of order – could pay a dividend.

And in fact the incidents ceased at once. The ardent appeals of the Catholic leaders, reinforced by Jean Lerolle, the president of the Catholic Association for French Youth, to resist fell on deaf ears. And the condemnation by Rome on 10 August 1906 of the *associations cultuelles* – in the encyclical *Gravissimo officii* – did not prevent the French bishops from seeking a *modus vivendi* with the government, which was duly achieved in the spring of 1907. In the Catholic view, the crisis had somewhat strengthened the authority of intransigent Catholics, both clerical and lay. It had lasted only two months on the militant level. The May elections in any case demonstrated the ultra-minority character of the incidents; the Catholics did not gain any advantage from them anywhere. Contrary to what was written in the Jesuit review *Les Etudes* on 5 September 1906, the Separation did not 'plunge the country into a series of revolutionary measures'.

Workers' strikes and trade unionism

The France of days-gone-by had furnished, if not all the 'officers', at any rate the 'troops' for the demonstrations against the inventories. It was the new France, the daughter of the steam engine, that expressed herself and organized herself in the wave of strikes and in the trade union advance of 1904–7.

The workers on strike

In 1906 there was one striker for every sixteen industrial workers: thus at the beginning of the century the strike had become part of the normal course of events for the proletariat. There were hundreds of thousands of strikers every year and even more people who showed their solidarity with the workers in their struggles. 'Communist soup kitchens' were organized, local or professional collections and subscriptions were raised and arrangements were made to look after the strikers' children. Music-hall songs, almanacs and drawings popularized striking; striking rather than strikes, for the strike illustration almost always called on the same symbolical objects and often used the space in the same way – barring it with a black wall of strikers or making a mounting wave of strikers cross it. Strikes began to make a stronger impression on public opinion as they grew longer. The maximum was attained in 1902: nearly twenty-two days on average, more than three times what it had been thirty years earlier. Most strikes were offensive strikes and they made the best possible use of a flourishing economic situation. On top of the traditional strikes in support of pay claims – always a priority – and of strikes caused by anger or solidarity and demanding the re-engagement of a comrade or the dismissal of a foreman, came the struggles for a shorter working day. In 1904–7 a peak was reached from every point of view. In 1904, after three quiet years, the number of strikes surged ahead: there were 1,026 strikes – almost twice as many as in 1903 – 271,097 strikers and nearly 4,000,000 days lost, against 2,400,000 in the previous year. The provinces were far in advance of Paris. After a definite drop in 1905 the movement gathered strength in 1906: 438,500 strikers – a record which was not to be beaten until the Great War – took part in 1,309 strikes of an average duration of nineteen days. The department of Seine was at the top of the list this time, and by a long way, with almost a quarter of the total. At the same time the boundaries of striking France expanded. The departments of the north, where the sombre miners and the impulsive textile workers held sway (they had long been among the leaders), the Lyon region (on the move as far as Saint-Etienne), and the industrial cities of the Isère were joined by new areas: Britanny with the spectacular strikes at Fougères and Hennebont and the constant and violent agitation at Brest, and the iron and steel workers of Lorraine.

The spectacular character of several of these affairs proceeded first of all from their length, which often resulted in awful hardships. At the Forges d'Hennebont, from April to August 1906, 1,800 workers fed themselves for 115 days on nothing but crabs caught at low tide and bread parsimoniously distributed: 350 grammes per day per family at the start; 750 grammes per family, this time per week, at the end of the strike. Attacks on property such as the violent occupation of a factory at Limoges, the looting of the shops of recalcitrant bakers at Brest, or on persons – an attack on a mayor at Lens, the illegal restraint of an employer at Limoges – arose out of the workers' exasperation during a particularly long strike or when confronted by a particularly detested employer. Fatal violence was never the work of the strikers: at Cluses, on 18 July 1904, the four sons of a watchmaker fired on an authorized demonstration and caused three deaths; at Longwy in September 1905 and at Raon-l'Etape in July 1907 it was the forces of law and order that killed, and in the Lens Basin, after the Courrières catastrophe, blood only flowed after the arrival of the cavalry. We can all see the strikes of these years in the mind's eye: streets were occupied, flags were borne aloft, the *Internationale*, which had originated in the North, was sung everywhere, there were still songs made up to suit the circumstances, and revolutionary Italian chants were to be heard in Lorraine and the Midi.

The pressure created by street demonstrations was all the more necessary in that the employers had learned to organize themselves and more frequently used the weapon of the lock-out. It is true that in many cases – in the textile industry of Nord, for example – the only cartels between the firms were still sales cartels. But at Fougères the Shoemakers' Association, founded in February 1900 and embracing in November 1906 twenty-three employers out of thirty-five[5] felt strong enough to launch a long trial of strength in support of one of its members. When beaten, the employers then tried to organize all the industrialists of Ille-et-Vilaine and shared in the establishment of a mutual assistance fund against strikes with certain big employers in the iron and steel and textile industries. Lock-outs could also arise out of a temporary coalition: in Lyon at the beginning of 1905 almost all the car manufacturers made common cause with Berliet and won.[6]

Workers' trade unionism

The shock administered to public opinion by the wave of strikes of 1904–7 was not due simply to its size. More and more often the strike was planned and the trade union acted as leader of the orchestra. It could also happen that the organization grew out of the strike: by prolonging itself the strike set in motion a process which outlived it, and Parisian trade unionists taught provincial workers to protect at all costs the weapon which they had put in their own hands. From the strike committee to the trade union; we have entered the twentieth century. The workers' organization expanded inside the firm, into the locality and across the nation. Except for the mixed, denominational unions dominated by the employers whose influence gradually declined, all trade union trends benefited from the impetus imparted by strikes. None of these trends really promoted social harmony and their coexistence did more to reflect and multiply tensions than to appease them. The trade union organization had been regarded by Waldeck-Rousseau, and subsequently by Millerand and those of the radicals who were seeking anything more than a supplementary election platform, as a mechanism for regulating conflicts with the workers, a tool for negotiation between the classes and a promise of a more sober attitude. They had to change their tune.

It is true that there were trade unions which did not give much trouble. Those founded by Marguerite Durand, the editor of *La Fronde*, gave every satisfaction from this point of view. They attracted more attention by the militant feminism of their founder than by their union activities proper, and their anti-clerical bias gave them the entrée to the Ministry of Labour (Biblio. no. 267). On the other hand, the first Catholic trade unions, known as 'separated' because only wage-earners were members, were characterized by their strongly denominational character. Firmly opposed to any class war, they were still not very numerous: only a dozen of them assembled on 20 December 1904 at the first congress of Christian trade unionism. Paris, where the Union of Workers in Commerce and Industry was founded in 1887, Lyon and Nord were where they found support. Here, with G. Tessier and J. Zirnheld, we find the very modest origins of the present-day *CFTC* (*Confédération française des travailleurs chrétiens*). It was the trade union thrust of those years that led the *SEIC* (*Syndicat des employés du commerce et de l'industrie*), whose legality was recognized on 15 May 1905, to define itself as a union of 'proletarians' and no longer one of temporary wage-earners on the way to professional independence.

Sometimes the most apparently solid trade union powers were brusquely challenged. In Pas-de-Calais the authority of the two miner deputies, Basly and Lamendin (old campaigners of the negotiating table backed by well-tested trade union organizations), was attacked by some young miners whose influence was reinforced by the outburst of anger which followed the Courrières catastrophe in March 1906. The numerical strength of the 'young trade union' remained weak, but its challenge worried those who were betting on trade unionism to achieve agreement. On 1 May 1906 the 'young trade union' joined the *CGT*, thus breaking with the Miners' Federation's tradition of autonomy. The *CGT* was young itself, since it really only came into being at Montpellier in 1902 under pressure from militant workers tired of the dissensions between the Fédération des Bourses du Travail and the Fédération d'Industries et de Métiers, and also of those between the various socialist groups and the anarchist current which had infiltrated the unions on quite a large scale. We shall return to the *CGT* advance guard. Standard-bearer of a class trade unionism, it wanted to be the spearhead of the revolutionary troops, and its rapid growth – the 1,792 unions federated to it in 1904 were 2,399 by 1906, and the number of subscribers had increased by some 45,000 – the influence which it wielded, and the influence attributed to it made a strong impression on public opinion.

It was in opposition to 'Red' trade unionism that the so-called 'Yellow' (Jaunes) unions were formed. Founded at Montceau-les-Mines in 1899, they received their colours in January 1904 when a former socialist worker from Doubs, Biétry, affected by 'jaundice' since the end of 1901, founded the National Federation of the 'Jaunes' of France (*FNFJ*) and openly declared war on the *CGT* in the name of understanding between the classes and of the maintenance of private property. The *FNJF* profited at the start from a fairly extensive interchange, especially in Paris, with the denominational unions, without giving them any allegiance. The violence displayed by the 'Jaunes' – which was quite open at Brest and Fougères – and their obvious venality at Carmaux slowed down their growth, and the *FNJF*, whose leaders rapidly moved towards an extreme right position in parliament, did not succeed in obtaining legal recognition.

1 May 1906

Social tensions and general disquiet came to a head on 1 May 1906. Not that there was any question of a 'révolution manquée'. However, never had a nationwide workers' movement been planned so systematically and the fact that it coincided with the electoral campaign increased its impact still further. The origin of the movement was a tradition which was already old, since it went back to 1 May 1890, and in which French workers had played a considerable part from the start. It was also a tradition connected with the spring renascence, linking the workers' demonstration to that of old rural labour. It was the 'May hope' of Albert Thomas. Thomas was a young socialist, a reformer if ever there was one, but also one very attentive to the trade union movement.

Why 1906? The *CGT*, in a demonstration of will, decided to organize a 1 May 'not like the others', to 'canalize the whole trade union effort into one single claim'. The eight-hour day was chosen as the workers' great aim; working time and rest time were joined by the notion – a new one for the working class in big industry – of leisure. A fine drawing by Grandjouan published in *L'Assiette au beurre* of 1 May symbolized the ternary rhythm of days to come. Living was not just a question of surviving: since its congress at Bourges (1904) the *CGT* had tried to instil this idea into the consciousness of the millions. The Confédération made a tremendous effort: there were newspapers, posters, tracts, six million stickers posted everywhere, pamphlets and confederate meetings in eighty towns, not to speak of ordinary meetings. On the Paris *bourse du travail* there was a great banner: 'From 1 May we shall only work eight hours a day.' This slogan was pregnant with differing meanings: for the most moderate it expressed a wish or a hope; for Emile Pouget and Dubéros, the founding fathers of

1 May 1906, it was a decision beyond which loomed a general strike; and for Griffuelhes, the secretary-general of the Confédération, it was an appeal to adopt a combative attitude. It is true that the mediocre results of the subscription, the refusal of some federations – that of the textile industry, for example – to participate, and the 'more reasonable' aims fixed by others, such as the book industry, prove that the myth did not mobilize the whole working class or even the whole *CGT*. Yet in Paris many old trades were on strike by April. A huge strike movement prolonged the stoppage of 1 May in the building industry, in furnishing, among the printers and among those twentieth-century workers, the car men and the Métro men. Soon they were joined by skilled iron and steel workers. Forty-eight per cent of the strikes of this great year broke out around 1 May. And on 13 July 1906 the law making a weekly rest day compulsory was passed.

Even though the provinces showed less enthusiasm, the 1 May 1906 revealed new possibilities. It inspired widespread fear, whipped up by the panic campaign of *L'Echo de Paris* and *La Libre Parole* and attested by the provisions accumulated by the bourgeoisie, the cows and rabbits boarded out in stables and even the capital provisionally deposited in Belgium. This was utilized by Clemenceau, the Minister of the Interior, to manufacture an 'anti-republican plot' conceived in common by the extreme right and the extreme left: on 30 April a Bonapartist was arrested at the same time as the secretary-general and the treasurer of the *CGT*. Lépine, the prefect of police, had occasion to reassure the conservative and nationalist population of the capital by putting Paris into a state of minor siege: this was the start of the 'Mouquin riding-school' which every now and then lost its temper and made a brutal charge. Yet this widespread fear was fairly factitious. In the provinces incidents were confined to a few ports; in Paris the press campaign was not supported either by the radicals or the Catholics: 'the 1 May is not a threat but a promise', wrote Ferdinand Buisson in *Le Radical*. Doubtless a shudder ran down the spine of the notables and the fashionable ladies. And that the *CGT* was from then on regarded as a redoubtable adversary by the Minister of the Interior is certainly proved by the personal development of the old warrior. It is certain that the various social forces united by a common ideology at the time of the supremacy of the Bloc were now divided. However, the feeling prevailed that the divisions would only show clearly a little later. What happened round about 1 May 1906 was the preliminary to a future rupture.

New strata of the population in conflict

The dynamism and combativeness of these warm springs were not the monopoly of a working-class avant-garde. For nearly the first time since the beginning of the Third Republic important sections of the peasantry abandoned their rural placidity.[7] And for the first time agents of the State, civil servants in Panama hats, set about organizing themselves alongside labourers in caps. The arena for the contest was becoming larger.

The peasant proletariat

The electoral support of the countryside, long since attained in the 'departments of '48', had been one of the constant objectives of the republicans since 1871 and at the turn of the century this support had made possible the provincial transformation of radicalism. And suddenly these areas were disturbed by surprising somersaults. Between 1904 and 1907 these somersaults affected the market-gardening suburbs of Paris and Lyon, Brie and Valois with their big fields of corn and sugar-beet, the Landes with their forests, and the wine-growing Midi. All these were areas where, in one way or another, a real rural proletariat toiled. This proletariat's entry into the workers' struggles often took place on a massive scale and with considerable enthusiasm. Often, too, the flare-up was brief and attempts to win back the labourers were successful. Nevertheless, the rural agitation worried the government, especially when it spread to urban areas.

Dawning class-consciousness was directed against 'the big men, whatever party they belong to ... the notorious capitalists, white, blue or red', in short all the 'rich republicans', including radical-socialists, who exploited the rural proletariat at two francs a day and treated it as 'the lords did in days gone by'.[8] In the Midi in particular the way people lived shed the cold light of day on the reality of social relations and the fictitious character of 'politics'. Of course, reactionary politicians were able to profit from all this: such was the case in the Landes, where strikes by the resin-tappers that started on 9 February 1906 in Lit-et-Mixe were partially checked by Ducamin, a dubious character who was probably the agent of clerical and monarchist landowners. However, the strike had not been in vain; 'The resin-tappers are very different from what they were a few years ago', *L'Autorité* wrote sadly. Among the agricultural workers of Hérault and Aude (strikes of January and December 1904) and the market-gardeners of the Parisian suburbs, the conflicts, vigorously pursued and sometimes instigated by the *bourses du travail*, adopted the rhythm of the working class from the start and it was possible to hear the peasants singing the *Internationale*.

Thus there was considerable disquiet among the landowners and soon also in the government. In February 1904 the right denounced these 'agrarian disturbances...' as 'a real revolutionary movement'. The government was summoned 'to take measures to safeguard the right of property'. It obeyed the summons and several times sent troops into the 'Red' Midi. Numerous militants were arrested and convicted; the same thing was to happen in the Landes in 1907 to the promoters of unions that favoured the *CGT*. In the middle term the repressive measures did not succeed in breaking class-consciousness: the agricultural labourers produced a common journal, *Le Travailleur de la terre*, even before the Land Federation was completely integrated in the *CGT*. In the very short term, among these often illiterate agricultural workers – they were often immigrants – setbacks and repression sometimes combined to favour the temporary resurgence of 'the unity of the land'. This was nowhere to be seen more clearly than in the wine-growing Midi. However, this return to the marriage of the classes may have brought social harmony, but it did not bring political calm or civic order.

1907: the revolt of the Midi

At the beginning of the twentieth century Mediterranean Languedoc was a land of the vine.[9] Native to the dry, stony hills and reconstituted after the phylloxera plague, it occupied 47 per cent of the cultivated land of Hérault, 33.2 per cent of that of Aude and 30.45 per cent of that of Pyrénées Orientales. From Perpignan to Arles stretched a continuous zone of monoculture which had become, except in Gard, massively industrial and capitalist through the concentration of property and cultivation. A huge rural proletariat consisting of small farmers who had been ruined, poor peasants who had come down from the highland areas, and Italian or Spanish workers lived in very difficult circumstances and formed a burden on the labour market. The extreme instability of production was bound up with the unpredictable nature of the weather, and the considerable tendency to over-production reflected the desire for quick profits which had even turned owners of prosperous silk mills to the vine. Sales were subject to competition from Algerian wines and from 'sugared wines' passionately denounced as fraudulent products when the harvest was good by the very people who, when there was a spring frost or disease, did not always refrain from indulging in the same practice.

However, the close links between a good part of the proletariat and the middle-sized and large landowners had been maintained. Many of these new agricultural workers had retained small plots of vines and did not find it easy to part company with the interest of wine-producers in general. The Confédération Générale Viticole, consisting of mixed unions, developed an inter-class ideology of 'defence of the vine'. This policy came to a head in the spring of 1907 under the cumulative effect of the addition of sugar to mediocre wines, two consecutively excellent harvests and regional underconsumption due to the decline in wages. The whole area was affected by the sale of wine at a loss, by the drop in wages, by unemployment among the agricultural workers, and by the reduction in the takings of small tradesmen and local craftsmen. Wine united all those concerned. The 'revolt of the beggars' was not simply the revolt of the beggars; the agricultural proletariat added its weight, its militant attitude and its bright colours.

In March 1907 a leader appeared at Argeliers, near Narbonne, one Marcellin Albert. A landowner though a small one, he inspired confidence in the big men as well as in trade unionists and, being a café-owner into the bargain, he embodied village sociability. Albert was to be christened 'the redeemer'. In Narbonne there was a socialist leader called Doctor Ferroul. New modes of action were adopted: mass meetings were held from 7 April to 9 June in all the towns, assembling the men from the country and those from the big cities. At these meetings the spoken word was king; all possible political and religious options were discussed and confused. What did the demonstrators want? Neither precise reforms nor revolution. They simply wanted some attention from highly placed people in Paris, where no one knew anything about the Midi. The truth was that the mixture of different classes forbade any genuine demands except a rather derisory appeal for a fight against fraud. However, Paris did not get very excited and the deputies for Languedoc – Albert Sarraut, member for Aude, was Under-Secretary of State at the Ministry of the Interor until 19 June – left it to the socialist Aldy and Jaurès to speak.

The chain resignation of municipal councils, then the first military disturbances – difficult to avoid, granted the regional character of recruitment – unleashed Jacobin disquiet after 10 June. The radical press had found its enemies: 'the reactionary anarchy of the crowds', the revolt against 'national sovereignty'. Called on to act, Clemenceau acted with that mixture of brutality and trickery which characterized his style of repression when he was in power: Ferroul was arrested, there was a murderous intervention by troops at Narbonne and numerous people were injured at Montpellier. However, there were also negotiations with the 17th Regiment of infantry, which had fraternized with the demonstrators at Béziers. A law on fraud was – at last! – passed and promulgated on 29 June, arrears of tax were remitted and Marcellin Albert was skilfully discredited.

Devoid of social or political aims, the crisis in the Midi had overflowed classic bounds and, without endangering national unity, had revealed the special character of southern traditions revitalized by the misfortunes of the vineyards. It had revealed the régime's inability to perceive threats and movements of opinion in good time. It had rendered the crisis of the Bloc more serious. Ferroul was to be president of the Confédération Générale Viticole; by 1908 the departure of agricultural workers from the *CGT* federation had been halted; and the song by Montéhus to the glory of the 'good soldiers of the 17th' was to become part of the traditions of the 'Red' Midi.

Civil servants and the CGT

The sharp crisis which developed at the same time among certain classes of civil servants threw up better perceived and more lasting contradictions between socialists and radicals. Civil servants had increased considerably in number since the beginning of the Republic. The Ministry of Education and the Post Office (*PTT*) in particular had grown by some 70 per cent in twenty years. The total number of civil servants was between 415,000 and 800,000, depending on whether or not one counted the armed forces, the local government officials and the tobacconists, who were almost as numerous. Regular monthly salary, pension: the civil service polarized the professional aims of the strata that were finding it difficult to rise in society, especially in the departments of the south-west and centre which were devoid of industry. As *Le Temps* wrote on 15 May 1909:

> For workers familiar with unemployment, the civil servant is the happy mortal who knows nothing of industrial crisis and the cruelties of competition. For the small tradesman the civil servant is the man on whom the customer will never default and who can always count on reliable resources. For the peasant he is a gentleman who has never shivered with terror when he saw the hail cloud pass over his field ready to burst.

However, since the beginning of the century the 'advantages' of the civil service had not been quite so obvious. In certain sectors the deterioration of working conditions aroused profound discontent: in the Post Office, while postal traffic had increased by 30 per cent between 1901 and 1905, the staff had increased by only 16 per cent and tuberculosis was having dire effects in small, unhealthy offices. The salaries of young government officials had not changed since 1844; a local police official received about three francs a day, the wage of an agricultural day-labourer. As a result, promotion became an obsession, but this was governed by arbitrary decisions, as were moves from one job to another. Even for judges security of tenure could not be relied upon implicitly.[10] Everywhere fear of the 'chef' was the beginning of wisdom; what assistant teacher did not tremble before his headmaster? Then came the sub-prefects and prefects, the slave-drivers of the department. Finally, the stagnant ponds of constituency voting lent weight to local grudges and to influential electors capable of securing the intervention of the deputy, whose power was described by Paul Boncour, a young lawyer with socialist sympathies, in these terms: 'There is not a road-mender who has not been interviewed by him, not a postman who is not under his orders, not a schoolmaster whom he has not threatened with a transfer' (quoted by H. Chardon, Biblio. no. 284).

Recruited in larger numbers, and from a level in society closer to the proletariat first because of the increase in numbers and second because of the education laws which made the leaving certificate general and (since 1886) raised the value of the elementary diploma, civil servants found it

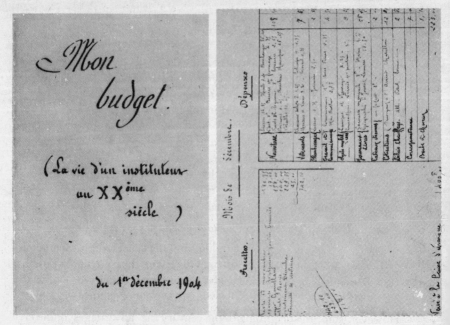

Earning one's living: a schoolmaster's account book, 1 December 1904

Source: J. Ozouf, *Nous, les maîtres d'école* (Julliard-Gallimard, coll. 'Archives', 1967).

more and more difficult to put up with these multiple servitudes. 'Faith in secularization', still alive, no longer formed a sufficient brake on the dissatisfaction of schoolteachers. And the workers in the postal services, certain sections of which – the telephone, for example – had formed part of the private sector until the end of the nineteenth century, had no reason to feel like the trustees of a national mission, especially as their service included some 'appointed' workers who had belonged since 1901 to the Union Fédérative des Travailleurs de l'Etat. Thus was born the idea of escaping atomization by forming a group. The professional associations encouraged among the teachers – they were called *amicales* – by governments keen to combat the influence of the clergy had developed rapidly since 1900 as a result of three factors: the Dreyfus affair, which had given a radical tone to behaviour; the desire of the Bloc governments to create in the civil service an organized base favourable to their policy; and the law of 1901 on associations. Often, but not always, dominated by the hierarchy, not federated to one another, cut off from the working-class avant-garde, these associations were enough for most schoolmasters, for whom 'the term "trade union" smells of gunpowder' (J. Ozouf, Biblio. no. 196). But for a small minority of teachers and for a much larger number of postal workers they were to serve as elementary classes in trade unionism.

Battle was joined in the full glare of public opinion in 1905–7. That was when the first civil service strikes started: policemen at Lyon (1905), junior post office workers in Paris (April 1906), were harshly repressed. The first trade unions among primary teachers were formed in 1903. On 13 July 1905 a dozen of these formed, round the nucleus of L'Emancipation de l'Instituteur, the first federation of teachers' unions, which held its first congress in April 1906. It was also in 1905 that certain subordinate postal workers, whose general association had just refused to turn itself into a trade union, split off from this association. The result was the creation of the Central Committee for the Defence of Trade Union Rights of State Workers, which was backed by the Union Fédérative. The Bloc governments hesitated for a long time, as was shown, up to the end of 1905, by their inaction in face of the young unions and the considerable divergences which arose among the political forces of the left on the content of a possible statute governing civil servants. The discussions, which were officially opened in December 1903 by Louis Barthou, soon excluded the right to strike, which was rejected by the vast majority of civil servants, and centred on the legitimacy of unionism and of membership of the *CGT*. Some people saw no guarantee against arbitrary behaviour except in a common statute or set of regulations; they were supported by the socialists and some of the radicals, but the authorities little by little decided to reject this claim. The dismissal in April 1907 of postal workers like Quilici and of teachers like Nègre showed a repressive vigour for which Clemenceau obtained from the Chamber – not without difficulty – a blank cheque (14 May 1907). But none of the three draft sets of regulations reached a public session and although the civil service unions were not recognized no text forbidding them was adopted; the electoral *clientèles* were against going so far. Did the radicals 'betray' the civil servants? What is most apparent is the divisions in the Bloc and the powerlessness of the State to resolve problems arising out of changes in its functions. The State could no longer present itself simply as the agent of the national will demanding unquestioning obedience from its servants. Having simply become the employer of a multitude of people, the frontiers of whose functions and positions it was difficult to define, it was a prey to all kinds of contradictions. The government could perfectly well show its authority when confronted with these contradictions but the nature of republican alliances did not allow it to resolve them. The machine went on working and no threat came in the short term from the civil servants. But here too it was clear that the Bloc had exhausted its strength.

The world is on the move

Deeply as fractures in society affected the history of the dissolution of the coalition of the left, the slow crisis which began in 1904 also developed in a different context. An important section of the radicals did in fact remain right to the end sensitive to the need for 'democracy' to remain united; they were ready to accept strikes and to come to some arrangement with the *CGT*, even for civil servants. The Tangier crisis, with the attitudes which it provoked in the principal leaders of French socialism and trade unionism, had to happen before the whole of the non-socialist political class began to grow worried and radicalism almost as a whole began to stand back.

The national consensus

Only somewhat dull echoes from the world outside reached Frenchmen's ears. Once the consequences of Fashoda had been dealt with, the government, apart from a few confused speeches when a new minister appeared before Parliament, kept profound silence on its foreign policy. From June 1898 to June 1905 this policy was directed by Théophile Delcassé. Delcassé, deputy for Ariège, whose policy aimed at isolating Germany and at developing colonial expansion, was reputed to have a taste for mystery, but the secrecy of the Quai d'Orsay was not only his doing. The agreements made with Italy in December 1900 and July 1902 remained unknown. It was the same in April 1904 with the clauses of the Entente Cordiale and on 8 October 1904 with the secret annex to the Franco-Spanish agreement which officially proclaimed the maintenance of the integrity of The Riff, Morocco. Both Chambers were content with this attitude. The manifestos of candidates in the elections of 1902 hardly mentioned these problems. Except for *Le Temps*, the *Débats* and from April 1904 *L'Humanité*, the press itself attached only minor importance to them. What was known of the Bloc's foreign policy was, at bottom, largely approved: 'In whatever direction we look we see beyond our frontiers only smiling, or at any rate peaceful, faces.'[11]

The Russian alliance alone aroused some disquiet, at any rate among the militant socialists, particularly Jaurès but also Vaillant. They were horrified at the anti-semitism responsible for the first pogroms of the century – at Kichinev in April 1903 – and also felt a permanent solidarity with the Russian revolutionaries who were victims of Tsarist repression. For his part, Jaurès was extremely upset by the *petit-bourgeois* vanity and the sterile hatred of Germany which he discerned even in the remarks of his friend Pelletan. So he thought that the Triple Alliance could act as a useful counterweight until the wide horizon of disarmament was reached.[12] Any criticism of the Franco-Russian alliance broke the national consensus, the 'sacred union' on foreign policy, the keystone of the régime. *Le Temps*, *Le Matin* and *Le Radical* all let Jaurès know this in no uncertain terms.

The Russian Revolution

The Russo-Japanese war and especially the Russian Revolution increased tension. After the Bloody Sunday of St Petersburg (9–22 January 1905) the contradiction between the solidarity of the workers and that of the ruling classes sprang to the surface. At the same time various different views began to take shape. Surely this unknown revolutionary Russia would be the standard-bearer of the hopes of a new age? Demonstrations, repression, strikes, armed insurrection: it was not very difficult for the sons of communards, for whom the annual climb to the 'mur des fédérés' was liable to become something of a reminder, to see their past again in these tragic events. And what about their future? 'It is on the banks of the Neva, the Vistula and the Volga', Anatole France declared on 16 December 1905, 'that the fate of the new Europe and of future humanity is being decided at this moment.' We do not know how deeply this feeling was rooted in the consciousness of the people. In any case, the Russian Revolution could be interpreted in many different ways: Jaurès saw it as the point of departure for a rapid victory of socialism via the path of 'European democracy', thanks to the collapse of the old empires. As for the workers on strike, it is not ridiculous to connect the new forms which their combative attitude took with the atmosphere of exaltation strengthened in them by the events on the Neva.

From Tangier to Stuttgart

However, the crisis of the left only attained its full scope under the threat of war. It was the diplomatic crisis publicly launched on 31 March 1905 by Wilhelm II's speech at Tangier and on 6 June by the enforced resignation of Delcassé that was to lead in two years to the isolation of socialism and revolutionary trade unionism. Analyses which until then did not affect decisive political choices were crystallized, so to speak, by the event and assumed a new meaning. Before 1905 anti-militarism had been essentially for internal, social use; it was aimed at the nationalists and at the intervention of the army in strikes; consequently it did not come into action in foreign policy. War remained an academic hypothesis. But now the situation had changed. The Bourges *bourse du travail* asked federated organizations to respond to a possible declaration of war 'by a general, revolutionary strike, that is, by revolution'. At the end of April 1905 Gustave Hervé launched – by very modern methods of publicity – 'anti-patriotism': if 'our country is our class', a military strike was the only response to war. By refusing to eject Hervé, though it did not for that reason welcome anti-patriotism, the young *SFIO* took the risk of being identified with him. After the socialist congress at Nancy and the international congress at Stuttgart in August 1907 (at which Jaurès assumed for the first time before the International his rôle of uniting all the socialist forces against war), how were the radicals going to react?

The disintegration of the Bloc

This was due to the convergence of all the factors discussed above.

The political crisis opens on the right

From January 1904 to January 1905 there was hesitation on the Bloc's right wing, where there were signs of a coalition between the Democratic Alliance and a certain number of radicals, the 'dissidents'. Their objectives were to consolidate the influence of that section of the world of business which had endorsed the anti-clerical campaign; and to reduce the socialists explicitly to the rôle of support force. They wanted to prevent the socialists from appearing as the spokesmen of the social strata in conflict and, at the same time, as participants on an equal footing in the political institutions of the bourgeois Republic. To accomplish this purpose it was essential to eliminate Combes, whose ministry posited, in the country as a whole, a non-aggression pact with the socialists and, in the Chamber, the discipline of the Bloc. The movement took shape but was not confined to the Palais-Bourbon. Yet it was there that the intrigues were conducted. One can take the year 1904 as a typical year in which to study parliamentary activities during the Belle Epoque, precisely where they took place and the equivocal language in which they were expressed.

Parliamentary power lay first of all in the committees where serious questions – those concerned with money – were discussed. The radical Paul Doumer, former governor-general of Indo-China, chaired the budget committee from where in March 1904 the great attack on Pelletan, the Navy Minister, was mounted. Pelletan, a left-wing radical-socialist, was accused among other things of slowing up the execution of orders for the fleet. Less central, but scarcely less important and indeed more explicitly tied up with big business, was the Public Works Committee, chaired by another radical, Guyot-Dessaigne, deputy for Puy-de-Dôme and former Minister of Public Works. He also chaired the committee on the army. Whether this was effect or cause, he developed in a direction very hostile to the socialists. The Committee on Foreign Affairs, Protectorates and Colonies was chaired by Etienne. The deputy for Oran, elected unopposed, the leader of the 'colonial party', was one of the founders of the Democratic Alliance. Closely tied to Rouvier, he chaired a committee whose operations were particularly effective. Finally at Social Security was Millerand, ejected in January 1904 from the Seine federation of the *PSF*. It is not surprising to find these men in the front rank of those who intervened, in 1904 and at the beginning of 1905, to destroy the equilibrium of the Bloc.

After the committees came the parliamentary groups. It was in these that tactics were decided and candidates provided for important jobs, the presidency of the Chamber in particular. On 12 January 1904 Henri Brisson was only just re-elected to this post, and Jaurès, the outgoing vice-president, was beaten in favour of a radical, Gerville-Réache. His defeat heralded the end of the Bloc's discipline. It was irreversible; and the executive committee of the radical party, which met on 27 January, decided to say no more about it. Socialism was thus excluded from an official institution, the presidency of the Chamber. Splits and realignments then began in the parliamentary groups; to keep the Bloc in existence, the radical-socialist left separated from the radical-socialist group and a year later the democratic left parted company with the Democratic Union. Amid all these deceptive nouns and adjectives, who could tell who was precisely who?

The list of dissidents gradually grew longer. The socialists were accused, apropos of a manual of history by Gustave Hervé, of lack of patriotism about the colonies; Combes was reproached with the lack of social reforms and, at the time of the record card affair (October 1904), of listening to informers. Events gathered pace at the beginning of 1905. On 10 January Doumer was elected president of the Chamber against Brisson by 265 votes to 240; he was not expelled from the radical party until July 1905. On 18 January Combes, whose majority had been continually eroded, offered the resignation of his cabinet to the President of the Republic; the dissidents had triumphed. But this could hardly be admitted since in the country as a whole there was no majority yet for a change of government. The Separation law had not been passed, the socialists were not united, and the social and international crisis had not really started. Consequently the Rouvier government which appeared before the Chamber on 27 January was headed by a former minister of Combes and gave no place to progressivists or open dissidents from the Bloc. However, although the property owners felt reassured by the arrival in the prime minister's office of Maurice Rouvier, whose hostility to an income tax was well known, his appeals for a majority – enlarged, if possible – and even for national concord in order to implement the Separation sounded strange not only to the socialists but to many radical-socialists; 154 of them refused to give a vote of confidence to the new ministry or else abstained, and out of the 373 votes that the government collected half came from the former right and dissident radicals. In parliament the Bloc was dead.

The creation of the SFIO, April 1905

Socialist unity, achieved a few months later, reinforced an already existing rupture. The road to a 'second unity' among the various political organizations claiming to be socialist – the Socialist Party of France, the French Socialist Party, the Revolutionary Socialist Workers' Party and various autonomous federations – had been opened in August 1904, at the request of the Socialist International, assembled in congress at Amsterdam. The tactics of Jaurès had been condemned at this congress. A few weeks of reflection convinced him that socialist unity had become a priority, even if this involved opposing part of his own party. Besides parliamentary events – and apart from his personal friendships – everything led him to take this course. In his own party, which was reduced to some 8,000 members and was cut off from the most combative strata of the proletariat, some young militants – Jean Longuet, Pierre Renaudel, Louis Révelin – wanted to get out of the radical-socialist marsh; above all, new times were coming with the increase in strikes and the anti-militarist movement, just when, from Manchuria to Moscow and Morocco, the danger of war and the prospect of revolution, which had loomed vaguely in the last few years, were becoming more real.

At the suggestion of the *PS de F*, from November 1904 a unification committee started to draft a declaration of unity on which agreement was reached at the summit on 13 January 1905, three days after the election of Doumer to the presidency of the Chamber. At the unification congress which was held in Paris at the Salle du Globe from 23 to 26 April 1905 the declaration became the charter of the unified party. From the point of view of the alliance with the radicals the essential element lay in the assertion, henceforth statutory, according to which 'the budget as a whole' had to be rejected by the unified parliamentary group. The formulas employed did not forbid deputies to vote with, or even for, the radicals, but they eliminated not only the participation of a socialist in a 'bourgeois' government but also structural and stable alliances. Thus the unified deputies left the Délégation des Gauches, as Jaurès had already done in February 1905.

What did the socialist base think of the Bloc? At the first congress of the unified party, which was held at Chalon-sur-Saône from 29 October to 1 November 1905, it became clear that the socialists' predominant concern was not only to make themselves into a clearly separated political force but also to have themselves recognized as one: the congress passed by a large majority the motion tabled by Cambier, which obliged party federations to put forward candidates everywhere at the next parliamentary elections. The congress left the federations free to make their own choices at the second round 'in the interests of the proletariat and the socialist Republic'. This meant, although it was not stated explicitly, keeping the path of 'republican discipline' open: at the first round one made a choice, at the second round one eliminated. Thus all that remained of the Bloc was a useful electoral practice, but one powerless to inspire a positive policy.

The electoral victory of the radicals: May 1906

However, the election to the presidency of the Republic on 17 January 1906 showed clearly that, even at the first round, the left remained capable of acting together provided that the person concerned was a reassuring one. What could be more reassuring than a senator, and of all senators the president of the Senate, charged with the responsibility of taming the turbulent towns with the rustic wisdom of the communes of France? Armand Fallières, senator for Lot-et-Garonne, was thus elected President of France by 449 votes to the 371 cast for the President of the Chamber, Paul Doumer. Three and a half months later the elections of 6 and 20 May showed that good republicans still did well. The right, which hoped to reverse the trend, put forward in most cases one single candidate in each constituency. On the left, on the other hand, division reigned; the Democratic Alliance had pronounced an anathema on the socialists.

A sign of the strong polarization of opinion was the fact that abstentions were only 20.1 per cent – even fewer than in 1902 – and 427 candidates knew their fate after the first round. And a sign of the fairly general maintenance of the electoral bloc in the country was the fact that usually republican discipline had played its part. Finally, a sign of the apparent reinforcement of the majority of 1902 was the fact that it obtained 420 seats. In thirty-two departments it held all the seats. The right was crushed and lost about sixty seats. Even by votes it had shrunk considerably in the Massif Central, though perceptibly less in the Midi. The old right was dying in its western fiefs; the new republican notables of the towns had extended their influence widely enough over the countryside to win a decisive victory over the people from the châteaux and the Church. As for the new rightist groups, they were scarcely formed or too unstable. On the left, the advance benefited all parties: the *SFIO*, which, with fifty-nine seats, returned to the Chamber stronger than the separate parties of 1902 in spite of the 'haemorrhage' caused by the appearance of the 'independent socialists' (Rhône, Loire, Parisian region); the Democratic Alliance; and even more the radicals. It was becoming feasible for the parliamentary groups representing these two last trends to form a 'governing majority' without socialist support and without the co-operation of the right. It was what is called the victory of the radical and radical-socialist party, which would never again have 250 deputies. It seemed as if the era of the Bloc was going to be succeeded by that of radical hegemony supported by the Democratic Alliance.

But what kind of radicalism was it to be? The party still only existed in its

600 to 800 cantonal committees, which were allowed almost total autonomy by the departmental federations, only about ten of which had a real
existence. Southern radicalism, the most 'advanced' sort, had begun to
grow short of breath: in Haute-Garonne, out of seven outgoing deputies
only two – as opposed to six in 1902 – had won at the first round, and the
Action Libérale had taken the seat at Villefranche. In Paris the radicals,
with few exceptions, only appeared on a vigorously 'anti-collectivist' and –
as demanded by the powerful Committee for the Provisioning of Paris –
anti-trade-union platform. On the Côte d'Or, the outgoing socialist
deputy, Bouhey-Allex, although a very moderate and popular man, had
been beaten by a rich radical brewer called Messner, president of the Dijon
Chamber of Commerce and vigorously supported by the Republican
Committee for Commerce and Industry. While losing some radical-
socialist votes, he had received sufficient assistance in the way of votes from
the right. The nucleus of radical-socialists after the style of Pelletan or
Ferdinand Buisson had diminished. The nebulous cluster of voters for
whom the order of the day was 'an understanding between the radical-
socialists, the radicals and the republicans', that is, 'keep out the socialists',
had expanded. The Republican Committee for Commerce and Industry
became this cluster's nucleus.

Thus the elections of 1906, which saw the victory of radicalism, also
constituted a fresh stage on the road to the disintegration of the Bloc in the
country.

The Clemenceau government

However, the triumphal election of old Brisson to the presidency of
the Chamber when Parliament met again seemed like a return to a past that
people had regarded as gone forever. It was only an act of homage. The
Sarrien government, formed on 14 March 1906 in the middle of the
Inventory crisis, continued. Headed by a provincial radical whose only
virtue was his political flair, the cabinet found its strong men in the
well-known leaders of the Democratic Alliance: Poincaré at Finance,
Etienne at War, Thomson at the Navy, Barthou at Public Works and
Leygues at Colonies. As Minister of the Interior, Clemenceau had prepared and won the elections. However, it was clear that the composition of
the government did not correspond to the radical upsurge revealed by the
elections. Sarrien's resignation and the arrival in power of Clemenceau, on
25 October 1906, would, so people thought, rectify the situation.

The former mayor of Montmartre, the tumbler of opportunist governments, the swashbuckler, the redoubtable and redoubted journalist and
orator, was sixty-five. The last great man of the radical old guard, a
republican under the Empire, the atheist doctor whose few – and exceptional – friends were Gustave Geffroy, founder of the Académie Goncourt,

and Claude Monet, had never tasted the joys of power until March 1906. Eliminated from the Chamber after Panama as a *panamiste* and lackey of England, he had left parliament just when the radicals of his generation – Lockroy, Brisson, Bourgeois – were accepting official honours. And he had only returned in 1902, rehabilitated by the Dreyfus affair, elected once again by 'Red' Var, but this time as a senator: Senator Clemenceau . . . The Senate was only a spring-board; mainstream radicalism in fact lacked men: Herriot had only just been elected mayor of Lyon. Clemenceau did not believe in the radical party, and in any case wanted no part of it: he never minded giving it a rap on the nose and never set foot in the executive committee. What need was there to be interested in the party in order to represent radicalism? For a new Chamber, a new old man. It was true that, as Minister of the Interior, he had just sent in the troops to the pitheads of Nord and on the eve of 1 May he had shown that he was a good manufacturer of plots of all kinds. It was also true that in the summer of 1906 he asserted the necessity of mixing 'reform and conservation' in the right doses when one governed, but in days gone by he had flirted with the anarchists, he had fought the 'wicked' laws and he was an individualist who wanted to be 'social' if not socialist. And when in June 1906 the theoretical debate between socialists and radicals had begun before an astonished and fascinated Chamber, it was Clemenceau who, still young in spirit, had answered Jaurès, matching 'utopia' with 'realism', society which must be transformed with man who must be transformed, and collectivism with individualism. Thus when Sarrien recommended Fallières to ask Clemenceau to replace him, Jaurès arrived at the same choice in *L'Humanité*: it was time, he said, for the 'leader' of the radical-socialist majority to come into power; he could 'implement his programme' and then it would be seen that socialism was the necessary sequel to it. After radicalism, socialism; a break, perhaps, or better still, as Jaurès hoped, the possibility of continuity.

So the new government's declaration in the Chamber in favour of 'a dignified peace' and of the inauguration of 'a democracy in the government' won it 376 votes; the whole socialist group abstained – a way of giving the new ministry a little credit. The government was indubitably more radical – it had seven radical ministers, among them Stephen Pichon, a personal friend of Clemenceau, at Foreign Affairs, and three radical secretaries of state, including the spirited Albert Sarraut, who brought with him the support of his brother Maurice and hence that of the powerful *Dépêche*. There were fewer stars from the democratic Alliance and it was a more 'social' cabinet than Sarrien's. The young Viviani, who had quietly quitted the permanent administrative committee of the *SFIO* and whom Clemenceau regarded as 'a sort of Millerand with ideals into the bargain', went to the new ministry of Labour and Social Security. The new minister called on the staff of his department to show the workers 'a visible prejudice in favour of cordiality and sympathy' (*La République française*, 21 October 1906). However, class conflicts were very soon to win the day.

Clemenceau's mode of administration was going to produce a hate-filled rupture between the radical government and the working-class, the most progressive civil servants and the vine-growers of the Midi. He did this first by employing troops systematically, either to replace absent technicians by military engineers (during the electricians' strike in Paris in March 1907) or more often 'to maintain order'. It was only rarely at that time that there were no deaths: the assassinations of workers culminated at Draveil (2 June 1908) in two dead and ten wounded and, at the launching of the same long building strike, at Villeneuve-Saint-Georges (30 July 1908) in four dead and hundreds of wounded.[13] Radicalism in power also turned against the new ringleaders. It arrested the trade union leaders, even socialist leaders, whatever their direct responsibility in the current struggles: Docteur Ferroul at Narbonne, and after Villeneuve-Saint-Georges almost all the leaders of the *CGT*. At the very least it launched numerous prosecutions against them, which resulted in fines and heavy prison sentences. In the case of the postal workers and teachers, people from another world, fortunate in their security, Clemenceau used often massive dismissals. Does power turn people mad? 'There is nothing more unfortunate than being the strongest', he was to write later, 'but this ill fortune is not without its pleasure.'[14] Saviour of the order threatened by the workers' movement, he likened himself now to the general at his look-out post: 'You are behind a barricade, I'm in front of it.' But the characteristic peculiar to Clemenceau in this lasting breach of confidence and in the mess he made of what many socialists hoped would be a harmonious effort resided in his delight in police work. From Marcellin Albert to Lucien Métivier, no one understood better than he how to develop an atmosphere of secret intrigue, how to discredit men, how to make people think they were being spied on, so that he could have more room to manoeuvre. He treated the wage-earners' battlefield like the Palais-Bourbon or some little anarchist group.

It can be imagined that no one provoked more hatred among the left than he. It was not only the leaders of the *CGT* who described the Clemenceau ministry on posters as 'a government of assassins'. He was called 'dictator', 'the best policeman in France' and soon became 'the red beast', 'the emperor of the informers'. From the beginning of 1907 to the autumn of 1908 there was hardly a socialist or anarchist group or trade union in which motions were not passed denigrating him and rejoicing in his imminent hanging: the guillotine, the creation of the Revolution, would be too honourable. It is true that it is a long step from words to actions and that no one tried to assassinate him, but when speeches attain this degree of continuity, generality and violence can their content be regarded as mere rhetoric? In a satirical paper as widely read as *L'Assiette au beurre* the drawings of Poncet and Grandjouan denounced for the first time in 1907 the official collusion between the police – a traditional object of attack – and the government. A new picture of the leader of the radical party emerged; he became the doctor with a death's head and big hands dripping with blood which caused *Marianne* to abort: 'Certainly you're pregnant with a new society, but you'll abort! I'm known for that!' (*L'Assiette au beurre*, August 1907).

Clemenceau was not the only one concerned. As a matter of fact, in May 1907 he was among those who were opposed to the dissolution of the *CGT* desired and even demanded by numerous radicals.[15] He was to renew his opposition after Villeneuve-Saint-Georges. Even the strikes were not the only point at issue. The poster 'Government of assassins' appeared in February 1908 and the prosecutions which it provoked were undertaken because it denounced the Moroccan massacres. When Gustave Hervé, the impetuous editor of a weekly with a reputation for hot-headedness, *La Guerre sociale*, had been sentenced on 24 December 1907 to a year in prison and a fine of 3,000 francs he owed his conviction to his attacks on 'Moroccan brigandage'. Jaurès only began to provoke hatred when, after the congresses of Nancy and Stuttgart, he appeared as the man who was betting on the strength of the workers to stop France's 'policy of conquest and pillage'. On these occasions the radicals, who were sometimes divided when it was a question of prosecuting the ringleaders of strikes, united almost completely. Henry Bérenger's *Action* was worried at the beginning of 1907 about the arrests of trade unionists; after Stuttgart it sharply denounced the choices of Jaurès, who was regarded as having given his allegiance to Hervé. *La Dépêche de Toulouse* itself expressed its grave disquiet. On the eve of the radical party congress (10–13 October 1907) the party bulletin published a series of individual points of view about Stuttgart. There were few who could speak with as much sang-froid as Buisson, Lafferre and Pelletan of their differences with the collectivists: familiarity with schoolmasters and freemasonry, and the traditions of '48 were still good guardrails. Among the others excitement bordered on delirium. The congress was to close with a pathetic affirmation, the conclusion of which it is worth quoting: 'we ask you, citizens, by all you hold sacred, to swear to combat the propagandists of anti-patriotism all round you... We are a party of reform, a party of the people; circumstances have compelled us to say that we are also a party of Frenchmen.'

Separation had marked the end of a common struggle. The anti-clerical policy had conformed to the wishes of various different social strata with their contradictory interests. It had been accepted and often positively desired by millions of men the majority of whom married in church and had their children baptized. It had responded to the aspiration towards 'reason' which had spread across a vast network of speculative societies and educational associations. There was scarcely a village, however far from Paris and Parliament, which had not opposed the Church. It was also in the name of the undisputed rights of reason that anti-militarism and the questioning of the privileges attached to the notion of *la patrie* had been able, during the first few years of the century, to find acceptance, even encouragement, from many radicals. The case of Gustave Hervé in Yonne can be regarded as typical: emerging from radicalism, this 'commercial traveller in socialism', a representative, in the eyes of the State apparatus, of extremist ideas, spoke the same language as the radical chemists, teachers, printers and peasants of his department. An anti-militarist journal intended for school-leavers, *Le Pioupiou de l'Yonne*, was prosecuted several times at the assizes and acquitted every time by the jury. Jaurès himself came to accept the discussion of the idea of *la patrie* like that of any other concept: there was no longer any Church and the light of reason was that of the whole people; nothing should escape their notice. Seen from this point of view, Combism, whose inferior aspects are quite obvious, becomes a widely assumed intellectual attitude avoided really only by those whose lives were sustained by the Catholicism of the time, or even – still – by certain socialists who professed Marxism.

Three years later a new page was turned. The alliance of various strata of the bourgeoisie with the political forces representing the working class did not survive the retreat of the religious orders and the Separation. If the traditional right was crumbling, it was not because its electors had gone over to the left but because the objectives it had shared in a period of prosperity with a large section of the old left were, so to speak, attained. This movement occurred at a time when the social conflicts bound up with the rapid development of industrial society were becoming worse and when international contradictions of a new dimension were beginning to appear. This time the Republic of Ferry had been outstripped. New conflicts that had been forming slowly were emerging. But amid what confusion!

10

The days of imperialism

Until now we have looked at the first few years of the twentieth century from an essentially political point of view. We have weighed the start of working-class struggles in the scales of the Bloc des Gauches. In doing so we were reading the history of majority opinion and its passions. It is possible to attempt another reading of the period which opened about 1898 but fully assumed its new characteristics only from 1905 onwards. That was the time when France achieved decisive access to the happy days of growth. For the moment we shall not note the results either in absolute terms or as a percentage; this will be done when the balance sheet is drawn up, in 1914. But we must examine now the ways in which profits were made and the mentalities which they reveal or conceal. In fact during the same years the foreign policy of France took a sharp turn, and colonial expansion, restarted with difficulty in Morocco, coloured in a new fashion what it is the custom to call the development of the empire. The liquidation of the Bloc des Gauches, which coincided with these events of world importance behind which loomed fatal rivalry and approaching war, ended in visible decay. At the same time, in those sections of the bourgeoisie which were traditionally the standard-bearers of the scientific approach and intellectual austerity, the cultural crisis which had begun fifteen to twenty years earlier grew worse. The situation outlined by these different phenomena is sufficiently special to justify treating it as a whole. When we use the expression 'the days of imperialism' we do not mean to imply that it automatically reveals chains of causality but simply that it designates what will come to appear the essential element.

The formation and investment of captial

If we admit the value of Marxist analyses of imperialism as first formulated at the beginning of the twentieth century – not in France but particularly in Austria around the pioneering Hilferding (*Das Finanzkapital*, Vienna, 1910) and in Germany around Rosa Luxemburg – it will be appropriate to enquire first about the conditions under which capital developed. Some recent works make it possible to see a little more clearly into the process.

Industrial capital and financial capital

In 1906,[1] nearly half the workers, 49.2 per cent, were still employed in establishments of less than five wage-earning workers. The very small enterprise continued to dominate France and its decline, though perceptible, was small in comparison with Germany or England. Dispersal also characterized some new industries: according to J. Tchernoff (*Les Ententes économiques et financières*, 1933), there were 2,380 companies producing electricity, and electricity provided a revival of activity for precision engineering, for example. At the other end of the scale the big firms were developing. Firms with more than 500 workers employed 10.8 per cent of the wage-earning labour force. Among such firms were the railway companies, the Lorraine iron and steel industry – in particular the Société des Aciéries de Longwy and the Forges et Aciéries de la Marine et Homécourt – Schneider, Forges et Camargue, Saint-Gobain, Rhône-Pulenc, Air Liquide, and so on. Even here there were no real giants; the dominant trend was for middle-sized companies. The case of the coal-mining companies was both typical and special; special, because it was the State which, since the decrees of 1852–4, forbade them to merge; and typical, because here as elsewhere – even if it was truer here than elsewhere – concentration was weak and because this did not necessarily put a brake on profits. Let us take one example: the Société de Courrières (Pas-de-Calais), which was not among the biggest, made a profit of 5.4 million in 1899 and 7.3 million in 1913; the shareholders were highly delighted.

It is a fact that employers and the State took more interest than has been suggested in the progress of firms. The number of engineers trained at the *Polytechnique*, the *Centrale*, the *Mines* and the School of Naval Engineering rose from an average of 292 a year between 1895 and 1899 to 351 between 1910 and 1914. Alongside the technical education organized by the State existed that given by schools run by industrial firms or chambers of commerce. Above all, the independence of the firms did not prevent the formation of cartels. But this took different forms: it was temporary for the cotton mills of Nord – the cartel was cancelled as soon as there was another good year – but more far-reaching for the coal mines. However, although commercial integration, intended to improve the competitiveness of Nord and Pas-de-Calais on the national market, was pushed quite far – the fixing of minimum tariffs, sharing-out of tonnages to be sold – the opposition of the middle-sized companies, anxious to preserve their autonomy, prevented all apportionment of production quotas. The agreement concluded in July 1901 resulted in the creation of the Entente des Houillères du Nord et du Pas-de-Calais, thanks to the tact of the head of one of the biggest companies, that of Lens. As for the Central Committee of the Coal Mines of France, which dated from 1892, it devoted itself mainly to obtaining from the authorities the legislation that best suited the interests of the employers. Such also was the rôle of the powerful Comité des Forges directed by R. Pinot, on whose board H. Darcy, the president of the Coal Mines Committee, also sat, but its hold over the iron and steel firms belonging to it was much greater. These firms did not hesitate to take part in international agreements to share out the world market.[2] Whether strongly concentrated like the iron and steel firms, or weakly concentrated like the coal mines, all these firms achieved their highest profits in 1911–14 and often in 1913–14.

French firms also wanted to preserve their independence of the banks. A company as powerful as Schneider chose, for more security, to retain its status as a limited partnership. One solution was for the firm to finance itself. Of course, to secure a high level of financing it was necessary to distribute to the shareholders – most companies were in fact joint-stock companies – only a modest share of the profits: the structural weaknesses behind the brilliant façade of the Charbonnages du Nord were partly explained by the considerable volume of profits paid out to ever more numerous shareholders.[3] But the huge size of the profits often made it possible to satisfy both the shareholders and the needs of the firm. Out of 2,250 milliards invested on average every year from 1900 to 1913, 71 per cent came from the surplus accumulated by the firm and reinvested. This extremely high percentage recurs in all branches of industry and in firms of all sizes (Biblio. no. 214). Only 29 per cent of investment was financed from outside, by shares or debentures underwritten by the banks. This major fact spotlights the independence maintained by industrial capital in relation to banking capital and consequently the slow rate at which the merger into 'financial capital' took place.

Since 1870 in fact, the big joint-stock banks – the Crédit Lyonnais, the Comptoir National d'Escompte de Paris, the Société Générale and the Group du Crédit Industriel et Commercial – had withdrawn one after the other from industrial investment. There was neither participation and control nor – or only very exceptionally – middle-term loans. 'Industrial firms . . . even the most wisely run ones, involve risks . . . incompatible with the security indispensable in the employment of the funds of a joint-stock bank': this pronouncement by Henri Germain, the head of the Crédit Lyonnais, a few months before his death in 1905, was widely accepted and obeyed. Obviously it was not the same with the national merchant banks formed as a result of the exigencies of economic growth: examples of these were the Banque de Paris et des Pays-Bas, familiarly known as 'the Paribas', founded in 1872 and the oldest of these banks; the Banque Française pour le Commerce et l'Industrie, created by Rouvier in 1901; the Banque de l'Union Parisienne ('Parunion') which Schneider very quickly got his hands on when it was formed in 1904. As for the regional banks, they were often limited partnerships and boldly financed the Lorraine iron and steel industry – Société Nancienne – the industries connected with Hydro-electric power – Banque Charpenay at Grenoble – and the various industries of Nord – Crédit du Nord. But almost always, far from controlling industrial enterprises, they were at their service; such was the case with Parunion for Schneider and with the regional banks. French industry remained master of its own fate. Thus in relation to the Marxist analysis, which was labelled as 'financial capital' the merger between industrial capital and banking capital, French industry 'lagged behind'.

Banking capital and investments

The banks themselves also functioned as businesses. Their aim, too, was to make the highest possible and surest profits; and they succeeded in doing this. J. Bouvier, F. Furet and M. Gillet, in their study of the movement of profits in France in the nineteenth century (Biblio. no. 214), have looked at banks as well as at coal mines and iron and steel firms, and they have been able to show that at the beginning of this century the profits of the banks followed the same rhythm as those of other businesses, naturally with some inequalities.[4] The capital they assembled formed a real economic striking force. In 1913 the Crédit Lyonnais alone had over 2,000 million francs on deposit. The four biggest credit establishments together held a total of 5.6 thousand million. To that must be added 2.87 thousand million assembled in ninety-three other banks and the deposits of the Banque de France and the Crédit Foncier: altogether 9.3 thousand million. At the beginning of the century these establishments considerably developed their networks of branches, sub-agencies and offices. There were 860 of them in 1907; in 1917 there were to be 1,280.[5] They penetrated calm sub-prefectures where the regional banks were sometimes their active competitors. Their vocation or their function was 'to bring to light and gather in all the unemployed capital, even the smallest sums, to pay interest on it and then apply it, especially for discount, to the needs of commerce and industry'.[6] Lawyers, duly given a financial interest, served as intermediaries, well acquainted as they were with rural people who would hesitate before a bank that was strange because it was Parisian. An extremely dense network covered France at that time and gathered in the money which until then had lain in woollen stockings or had served 'la terre' – a myth, but also a reality. All round, in spite of the proportion of savings which still went to the lawyers, the postal savings banks or the agricultural savings banks, the lion's share was now syphoned off by a powerful banking system, the organization of which was doubtless more advanced than that of industry. It has proved possible to show that in Phase A[7] a certain de-concentration took place, to the detriment of the big credit establishments and the local banks, and to the profit of the regional banks. However neither this tendency to a certain decentralization nor the division of work nor again the institutional differences between types of banks could obscure the formation and development of stable banking groups or of syndicates organized for a particular financial operation.

Where was this huge mass of capital invested? The theses of J. Thobie and R. Girault and the works of R. Poidevin and R. Cameron answer this question. All these writers confirm the size of the exports of capital, which started well before the end of the nineteenth century but accelerated considerably from 1898 onwards: it was then that France began to practise imperialism, particularly in this domain. During the course of fifteen years more than a quarter of the capital exported went off to Russia, France's privileged ally and first customer: 12,000 million out of a total of 45,000 million. Turkey, which was not bound to France by any military alliance but had come to treat France as her principal supplier, received 7 per cent. The revolution of 1908, which was successful, at any rate temporarily, did not disturb the system of dependence to which Turkey had been reduced any more than the Russian revolution of 1905, at the end of which the Tsar retained power, fundamentally changed relations between Russia and France.

The sums exported, which came mainly from the rich bourgeoisie, served two principal purposes: public state loans (originally particularly lucrative pieces of business, either in the form of long-term loans or to permit the servicing of the national debt), and direct private investment. The former were undeniably parasitical. But the share of public investments which financed industrial enterprises abroad, for a long time fairly slender, went on increasing when growth became established in France. In 1914 it amounted to 21.9 per cent of the funds placed in Turkey and 19 per cent of those that went to the Empire of the Tsars. The industrial investments in Russia were channelled – 65 per cent of them – into the heavy iron and steel industry, the mines and oil, all industries vital to the economic future of the country. The revenue from them was very unlikely to be affected by transitory fluctuations of fashion. On the eve of the Great War the armaments business was becoming increasingly more important. The very big French firms involved thus found, especially from 1906,[8] a means of establishing a solid link between industrial capital and banking capital. They no doubt thought that it was in their interests – and it was the same in Austria–Hungary and the Balkans – to set up branches of their firms rather than export merchandise made in the mother country by French workers always liable – who can ever know? – to join a trade union and demand increases in their wages. Thus exports of French merchandise to those countries where 'France' had massive investments were low – less than 5 per cent of the goods which these countries imported. However, one cannot draw from this fact pessimistic conclusions about the dynamism of French capitalism. Banking capital and industrial capital were here in agreement, not in order to provide external outlets for national industry, but to procure the means of most effectively exploiting the countries where they invested.

There remained those not invited to the party, who could smell big profits being made, particularly the middle-sized firms which had been unable to find a place in the big consortia. They are to be heard whimpering and asking more and more firmly that money should only be invested abroad in return for firm commitments from the country requesting the money: orders for material, and so on. There was the need to overcome foreign competition as well. This business was becoming a State affair; so the State must intervene actively.[9] The French government did not lack means; the most frequently employed was the authorization or refusal to have a foreign loan quoted on the Paris Bourse.[10] But when the assurances demanded concerned a weak country and not a powerful ally, or one supposed to be powerful, diplomatic pressure or even a naval show of strength could be useful. But the government still had to make up its mind to use these methods.

In all this there were numerous contradictions connected with the complex interplay between diplomacy and business, with the personal financial choices of this or that minister and with the unequal development of national capitalism. Finally, state interventions did not aim only at securing orders. It is in Turkey from 1905 that J. Thobie believes this 'common front' functioned best, a common front of finance, industry and diplomacy, the industrialist being assured by agreement of obtaining the desired orders. It was there no doubt that the most classical interpenetration of banking capital and industrial capital was achieved. Exports of French goods to Turkey represented over 9 per cent of that country's total imports – a much higher percentage than for Russia.

Turkey, Russia: in spite of some differences the general line was fundamentally the same. Exports of capital played a much more important rôle in the genesis of French financial capital than the exchanges between industrial capital and banking capital on the national market. The State was led to intervene in many ways in this process. This interpenetration is one component of imperialism.

The colonial empire

The concept of imperialism, when taken in the sense given to it at the beginning of the century by Marxist theorists, is not contained within the narrow meaning that others, who only employed it in conjunction with the adjective 'colonial', were beginning to attribute to it. One can even say today that the adjective was in part incongruous, but only in part.

The colonies and the national economy

In fact in 1914 the French colonial empire – 10.6 million square kilometres; 55.5 million inhabitants – was responsible for only 12 per cent of the trade of the mother country, exports being rather greater than imports. Algeria and, far behind, Tunisia, Indo-China and the recently conquered Morocco were at the head of the list. Nor was the empire an Eden for the export of capital: less than 9 per cent of all the French capital exported ended up in the colonies. And although the total of French investments had quadrupled in ten years, the empire's share on the eve of the Great War was scarcely larger than that of Turkey and smaller than that of Latin America. Between 1898 and 1914 the empire did not generally function either as somewhere to invest capital at a great profit or as somewhere to sell goods.

It continued to be consolidated thanks to the effecting of a number of territorial – that is, military – links, the effectiveness of which depended on the diplomatic contacts of the forces involved and on the size of the compromises that could be discussed with the other major colonial powers. Marchand had to evacuate Fashoda to the advantage of the British (November 1898), but the three expeditionary columns that had set out from the Sahara, the Congo and the Sudan were able to join forces in Tchad after destroying the empire of Rabah in April 1900. People were to talk for a long time, but more in Africa than in France, of the crimes committed *en route* by the men of the Voulet-Chanoine mission.[11] Thus the junction between Africa of the southern Sahara and Maghreb Africa was achieved.

Towards 1900 colonial expansion became generally acceptable to public opinion. The violent campaigns of the 1880s had subsided: the 'colonial party' had won. However, acceptance did not mean enthusiasm. Did the hum of parliamentary talk about the colonies really reveal, as the radical Gaston Doumergue said it did, 'benevolent indifference'? In any case it came to a head over Algeria which was officially regarded as an extension of metropolitan France. The colonists, especially the lobby led by Eugène Etienne, strove above all to avoid any innovation favourable to the native population. They succeeded easily in this aim and the long proconsulate (1895–1911) of Jonnart, the friend of Waldeck-Rousseau, was punctuated only by empty rhetoric. The question of money made the difference all the more profound. Most French members of parliament were haunted by the idea of an increase in the budget. Colonies, all right, but no money for the colonies. They had to find from their own funds the resources necessary for their domination by France and for their development.

Colonial affairs

This left the door wide open to private exploitation and to 'colonial business'. Since the State could not abandon all its interest in territories where it kept troops, territories whose exotic tints suffused a whole range of literature, the political class was to find itself closely involved in this exploitation. In the time of Waldeck-Rousseau and during the happy days of Combism, official silence on colonization was accompanied by a vague symbiosis between numerous deputies and colonial affairs. Little by little radicalism began to get a grip on the management of the colonies. In spite of sharp competition this grip was tightened after the fall of Clemenceau (July 1909) by the arrival in parliament of new men who generally sat with the radical left. If we wish to understand the profound changes that affected radicalism between 1899 and 1914 we ought to examine the links which radicals influential in the political machine established with the economic development and administrative management of the colonies. But the evidence necessary for such an examination has not yet been assembled and we shall therefore have to limit ourselves to the mere outline, an inventory of names, conscious though we are how unsatisfactory from a historical point of view such a 'method' is.

Here, then, are some of the men to whom people like Etienne and Thomson – 'the phosphate man', as the deputy for Constantine was called – had to give way. There was Albert Sarraut, brother to Maurice who ran the powerful *Dépêche*, deputy for Aude where he was re-elected in 1910 against the socialist Ferroul, Under-Secretary of State in Clemenceau's cabinet, Governor-General of Indo-China from 1911 to 1914. There was Léon Mougeot, whose career was typical. As the young deputy for Haute-Marne at the time of the conquest of Madagascar, he was the bitter opponent of the Compagnie Occidentale de Madagascar, nicknamed the 'Suberbie'. He was Secretary of State at the Post Office in the governments of Brisson, Dupuy and Waldeck-Rousseau (1898–1902), he was Minister of Agriculture under Combes and then became a senator. A very rich colonial landowner, he was called 'le seigneur Mougeot' in Tunisia. In 1913 he held, among other jobs, the chairmanship of 'Suberbie', in which post he displayed a meritorious keenness to save it from the difficulties in which it had become bogged down.[12] And there was Justin Perchot: a rich building contractor much involved in public works, in 1909 he acquired *Le Radical* and became deputy, then senator for Basses-Alpes. He was one of the big powers in the party; he had important interests almost everywhere, but especially in Indo-China and Morocco. These men are only the ones most in the public eye. We shall meet others in connection with this or that affair.

We ought to have begun with Paul Doumer.[13] After all, he remained a radical until 1905 and his elimination was not due to his colonial work but, as we saw, to his candidature against Brisson for the presidency of the

Chamber. The name of this future President of the Republic, undeniably a son of the people, protected by Hanotaux, without any political convictions at all, is closely associated with Indo-China. His aims there were partly, but only partly, in harmony with the unexpressed wish of the Chamber: not a sou for the colonies. Partly, because during his years in the Far East (1897–1902) he succeeded in installing a coherent state apparatus financed 'without pain'[14] by new indirect taxes, in particular by the excise duties he imposed on salt, opium and rice alcohol. But only partly, because his great project for a railway in Yunnan, the prelude to an annexation which was never to take place, raised some concern for diplomatic, financial and technical reasons. In June 1901 Doumer finished by winning the game: he forced on Parliament, out of context, an agreement extraordinarily favourable to the four banks which were going to finance the project. The passion for power and greatness was associated on this occasion not so much with the wishes of the banks as with the interests of the iron and steel industry. The study made by M. Brugière of the Doumer offensive demonstrates some of its mechanisms, which were typical of this kind of operation: formation of a pressure group – the Comité de l'Asie française, run by Etienne – an effective press campaign and even banquets for people in the entourage of the President of the Republic, a discreet rôle for the Minister for the Colonies, A. Guillain, a progressivist who just happened to be vice-president of Forges et Aciéries de la Marine et Homécourt,[15], and so on.

Doumer's enterprises in Indo-China aimed to lift it out of its torpor and to turn it into a land open to capitalist colonization. The relations between national policy and colonial affairs also touched on more ancient sectors. First of all there was the control of landed property. At the beginning of the century the work of despoiling the indigenous population, carried on systematically in Algeria since the Second Empire, proceeded on the basis of legislation passed 'to snatch the Algerian soil out of its immobility': between 1900 and 1920 the Algerians lost some 2.5 million hectares, most of it going to the Domains but a considerable part to the colonists.[16] But it is in Tunisia that, apropos of one of those scandals that occasionally dredge up the truth, the connections between the men in power and the dispossession of the natives have recently been studied in the most precise fashion. Without recounting, even in outline, what has been called the 'Couitéas affair',[17] we shall examine briefly the mechanisms it reveals. They first spotlight the importance in Tunisia of 'parliamentary colonization', which started when Paul Bourdes was Director of Agriculture in Tunis. Among the thirty or so individuals who acquired, then or later, huge estates very cheaply there were nine deputies and eight senators; seven of them, including Mougeot, had been responsible for presenting the budget of the Regency (of Tunis), some of them several times. The good and bad luck of

Couitéas also indicates the importance of the rôle played inside the system by personal relations constituting distinct circles, relations quickly renewed and capable of overlapping. The important support enjoyed by Couitéas, a 'new man' in every sense of the term, came to him from the friends he acquired through his lavish hospitality. He quite easily induced Stephen Pichon – Resident-General from 1900 to 1906 before becoming Clemenceau's Minister for Foreign Affairs – to compromise himself on his behalf. A second circle consisted of the radicals in the government who exploited their private friendships as well as their official responsibilities: in 1904–5 the personal secretariat of Senator Ernest Vallé, Keeper of the Seals in Combes's government, intervened several times on behalf of Coutiéas with the Ministry of Foreign Affairs headed by Delcassé.

It would be very unjust to say that the radical Republic was responsible for this mode of behaviour, which in colonial affairs, where distance, ignorance, indifference and private interests had a cumulative effect, produced more serious results than in metropolitan France. The radicals in power inherited a system installed by the opportunists. But it must be recognized that after often denouncing it they did not change it and that the artlessness affected by many of them – Maurice Berteaux, for example, a rich stockbroker famous for his 'good fellowship' – possibly even aggravated it. The ruptures caused in France by anti-clericalism counted for less in colonial circles;[18] moreover there arose on the borders between the radical party and the Democratic Alliance a vague political zone all the more closely connected with business in that it attracted all those who at one moment or another in their economic enterprises needed the co-operation of the State.

In Tunisia the lands taken from the indigenous population by the colonial parliamentarians and their friends and protégés were usually developed as olive groves, with a view to high returns even when old methods of cultivation were used. In black Africa, on the other hand, and in particular in the 'French Congo' the most archaic procedures of colonial exploitation were adopted from 1898–1900. It is true that the concessionary régime, under the influence of the unexpected upsurge of the nearby 'Independent State of the Congo', abandoned the pre-colonial type of situation which for fifteen years had characterized the lands conquered by Brazza. But as constituted, at the request of the Ministry for the Colonies, by an extra-parliamentary commission which drew up a typical specification, it confined itself to adopting once again the statutes of the old charter companies of the first colonial empire. The only difference, one enforced by the radicals, was that the companies theoretically had no rights based on the 'royal prerogative'. They were straightforward 'colonization enterprises' which, in return for payment to the State of a fixed rental and a percentage of the profits, received a monopoly in the development of the

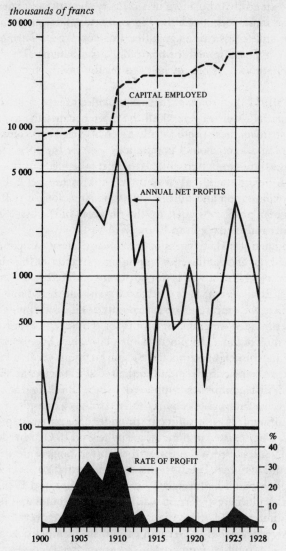

Rates of total profit for concessionary companies in the Congo

Source: C. Coquery-Vidrovitch, *Le Congo au temps des grandes compagnies concessionaires, 1898–1930* (Paris, Mouton, 1972), p. 510.

products of the soil. For the rest, and this is the essential point, the French Republic, unlike Belgium, declined to pay any investment expenses. It is not then surprising that the some forty companies which were formed in record time did not receive any encouragement from the banks. Colonists who wished to extend their business in a country they already knew were joined by a few merchants from the big ports and later by journalists recruited for possible press campaigns; that was how André Tardieu, who was attached to *Le Temps*, joined the board of Ngoko-Sangha. The Bank of Indo-China sometimes put one of its men on the board, but only very occasionally.

From 1903 to 1911 the profits of these companies ranged from 25 to 38 per cent. The shareholders benefited all the more because the companies did not re-invest any of these profits. Only a policy of rigorous compulsion, ruinous for the life of the colonial populations and for the survival of the natural resources – rubber in particular – made it possible to obtain results like these. Even before the Great War these enterprises were collapsing. This policy of exploitation and pillage was obviously a long way from the concern for regular profitability felt by the directors of the big industrial and banking firms in metropolitan France.

The old-fashioned destructiveness of the concessionary companies tells us a good deal about the routine, pre-capitalist character of the 'development of the empire'. However, it is not adequate to define it. In the years immediately before the Great War the banking and industrial monopolies began to infiltrate the empire at several points. The development of the Hongay mines provided magnificent profits for the Société Française des Charbonnages du Tonkin and from 1911 the plantations of rubber plants, at first restricted to the neighbourhood of Saigon on the grey soils where civil servants invested their savings, spread to the red soils of central Vietnam, where the capitalist companies supported by the Bank of Indo-China invested. These vast enterprises required from the start a quantity of labour that local recruitment did not suffice to provide. The post-war problems existed already. They existed in Algeria, too, where on 16 October 1913 the government-general signed an agreement with the Société de l'Ouenza which gave it mining rights. The agreement provided that 20 per cent of the company's capital would be furnished by French banks and French iron and steel firms. And the rest? Krupp was in the background and it was in vain that in January 1914 the socialists denounced a government that handed over Algerian riches to German capitalism: competition between the big companies could be tempered by compromise.

The debasement of political life

Whether it was caught up by the impetus of industrial growth, interested in investing abroad, or connected with the colonies, the whole business world found itself having more and more to seek support from politicians and to develop convincing arguments. Whether there were scandals or not, the rivalries between these men and these groups remained opaque to a public opinion accustomed to think of political life in ideological terms. The militants who sought to make out the elements involved and to determine the mechanisms – men like Carlier, Jaurès and Merrheim – were very few in number. The efforts they made from 1908–9, in particular, to define in a concrete way the international character of the monopolies which the working class was beginning to oppose, remained embryonic and limited. But this obscurity was not incompatible with the confused perception of a change. Filtered through the press, blurred by the political transcriptions of the language, the new lines along which capitalism was developing formed one element in the debasement of political life which slowly set in after the bloc had disintegrated.

The disintegration of the parties

In reality the disintegration of the organized political forces had begun on the left well before the publicized decease of the Bloc. The independent socialists' break with the young *SFIO* had disturbed working-class consciences: at Saint-Etienne around Briand, at Grenoble around Zévaès, at Lyon and in Gard, the socialists who had left the unified party continued to call themselves socialists and kept a good proportion of their electors. Certain departures – that of Viviani, for example – had occurred so late that it was very difficult to be certain of the precise date. For the rest, was the party really unified? Up to 1908 it was possible to doubt it. The personal behaviour of Clemenceau as prime minister, from October 1906 to July 1909, made visible each process in the evolution of the radicals, a process which had been partly obscured by the electoral success of 1906 and by the very weak organization of the party. At the same time the personage of Clemenceau opened the door to interpretations of the crisis based on personal character. These were superseded by a more accurate understanding after the long and bitter debate in the Chamber on the bill for a tax on income drawn up by Caillaux. This proposal was politically democratic and socially moderate. Yet there were numerous reservations among the radicals. Pichery, the deputy for Romorantin, summed them up quite bluntly: 'We want this new tax on income to be prepared with great caution, so that it does not involve harassment or inquisitions, does not breach the secrecy of personal fortunes and does not hinder the conduct of business.' Moreover, the politicians knew that the radicals in the Chamber did not run much of a risk in passing the bill – which they did by a large majority on 9 March 1909 – since in any case it would be rejected by the Senate. Accordingly the fall of Clemenceau did not bring an end to the crisis in the party.

Pelletan had analysed the reasons for it:[19] the radical deputies were elected by 'the people', but 'in the circles they frequent, in their ordinary relationships, in their families and their daily life they belong to those middle classes which will pay the complementary tax[20] when our bill for fiscal reform is passed'. Were the deputies the only ones in this category? It was surely very often necessary to put the members of the committees and the minor local notables in it, too. In any case, the middle classes organized their defence during the months when the tax question was debated publicly. Organizations hitherto separate federated to bring pressure to bear on the deputies. Thus was formed the Committee for Fiscal Study and Defence, which embraced among other bodies the Committee for the Provisioning of Paris, with whose anti-socialist bias we are familiar, and the Association for the Defence of the Middle Classes founded by Maurice Colrat, a lawyer from the Poincaré stable. The organizers of these movements were undeniably more to the right than the majority of radicals, but they fished in the same pond and one had to get oneself elected. Alongside the speculative societies which had been so lively in the days of Combism there now flourished societies for the defence of various interests. Their pressure pushed the radicals in directions that made good relations with the socialists more and more difficult. It is true that this pressure was not everywhere equally successful: a large proportion of the radicals resisted it, but without drawing any but somewhat repetitive conclusions – radicalism must remain true to itself. Could it? We are still not very familiar with the springs of these middle-class movements. They were probably stronger in urban environments and possibly weaker in areas where a vigorous newspaper like the *Dépêche* maintained a strong leftist influence. But even the great daily of the south-west, which certainly favoured a progressive tax on income, was distancing itself more and more from the socialists.[21]

Whatever the causes of it may have been and whatever its scope, the crisis of radicalism expressed itself in a weakening of the ideology in the deputies and often in the electors. This complicity has been made obvious in Loir-et-Cher, where G. Dupeux has noted the coincidence between the spread of hotly contested sponsored candidatures and the movement of deputies towards a moderate radicalism. Secularization was certainly not forgotten and the renewed offensives of the hierarchy against secular schoolbooks and teachers occasionally restored its combative vigour.[22] But it is questionable whether those of the new unbelievers – in Paris the graph of Catholic weddings and of baptisms dipped steeply between 1905 and 1914 (see page 103 above) – who became radical voters had anything like the ardour of the combatants of 1900. Now the middle classes, which were so heterogeneous, could hardly sustain the established republican order without a unifying ideology. Anti-socialism and nationalism could be heard knocking on the door. In 'pink' Toulouse, where the *Dépêche* was printed, and for which Jaurès still wrote, it was in this direction that the new radicalism tended from 1905 onwards.

The elections of 1910 demonstrated the political unease at the heart of which the radical party was operating: there was a relatively high abstention rate – 22.5 per cent and more than 200 new deputies, radical or moderate. It is true that the new constituencies, mainly urban ones, were won for 'the Republic' – at Bayonne, for example, in the difficult Basque country. But on the radical ticket very often two, three and sometimes even four candidates had opposed each other, and many of them had openly defied the official programme of their party; its concepts were alien to them, and it was often these candidates who had won. Altogether the socialists won about twenty seats, often in young, dynamic constituencies: such was the case at Grenoble, where Mistral was chosen by an electorate in which 35 per cent of the voters were workers, over 20 per cent clerks and 12 per cent the managerial class. The radicals fell back perceptibly, either to the advantage of the socialists or even to the advantage of the right. Above all, the general disintegration was incredible. The parties were split up into uncertain fragments and the parliamentary groups multiplied; there were nine of them in the Chamber, including one of 'independents' – the 'wild men' – situated more or less between the radical left and the radical-socialists. Briand, the Prime Minister, did not belong to any group.

This was the start of the time in the history of France when there were radical governments containing radicals but not led by radicals nor even any longer dominated by a radical majority. It was a long period, scarcely interrupted just after the Great War by the 'blue-horizon' elections. That in these circumstances the civil service acquired increased importance seems probable, for in fact governments indulged in a sort of waltz. The ministerial stability that the radical Republic had known from 1899 to 1909 was over. Briand was prime minister, then Briand again, then Monis, then Caillaux – not for long! – Poincaré – a sign of the times – then Briand again, Briand yet again, Barthou, Doumergue, Ribot for three days! Finally Viviani, and by then the war had arrived. These swift changes were a gift to anti-parliamentarianism, but anti-parliamentarianism was out. Economic growth was healthy, the nation was loyal and the tax on income waited in its coffin for the three-year law to create an irrepressible need for money before emerging from its sleep.

'Briandism' and proportional representation

Briand was called 'the sleep-inducer', 'the man of appeasement', 'the saviour'. In that autumn of 1910 when he had just crushed the railwaymen's strike, without a shot – 'look at my hands' – but at the cost of a mobilization of the strikers which made them liable to court martial and created an extremely serious precedent, the man who formerly had been a militant advocate of the general strike arrived in the foreground of events. We do not know Briand very well. His political capacity and oratorical gifts are undeniable, but we know little of his ways of thinking and the reasons for his actions. In giving the name 'Briandism' to the decay of political life which still went on after 1910, Jaurès perhaps overestimated the rôle of his former friend. But this is not obvious. Briand was certainly not at the root of the depressed condition and political impotence of Parliament and the government. The deep-lying reasons for this were in fact not solely French, but European: France had her share of the new contradictions arising out of the upsurge of profits, the painful rise of the working classes and the clash of nationalisms. But France tackled them with an ancient and complex heritage. Briand's strength came to him, temporarily, from the fact that he did not belong to a profession, much less to a party and least of all to his past; he was the opposite to an heir. Very hostile to organized forces – from the Church to the *SFIO* or the *CGT* – he had sufficient knowledge of French parliamentary reality always to tot up his 'republican majority', even when he seemed like the saviour to many men classified as 'right' who hastened to give him their votes on days when they feared the collapse of society. A rallying point for scattered individuals and, so he thought, defeated classes, he was to take on the succession from the weak and divided radicals, among whom as a matter of fact, he had many admirers,[23] to lead the radical Republic to 'Poincarism' and the most equivocal 'moderatism'. From July 1909 to March 1913 he was present in all governments except the brief radical interlude of 1911, and his rôle was to be decisive in the election of Poincaré to the presidency of the Republic.

Was there a political solution to the party break-up that favoured a system of sponsorship? Some people put their faith in a new method of voting: proportional representation with voting for a list of candidates. The founders of the Republic liked to quote Gambetta, who had proclaimed voting for a list, the only method of securing the triumph of 'the idea' over personal rivalries. The progressivists saw it principally as a means of giving representation to minorities bullied by majority voting and of arriving at a 'policy of toleration, justice and truth'.[24] From 1905 Charles-Benoist, a very well-known Catholic journalist – he also taught at the School of Political Science – devoted himself to it. On the extreme left, above all, the socialists declared themselves warm supporters. They saw it not only as a means of obtaining in the Chamber a representation more in harmony with their support in the country, but also as the only means of pushing back the reign of confusion, the régime of sponsorship and the political decay bound up with Briandism. Jaurès hoped that it would lead to the reconstitution of a coherent radical party, which the democratic evolution of the country required. The Guesdists declared that they expected it to put an end to the 'blocking' compromises of second-round alliances. The campaign was a long one. In 1907 a parliamentary group for proportional representation (*RP*) was formed in which Jaurès, Charles-Benoist and Ferdinand Buisson found themselves side by side. Once again it all came to nothing: after the disappointing conclusions of the great debate of October – November 1909, the discussion started again in the country as soon as the elections were over, only to end in March 1913 in a fresh setback.

Few coalitions have been as heterogeneous in their composition and even in their intentions as that of the 'rpéistes' (supporters of proportional representation). And few have finally been so useless. The reason was that those who had seen it as a remedy for Briandism had underestimated the reactions of radicalism. It was true that the radicals had condemned constituency voting on innumerable occasions and spoken of electoral reform. But what kind of reform? When they discussed it at their congresses from 1906 onwards the proportionalists never received the support of any but a small minority. What was worse was that among the latter were to be found secular saints like Ferdinand Buisson as well as politicians on the right of the party like Jean-Louis Bonnet. The charms of the constituency seemed very much alive to the majority of deputies; it was there that they had their real bases, their committees. Among the most enthusiastic supporters of constituencies were Pelletan and Combes, two old campaigners. Far from clarifying the situation or halting the process of decay, the campaign for *RP* aggravated it; it had created new, artificial splits in the radical party without causing the old ones to disappear. And it had strengthened the personal position of Briand, a master of equivocation: after denouncing 'the stagnant little ponds' of the constituencies on 10 October 1909 in the famous Périgueux speech, he declared that the country ought to reflect on the problem and transferred the fifty votes necessary for the bill's rejection.

The movement for social peace

Briand's real aim was to suppress ideological and class confrontations. That was the basis of his political practice. For this reason, too, from 1906 his initiatives are to be counted among those that aimed to ensure the advent of social peace. These initiatives were naturally not new. The currents of thought that had emerged from social, integrationist, royalist Catholicism had diversified by the end of the nineteenth century. The solidarism fathered by Léon Bourgeois[25] propounded the thesis of the 'quasi-contract of association': it asserted that society was nothing but the chain of individuals associated in a common task to which everyone has obligations. For solidarist radicals, private property and work could not be separated: the radicals, said Ferdinand Buisson, were 'a class of owners who work and of workers who own'; that was the doctrinal foundation of their hostility to any kind of collectivist solution. As for Millerandism, it had on the contrary put first the State's duty to intervene in the relations between the classes in order to obtain social peace. In 1908 Millerand published a collection of essays, *Travail et travailleurs*, in which he criticized 'liberal egoism', denounced strikes as pointless, and emphasized the primacy of the national community represented by the State over class interests. But Separation, the crisis of radicalism and the greater bitterness of competition provoked a revival of these themes.

The common objective was to reach an understanding between capital and labour, since, from the intensity of the workers' struggles and the vitality of the theories that gave them a general application this seemed to be the key to any social peace. The pressure of strikes, which had slightly relaxed in 1907–8, worsened again as soon as the economic situation started to improve; while it led to the failure of certain initiatives, it gave others additional arguments for trying to lead a combative proletariat to adopt wiser counsels.

Briand's attempt at social participation, 1909–1910

The information collected by M.-G. Dezes (Biblio. no. 221) has permitted a better understanding of the secular reformist movement which blossomed around Briand in 1909–10, and gave Briandism a fresh field of social activity. It had various origins: the maintenance in the *CGT* of a reformist current that was in a minority but active; a growing interest in the world of labour among sociologists and lawyers; and Briand's desire not only to surround himself with brilliant colleagues but possibly also to base his political influence on them. By autumn 1909 the principal instruments were available: the Comité d'Union Syndicaliste, which had been founded in July 1909, embraced the reformers in the *CGT*, from Coupat to Niel, and had a weekly paper, *L'Action ouvrière*; and the Comité de la Démocratie Sociale, which was run by two admirers of Briand, his political secretary, Léon Parsons, and the lawyer Etienne Antonelli. Until the end of 1911 it had its own publication, *La Démocratie sociale*. Prime minister since July 1909, Briand gave the movement his clear endorsement in the speech at Périgueux by comparing with the 'small job of committees' the wide current of 'general interest' and the prospects of 'social democracy'.

Mere words? A wind that would soon blow itself out? Certainly, but something else as well: Briand and his supporters were seeking to produce a programme which reasonable trade unionists could take over and which would divert the workers from strikes and employers from repression. They regarded social conflicts as based on false premises and solidarity between the classes as stronger than the opposition between them. By taking action, therefore, one would eliminate illusions and conform to the underlying realities of society. The key word of Briand's team was 'participation', a word already employed by Sismondi. The aim of the 'participatory revolution' was to facilitate social mobility and the means was the holding of shares by workers complemented by powers of control giving an equal place in the firm to labour and capital. Those who ran *La Démocratie sociale* doubtless wanted to go further: encouraged by socialists connected with trade unionism like Albert Thomas, they envisaged the creation of a labour party. Briand's political practice limited these ambitions.

It was also going to help to make the whole project fail. Not only did the employers fail to co-operate in any way and not only did Jaurès, interested at first, rapidly part company from them – in particular, he regarded participation at managerial level as ridiculous – but above all the suppression of the railwaymen's strike put an end to dreams of social peace. Briand had chosen his camp; the socialists and trade unionists, including those most interested in reform, chose theirs.

The Christian movements for social peace

At Périgueux Briand had extended a cautious hand to Catholics who accepted the Republic. In these circles, too, movements concerned with social problems developed. Their only organized political form of expression was the Action Libérale Populaire (*ALP*). Hostile to any state intervention, this movement oscillated between radical rejection of class conflict incompatible with the 'sweet light of the blue sky of France'[26] and the distribution of advice intended to avoid conflict by a 'more complete merger of the employing and working elements'. But the groups who claimed to represent social Catholicism were not in any way connected with the *ALP* and displayed, between 1906 and 1914, other riches. There were social weeks, founded in Lyon by Marius Gonin; and there was the Action Populaire, which was particularly active in Nord, where Father Desbuquois organized 'social secretariats' in the big towns. Tempted at first by the 'Jaune' movement, *Action* Populaire subsequently took an interest in Christian trade unionism. Then there was the Association Catholique de la Jeunesse de France (*ACJF*), which gained a national public; with some 3,000 groups and 140,000 members in 1914, it recruited not only among the ruling classes but also among the Catholic peasantry and among clerks. Decidedly royalist in some parts of the Midi – in the Ardèche, for example, where its organizer, H. de Gailhard-Bancel, was a somewhat colourful character – accepting the Republic elsewhere, it bore witness to the lack of achievement and the resistance to change of Catholicism.

The task of these movements was at first one of propaganda. Without any hold on the apparatus of government and without any real influence on the working class, they could not feed the ambitions of men like Antonelli or Parsons. From 1909 a review with a wide circulation, *Le Mouvement social*, complemented the brochures and almanacs of the Action Populaire. The aspiration to social peace was reduced to the organization of discreet enquiries – in 1904 the *ACJF* 'forgot' to put a question on the wages of young workers – and to warm expressions of social goodwill. This did not get anyone very far. The political club round Briand lacked a movement and the Catholic movements lacked any political and social theory. When the economist Charles Gide, backed by the majority of Protestant Christian socialists, guided the Nîmes School toward a consumer morality, diverting it from the liberation of the producer, his aim, too, was to check the rise of collectivism[27] and to strengthen social harmony. At any rate he took a clear stand against capitalism.

Cultural depression?

The vain hopes of social peace, the retreat of the ideologies which we call radical and the hold of big business on public life were accompanied by cultural changes that had begun to appear twenty years earlier. The Belle Epoque gave them the chance to blossom. The lustre of Parisian letters should not be allowed to conceal the unthinking preservation and dissemination of the cultural values of the past, whether or not produced by the notables. It scarcely hides their debasement, which was closely linked to the ideological reversal of the élites.

Traditions maintained

The mass culture which began to spread was grafted onto a society in which, though peasant traditions may have been threatened, the manners inherited from the past were still very much alive. It is difficult for us to realize just how pervasive was the atmosphere of violence. In the military prisons, the activities of the *Biribi* ('Red Caps', military police) – denounced by the revolutionary press – often resulted in prisoners committing suicide.[28] Torture was still employed in spite of the regulations published in December 1899, and the rations of a man put in a correctional cell were smaller than those of an inmate of Auschwitz. For that one can still accuse the authorities, but when on 8 December 1908 the Chamber decided by 330 votes to 201 to retain the death penalty, it prolonged the executioner's functions – in spite of an unfavourable report from Briand, the Keeper of the Seals – under 'the pressure of the grocer, the tailor and the candlestick-maker'. When *Le Petit Parisien* had organized an opinion poll in the previous year, there were over a million replies in favour of the death penalty and about 328,000 against it. And how many torturers were there among the 'educators' in those freezing clerical or secular prisons known as boarding schools?

Traditions were also maintained in those bastions of official taste, the State and its institutions. H. Dujardin-Beaumetz, a right-wing radical, was Under-Secretary of State at the Ministry of Fine Arts from January 1905 to January 1910 – has anyone held the post any longer? This prefect's son certainly abolished the censorship commission which until June 1906 attempted to dictate what songs should be sung and what plays should be staged in Paris; its impotence had become almost ridiculous. But his fame is based more, today, on his firm opposition to the purchase by the national museums of any work by Cézanne. Love of the 'great subject', dark colours and the most obsolete academism distinguished official taste in painting. It was the taste of the Institute and the Salons; and it was also the taste of the self-satisfied bourgeoisie. The trouble was that great subjects were hard to find; so they were drawn from the past. In literature the principal reviews contained to disseminate the same somewhat heavy texts. France congratulated itself on remaining the country of classicism: 'The classical spirit belongs to all countries, but it belongs above all to ours.'[29] Measure, good sense: that is what people looked for in Corneille and Racine; one can understand Péguy's ferocity. Established bodies, with the University in the centre, functioned like machines for reproducing the values worked out during the course of the nineteenth century by the well-to-do bourgeoisie; secular in *La Revue de Paris*, these values evolved in the direction of Catholic spirituality in *La Revue des deux mondes*.

Progress of the culture of the notables

The culture of the notables not only retained its dominant position but even extended it at the beginning of the century in the direction of new circles. The mass magazines, much more numerous now than in the first few years of the Third Republic, reached even the *bourgs*. *Lectures pour tous* was born in 1898, launched by the firm of Hachette, which also started *Je sais tout* in 1905. From 1905 the Tallandier group also published *Lisez-moi*, while it was *Le Petit Parisien*[30] which published *Nos loisirs* from 1906, in harmony with the law which that year made a weekly rest day compulsory. In parallel the rise of the Paris dailies continued, to the detriment of the political press. It was at this time that the four big papers – *Le Petit Journal*, *Le Petit Parisien*, *Le Matin* and *Le Journal* attained their biggest readerships: the number of copies printed – 4.5 million – represented over 40 per cent of the copies printed by all the French dailies. *Le Petit Parisien*, together with *Le Petit Journal*, had won a loyal provincial public. The big regional papers were also at their zenith. The great thing was not to displease these mass readerships; *Le Petit Parisien* wanted to be the 'regulator of collective passions'. It was also a question of handing on stereotypes, models to integrate people in society. This rôle fell in particular to the serialized novels which often occupied the lower halves of two, three or four pages of the paper.

In this way the dominant features of the dominant culture reached new circles: a taste for archaism,[31] the rural values exalted by innumerable inferior novelists writing in the style of Henri Bordeaux, confidence in work as a source of prosperity and 'natural' social hierarchies. This culture certainly had points in common with what was taught in the state schools. But at the same time, cut off from educational disputes and characterized by aims independent of the secular cause, it turned towards social and political conservatism.

Urban changes

In town, official conformism was subject to numerous pressures. Did the bourgeoisie respect the values that it proclaimed? It is permissible to doubt it. Was not vaudeville – from Courteline to Feydeau – not largely preferred to the Comédie-Française, and, if people went to the Comédie-Française, did they not prefer *L'Aiglon* to *Polyeucte*? It is not very agreeable for a dominant culture to find itself dropped in favour of what are generally known as minor genres.

Since the turn of the century the cinema had also joined the competition. After becoming a mere fairground curiosity for some time, the cinematograph returned to town thanks to Méliès, the creator of the scenario and the production. It returned a little late, because the theatres that specialized in showing films demanded long, realistic ones. The intelligentsia hesitated: was the cinema art? The middle classes took their wives, and so did the workers. There was nothing very new in the ideological content of the cinema. But all kinds of ancestral attitudes were going to be upset by these darkened halls. Here again the unacknowledged often supplanted what was loudly admired.

Finally, the cultural depression was linked to a third change: the evolution carrying the urban élite away from the scientific approach, from rationalism and from the ideology proclaimed in the schools and even – though to a lesser degree – in the literature designed for mass consumption. The 'crisis' of the scientific approach had begun in the 1880s. Without going back to its origins we must see how, in a restricted but influential circle, it had assumed some spectacular aspects.

The upsurge of mystical spirituality

The conversion of young intellectuals that had begun with Claudel continued in the first few years of the new century with that of Francis Jammes, Max Jacob, Jacques Maritain, Louis Massignon and Ernest Psichari. Psichari's conversion involved the family of Renan. Péguy quietly returned to the faith of his childhood. Some painters were converted, Rouault, for example, and musicians, too. Each of them moved towards God at his own pace. But among these 'converts of the Belle Epoque' – curious birds hatched by rationalist fathers – the discovery of faith was accompanied by an intense interior life and an exalted mystical practice. The ages of these converts, which varied considerably, suggests that it was the moment that was decisive, not the generation. This wave of conversions probably remained a largely Parisian phenomenon – certainly a limited one. However, besides the fact that the Church rang its bells, the new Catholics belonged to circles where people knew how to write. Péguy had his own review, Jammes's elegies were published widely.

This phenonemon, and it was not peculiar to France, formed in France part of a bigger whole: a return to mystical spiritualism (in the philosophical sense of the term). University philosophy had never broken with spiritualism. Secular and rationalist with Renouvier or the young Alain, it now became mystical with Maurice Blondel and Henri Bergson. The case of Bergson is important. Since 1897 his course of lectures at the Collège de France had been extraordinarily successful: philosophers, scholars, writers, students and fashionable women jostled each other at his lectures. It was, in Péguy's words, 'A return to metaphysics in the world'. And in fact *L'Evolution créatrice*, which Bergson published in 1907, pointed straight towards God along the path of 'l'élan vital', rehabilitating intuition and mystical experience. By echoing his teaching, journalists gave it extremely wide currency.[32] Now Bergson was not a Catholic, but his philosophy bears the stamp of the age. By praising intuition it made the charms of Impressionism comprehensible; it moved in the same direction as Symbolist poetry; and it was in accord with Tolstoy's ideas. By rehabilitating the irrational, it found an echo in a current of thought which we saw at work in the Dreyfus affair and it legitimized the mystical practices developing in the Church: miracles, apparitions. By rejecting the arid influence of the Kantian categories, Bergson furnished an explanation for the scientific changes in progress.

It is obviously impossible to isolate the causes of a movement the components and scope of which are still not very well known. But it seems possible that it was connected with the disquiet inspired by the social, political and intellectual contradictions of the twentieth century on which the radical Republic was now embarked. The days of calm progress were over; those of crises began amid disquieting though, for some people, cosy circumstances.

Towards the Great War

Nationalism

The mystical current also played its part in the nationalist movement which had become active again by 1905 and which markedly increased its activity after 1911. The Dreyfus affair had made it possible to classify the nationalist current as clearly belonging to the right and to keep it away from the corridors of power. Many of those who sympathized with it had been reconverted to republicanism; moreover, they were republicans in the first sense of the term. The radical party had had to welcome a fair number of them, but it was not the only party to do so. In three regions – the departments of the east, those of Brittany and its surrounding area and certain departments in the southern part of the Massif Central – republican deputies had been voting since 1898 with the nationalist right.[33]

The themes emphasized by neo-nationalism tell us much about it. It hated two things: Germans and bad Frenchmen. This latter term denoted those unwilling to let themselves be carried away by the chauvinistic current, especially if their conduct could be damaging to the big interests. Such people included members of the *CGT* and socialists, accused *en bloc* of 'having no country', and politicians classified as pacifists – Caillaux, for example, and his dangerous plan for income tax. Neo-nationalism was against socialism, even the socialism embodied in the intermediary figure of Caillaux. But it also took a very strong stand on Germany, which provoked numerous enquiries and studies: the danger it presented for France was defined as pressing and multiple, 'simultaneously continental, maritime, colonial, economic'.[34] The spotlight on Germany, which was something new, obviously turned people's attention to Morocco, the remains of which were being bitterly disputed between the two countries from 1905 onwards: colonizing nationalism and anti-German nationalism, adversaries at the beginning of the Third Republic, now joined hands. It also turned people's attention to Alsace-Lorraine, but in an ambiguous fashion. In spite of the novels of Barrès or Bazin – *Colette Baudoche, Les Oberlé* – and in spite of the dissemination, from 1912, of Hansi's albums comparing the gentle French domination to the brutal rule of Germany, references to Alsace-Lorraine were made to serve anti-German nationalism rather than the desire to regain the 'lost provinces'.[35] On the other hand, German competition was explicitly and frequently mentioned. It is true that not all sectors of French capitalism were under the same threat: the Lorraine iron and steel industry was threatened to a greater degree than the coal mines of Nord and Pas-de-Calais whose main competitors were English and Belgian coal. Nor could one say that the banks with multiple investments were particularly threatened. But the place occupied among the weapons of nationalism by the rivalry between 'German junk' and French 'high quality' production made it profoundly imperialistic.

The 'how' is almost as important as the 'why'. Here neo-nationalism bordered on mysticism. People compared the soldier who obeys instinct with the ratiocinative intellectual, the centurion who guarded French culture with the university which was ready to hand it over to the Germans. Péguy, the former Dreyfusard, and Psichari, Renan's grandson, competed with each other along this path. Conversion became a proof of patriotism. The profession of arms, in the colonies or on the Vosges, was superior to all others. And for the soldier to fulfil himself completely he needed war: 'It is pure delight for a soldier to see the national idea come into being, grow and increase on the field of battle... Dear France, dear country, you will doubtless live through some grave times.'[36] By beatifying Jeanne d'Arc, Pius X showed clearly enough that Catholicism was the backbone of patriotism. Of course, various differing attitudes were possible: the nationalism of Poincaré was relatively moderate, that of Barrès was idealised. One could be both a nationalist and a republican – such was the case with Péguy – but the followers of Maurras regarded this as a weakness which certainly had to be tolerated but nevertheless was to be condemned. All round, the nationalist current displayed a real unity. Disseminated by a press not lacking in funds, it counted for something in the nation and particularly in foreign policy.

The policy of Delcassé, 28 June 1898 – 6 June 1905

The choices made and implemented by Théophile Delcassé orientated France's foreign policy up to the Great War. Never in the Third Republic had a minister of Foreign Affairs remained so long in office. And never had one apparently been so free to do as he pleased: public opinion was not much concerned with international problems and the Chamber, where in any case Delcassé was quite popular, only exerted a moderate control. He was assisted by some remarkable ambassadors: Camille Barrère, and Jules and Paul Cambon. It was on the responsibility of Delcassé – he was young, only forty-six in 1898, and he had arrived at the Quai d'Orsay right in the middle of the Fashoda crisis – that the Triple Entente took shape, the keystone of the policy of European diplomatic and military blocs. It was also under his aegis that France embarked on an undeniably new policy of the annexation of Morocco.

Where was the novelty, it may be asked? Up to the end of the nineteenth century France had hesitated between a policy of colonial expansion which brought her into competition with England and a continental policy aimed essentially against Germany. The – secret – agreements of 18 August 1892 with Russia were part of the second policy. The first policy dictated among other things the Marchand expedition, organized by Hanotaux, Delcassé's predecessor at the Quai d'Orsay; it had had to be brought to an inglorious end. Delcassé's 'great policy' consisted in taking the view that the two aims outlined above were not contradictory and that their simultaneous realization postulated the elimination of points of friction with England, the reinforcement of the alliance with Russia and a special effort to detach Italy from the Triple Alliance. Such were the main lines of the plan which he explained as early as February 1899 to his colleagues.

This plan raised several questions. The first concerned the priority of the colonial objective. In 1894 Delcassé had been Minister for the Colonies and he was connected with the complex pressure group known as the 'colonial party', whose leader was the deputy for Oran, Eugène Etienne.[37] In 1898 the colonial party made the attachment of Morocco to France objective number one because of its geographical situation and its probable mining resources. However, it did not think that this aim could be achieved without the support of Germany given English interests at Gibraltar. On this essential point Delcassé did not follow his friends; the choice he made and the way he implemented it were clearly directed against Germany.

The second question that needs to be asked is, was the 'colonial party' a bloc? Serious rivalries made themselves apparent between the French businessmen interested in the 'peaceful penetration of Morocco'. P. Guillen has pointed out the violence of the conflict from 1902 onwards between the Compagnie Marocaine, Schneider's creation, and a banking syndicate run by Paribas;[38] it was a case of industrial capital against banking capital. Not without hesitation the French Foreign Office chose the consortium organized by Paribas, the only one able to respond to the enormous loan the Sultan was obliged to raise. When Schneider found the necessary money by coming to an understanding in 1904 with the Banque de l'Union Parisienne, open conflict broke out: it was settled by Delcassé, who on 9 May 1904 told the secretary-general of Le Creusot that he could not allow his firm to impede a decision in which the national interest was involved. The loan, signed on 12 June, ruined Morocco, ensured the consortium huge profits and its ally, the French government, a pre-eminent position in Morocco. Two conclusions can be drawn from this episode: first, that it was the political power that laid down the law to business; and second, that it could only settle the affair by linking itself to the major interests of banking capital. These two conclusions are not contradictory.

Seen in this light, the Entente Cordiale itself can look like a means to facilitate the victory of banking capital: Paribas was in fact linked to the English banks, and the signature on 8 April 1904 of the Franco-British diplomatic agreement removed a serious obstacle to the full accord of the Quai d'Orsay and the consortium. Obviously the Entente Cordiale had a far greater importance; it marked a lasting turning-point in French diplomacy. However, at that date it was only a question of a colonial and imperialist swop; France agreed 'not to hinder Great Britain's activities in Egypt' while England recognized that 'it was France's task to keep the peace in Morocco'. The concept of a protectorate was mentioned only in the secret articles. This share-out, complemented by other clauses of the same type, opened the way to diplomatic agreements but did not include them. However, Germany was not deceived, all the less because she knew that in December 1900 Italy had 'tried a waltz' with France.

The successes gained by Delcassé encouraged him in his decision to act promptly in Morocco without worrying about the possible reactions of Germany, which did not yet have any big interests there. What he wanted was the recognition by the Sultan as soon as possible of the French protectorate. This was to take eight years; during these eight years this plan, which was pursued just as keenly by Delcassé's successors, was finally to create an atmosphere of profound distrust between France and Germany. The French socialists were quite right to denounce, at this level of international relations, one of the fundamental threats to peace. Yet Germany counted mainly on using Morocco as a means to break up the Entente Cordiale by forming a continental Germano-Russian alliance which France would have to join in exchange for the acceptance by Germany of her freedom of action in Morocco.

For the time being Delcassé's Moroccan initiative led slowly to a German counter-offensive: it was the speech of Wilhelm II at Tangier (31 March 1905) which was itself to bring about the fall of Delcassé. Convinced that Germany was bluffing, Delcassé pressed the Sultan to accept the protectorate, said he was certain of British support and refused any concession to Germany. It was this choice which was opposed by Prime Minister Rouvier, the socialists and a large section of radical opinion, from Clemenceau to *La Dépêche de Toulouse*. On 6 June, during a dramatic cabinet meeting, Rouvier, who had just had a secret interview with a German diplomat, obtained Delcassé's resignation as demanded by Germany.

There were important consequences. At bottom, Germany had not obtained satisfaction. The plan for a continental alliance failed because of the huge international loan floated by Russia in which France's financial means easily ensured her the first place.[39] The international conference at Algeciras (15 January – 7 April 1906) gave France special rights in Morocco and accepted that the State Bank which was going to be formed in Morocco in 1907 should pass in all essentials under the control of Paribas. But French public opinion had received a shock. The resignation of Delcassé right in the middle of an international crisis was presented by part of the press as an insult. It released a wave of anti-German nationalism. The following months saw a big paper like *La Dépêche de Toulouse* harden its attitude to Germany and promote for France the policy known as 'the orchestra stalls policy': half-way between the 'firebrands' and 'the pacifists', France should keep her hands free but refuse any rapprochement with Germany.

From 1906 to 1913 France's foreign policy was certainly going to pass through various different phases, but in essentials – strengthening of the Franco-Russian-British bloc, slow progress towards a protectorate in Morocco, support for big business – it presented a certain continuity.

The slight variations in the application of this policy were important. The line taken by Clemenceau's government, in which foreign affairs were entrusted to Stephen Pichon, one of Clemenceau's personal friends,[40] was distinguished both by the personality of the old campaigner and by his parliamentary majority, the disintegration of which was far from complete even if the vitality of the Bloc was in a fatal decline. Although he was responsible for some pretty big military and diplomatic moves in Morocco, Clemenceau attached less importance to it than to Germany; however, the disquiet and even hostility that Germany aroused in him did not go as far as bellicosity. To consolidate the system of alliances outlined by Delcassé, French diplomacy used its good offices between its ally Russia and its friend England: the Anglo-Russian agreement of 31 August 1907 – this, too, was a swop and share-out operation – gave consistency to the Triple Entente. During the Balkan crisis of 1909 Stephen Pichon warned the Russian government that France would not give military support to its attitude to Austria–Hungary because 'the vital interests of Russia' were not involved. The Tsarist empire, whose economic recovery was only just starting – thanks in particular to the French loan of January 1909 – was unable to proceed further. The consequences of this attitude were to be complex: on the one hand Russia was to bear a lasting grudge, sustained in the following years by French firms' policy of investment, and on the other the effectiveness of a French *démarche* in favour of peace had been proved.

However, Jaurès, who harassed the Clemenceau ministry on its general policy and in particular on its Moroccan policy, rightly pointed out that this '*démarche* for peace' was the expression of an ambiguous policy. Neither in Morocco, in spite of the Franco-German financial agreement of 9 February 1909 – viewed with favour by Wilhelm II in the context of French influence on Russia – nor on a general level were the choices made clearly. In fact the initiatives of the 'Africans' in Morocco were generally supported and the rivalry between French and German capital grew.

Today we are better acquainted with those rivalries and the possibilities of settling them temporarily. The conflicts appeared during these years, both before and after the fall of Clemenceau, in several parts of the world. Let us take a few cases. In Turkey, the refusal of the French government to give a quotation on the stock exchange to the Ottoman government, which was in search of a loan (October 1910), led to the subscription of this loan in November by a Germano-Austro-Hungarian consortium: Paris had been deceived by the Turkish government, which had publicly declined to accept the control of its finances the French government had taken for granted.[41] In China it was on the basis of the Entente Cordiale that in April 1911 a banking consortium was formed whose avowed aim was to gain complete control of Chinese finances.[42] In Morocco the 'economic collaboration' – that is, the joint exploitation of the country – provided for by the agreement of February 1909 was functioning very badly; the groups of French and German mining and iron and steel engineers were clashing openly.

It was against this background that in April 1911 the Monis government – a radical government in favour of which the whole socialist group had abstained – decided to occupy Fez in flagrant violation of the Algeciras agreement. Germany responded by sending a symbolic gunboat to Agadir on 1 July. The crisis was extremely serious: the two countries were on the brink of war in spite of the efforts of Caillaux, prime minister since 27 June, who engaged in secret talks without informing his Minister of Foreign Affairs, Justin de Selves. In the end a new swop agreement was signed on 4 November: Germany accepted in advance the French protectorate (over Morocco), the establishment of which from then on was only a formality, and obtained in exchange an important section of the Congo between the Cameroons and the Belgian Congo. To give the bargain a more regional character, Germany ceded to France the little 'parrot's beak' to the south of Chad. The diplomatic and military blocs emerged from the crisis strengthened. Nationalism had been exacerbated both in France and in Germany.

In 1912–13 it was in the Balkans that the crises preceding the war erupted. The principal Franco-German dispute had been settled, but neo-nationalism had never been so virulent and the rivalries between financial groups did not cease, even though it was clear that a section of banking capital did not have the same interests as industrial capital and defended a policy more favourable to compromise. The election of Poincaré to the presidency of the Republic against the radical Pams and the socialist Vaillant (17 January 1913) did not strengthen the pacifist camp, to say the least. For ten years political crises had constantly interfered with economic tensions.

11

The avant-garde movements

The dullness of the Belle Epoque should not induce us to forget the new forces that began to appear during this period. Various avant-garde movements – sumptuous, modest or aggressive – stand out against an often greying background. France was still far from being an industrial society, but its entry upon the era of imperialism and the delays and blockages affecting what was an irreversible movement (though it was not always perceived as such) allowed the opportunity for some bold young shoots to spring up. Most of them were to blossom immediately after the Great War. The most vigorous are still throwing out new shoots today. Amid these movements, ideologies and creations, the twentieth century began before 1914; in the first decade of the new century almost all the things that were to constitute the unique character of the inter-war period were in embryo.

Political and social avant-garde movements

Action Française, the Sillon, the *SFIO* and the *CGT* – from the extreme right to the extreme left these movements began to stand out during the course of a few years (from 1899 to 1905). They were in the van of currents of opinion and beliefs which existed before them, and which were not eliminated by their appearance. Whether they were destined for a short or a long life, they subsequently organized themselves without losing the strong ideological content with which they were charged.

A new extreme right: Action Française

From 1905 the Intelligence Service began to show an interest in a movement launched five years earlier but which until then had not attracted any attention, namely the Action Française. Coeval with the various leagues, the *AF* came modestly into being during the Dreyfus affair. At first, in the spring of 1898, it was only one nationalist committee among others; its leaders, a Jacobin journalist called Vaugeois and an anarchist writer by the name of Pujo, were by no means monarchists. Their meeting with Maurras at the beginning of 1899 led them to break with the Ligue de la Patrie Française, which was regarded as too 'soft', and to found in July 1899 a 'little grey review' which was to appear twice a month until 1908. Charles Maurras, a convincing, even imperious character, whose first articles extolling 'le faux Henry' had appeared in the old-fashioned *Gazette de France*, carried out in the new review a resounding 'Enquiry into the monarchy' and slowly drew his companions in anti-Dreyfusism towards 'total royalism'. La Ligue d'Action Française was founded in 1905, but its first congress was not held until two years later. The funds collected – particularly those from the Daudet family – made possible the publication, from 21 March 1908, of a daily *Action française* sold in the streets by 'Camelots du Roy'. For ten years the movement made constant, but not striking, progress. Until 1914 Action Française was to remain a tiny group.

The novelty of the movement was that, even when the Affair was over, it continued and pushed to the point of caricature the behaviour of the anti-Dreyfusard leagues. The violence and insolence of its publication cut across the formal tone of the old monarchist press and were inspired more by *La Libre Parole* in the heyday of Drumont. It specialized in libellous campaigns: the republican University (1908–11), the German–Jewish spies (September 1910 – April 1912). The Ligue also knew how to create agitation in the streets – during the transfer of Zola's ashes to the Panthéon on 4 June 1908, for example – in public squares, where the statues of the chief Dreyfusards were attacked with hammers, and around theatres, where it demanded and sometimes obtained the withdrawal of 'Jewish' plays.[1] In the Latin quarter it revived (against the socialist Charles Andler or the radical Thalamas) the battlefield atmosphere of 1898–9. It professed to be the expression of an indignant younger generation, whose rude virtues it compared with the stifling republican dullness or even, but on the sly, with the somnolence of provincial châteaux. Action Française was also avant-garde in its intellectual ambitions. The *Revue critique*, founded in April 1908 by J. Rivain and others from the Cercle Joseph de Maistre, remained for a long time in the ambit of the *AF* and the daily's columns printed the intelligent chronicles of Jacques Bainville and the didactic brickbats of Maurras. Even when the offensives only half succeeded – as in the case of the attempt during the winter of 1905 to recruit to the cause Fustel de Coulanges, the historian of the ancient city-state – they were the occasion for the completion of an effective cultural apparatus: the Institut d'Action Française (February 1906), and the Rivain bookshop.

'Maurrasism' succeeded in fact in grafting royalism on to the nationalism of the leagues; they had thought that the Republic could be reformed, whereas it was necessary to attack not just its deviations or its institutions but its spiritual foundations. National unity could not be achieved, according to Maurras, in a Republic that was the daughter of the Revolution. The monarchy alone embodied the essence of the State and gave to politics its natural place – first place. The French Revolution had opened the era of disintegration *vis-à-vis* both individuals and social classes; it had hallowed the primacy of economics, the direct progenitor of the detested collectivism. So first of all must come the restoration. This return to France required the elimination of foreigners, those metics who disturbed its being. The country needed to exclude people in order to define itself. 'It would all be impossible or terribly difficult', wrote Maurras in *Action française* (28 March 1911), 'but for the providential existence of anti-semitism. That settles, smooths and simplifies everything.' The Jew – or any other foreigner, but the Jew was the most convenient foreigner – was as necessary as the king to the idea of France. This doctrine implied a strong, repressive State, based on the army and the Church. An atheist himself, Maurras needed the Church and Catholicism as state religion.

The language of Maurras was not that of fascism. There was no lyricism in it; it cultivated a supercilious rationalism and was categorical in form, though claiming to express empirical truths. It reflected a conservative sense of Catholicism. However, a movement can hardly be defined by its language alone. The social bases of Action Française – we know what they were only at the level of members or of the closest sympathizers – remained narrow. Towards 1910 there were about forty sections in Paris and possibly 200 in the provinces, none of them with very many members: altogether a few thousand adherents. In the processions there were 3,000 people at the most. Outside Paris the territory of the movement, encouraged from the end of 1911 by the pretender to the throne, a mediocre character, was almost identical with that of the old royalism: the 'White' departments of the west, the south-west and the Midi; Nord and Pas-de-Calais; and the valley of the Rhône. More than half the sections were headed by nobles and a fifth of the resources of the movement came from titled families. Then came members of the clergy of whom there were many, officers and lawyers, and a small number of the urban bourgeoisie. After the cadres, the rank and file. There were few peasants, practically no workers, and hardly any industrialists so long as the sun of profit shone. The presence in Action Française of the small tradesmen, the bank clerks and the commercial travellers who at the end of the century formed the basis of the nationalist leagues might tempt us to see a pre-fascist current in it. But its unsuitability for the masses and its framework of Catholic notables rooted it strongly in the national conservative tradition. What was new and significant for the future was the success of the nationalist graft on the old monarchism, the recruitment of young militants and often of brilliant intellectuals who had returned to Catholicism, and the enlistment of notable personalities, from Henri Bordeaux to Jules Lemaître, from Gustave Fagniez, the co-founder of the *Revue historique,* to Antoine Baumann, the executor of Auguste Comte. These had never before been seen at the side of royalists and now here they were not hesitating to lend their names – associated, it is true, with those of Jeanne d'Arc and Louis XIV – to appeals for a possible *coup de'état* and to the wielding of the cudgel in the streets.

Against a background of Christian democracy: the Sillon

Although pure hagiography is no longer in fashion,[2] it remains difficult to conjure up an accurate picture of the Sillon, a curious offshoot of Christian democracy. The history of the movement tends to be confounded with that of its 'leader', Marc Sangnier. Born in 1873 into a fervently Catholic family belonging to the rich bourgeoisie, Sangnier studied to enter the *Polytechnique* at the Collège Stanislas in a religious circle that supported the Republic and was profoundly spiritual. The start of his militant career consisted of a group of school-friends called La Crypte (1893) and of a little review, *Le Sillon* (1894). The Sangnier fortune enabled their son to leave the army in October 1898 to devote himself to the movement of which he had dreamed as an adolescent and to subsidize it quite generously. The main stages of the movement were to coincide with Sangnier's decisions. These stages were the manifesto of 10 October 1899 in which the programme of the Sillon was outlined; the 'crisis' of 1905[3] which strengthened the influence of the Sangnier family; and the new, more political, or even electoral, trend of the movement after 1906. This dry chronology does not really do justice to the charismatic influence of 'Marc'. His 'friends' and 'comrades' were first and foremost his disciples, almost his devotees. François Mauriac, in *L'Enfant chargé de chaînes*, has spoken of the 'look that touched people's souls' and of the 'long, delicate hands ceaselessly reaching out towards the hands of the person to be won over'. Was Sangnier's influence bound up, as has been suggested, with the permanent sublimation of a lively sensuality?[4] It was assisted in any case by a fluent eloquence and an essayist's craftsmanship in drafting written documents.

Even so, attractive as he was, his influence was so strong only because he was able to adopt the tradition of intransigent Catholicism[5] hostile to the Orleanist 'liberalism' of men like Dupanloup, and also at the same time to take over the young Christian democratic tradition, even that of the *ACJF*, and to crystallize latent dreams. Up to 1906 the bishops were generally happy to recruit new forces for the battle against anti-clericalism – new forces which in addition had shown their indifference to Dreyfusism. From 1899 to 1905 the Sillon's ideology did not differ substantially from that of the 'second Christian democracy' of the democratic priests – men like Naudet, Garnier and Dabry – or of the *semaines sociales* organized by Marius Gonin at Lyon in 1904. It was a question of struggling vigorously for the rights of the Church but at the same time of clearly accepting the Republic and its consequences and of ensuring a place for Catholics in society, no longer through the traditional good works but through mutual education and moral training. Where then did the avant-garde aspect of the movement come from? The Sillon provided a response to the expectation of a new generation of Catholics, whether educated in secular schools or not, in search of new forms of social life; it adapted itself to the sensibility of young curates seeking a deeper, almost missionary commitment and contact with the people.[6] We know this from the study of branches of the movement which appeared in the east, the north, the valley of the Loire and above all in Brittany; some thousands of young people, of very different social origins, learned to 'love the Sillon', to recognize themselves in this 'common soul'. These young men became socialists through various activities – study circles, popular institutes, soldiers' funds, co-operatives of every sort. The members of the 'Young Guard' swore to devote their lives to God and the Sillon and, dressed in a black uniform with a red cross, protected meetings of the Sillon against the anti-clericals and sold the movement's newspapers. The Catholic ceremonial surrounding their initiation functioned as an initiation rite and confirmed them in their belief that they formed the knights errant of the modern world.

By 1906 Sangnier had foreseen the possibility of a religious peace, and he swiftly drew his conclusions: it was time to give an autonomous political dimension to the deep desire for democracy, that is, for participation in the whole life of the state, which the Sillon had developed in its militants. This objective necessitated changes in the structure of the movement for it had to become a secularized and more centralized political party. Contacts were made with Protestants – with Pastor Soulier, for example, president of the Young Men's Christian Association – and even with free thinkers like Albert Nast, with a view to the creation, first of all, of a 'bigger Sillon'. Sangnier sought to address himself more and more to the working class, to whom he now denounced 'capitalism'. Over 6,000 subscriptions were collected in order to add to the bi-monthly *Sillon* and the weekly *Eveil démocratique* the daily newspaper indispensable to such an enterprise: the first number of *La Démocratie* appeared on 20 July 1910.

This new project involved the condemnation of the Sillon by the Church. The letter which Pius X sent to Marc Sangnier on 25 August 1910 was the culminating point of a long period of tension. The Sillon was accused of lending its protection to socialism by giving priority to democracy over 'authority, the Church's vital product'. It was also accused, when so many priests were involved in it, of evading control by the Catholic hierarchy. We know today the part played in this condemnation by the conservatives or 'integralists' of Rome – the Pope himself – and France: the Bishop of Nancy, Mgr Turinaz and abbé Barbier, all closely connected with the Action Française.[7] But it is doubtful whether the men of the conservative network of 'La Sapinière' were the only ones concerned; many bishops were worried. What was more serious was that regional branches of the Sillon –

those of the east and Limousin, for example – had disappeared and that founder members like abbé Desgranges had left the movement. It is true that numerous people – some thousands – were loyal to it. But it was the major part of the French Church which in 1910 was not prepared to tolerate the secularization on a democratic basis of a movement largely denominational in origin. After the immediate submission of the Sillon, Sangnier was to found in 1912 a small party called the Jeune République without incurring criticism from Rome; Catholics were free to take part in the political struggle, even if it was democratic in the complex sense which the Sillon had given to this word, but not churchmen.

The socialist avant-garde: the SFIO

The beginning of the century saw the crystallization on the left of the French political chess-board of the two socialist avant-garde movements, the *SFIO* (Section Française de l'Internationale Ouvrière) and the *CGT* (Confédération Générale du Travail), which relied for their support on the progressive members of the working classes who had been the standard-bearers for the various brands of socialism.

At the time the *CGT* did not hesitate to challenge the pioneer character of the *SFIO*. The statutes of the new party and its origins did in fact make it very much a part of the political life of the Third Republic: organized on a local basis, the *SFIO*, a party of the direct type, had no factory groups and preferred to aim at winning over the electors. The difficulty which the party found in intervening in social conflicts did not come only from the barrage organized by the *CGT*, whose preserve these conflicts were, but also from the way in which it was organized: what is the good of preaching if there is no one there to spread the message? In any case the Guesdists were the only ones who recommended this kind of intervention; but it was in order to criticize the revolutionary strategy of the *CGT* and to assert the tactical superiority of the voting slip to the strike, if not the gun, that they still raised their hands in salute, though from a distance. In addition, where the small peasants were concerned, doctrine was uncertain; at the Second International this difficulty was not peculiar to French socialism. Finally, although from 1908 unity was no longer really in doubt, the *SFIO* remained divided into factions sometimes inherited from the past – Guesdism – and sometimes closer to the problems of the present – 'working-class socialism', the 'insurrectional' tendency. The parliamentary group through which the influence of the party could make itself felt in affairs of state was far from displaying the coherence officially desired. Almost unanimous when it was a matter of condemning anti-working-class repression in front of the 'elected representatives of the bourgeoisie',[8] it was sometimes divided on problems of parliamentary tactics,[9] even on fundamental questions. The law which on 31 March 1910 finally ratified the first pensions for workers was supported by twenty-five socialist deputies – they followed Jaurès – while twenty-seven opposed it with Guesde. Vaillant and his friends abstained.

The reasons for these weaknesses were complex. The extreme ideological diversity of French socialism had not disappeared. The adoption of a few popularized Marxist themes did not signify that Marxism had acquired a dominant position: the translation of Marx's works had made little progress, the socialist press was less and less informative in this respect, the party's bookstall was still just as eclectic and France did not witness the appearance of any Marxist radicalism of the sort that was flourishing in other European countries. The sociological composition of the *SFIO* no doubt had a good deal to do with this. The party certainly continued to make progress in the dynamic industrial zones – the departments of Nord and Pas-de-Calais, the suburbs of Paris – but not in Meurthe-et-Moselle. Rhône, Loire and Bouches-du-Rhône made recruits but not to the extent that might be expected if there had been a real interchange of ideas between the working class and the party. On the other hand, fairly large inroads were made in the rural areas – the Mediterranean Midi, Aquitaine and the periphery of the Massif Central – to the detriment of radicalism. The general line of the party, sometimes strengthened by original legislative proposals – with regard to the share-croppers of the Bourbonnais, for example – seems to have been responsible for this rather than its intervention in peasant conflicts, and the electoral growth of the party emphasized through its frequent disputes with militant elements the party's parliamentary nature.

Yet the *SFIO* certainly looked like an avant-garde party, first and foremost because of its small size – 44,000 members in 1906, 63,000 in 1912; the number did not reach 90,000 until July 1914 – which provoked ironic comments from the big battalions of German social democracy. The same impression was given by its organization: this obliged groups to belong to departmental federations which were responsible for ratifying candidatures and for monitoring the local press and were directly represented at the quarterly national council and at the annual congress. At the top the party apparatus was fairly light: it consisted of the permanent administrative committee, elected from 1907 in proportion to the various tendencies represented in the party, and, round Louis Dubreuilh, the secretariat. *L'Humanité*, founded on 18 April 1904 by Jaurès, had been placed since the beginning of 1907 'under the control of the party' and gradually became its official mouthpiece. What is more, militant socialists in this strongly parliamentary party often had other aims than winning an electoral victory. At the beginning of this century many workers were still being dismissed from factories and many teachers were sent to the most isolated village in their department because they belonged to 'organized socialism'.

The bases on which the party recruited publicly sometimes allowed Christians not only to belong to it but even to indulge in militant activities: thus several of the Protestants who at the beginning of 1908 founded the Union of Christian-Socialists were members of the *SFIO*;[10] the best known of them was Paul Passy.

Finally, released from the anti-clerical battle by Combism and the separation of Church and State, French socialism came for the first time to elaborate a general political line and to tackle the totality of the problems facing society. Debates within the party did not concern reform and electoral practice, now more or less accepted, or theoretical considerations, such as the concept of the State, the development of public services – from municipal monopolies to nationalization[11] – and even the need to cross national frontiers and go beyond a narrow France-centred attitude. These debates revealed thinking that was trying to sort itself out amid the contradictions arising out of industrial society and imperialism. However, optimism triumphed: it was the expression of industrialist confidence in progress and was strengthened on the eve of the Great War by the party's electoral success and by the leadership which the *SFIO* was becoming capable of disputing in the International with German social democracy. In spite of the painful times he experienced, in the eyes of the people Jaurès symbolized the socialist hope.

The CGT

At the beginning of the century the *CGT* appeared incontestably to represent revolutionary aims. It owed this reputation primarily to the disquiet aroused in industrialists, owner farmers and the State-as-employer by its double structure – local *bourses du travail* and national trade union federations – which had been affirmed by 1895. The incredible trade union activity of the beginning of the century was gradually organized, by dint of a huge effort, into federations first of trades, then of industries. For example, the building federation, which until 1914 exerted inside the Confédération an influence comparable to that of the textile federation in the 1880s, numbered some 80,000 members. But it was the *bourses du travail* and their first secretary, Ferdinand Pelloutier – who died prematurely in March 1901 – that began to produce a specifically trade union ideology, the evolution of which up to the Great War was largely linked to working-class practice.

Yet the theme of the general strike, which, via active local sub-committees, gradually permeated the trade union avant-garde at the turn of the century, did not correspond with practice; the setbacks of 1898 (railwaymen) and 1902 (miners) are sufficient proofs of this. The success of the general-strike ideology was due to the fact that it made the section of the proletariat seeking to escape from Millerandism conscious of its power;

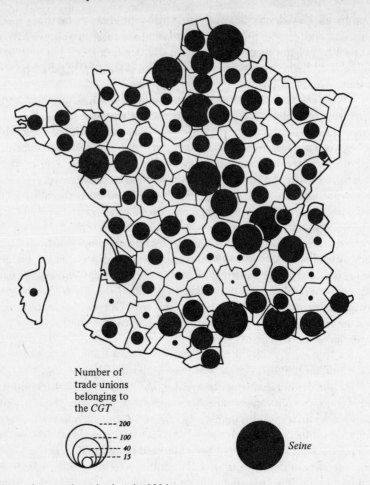

Number of
trade unions
belonging to
the *CGT*

---- 200
--- 100
--- 40
--- 15

Seine

Working-class trade unionism in 1914

Source: Atlas historique de la France contemporaine, edited by René Rémond (Paris, A. Colin, 1966).

it helped to make the working class into a separate class. The arrival at the head of the Confédération in 1901–2 of a new team – a Vaillantist, Griffuelhes; an anarchist, Pouget; and a studious but rugged boiler-maker from the department of Nord, Merrheim – more or less coincided with the radicalization of working-class struggles: the leadership of the Confédération took over partial strikes, which were often successful in Phase A, and emphasized the educational value of daily strike action. Officially reaffirmed, the general strike tended more and more to become a myth that condensed proletarian energies (Georges Sorel). 'Direct-action trade unionism': this description underlines the differences between the 'two socialisms', that of the *CGT* and that of the *SFIO*. The young Confédération refused to acknowledge the State: it desired to strike at the employers directly, without going through the mediation of parliamentary political action. This is the meaning of the famous text which was adopted in October 1906 and which has passed into the history of trade unionism as the Amiens Charter: 'Economic action must be taken directly against the employers; as trade union groups, the confederate organizations do not have to worry about the parties and sects which, outside and alongside the unions, can freely pursue the transformation of society.' In principle, this was no more a declaration of war on the *SFIO* than on the anarchist 'sects'. But the tone and style of direct action by the *CGT* were defined by the most turbulent unions – dockers, workers in the arsenals, navvies and masons. The municipalities were worried by all this, even if they were socialist, as was to be seen at Brest: though sympathetic to the *bourses du travail*, which they subsidized, they felt institutionally bound to ensure that order was respected. They were also naturally keen not to lose local power at the next elections; and *CGT* agitation upset people outside the working class and could thus lose votes.

The Confédération then hardened its attitude, taking pride in its good minority conscience: it was conscious militants who made history, not the masses who were good for nothing but voting. Although the confederated trade unions recruited fewer new members after the flare-up of strikes in 1904–7, this was not necessarily worrying. Unlike socialism, the quality of trade union activities was not measured by this standard. Accordingly the *CGT* jealously preserved an internal system of power which gave a majority to the small federations, the most 'revolutionary' ones, and kept in opposition, the building workers excepted, the big industrial federations, such as the book workers and the textile workers, and the unions which had a reputation for power, such as the railway workers. The miners' federation, with a socialist leadership, did not join the *CGT* until 1908, and not without new crises looming up on the horizon. It is perfectly true that it was not – far from it – the old, splintered trades which alone laid down the Confédération's strategy: the building workers and the iron and steel workers – the Metal Federation had been formed in 1909 – were the heart and soul of revolutionary trade unionism. However, it is a fact that membership, which rose steeply from 1902 to 1908, subsequently stagnated: the *CGT* was never to exceed the 350,000 or so members it had attained in 1908.

It then entered a period of concealed crisis; the repression to which it was subjected after the affair of Villeneuve-Saint-Georges was a sign rather than the cause of this. After the brief episode of a reforming leadership (Niel, 25 February – 28 May 1909), Léon Jouhaux, a young libertarian from the match-makers' union, began work as secretary of the Confédération on 13 July 1909. In spite of the reservations inspired by his personality, it was the beginning of a long reign. The dawn was an uncertain one; like the *SFIO*, the *CGT* hesitated and looked for the right path to follow. Around the figures of Coupat, Keufer and Albert Thomas, the little *Revue syndicaliste* had crystallized (since 1905) the researches of the reformers: those who believed in classes, not in the class struggle. Around *La Vie ouvrière*, launched in October 1909 by the team assembled by Pierre Monatte, were grouped the revolutionaries anxious to think more deeply about the French and international environment in which trade unionism operated and about the employers' new kinds of power. This trend turned out to be the most long-lived one: the revolutionary tendency drew away from the sort of revolution that was often verbal and confined to France and began to turn towards analyses that were both meticulous and general and towards new international prospects.[12] Here lie the roots of the movement which, after the Great War and the Russian Revolution, was to lead so many authentic revolutionary trade unionists towards the Third International.

From the CGT to the SFIO

However, even during the years when the two organizations were most in conflict (1904–8) they shared a sort of common mentality. To some extent it was the not very explicit mental attitudes which kept both the party and the Confédération rooted in the soil of republican, civic France. But this was a land of men; what was to be done with women in a party largely devoted to trying to win elections? Until 1912 it did not offer them any organized welcome.[13] So the figure of 200 women members in Seine in 1910 and that of 2,000 for the whole party in 1912 must be regarded as maximal. A few specialists – Bracke, Sembat, Thomas, Jaurès – wrote or spoke here and there in favour of votes for women, but no real effort followed these words. Only one woman, Madeleine Pelletier, a doctor and feminist, was really militant in the *SFIO*. In reality the party was frightened of the idea of careers for women and on this point its members were closer to Proudhon than to Marx. Anti-feminism was still more explicit in the *CGT*: it is true that the percentage of women members rose from 5.2 in 1900 to 9.8 in 1911, but they never occupied any but posts of modest responsibility. Here the objection was the competition of women workers, always underpaid, with men. The aim was not to increase women's wages but to pay men enough to remove women's need for a 'supplementary' wage. Men should go to work and women should stay at home. Against this male-centred attitude, which lasted longer in the Book Federation than anywhere else, the neo-Malthusian campaigns conducted by the most revolutionary *bourses du travail* did not make much headway: by calling on couples to practise birth control, the neo-Malthusians wanted mainly to keep up wages and to avoid wars through lack of cannon fodder; they were not interested in liberating women.[14]

The *SFIO* and even the *CGT* were also adult affairs addressed to adults. Young people did not feel quite at ease in them. So far as the *SFIO* was concerned, this even verges on understatement. The youth groups – Vaillantists, Allemanists, Guesdists – were alive enough and quite numerous at the turn of the century, but they subsequently faded away; their lukewarm enthusiasm for electoral activity worried people. The party dreamed more of supervising them than of inciting them to action. In the end the Seine federation itself refused to grant them any organization of their own. They were pushed into the margin and vague socialist attempts from 1907 at a sporting organization did not suffice to endow the party with the young militants whom apparently, in spite of the insistence of the International, it did not want. There was a warmer welcome in the *CGT*. The first youth groups appeared around 1903–4, linked to the *bourses du travail*. They tended to pursue activities connected with the physical and moral health of the proletariat, of 'la race', as people called it: anti-alcoholism, elementary rules of hygiene, and so on. There was also a certain amount of anti-militarism. This was of course an expression of working-class anger at repression, but it was also a genuine denunciation of military life, regarded as brutal, and the passive obedience to a hierarchy bound up with 'the glory of the sword'. However, from 1906 the 'young trade unionists', too, entered a grey period and more or less sank into apathy.

Finally, it may be asked what the socialist avant-garde had to say about the distant peoples colonized by France. The silence of trade unionists on this matter reflected their indifference: overseas, moreover, trade unionism recruited to all intents and purposes only European workers. It was the same, apart from one or two exceptions – Martinique, for example, which sent a native socialist deputy, Lagrosillière, to the Chamber – with the 'colonial' socialist federations. These were not in any case very strong, and the party's 'inspectors from headquarters' seldom had the desire or the means to see further than their local informants. A man like Félicien Challaye took the trouble to look and reflect, but the interest of most messengers remained superficial or episodic. There were few militants who took the trouble, as Paul Louis did (*Le Colonialisme*, 1905), to locate the colonial problem in relation to the evolution of capitalism or who were led by their knowledge of the great civilizations outside Europe and by their intellectual generosity, like Jaurès, to a multi-cultural vision of humanity. It is also true that there were few like Lucien Deslinières or Maurice Allard, who shared the Africanophobe attitude of the great colonists (cf. the texts cited in Biblio. no. 230). Usually the native population was regarded as 'still in the period of childhood',[15] and socialists had to offer help and protection towards the enlightenment represented by the Republic. Industrialism joined forces with the Jacobin and anti-clerical tradition to nourish a profoundly Europe-centred attitude.

Yet similar convictions clearly distinguished the working-class and socialist avant-garde as a whole from the main body of the republicans. There was a hatred of war, even among the most 'patriotic' socialists such as Eugène Fournière, the editor of *La Revue socialiste*, a profound mistrust of justice and the 'class' police, and of the army, too, even though here attitudes were rather more complex. The Sou du Soldat,[16] formed in September 1900 by the *bourses du travail*, was an occasion for reminding workers who had the misfortune to be called up for the army of their duty to their class – rather than their duty as internationalists, it is true – and the *Manuel du Soldat*, written by Yvetot, denounced the army as a school of vice and crime. Apart from the phraseology, regarded as sometimes excessive, the socialists were on the whole in agreement with this manual, and the remarks of Jaurès in *L'Armée nouvelle* (1910) were reckoned to be too conciliatory. Finally, and this is the essential point, both the *CGT* and the party awaited the liberation of the workers from the expropriation of the capitalits (Amiens Charter) and the socialization of the means of production and exchange (statutes of the *SFIO*), and this in the framework of the international accord of the world of labour. The time had passed when these rudiments of the 'doctrine' were constantly reiterated, and the hope of a revolution in the near future had faded. But the desire for revolution had not faded.

On the levels both of reflection and action a group – let us call it for the sake of convenience 'leftist' – had broken away from these avant-gardes at the time when the working-class movement was growing more radical. From 1904 to 1908 *Le Mouvement socialiste* became, under the impetus of Lagardelle, the review of 'working-class socialism' at the cost of a bold re-reading – or revision – of Marxism: the review provided a theoretical basis, in an intelligent, pontificating and often striking way, for the *CGT*'s working-class attitude and its desire to make the proletariat into a watertight class by giving it the workshop as its framework and separation from all other sections of the population as its goal. Lagardelle and his friends set the atomization of the citizen over against the collectivity of the producer. For some years the theoretical imagination of French socialism lay to the left of him, at the confluence of the *CGT* and the *SFIO* – to which Lagardelle belonged. The same was true of its practical imagination; the focus of this was *La Guerre sociale*, which Gustave Hervé launched in December 1906 with Miguel Almereyda, a militant anarchist known for his activity in the International Anti-militarist Association. Written in a mordant style and soon printing 50,000 copies, Hervé's paper became the mouthpiece of the 'insurrectionists', who were joined by militants who at the beginning of the century had put their faith in the revolutionary flame of Guesdism. They indulged not only in insolent language and the denunciation of compromise but also in street violence and intervention in strikes. The *CGT*, unwilling to yield to any pressure, kept its distance after the affair of Villeneuve-Saint-Georges. But Hervé's line also found support in some predominantly peasant departments.

The fact is that both Hervé's attitude and working-class socialism corresponded to a genuine extreme-left bias which embraced the anarchists who were still numerous,[17] 'advanced' socialists and some revolutionary trade unionists. The golden rule for those among the 'Hervéists' who were members of the *SFIO* was 'always keep to the left of the party'.[18] At a deeper level, this trend was distinguished by its hostility towards the State, which was regarded as a hard employer and in addition as a thief, a war-monger and, in the colonies, a torturer. These reactions revived an old anti-State attitude. However, they were extremely heterogeneous and doubtless ill-adapted to the basic phenomena that were beginning to appear in the organization of production and of the working class – ambiguous functions of the State, trade union concentration, and so on. Consequently they failed in 1910 to give birth to a revolutionary party whose official publication would have been *La Guerre sociale*. The move by certain people – the anarchist Janvion, the philosopher Sorel – in the direction of Action Française was doomed to failure in a country where socialism was so profoundly republican. Lagardelle gradually lapsed into silence, Hervé was to 'rectify his aim' and in 1913 the anarchists attempted – somewhat late in the day – to organize on a national scale the innumerable tiny groups through which their vitality was being squandered. The *SFIO* and the *CGT* had turned out to be the strongest movements. From this point it was within their ranks that new analyses were made, while the attempts made since 1906 by Jaurès and Vaillant to bring the two closer together continued. The two leaders succeeded in getting the majority of the party to pay lip service to the Amiens Charter as the sign of a wish for revolutionary autonomy which must be preserved, and it was via the *CGT* that the concept of a general strike against war permeated French socialism. One could then see what the two movements had in common: on polling day, for whom did members of the *CGT* vote? In the provinces, how many militants, the barrack-room lawyers of the proletariat, were both socialists and trade unionists? And in the eyes of the Belle Epoque establishment, were they not all 'anarchists'?

Avant-garde culture

At the beginning of the century Paris was playing the rôle of world capital of avant-garde culture. According to Robert Musil, 'those who have begotten the age' were gathered there. This reputation was no doubt exaggerated. To confine ourselves to Europe alone, it was in Munich that the first exhibition of the 'Blaue Reiter' opened in December 1911, in Geneva that Ferdinand de Saussure established the science of general linguistics (1906–1911), between Vienna and Berlin that Schoenberg started to break with tonal music (from 1908) and in Prague that Kafka began *Amerika*. In France itself the capital did not have a monopoly of the avant-garde. The mayors of Lyon – Augagneur and particularly Herriot who succeeded him in 1905 – gave a young architect, Tony Garnier,[19] his first real chance. Garnier's first plan for an 'Industrial City' was made in accordance with the concept of towns on a human scale of which Fourier dreamed. In 1914 Lyon welcomed the first International Urban Exhibition. Yet the concentration of publishing, the art market, the learned institutions (Collège de France, *Ecole pratique des hautes études* (*EPHE*), Muséum), the *grandes écoles*, and the literary cafés confirmed Parisian leadership in creativity and cultural – not only aesthetic – daring.

In dealing with a subject like this there is a great risk of ending up with a catalogue, if not a prize list or at best a chronological table; all the more so since the material indispensable for a reflective survey has not yet been assembled and the cultural links look more problematical than solidly buttressed. Nevertheless, the French cultural melting-pot deserves exploration.

From the scientific approach to the scientific renewal: Modernism

The mutations of scientific positivism were contemporaneous with its victory. But their use functioned at very different levels, and there were areas where the scientific approach still caused scandal at the beginning of the century: the Modernist crisis bears witness to this.

The Modernist movement was not confined to France, but it was in France that the 'Loisy affair' erupted. It originated among the biblical scholars (the 'nice people' of whom Lucien Febvre was to speak). They were not very numerous, but their work found an echo not only in the learned reviews but also, since Renan's *Vie de Jésus*, in periodicals with a wider circulation. A priest since 1870, Alfred Loisy, who had already had some disputes with the hierarchy on account of his teaching, held a chair at the *EPHE*. His 'little red books' came out right in the middle of the Combist era: 1902, *L'Evangile et l'Eglise*; 1903, *Autour d'un petit livre*. The controversy which they aroused brought Loisy under fire from Rome: of sixty-five 'doctrinal propositions' condemned by the Holy Office on 4 July 1907, thirteen referred to *L'Evangile et l'Eglise* (the decree *Lamentabili*). Soon afterwards the Pope issued a total condemnation of Modernism (in the Encyclical *Pascendi* of 8 September 1907). A few months later Loisy was to be excommunicated. The episode is interesting for two reasons: the ideas expressed by Loisy, and the extent of the support which he found and of the passions which he unleashed. Could one be both a Catholic and a scientist? Loisy, while indulging in controversy with liberal Protestantism,[20] no doubt hoped to induce theology to accept the critical gains of biblical exegesis and thus to prompt some relaxation of the Church's rigid attitude. But the difficulties he encountered led him to assert that biblical criticism must preserve its autonomy in relation to the magisterium of the Church. It was this secularization of knowledge that at the beginning of the century the Catholic Church could not accept.

However, Loisy was not isolated. Much encouragement came to him from Catholic circles whose principal preoccupation was not exegesis. Well-known democratic priests, Christian democratic laymen such as Georges Fonsegrive and the liberal bishops of Albi and the Tarentaise among others approved of his effort if not of all his conclusions. Jacques Rivière was to speak later of the 'sort of electric shock administered to people's minds'[21] by the little books. We can perceive only vaguely the content of the faith of those who supported Loisy or of those who parted from him *en route* – like the philosopher Blondel. But the debate, by challenging the idea of the Gospel as the faithful echo of the words of Jesus, touched the very springs of spirituality in ardent believers.[22] Moreover, Modernist criticism was drawn into a very serious discussion to which Christians in republican, scientific France were invited; it seemed like an indispensable *aggiornamento* if Catholicism wanted to envisage the intellectual reconquest of the bourgeoisie. Thus Modernism came up against a heterogeneous coalition which ensured its defeat for the time being. Some turned their efforts at renewal towards the quest for a different kind of spirituality – Blondel, Laberthonnière – or another mode of participation in social life – the Sillon. Others, such as Richard, the Cardinal of Paris, were concerned above all that the faithful should not put frightening questions to themselves. The most obstinate people – old and new 'integralists', from *L'Univers* to *L'Action française*, full of obedience after the Pope had spoken – condemned in Modernism 'all modernisms'. Beaten in the Church, the Modernist avant-garde nevertheless kept and perhaps even made friends, both in the ranks of liberal Catholicism and among those – from Edouard Le Roy to the father of Grandmaison – who, while submitting, continued to wish that the intellectual life of the Church should not remain bogged down in dusty dogmas.

Renewal in the humanities

The Modernist battle took place simultaneously with a renewal in the humanities which was rooted in a very different, secular milieu. Its promoters, without renouncing a rational view of the world – quite the contrary – attempted to discard what was beginning to look naïve to them in scientific determinism. Reviews such as *L'Année sociologique*, launched by Durkheim's team in 1896, or the *Revue de synthèse historique*, founded by Henri Berr in 1900, published fundamental methodological studies. Three innovations – essential ones – made their appearance. First, there were works of serious reflection on society, stimulated by an awareness more often dimly felt than formulated in precise terms that the social fabric was breaking up; these works would be incomprehensible but for the spread of Marxism, though this does not mean to say that they were inspired by it. Second, there was the rejection of belief in the existence of facts of nature, the range and causal connections of which it might suffice to establish. And third, there was the aspiration towards a synthesis beyond the splits between the various disciplines. At the heart of this renewal was history, the queen of the nineteenth century.[23]

It was in relation to history that the new geography acquired its definition round the figure of Vidal de la Blache. A historian by training, he brought to geographical research and study a vision of history very different from that of Lavisse, although the famous *Tableau de la géographie de la France* of 1903 formed the opening to the *Histoire de France* edited by the semi-official historian of the Republic. The regional landscape, the first subject of the study, was not 'something given by nature' but 'the product of man's activity', the work of history. Vidal's vision of the world traditionally puts man, as a priority, in the landscape. However, at the beginning of the century it was innovatory to the extent that it founded a mode of historical knowledge that avoided both catalogues and statistics.

History was also the reference point of the new kind of literary criticism that began to make its appearance; this criticism wanted to unravel the tangle of the subjective criticism of men like Lemaître or Emile Faguet while avoiding second-hand sociology in the style of Plekhanov. In his *Introduction à l'histoire littéraire* (1898), Paul Lacombe emphasizes the function of demand in literary production: the consumer determines the direction taken by the producer. He suggests a number of categories suitable for defining various kinds of public opinions, and the concept of class seems to him to play a part, provided that it is analysed in a fairly sophisticated way.

This renewal of research stimulated by social documentation affected first and foremost the subjects regarded as historical. Such was the case with that privileged subject, the French Revolution. By publishing from 1900 to 1903 his *Histoire socialiste de la Révolution française*, Jaurès put it once again at the heart of politico-scientific reflection. The brilliance of the style and the wide scope of the information presented are not the only virtues of this work, long pondered and written at a breath-taking rhythm. The book is striking in the novelty of its conceptual framework: the real heroes of the drama recounted are the classes which Jaurès sees at work in the depths of the provinces as well as in Paris, in the distant world of the Isles as well as in the Europe that shuddered in the wind blowing from France. At about the same time François Simiand, another socialist, devoted himself for the first time to the study of coalminers' wages. Simiand challenged purely histori-cal history, and he took his stand at the crossroads where sociology, economics and a new kind of history met, with the explicit intention of giving full value, at the expense of 'individual facts', to the 'facts which are repeated', the 'facts of society'. His efforts were directed to the study of relations, whether involving conflict or compromise, between employers and workers.[24] To study the economy in a 'positive' way, he said, was to study its reality, which was social.

The new history may háve escaped the professors of the Sorbonne, but outside the universities, away from the examinations that conferred titles and jobs, it would be difficult to measure the leading part played by sociology. It owed a great deal to Durkheim (1858–1917) and his first disciples – Marcel Mauss, Maurice Halbwachs, Simiand and Bouglé. It enjoyed rapid recognition by the universities, in post-graduate teaching.[25] Its founders doubtless thought of their discipline, in the style of the natural sciences, as a sort of 'social physics'. But they were the first to admit that there is no such thing as crude, observable fact: every fact is a construct and sociology's first task is to constitute its material. We have not yet exhausted this discovery, which is at the heart of the *Règles de la méthode sociologique* (1895). It sounded the death knell of the old scientific approach.

Renewal in the physical sciences

About the same time radical changes threw the physical sciences into a ferment. However, their formalized language and the frequency of conferences and seminars facilitating confrontations make it ridiculous to separate, in this domain more than in any other, French science from what was happening abroad. It was in Berne, and later at the Zurich Polytech-nic, that Einstein, in 1905, laid the bases of restricted relativity before proceeding to the assertion of general relativity. On the other hand, the work carried out from 1895 by Pierre and Marie Curie link the other great discovery of those years, that of the new properties apparent in matter, to France and, more concretely to the School of Physics and Chemistry of the City of Paris. The books of the mathematician Henri Poincaré confirmed in the eyes of the cultivated but non-specialist public the emergence of fundamental reassessment, of a new 'Copernican revolution'.[26] It seemed that the Newtonian explanation of the world was collapsing. Einstein's discoveries led to the rejection of the implicit presuppositions on which Euclid's geometry and Newton's mechanics rested. The space and time of the physicist ceased to coincide with the *a priori* forms of sensibility hallowed by Kant. What were affected, or even destroyed, were the age-old habits of representation used by the scientist and disseminated wholesale by the academic establishment. Was it necessary then to 'doubt science' just at the moment when discoveries like those of the Curies were on the contrary revealing the capacity of scientists to bring to light previously unknown elements? Bergson's finally ironic answer emphasized the impotence of a successful philosopher to recognize such radical novelties. Science was reconstructed on different foundations, and scientific progress ceased to appear as the fruit of a continuous accumulation of knowledge; it consisted first of reforming the faculty of knowing. Positivism was outstripped not by a return to the irrational but, as sociology recommended, by a different method of approach to the rational.

The aesthetic avant-garde

The crisis in cultural values affected at the same time the classical representation of space, the organization of language and the apprehension of time. Alongside the new physics came the new painting and the new poetry. While refraining from specious reflections on the relations between the theory of relativity and Cubist space,[27] the historian struck by such concomitances cannot evade the prospect of a common requirement: the avant-garde work of art intervenes as one of the constituent elements of the socio-cultural fabric; it establishes in it, not without difficulty, its own system of values. This was perhaps never so evident as between 1907 and 1914.

No art, not even avant-garde art, is possible without a minimum of instances of recognition and of means of commercialization. At the dawn of the century the possibilities for experimental painting were more considerable than those available for the written word. Ever since the official monopoly in approbation had been broken by a few art-dealers at the time of Impressionism, avant-garde painting had some chance of being seen by art lovers and of being sold. D. H. Kahnweiler and Bernheim junior, by systematically using exclusive contracts, took risks but in the hope of making a profit: the auction of *La Peau de l'ours* on 2 March 1914 proved that modern painting had found a public.[28] The structures were in place that were going to establish the avant-garde art inside the capitalist market. The world of publishing and literary criticism was much more timid. Grasset certainly published *Du côté de chez Swann* in 1913, but at the author's expense. As for the *Nouvelle Revue française*, which started publication in 1908, it launched on the market *Le Grand Meaulnes* by Alain-Fournier and *Barnabooth* by Valéry Larbaud, but its editorial board, from Gide to Schlumberger and Rivière, was nervous of the kind of boldness that aimed at the deconstruction of language.[29] Contrasting 'the order of art with the art of order',[30] the review displayed great open-mindedness, but endowed Literature with what this concept implies in the way of old-fashioned rhetoric.

Thus it is advisable to look first at the artists. The renewal of their vision of the world was effected in any case under pressures outside them. From Blaise Cendrars to Larbaud, exoticism changed dimension if not yet perspective: the theme of Ulysses was revived by the Orient Express. Above all, the creations of the colonized peoples were subjected to a fresh look. Without knowing it, painters followed the same path as Maurice Delafosse, an African administrator mad on ethnology, or Victor Segalen, a naval officer. By writing *Les Immémoriaux* in 1907 and by entrusting the rôle of narrator to Terii, the Maori, Segalen broke with traditional exoticism and put the colonized at the centre of a universal space.

About the same time 'negro art', which until then people had agreed to regard as 'primitive',[31] entered the aesthetic consciousness of young painters and sculptors. In anonymous Africa they discovered the key to a new dignity: that of the work – masks, statuettes – which exists in itself, without literary support.

There were two consequences. On the one hand, the exclusivity of Western values was challenged: the recognition of otherness radically challenged what might be called the colonialist 'spirit', even if no profession of political faith flowed from this immediately. On the other hand, the academic organization of space, the space which had constituted the work since the Renaissance, was shattered. Such was the first result of Cubist efforts, as a result of which the questioning of the West's plastic vision grew more profound. After the Cézanne exhibition of 1907, the first Cubist group formed in 1908 round the Bateau-Lavoir: it consisted of Braque, Picasso, Delaunay and Villon. 'Noble' subjects and themes were abolished through experiments which differed from one painter to another and changed year by year. *Les Demoiselles d'Avignon* (1907) and the portraits of Kahnweiler by Picasso reconstructed the space occupied by the body. *La Danse*, by Matisse (1909) showed a curved space seen from outside. The system of spatial signs was not the only thing to be renewed: the poets, from Max Jacob to Apollinaire, in the process of breaking with Symbolist language (rendered banal over the previous twenty years), destroyed the old poetic mode of expression by the free association of words, and created the instrument necessary for a new way of thinking and feeling. Juan Gris did the same thing with collages. By publishing *Les Peintres cubistes* in 1912 Apollinaire built a bridge between criticism, poetry and painting which led towards new territories where not only traditional space but the whole socio-cultural order is mocked by formal researches of great intensity.

Poetry and painting – romantic prose as well – also worked to break out of the strait-jacket of the placid, continuous rural and bourgeois age. The 'Manifesto of Futurism' published in *Le Figaro* of 20 February 1909 by the Italian Marinetti – an astonishing cultural agitator – proclaimed the accord necessary between modern poetry and speed, and the superiority of the 'roaring automobile' to the *Victory* of Samothrace. From the factory to the aeroplane, the rhythms of the modern world entered the novel, but as new themes rather than as new modes of expression. Better established and more sure of itself than the Italian or Russian ruling classes, the French bourgeoisie saw only superficial excitement in breaches of form, and the production of novels could not do without its support unless it could find a popular substitute, which was impossible. The conditions of production were more favourable to the expression of this aspect of modernity in poetry, music and the plastic arts:[32] the same dynamic of violence was expressed in the music of Erik Satie, in *Les Bûcherons au travail nus dans la forêt* by Fernand Léger and in *Le Cheval moteur* by Duchamp-Villon. But literary language, confident in the primacy which it enjoyed in the culture of the social élite, proved more resistant to innovation.

Thus it was only at the cost of severe cuts in the text that the total dramatic spectacle attempted shortly before by Wagner made a fresh appearance as a means of expressing the changes in aesthetic values: twice in a decade the opera, the focus of fashionable ritual, was the vehicle. There were two scandals: on 27 February 1902 *Pelléas et Mélisande* was received as an anti-Tristan son of Tristan; for Debussy, as for Wagner, music began where words ended. The 29 May 1913 witnessed the première of *Le Sacre du printemps* at the recently opened Théâtre des Champs-Elysées. This time words were quite simply excluded and it was between the music (by Stravinsky), the choreography (by Nijinsky), the scenery and the costumes that a bold complicity was established, thanks to Diaghilev, who in 1909 had brought the Russian ballet to France. This time the barriers between the arts were broken down.

On the eve of the Great War another avenue opened up, marked just as strongly by the rejection of nineteenth-century values. This avenue was taken by Proust as well as by Gabriel Fauré, Florent Schmitt and Mondrian who arrived in Paris in 1912. With Proust the traditional novel was well and truly dead. A decisive step had been taken on the road to the contemporary novel without a hero and without a 'story'. Once time consisting of events had been destroyed, the true life became not that of fugitive present, but that of time which has fled, of time past, which is to be recreated in all its fullness. Mondrian for his part pushed the desire to break with the plastic transcription of a space peopled with objects to the point of the suppression of objects, of the obsession with 'pure painting', in which the artist creates autonomous symbolic wholes known as abstracts. So ended a cumulation of critical waves which were born at different moments and which, temporarily overlapping – for no 'school' eliminated the previous one – endangered received values as a whole: the old academism, still very much alive; Naturalism, which had entered the past; and all the Impressionist and Symbolist modes of vision which the educated bourgeoisie was in process of accepting.

All round, the split between the aesthetic avant-garde and traditional modes of representation displayed on all fronts the desire to change the relations between the work and the person who listens to it, reads it or looks at it. Even in the theatre, which was hide-bound in tradition, the wish to turn the spectator into co-author made its appearance. The experiments of Jacques Copeau at the Vieux Colombier, where he abandoned scenic illusionism, were an appeal for the participation of the public. Nothing was given. The receiver was no longer simply to receive. The created form was no longer closed in on itself. The author, the 'creator', had ceased to be God the Father.

From one avant-garde to another

Between the political and social avant-garde movements and avant-garde culture the predominant note to be heard was one of discord, or even of sharp contradiction. This was largely owing to the almost obligatory position held between cultural innovation and militant political attitudes by the intellectuals. University teachers, journalists and writers sometimes had contact, but for the most part these circles lived side by side in total ignorance of one another. Socialists, monarchists or Sillonists, they had almost all had a secondary education and taken the *baccalauréat*, the entry ticket to bourgeois culture. Their ideologies might be quite different, even opposed, but they all had the same cult of the humanities and the same rhetorical training. Why dislocate the literary language? Why paint what no citizen could see, whether he was educated in one of Jules Ferry's schools or in one run by the Christian Brothers? In the children of the secular age this certainty was joined by additional mistrust of linguistic obscurities suspected of nourishing obscurantism of thought. And all these people lacked artistic culture: in their eyes art was something on the fringe of society. From Pierre Lasserre and Clouard, who from 1908 edited the *Revue critique*, to Anatole France, classicism or substitutes for it pulled in the money. It did not occur even to socialist intellectuals that socialism could be the vehicle for a new way of seeing the world. Culture had to be established on the basis of the legacy of the past: a return to the pre-Romantic past for the friends of Lasserre, who thought the enjoyment of these fruits should be confined to an élite, and for the friends of Jaurès access to 'haute culture' for the ordinary people previously prevented from enjoying it.

There were hardly any places where the militant intellectuals could meet the visionaries of a new world – artists or scholars. The members of the learned institutions, if they belonged to the left, had the League of the Rights of Man in common, and among the young people there were growing groups of collectivist students, but with a disproportionately large number of 'scientists'. But avant-garde literary and artistic circles formed little chapels, shut in on themselves. Painters and writers met in the cafés of Montmartre or at the Bateau-Lavoir in the rue Ravignan. The time had gone when they had access to *La Plume* or *La Revue blanche*. Whether they had a decent income or not, most young writers and painters led a life that seemed strange to university teachers like Lucien Lévy-Bruhl, Maurice Halbwachs or François Simiand. The taste for public life had possibly never been so alien to them. Picasso himself, whose early Spanish works had been marked by social violence and working-class distress, turned in Paris to other subjects and other friends. Young creative artists expressed their desire for rebellion in pictorial or literary writing.

For the rest, after the Dreyfus affair the call to the dissemination of culture and to political militancy faded among many intellectuals. The heroic period of the Universités Populaires was over, and both socialists and radicals tended to return to their beloved studies. The growing 'parliamentarization' of unified socialism was reflected in the party's silence about the new cultural problems, in the monotony of the books it sold and in the effective but somewhat old-fashioned character of its scientific approach. Encyclopedias of 'popular philosophy' occupied as much space in the party's bookshop as the writings of Marx; and moreover they sold better. Many intellectuals who had written for *L'Humanité* in the early days ceased to do so after unity had been attained and thus lost a contact with the militants that just after the Dreyfus affair they had to a large extent achieved. We are talking of critics such as Léon Blum and above all of specialists in the social sciences. It is true that the latter sometimes found places from which they could speak to the young, at the Collège Libre des Sciences Sociales or at the Ecole des Hautes Etudes Sociales, for example. The most active of them launched new series of books: *la Bibliothèque socialiste* was published from 1900 to 1907 by the Société Nouvelle de Librairie et d'Edition.[33] It was strongly influenced by the *Ecole normale supérieure*, or *Les Cahiers du socialiste* which more or less took over from it under the aegis of Albert Thomas from 1909 onwards. A very few taught at the Ecole Socialiste, the creation of which the group of collectivist students had succeeded in forcing, also in 1909. However, in spite of the existence of a School of Art directed by Ferdinand Herold at the Ecole des Hautes Etudes Sociales, Jaurès was essentially right when he wrote that 'the sort of thinking which expresses itself in artistic forms no longer understands, or hardly, the sort of thinking expressed in political and social activity'.[34] Moreover, he was personally not very sensitive to the pictorial challenge to the old order and scarcely more sensitive to the boldest aspects of the literary renewal: when he enthused in 1913 over a young writer it was Alain, not Proust, that he had discovered. However his consciousness of a lack, of a gap, illustrates how, at the beginning of the century, the party which regarded itself as the vehicle of the future of socialism was divorced from the researches which were producing a new vision of the world.

The efforts made inside or on the fringes of the trade union movement showed more originality. Trade unionism had inherited the links formed in 1880–90 between anarchism and numerous avant-garde creative artists. It is true that, from Octave Mirbeau to Signac and from Lucien Descaves to Steinlen, it was a question of a generation which had reached maturity and hardly renewed the way in which it expressed its social protest.[35] Nevertheless, the cultural specificity of the trade union avant-garde was real: the teaching dispensed by the *bourses du travail* put the emphasis on trades, the creative meaning of work and the values represented by the proletariat. It was the tradition of Proudhon, very strongly rooted in France and which Pelloutier had revived by proposing to create in each *bourse* a social museum. This cult of the beauty of work which enabled Péguy to think that he was more at ease with the workers than in the atmosphere of the Sorbonne, bears witness to the preponderance of qualified workers in the *bourse* sector of the movement. However, this obviously did not make it any easier for such people to understand a poet like Apollinaire, or Cubist painting. But for revolutionary trade unionists the workshop was not simply the place where objects were produced. It was there that 'ideas exclusive to the proletariat' were forged and that a new civilization could be worked out. This civilization rested on a morality; 'the morality of the sublime', said Sorel. The militants put it in different ways: 'let us train men and crack skulls'.[36] The sense of solidarity, the refusal to succeed in life as an individual were the principal features of this proletarian morality.

By asserting that they meant to promote it, the trade unionists restored to collective practice a function which it had lost: they made possible the re-emergence of the concept of social art as art born of the collective life and placed at its service. They defined it now as 'the aesthetic sense applied to the collective life' (Claude Roger-Marx, *L'Art social*, 1913), that is, to the life of the city, to the decoration of the factory, the house or the street. *L'Humanité* gave space to these problems. The modernity of the background to life was at last given more value than the after-effects of a countrified, academic past. The 'scenery of shields and swords' which the bourgeoisie liked was at last freely criticized. On the eve of the Great War the question was whether those interested in social art so understood could join forces with the Cubists in a common fight against the dusty décor of life and its traditional representations.

12

France in 1914

France is republican

At the start of the period of wars, crises and revolutions, and at the end of forty years of Republic, what was the state of the conflicts that had dominated the nineteenth century? How did things stand with the much vaunted equilibrium and harmonious prosperity of French society? In 1914 few European régimes looked as solid as the French Republic.

A constantly challenged régime

· Not that it had ceased to be challenged. Monarchists and Bonapartists had not disarmed, but their audience had contracted. *Le Gaulois* of Arthur Meyer, which during the Dreyfus affair had collected some of the readers of *Le Soleil*, remained the fashionable paper in country houses and drawing-rooms; it printed between 20,000 and 30,000 copies. In the provinces a few old newspapers supported by local dignitaries persevered until 1914. *L'Action française* above all had rejuvenated declining royalism and modernized its doctrine. At the elections of 1910 only seventy deputies did not stand as republicans; some twenty perhaps remained inexorably hostile to 'the beggar woman'. In 1914 fewer still. They came from the woods of the Vendée, from Ille-et-Vilaine and from a south-west which extended to the southern fringes of the Massif Central – the almost solely rural constituencies where there was a certain consensus between nobles and peasants.

The Bonapartists were in sharp retreat – into the south-western departments of Gers and Charente, and those of Corsica, which were its home ground; in 1914 the 'réunion de la presse bonapartiste' listed only a few dozen provincial newspapers and no national newspapers. But the anti-parliamentary attitude which had characterized it and which had reappeared in most of the anti-Dreyfusard leagues still floated as a possibility on the horizon of popular discontent. With the help of neo-nationalism it had even penetrated the sphere in which political power was exercised directly: a considerable section of the press urged Poincaré after his election to the presidency of the Republic to dissolve an ungovernable Chamber. In a society in which parliamentary life mobilized so much energy and in a country in which the memory of the Empire and of Boulangism had not completely faded away, an anti-parliamentary attitude easily appeared – sometimes wrongly – to be anti-republican.

A régime that grew more and more stable

Nevertheless, the régime was extremely strong, and not only because of the mediocrity of the claimant to the throne. The monarchist and Bonapartist deputies no longer formed independent groups in the Chamber and it was very difficult to distinguish them from many conservatives who supported the Republic. The loyalty of the working class had been gained from the start. Without being complete, the conquest of the countryside, Gambetta's dream, had been consolidated. Since 1900 numerous statues and busts of the Republic had been erected in village squares, sometimes adorned with inscriptions which recalled what the children of the locality owed to their political mother.[1] These inscriptions show more than acceptance; they display fervour. The Catholic and royalist journalist, Jacques Valdour, was impressed by the obvious respect in which the Republic was held by the strongly individualistic agricultural workers of Brie.[2]

This devotion was exercised within a now stable framework of institutions. The electoral system gave citizens the frequent opportunity of 'doing their duty' by voting. The failure of attempts to introduce proportional representation shows that the country remained attached to constituency voting in spite of – or because of – its alleged defects. As the council of the communes of France, the Senate had decisively rejected electoral reform in March 1913. Better even than the Chamber, it ensured the over-representation of the rural districts and watched jealously to see that social laws, so wasteful of the state's resources, as is well known, and possibly costly to employers, were kept off the statute book as long as possible. It also blocked fiscal measures that might be useful but were also dangerous. By 1907 the radicals, who dominated it through the 'radical left' group, had officially deleted its abolition from their programme, contenting themselves with the wish that recruitment to it should be widened. However, there was a more active political life in the Chamber, where manners were said to have become more democratic with everyone on Christian-name terms. Since 1910 members of the big commissions had been appointed, for both the Chamber of Deputies and the Senate, in proportion to the size of the parliamentary groups. The Assembly had been forced to adopt this system by the complexity of the mechanisms in which the republican State now intervened.

The State now concentrated less and less on the maintenance of order and the defence of the national territory. Both in the economy and in society as a whole its intervention was requested by numerous pressure groups whose composition has hardly yet been studied. The machinery of government had also been enlarged: Agriculture was made into a ministry in 1881, the Colonies in 1893 and Labour with Social Services in 1906. The stagnation of certain government departments was the subject, from inside, of sharp criticism: for example, some advocated the abolition of the Ministry of the Interior, which was regarded as overblown and expansion- ist.[3] The reorganization of the Sûreté (Criminal Investigation Depart- ment), regarded as somewhat dusty, was also recommended. It was at this time that the concept of administrative authority appeared (H. Chardon, Biblio. no. 284): 'We have not given the permanent technical officials, who alone can properly run the public services, the status and the responsibility without which this administration is only a sham. Why, it was asked, should the transitory members of ministerial cabinets understand how to run offices?

These interesting demands are still not very well known. They came mainly, it seems, from middle-rank officials of the central government. Above the office level the continuity of the State was ensured by a few great crops whose recruitment betrayed a political favouritism that was sharply denounced and the compromises swallowed by the Republic. The Council of State – after 1910 it had 114 members – the Inspection des Finances – to which Joseph Caillaux belonged – and Foreign Affairs still recruited only partly by competition. A quarter of the appointments as appeal judges and all those as councillors of State remained in the government's gift. As for the competitions, candidates prepared for these at the Ecole Libre des Sciences Politiques, founded in 1871. From the start the organization of the work in *écuries* (stables) eliminated those who were not heirs in the most restricted sense of the term. The requirements in the way of elegance and 'presence' led the nobility and the top ranks of the bourgeoisie to occupy a far superior position relative to their number and moreover to their real ability. Real dynasties administered France at the highest level and influenced governmental decisions by the information they assembled, the reports they presented and the policies they suggested.

Overseas, the colonial régime, which overlapped with that of the Repub- lic, was not on the whole the target of opposition movements powerful enough to endanger it. Incidents in Algeria such as the rebellion of the village of Margueritte in the spring of 1901 or, ten years later, 'the exodus from Tlemcen' certainly revealed the disaffection of the 'native popula- tion'; but they did not constitute any immediate danger and the Algiers administration, subject to permanent pressure from the colonists, did not draw any other lesson from them but the need for repression. On the other hand, this repression provoked protests from the 'Young Algerians'. These,

joining the movement in hundreds – but not in thousands – were secularized and dreamed of naturalization for their brothers. They were the
(rare) products of French secondary education; they worried the
Europeans in Algeria, but not the metropolitan authorities. The activities
of the 'Young Tunisian' movement, which was much more combative and
nationalist, were sharply curtailed after the incidents of 1911–12. At the
other end of the empire, in Vietnam, the armed resistance, which had been
pretty well continuous since the beginning of the conquest, finally petered
out. After demonstrations in 1908 against forced labour and personal
taxation had been crushed, the League for the Restoration of Vietnam, led
by an educated nationalist called Phan Ba-Chau, turned to terrorism but its
social base was narrow – the great mass of workers did not belong to it – and
in 1911 the future Ho Chi Minh embarked for the West. Indo-China did
not worry the French government any more than did Algeria.

A poor yield

The Republic was firmly established, but was it already suffering
from a hardening of the arteries? The poor legislative yield of the system
was striking. It was true that social legislation had made some progress.
For example, the Clemenceau ministry had not confined itself to repression: it had facilitated the adoption of measures calculated to help the insane
and to ease the marriage or legitimization of children born out of wedlock.
It was also during the premiership of 'France's top cop' that a law under
discussion since 1894 authorizing a married woman to do as she liked with
her wages was passed on 13 July 1907. Five years later (11 March 1912)
another law released minors less than thirteen years old from repressive
jurisdiction and provided for a régime of supervised freedom. Nor did the
radicals deprive themselves of the pleasure of winning the prize for 'social
laws' passed under the Republic; weekly rest day (13 July 1906) and
pensions for workers and peasants (5 April 1910). Nevertheless, the system
was extremely sluggish; it had taken twenty years to pass the law on
workers' pensions (H. Hatzfeld, Biblio. no. 296), and twenty years, too, for
the tax on income, 'the Sleeping Beauty tax'. The support of the organized
social forces, fundamental to success, was not unanimous: the *CGT* led a
public campaign against the law on pensions, not only because of its
derisory character – a 'pension for the dead'[4] – but also because of the
mistrust it felt for the 'robber State'. But working-class nerves were
constantly stretched by these interminable pregnancies that regularly
ended in sickly deliveries. This brings us back to the institutional mechanisms that allowed Parliament to do the contrary of what universal suffrage
wanted. The Senate halted the law on pensions for three years, from 1907 to
1910, and from 1909 to 1913 it blocked Caillaux's bill introducing income
tax. Means of burying measures were not lacking; the most usual one was to

send a bill back to be examined by a commission. The Chamber was not totally deprived of means of pressure on the Senate where fiscal measures were concerned; the Chamber could include the measure in the finance bill, which did not need senatorial approval; but it seldom made up its mind to take such action. The government itself had various means of exerting pressure at its disposal and it did sometimes employ them,[5] but in terms of tactics rendered more and more subtle by the absence of any stable majority and the rapid turnover of ministries. The régime was basically 'social', but its feeble capacity for reform showed that it was political in its techniques, and the sclerosis it displayed bore witness to difficulties in the parliamentary Republic which went beyond the 'governmental waltz', a theme much appreciated by the humorous press.

Progress and prosperity

France's strength also came, so it was said, from its wealth, from its equilibrium and from the changes which had ensured its modernization, especially since 1900. New research has brought confirmation on several points of a description challenged at the beginning of the century by the first socialists infatuated with growth – Albert Thomas, Francis Delaisi – and by some Anglophone historians.

National prosperity

For many French people of the period between the two wars the Belle Epoque was first and foremost the era of monetary stability. In 1914 the Republic remained faithful to the franc of the Revolution, of Germinal. The metallic money fixed by Bonaparte still formed a third of the money in circulation, the share represented by banknotes having a short time previously shrunk to the profit of bank money, of bank deposits. These heavy-sounding coins were still used for everyday transactions and it was these coins they that people kept in woollen stockings for safety. In practice, if not in law, monetary stability rested on the gold standard.

In terms not of collective consciousness but of objective reality national prosperity is measured first of all by production. The calculations of M. Lévy-Leboyer (Biblio. no. 299), who used the weightings of T.-J. Markhovitch (Biblio. no. 300), tend to show that the national product had tripled since the beginning of the nineteenth century and that its rate of growth, which had slowed since the end of the Second Empire, recovered real vigour round about 1895 and especially in the three or four years immediately before the Great War. Such a general formulation has the merit of emphasizing the essential. The increase in the gross national product, and still more clearly the increase in income, put France among the most vigorous modern nations. It was certainly a fair distance behind the United States and even Germany, where the average annual growth of the GNP over half a century was 2.8 per cent, but quite close to the United Kingdom, where the rate was 2.1 per cent. The French rate was 1.6 per cent.[6] Calculated per head and not as a total figure, the national rate of growth – 1.4 per cent – was slightly higher than that of the United Kingdom and slightly lower than that of Germany. Agriculture was included in this general progress. The old dyestuff crops and the rearing of sheep yielded to flowers, fruit and vegetables – a great novelty – to the vine, now cultivated in some regions on an industrial scale, to sugar-beet, the cultivation of which had been perfected, and to the growing of fodder crops. The production of fodder crops more than doubled in thirty years, and as a result the rearing of cattle for meat and milk made a real leap forward. But although the gross value of agricultural production increased by a half-milliard in a third of a century, and although agricultural income made rapid progress from 1900 onwards, the net product diminished over thirty years,[7] in marked contrast to that of industry. To study that major factor, industrial growth, F. Crouzet has constructed a particularly sophisticated index.[8] He notes that the average annual rate of growth from 1815 to 1913 attained 2.97 per cent if it is based on the most dynamic industries and falls to 1.61 per cent,[9] if one takes into account the whole of industrial production. Between 1896 and 1913 it moved to 2.4 per cent.[10] From 1905, four or five years before agriculture finally emerged from its prolonged misfortunes and benefited in turn – very late in the day – from the rise in world prices, the first index rose to 5.2 per cent and even the second reached 3.56 per cent. The upward surge of industry at the beginning of the century is still more marked if the comparison is made not with growth during the previous century but with the last twenty years of the nineteenth century, which were so badly smitten by stagnation and even by recession. The triumphs of industrial growth did not entirely coincide with the rise in prices which began in 1896. Still only fair at the turn of the century, and slowed down in any case by the recurring difficulties of 1901–4, industrial growth did not really get going until after 1905, and the new wind which blew through French industry reached its maximum strength in 1910–13. Industry then very nearly attained the magnificent rates of growth that had characterized the end of the July Monarchy and the beginning of the Second Empire.

The songs of praise for growth were all the more lusty as it mainly affected more recent industries. What lagged behind was the textile industry, particularly the oldest textiles – hemp, linen, wool – although the industry still provided work, even after all the changes in it had been made, for 41.7 per cent of the industrial population. Cotton, the great performer of the beginning of the century, showed more staying power, and the silk industry was fairly sprightly. Coal's performance was not exceptional

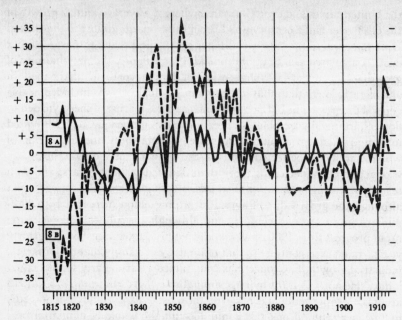

Two indices of French industrial production in the nineteenth century

Relative gaps, in percentages, in relation to the long-term tendency calculated according to the method of exponential adjustment

Index 8A, which unites 7 indices (including linen and hemp) represents the whole of industry working for the market. Index 8B, based on the first six indices (plus cotton and silk) represents in essentials new, dynamic activities.

Source: F. Crouzet, 'Un indice de la production industrielle française au XIXe siècle', *Annales ESC*, January-February 1970.

either. The production of coal continued to grow – it reached 42 million tonnes in 1914 – but this was essentially because of the Nord basin and the Pas-de-Calais, where the maximum rate of growth was attained against the trend and remained steady in the first few years of the century at 2.72 per cent per annum. Like food production and building, these industries were no longer star industries, although they were driving forces because of the large place they occupied in national production.[11]

The greatest dynamism was to be found in industries created at the end of the nineteenth century. With twenty-four factories and 20,000 workers, Saint-Gobain dominated the chemical industry, which in 1914 employed some 120,000 workers altogether. The upsurge of the iron and steel industry was dazzling at all levels; it employed about 900,000 people, not counting the iron miners. In 1914 four times more iron was extracted than in 1900 and the rate of growth of the production of steel, which had completely outstripped cast iron, reached 7.6 per cent per annum. It was a great triumph for the iron and steel industry of Lorraine. The rapid progress of hydro-electric power enabled the Alpine valleys to specialize in precision engineering, special steels, and aluminium of which France was the second biggest producer in the world. More classical forms of engineering such as the manufacture of armaments, Schneider's speciality at Le Creusot, also experienced a very high rate of growth. Finally, the star of the new century, the motor car, was making a promising start; between 1895 and 1914 the number of cars in France rose from 300 to 107,535.[12] French production was exceeded only by that of the United States, and if we add the allied industries – including Michelin tyres at Clermont-Ferrand – the motor car kept some 100,000 workers busy.[13]

France had entered the industrial era. It may be that its growth was retarded by the lack of interest shown by the banks in industrial investment and by the practice, employed in the vast majority of cases, of self-financing, but at any rate the crime of non-growth cannot be imputed to French industrialists. It is true that in spite of the great leap forward of the early years of the century France was now only the fourth greatest industrial power: the unequal development of capitalism did not operate in her favour. But there were many different reasons for this, and when French entrepreneurs looked at production and their profits on the eve of the Great War they would feel legitimate satisfaction.

A more comfortable life and more modern manners

In this wealthier France the standard of living had improved and manners were different. Let us limit ourselves for the moment to a few general considerations which will be corrected later on.

Standard of living: in 1913 it remained higher than in Germany. It was lower, it is true, than in England, but French progress, more substantial during the previous fifty years than Great Britain's, was tending to bring the 'average Frenchman' closer to his new friend. One thing is certain in the realm of nutrition, always a major problem, the consumption of bread, the national food *par excellence*, was declining, after reaching a peak in the 1880s; in the subsistence disturbances of 1911 it occupied only a secondary place. Even in working-class families meat competed to a large extent for the first place: according to the investigation of M. Halbwachs it represented at least a quarter of their expenses.[14] Wine triumphed: 11.4 per cent of the working-class families studied by Halbwachs devoted more than 15 per cent of their budget to it; it was drunk at home, at work and in the worker's café, the *bistrot*. At the other end of the social scale the size of the expenditure of 'bourgeois families' on choice wines and liqueurs is surprising. However, the consumption of wine, more than that of meat, is in France a cultural fact which does not necessarily testify to growing comfort, except, no doubt, in the country. Apart from these three things, the nation's diet, which remained seriously deficient in milk, sugar and fruit – Vitamins A and C – was on the whole better balanced than at the beginning of the Third Republic.

Advertising provides another sidelight on the changes in manners. 'I only smoke Nile', an advertisement for a famous brand of cigarette papers, appeared daily for years at the top of the front page of *La Dépêche de Toulouse*. Pharmaceutical products invaded numerous newspapers: it was the age of 'pink pills for pale people' and of 'la Jouvence de l'abbé Soury'. Above all, clothes, the new pleasure, percolated even into the countryside through mail-order catalogues. Daniel Halévy put leisure clothes on the same level – or almost – as the bicycle among the new tastes which he noticed when he visited the 'paysans du Centre' in 1910.

The bicycle! In the provinces it did not really catch on until the beginning of the century. To encourage sales, shops began to give free lessons, to hire out machines by the month, by the day or even by the hour, and to sell on the instalment system. This bicycle sales campaign went hand in hand with the growing popularity of sports: the Tour de France began in 1903. Patriotism was involved: it was by forming healthy bodies that people would reconquer Alsace and Lorraine. The Church was soon carried away by this slogan: church clubs and the *ACJF*[15] organized sports centres and gymnastic societies. Universities and state schools were slower to follow the trend. The time had come in any case when, to sell the 'Herculex electric belt', supposed to restore to the stronger sex a possibly threatened virility, the illustration showed a sportsman going flat out (*Le Rire*, 1903).

More modern still were the things – gadgets? – that abolished or shortened distances. The telephone, for example: a Parisian phenomenon in 1900, it soon spread to the provinces; in 1910 Nièvre had 200 subscribers. Car-owning became more widespread at the same period. An essentially urban product in 1900, by 1913 it had invaded the countryside: at that date 55 per cent of the cars in use in France belonged to those who owned land. The age of the 'auto pauper' came nearer with the founding in October 1900 by Henri Desgrange of *L'Auto-Vélo*, which soon printed 120,000 copies. It held up to public contempt the watery-eyed, doubled-up pen-pusher and demanded a pedestrian code. But in the country as a whole reactions remained very critical: the car was regarded as a lethal weapon and drivers as road-hogs.

A more socialized existence

Socialization began at the primary school, or even, for those who could get into one, at the nursery school, where Pauline Kergomard's ideas had been totally accepted: the child learnt to blow its nose, lace up its shoes, to say 'good morning', and to look at the world in accordance with a unique system of teaching confirmed by various decrees. Almost every young Frenchman passed through 'la grande école'. The number of illiterates discovered when young men were conscripted gradually dropped: 6 per cent in 1901, 4 per cent in 1914. The primary school taught, more authoritatively than the nursery school, not only the discipline of collective life and the ideology of succeeding in society by work, thrift and respect for the established bodies in a Republic, but everything that an adult was supposed to know. This encyclopedic approach was criticized by a few avant-garde teachers, by certain anarchists and by socialists like Jaurès: 'Be able to read well', wrote Jaurès, 'and the rest will follow.' In saying this he was acknowledging evidence of the lukewarm interest in reading observed in adults and trying to find a remedy for it.[16]

In 1914 the state schools had been established for thirty years. It was in the last twenty years that the context of adults' lives had changed. Since the end of the nineteenth century there had developed a network of associations which the laws of 1884–1901 had provided with legal frameworks. We shall not go back over working-class trade unionism, the organization of the parties of the left, whose structures were very uneven, or the multiple network of societies which made radical France something different from a radical government. On the eve of the Great War a socialist wage-earner belonged in principle not only to his political group but to his professional trade union and often to a co-operative: from the League for the Rights of Man to freemasonry, which was more active than ever,[17] many other groupings made demands on him. The organization of some clearly defined professional circles is significant. Thus from 1895 friendly societies multiplied among university graduates.[18] In 1908 there were 202 of them, embracing five-sixths of the teachers in boys' and girls' *lycées*: a phenomenon which pleased the Ministry so long as their behaviour was 'sensible'[19] and did not lead to the feared trade unionism. These teachers were grouped on various different bases: function exercised,[20] degree – the Société des Agrégés was formed in 1914 – or subject taught. The associations of specialists multiplied in 1910 when there was a rumour that the timetables of secondary education were going to be revised and the time given to some subjects reduced. Naturally each subject – philosophy, history, mathematics, classics – wanted to protect its own timetable. Membership did not automatically involve militancy: these organizations, whose members were united by the wish to defend certain very narrow interests, had a tendency to ossify.

Unlike trade unionism and the lay university, in conservative religious and social circles the proliferation of numerous associations continued to 1914. It was an old tradition that drew its vitality from feelings of nostalgia – for the destruction of intermediate bodies in favour of atomized citizens – and of hope – for the preservation in the rural areas of the social hierarchies.

The intermingling of the interests of the notables and of those of the Church was clear in the agrarian organizations and particularly in the powerful Union Centrale des Syndicats des Agriculteurs de France, known as the organization 'in the rue d'Athènes', a body well-known today.[21] It is true that it claimed to be politically and denominationally neutral. But the cult of the leader and the desire to maintain, 'with the help of God', social peace made this organization a powerful agent of conservatism. The creation in 1910 of a competing radical federation,[22] promoted by the capitalist farmers of the Parisian Basin and supported by Joseph Ruau, Minister of Agriculture from 1905 to 1910, no doubt formed a political counterweight. But in both cases, although the members were numerous – a million in the 'rue d'Athènes' – and were attracted by the real services rendered by the associations, it was the notables who were in sole charge.

A subject of admitted disquiet: the demographic situation

It is fair to ask whether the radical Republic really provided all French people with the prosperous and balanced life that we have just indicated. Had progress united the towns and the rural areas and had it treated all ages, sexes and classes equally? Before outlining old and new tensions, let us first see how things stood with the numbers of the subjects of this history – the French.

On the eve of the Great War the official silence on demography, which Dr Bertillon (Biblio. no. 278) – who blamed the celibacy of politicians – had been trying in vain to break since 1896 by founding the 'National Alliance for the Increase of the French Population', was at last broken. This was less on account of the needs of industrial growth than because of the prospect of war and the fears inspired by fecund Germany. The figures could indeed cause some worry to those who claimed to be inspired by patriotic motives. Not in absolute terms: with 39.6 million inhabitants at the census of 1911, France remained well populated; not so well as Germany, it was true, but as well as Great Britain and better than Italy. The disquiet was caused by the almost total stagnation of growth; during the last twenty years of the nineteenth century the annual increase had been on average 75,000, but since 1901 it had fallen to 50,000. The rate of reproduction of the population – 1.02 in 1891 – was only 0.96 in 1911. At the end of the nineteenth century the average French family had 2.2 children; on the eve of the Great War it had only 2. The impetuous upsurge of capitalism had not been paralleled in demography: the drop in the birth rate had not been halted. The rate had fallen to 19 per cent. The fact that the total figure of the population had not begun to drop was due to the immigrants and to the tardy, but since 1890–5 perceptible, decrease in the death rate. The spread of asepsis, vaccines and serums, in short the work of Pasteur and his disciples – Roux, Calmette, Guérin – was largely responsible for this. Obviously discoveries were not sufficient in themselves, any more than they were for industry; it was the school that disseminated the notions of elementary hygiene. Expectation of life had improved distinctly; it was now forty-nine. However, there was no reason to shout for joy: the general death rate – 19 per thousand between 1901 and 1910, 17.7 in 1913 – remained higher than that of the Scandinavian and Anglo-Saxon countries, of Belgium, the Netherlands and Switzerland, and it was particularly high for small children.

Why was this? The country was still haunted by diseases which people did not know how to arrest or which received attention too late. Such was the case with venereal diseases, particularly syphilis. The 'Neapolitan evil' still provoked shame. The greatest doctors – the Broca hospital specialized in dermato-syphilography – applied themselves to taking the drama out of it and to curing it. More freely admitted, tuberculosis was nevertheless concealed under all sorts of veils – loss of energy, anaemia.[23] There was tremendous debate on its origins, the conditions in which it spread and the remedies to be applied. Of twenty-five famous doctors,[24] nearly half devoted the best part of their lives to tuberculosis. Heat and sun were still advised – the Côte d'Azur or even Algeria[25] – but the first sanatoriums appeared in the Jura in 1900 and it was there that the first pneumo-thorax operations, an Italian discovery, were carried out. BCG was to be discovered in 1913. A third social evil – possibly the most important – was alcoholism. It was said to be responsible – though this is not certain – for the high working-class birth rate,[26] but it was in any case responsible for much of the child mortality. The areas where the vine was cultivated on a large scale were free from it; wine often functions as an antidote. The people of Languedoc are not alcoholics. On the other hand, alcoholism poisoned the regions where fruit juice was distilled, particularly those like Normandy, where the apple reigned supreme. The workers in the towns and the mines, poorly nourished, crushed by physical labour, sought a 'lift' from it. Spirit drinking is also encouraged by boredom and solitude. However, the consumption of alcohol started a decline which could be connected with the obligatory rest day and the general tendency to shorter working hours.

Death and its immediate causes were directly affected by social inequalities. Differences in the death rate were particularly noticeable in the big cities. The case of Paris has been studied on the basis of the figures for 1911–13. In the wealthy *arrondissements – VIIIe, XVIe, IXe –* the general death rate was 11 per thousand and the infant mortality rate was 51 per thousand; in the poor *arrondissements – XIIIe, XIXe, XXe –* the respective figures were 16.5 and 107.[27] For deaths from tuberculosis in general the difference between the very rich districts and the very poor districts was 100 per cent.

Not only was the death rate among the 'poor and their children much higher than among rich', but there were real class diseases, and tuberculosis was high on the list of them.

However, the major fact in the eyes of the populationists remained the decline in births, which was particularly marked in the valley of the Garonne.[28] It was a major fact because since the beginning of the century a new phenomenon was becoming apparent: the drop not only in the birth rate – that had been going on for some time – but in the fertility rate calculated on the basis of women between fifteen and fifty capable of bearing children. It was also a major fact in that it affected all social classes. The working class, so long a 'rabbit warren', as the anarchists put it, was in the process of changing. The calculations made in 1906 in industrial regions showed that the gap between workers and employers had narrowed considerably; as a matter of fact, it was the clerks who were the most 'Malthusian' section of the population. Finally, from a geographical point of view the phenomenon was general: only in Brittany, the northern region and the eastern part of the Massif Central did the birth rate remain high. From a technical point of view, the 'sin of Onan', which was often brought into the discussion, was not the main cause. Couples had recourse mainly to *coïtus interruptus*; this was the 'mournful secret' of which priests in Languedoc had been complaining even before the Revolution. But the most ardent populationists such as Dr Bertillon were not entirely wrong in accusing what they called 'the criminal propaganda of the neo-Malthusians'. The League for Human Regeneration, founded in 1900 by Paul Robin, a former pupil of the rue d'Ulm, a free thinker and an anarchist, organized the teaching of birth-control practices. After Robin withdrew from it in 1908 the enterprise was carried on by one of his earliest colleagues, Eugène Humbert. Papers, tracts, stickers, brochures and pictures called on people 'to have less children' and disseminated the techniques.[29] The active support of the anarchist groups, of some socialist groups[30] and of certain *bourses du travail* was gained. Chemists sold the products, and midwives and doctors lent their aid. The most politically committed Malthusians were concerned to make war more difficult by denying it 'cannon fodder' and to push up wages by reducing capital's army of reserves. They all aimed at 'substituting reflection for instinct, foresight for thoughtlessness, *homo sapiens* for the brute'.[31]

Thus neo-Malthusian propaganda had a mass appeal, at any rate in the towns. However, it does not sufficiently explain the national – and in fact international – and inter-class aspects of the decline in births. Religious correlations are not very conclusive and the relation of cause to effect is debatable; how many men and women stopped going to confession because they transgressed the sexual vetoes of the Church and not vice versa? It would probably be closer to reality to argue from the progress of rationality.

Philippe Ariès for his part has emphasized the new concept that people had of the place of the child in the family: the couple's happiness, so he says, tended more and more to reside in the child and its future, to which everything had to be sacrificed; the family thus made the child autonomous. It is certain that at that time psychology,[32] medicine – the French Paediatric Society was founded in 1899 – the nursery school and literature tended to look on the child as a separate being. In 1893 a provincial socialist paper recommended 'replacing the gods ... by a unique little god that we create ourselves: the child, that is, the human race of tomorrow' (*La Voix des travailleurs du Tarn*, 7 May 1893). It still requires explanation why this guiding concept spread from the bourgeoisie to the working class and the peasantry. Perhaps this development should be related to a certain improvement in the lot of the workers, with less insecurity and more frequent exchanges of views with others. In short, to the creation of a national market and a daily life less subject to fatality, ignorance and misfortune.

Old and new tensions

Rural areas and towns

Rural France still weighed more heavily in the demographical balance than the towns. In 1911 the population of the rural areas – villages and localities of less than 2,000 inhabitants – represented about 56 per cent of the total population. It had decreased only relatively, and fairly moderately: 10 per cent in thirty years. Round about 1900 it seemed to reach an equilibrium: those who subsequently left the countryside, and there were fewer of them, were attracted by new factory sirens (unless they came from the very backward regions). The subject of literary lamentations – *La Terre qui meurt* by René Bazin dates from 1899 – and of political ones, too – Méline never ceased to mourn the abandonment of the land to the advantage of the impious, unpatriotic city – the idea of the rural exodus must be handled cautiously. France was not yet a 'desert'. The active population employed in the primary sector still formed between 41 per cent and 43 per cent of the total, according to the statistics employed. It had declined less in percentage than the rural population and at the beginning of the century it reached its maximum in absolute figures – about 8.7 million.

Of those who had left, many did not belong to the primary sector, and others – the girls who went to find a job in the towns – were not classified in the country as part of the active population. In the villages life had become, so to speak, 'countrified'. It is true that locksmiths still worked in the Vimeu and watchmakers in the Jura, but in general the craftsmen who had formerly worked for urban businessmen had shut up shop. Many had gone off to work in the workshop, the mine or the factory and when those remaining died there were few to replace them. In the hills of the Beaujolais and the Lyonnais, the crafts of smiths and tilers, basket-makers and carters, tinsmiths and coopers were fast disappearing. It was the same in Picardy. Many 'gentlemen' had also left the villages in search of an activity better suited to the more expensive tastes of their families at a time when the income from land had everywhere declined. Doubtless new professions were appearing in the *bourgs*. Roger Thabault noted in 1906 that at Mazières-en-Gâtine there were two bakers, two small ironmongers and a seedsman. The civil service in particular was well represented, by teachers and tax-collectors, roadmenders and postmen, gendarmes and road engineers. The fact remains none the less that the village was devoted to primary production much more than in the past.

In France as a whole the technical progress of agriculture – fertilizers, selection of species – was slow, though doubtless a modest amount of equipment had been adopted on the plains. Even though the export of beef cattle showed a credit balance, not enough was produced to feed France. Investment had not been lacking in the early years of the twentieth century but the time lost in the second half of the nineteenth century had not been made up. There were many reasons for the long-lasting weakness in investment for modernization. With the small and middle-sized farmers the quest for an 'honourable' status no doubt played a part in hard times. Such a status came rather from the purchase of new land than from the updating of agricultural methods. Above all, that part of the bourgeoisie which lived on unearned income constantly took a large slice out of the revenues from land. The arrival of protectionism, a reassuring support for old-fashioned practices, and its reinforcement in 1910 did nothing to help. The relatively small size of the exodus from the land made mechanization unnecessary and the moderate republican State, anxious to preserve a political base that was more reliable than the urban population, long helped to lull the farmers to sleep. It showed its solicitude for the peasantry more by all kinds of small favours than by a general policy. The organization of the Crédit Rural and state subsidies for mutual assurance societies did not really develop until the beginning of the century; they testify to a livelier sense of initiative in the radicals than in their predecessors.

If we wish to understand the difficulties which, after a temporarily favourable economic situation, were about to assail the French countryside, we have to look at the towns as well. Not that there had been urbanization on a massive scale. There were few towns with more than 100,000 inhabitants – only sixteen, in fact. The only very big regional cities were Lyon[33] and Marseille, which each had a population in excess of half a million. Urban France was essentially the France of towns comprising between 5,000 and 20,000 inhabitants – sub-prefectures, sometimes prefectures. Guéret had 6,000 inhabitants, Gap fewer than 7,000 and Pamiers under 8,000. However, some towns, such as Grenoble, Nancy and Nice, which around 1880 had some 50,000 inhabitants, developed rapidly. They all had a regional function as well as a specific activity. Near the regional centres the small towns in the department served as staging-posts: Georges Dupeux has shown that two-fifths of the growth of Bordeaux was based on the reservoir of people in the surrounding countryside. All round the cities suburbs burgeoned, soon to be invaded by typically suburban houses: between 1900 and 1914 the commune of Ecully near Lyon expanded from 2,964 to 3,215 inhabitants. The newcomers lived in little cube-like houses, concealing along the narrow streets kitchen gardens, chicken runs and rabbit-hutches.

The city *par excellence* was Paris. With almost three million inhabitants from all over France, it was a giant city[34] in which the most modern kinds of public transport were beginning to appear: the first underground railway was opened in July 1900. While in the market-gardening suburbs such as Bobigny and Montreuil the working-class population grew among the cabbages, the peopling of the northern suburbs and that of the big western bend of the Seine inaugurated a new era. Another town sprang up there, anarchic in its unplanned growth, and forming a tragic contrast with the organized beauties of the heart of the city. There, fetid odours, filth and violence reigned supreme – 'the suburbs, a setback in urban history and already the terror of the bourgeois'.[35]

However, the city attracted people through its animation, its 'electric illuminations' and also through its cinemas, which multiplied after 1910. It also attracted people with the hope of more certain gain, of a weekly rest day unknown in the fields and of quicker success. It provided an image of vitality. It looked both seductive and dominating. And in fact a set of links between the village and the city developed which made the country dependent on the town and the primary sector dependent on the secondary and tertiary sectors. Doubtless the links were reciprocal: primary-sector France, through its size and slowness, put a brake on the development of industry and services. But for these and for investments, for purchases, sales and jobs it was to the town that the country people turned. The urban domination was that of capitalism. The sugar-beet producer's profit depended on the price fixed by the distiller or the sugar manufacturer and the dairy farmer's profit depended on the prices quoted by the dairies. Modernization increased this dependence: who fixed the prices of fertilizers and mechanical equipment? Obviously all those who lived from the land did not have the same capacity to resist these pressures; the small farmer could not adopt the solution available to the big-sugar-beet producer, that of becoming a distiller or a manufacturer of fertilizer himself. On the whole, faced with industrial and banking capital, the rural world was in a weak position to resist. It was no doubt this image of a rural society threatened and manipulated by the town that stimulated the fashion for rustic novels. It also stimulated the 'agrarian' feeling that served the rural notables so well and on which they capitalized in the unions mentioned above. The opposition between town and the country, not a new factor, had been renewed.

Regions and regionalism

There were also differences between the regions. Had they grown deeper? And if so, with what consequences? Let us confine ourselves to a few examples.

To the north of the Loire were the lands where capitalism held sway. From the Parisian Basin to Nord[36] and Lorraine were concentrated the biggest industrial complexes of the old and the new France. Large-scale agriculture was strongly developed there; it was a wage-earning agriculture concentrating on corn, sugar-beet and meat which required big investments and brought in good profits. The permanent agricultural labourers, crushed by poverty and indifferent to religion, were joined for the big annual tasks by a whole population of migrants. At the heart of this region was Paris and its growing red suburbs where a new range of industries was growing. In spite of the spreading institutional banking influence of the capital and in spite of the spider's web that it was tirelessly spinning, it had not devoured either the old, patriotic, Catholic Lorraine (the Lorraine of *Colette Baudoche* or *La Colline inspirée*) revolutionized by its new iron and steel industry, or the basin of Nord and Pas-de-Calais where business remained largely family affairs and the profit from coal-mining was very adequate. Good regional banking systems had developed there in the service of industry. But the conquest of the national – even the international – market[37] developed in the managerial classes a spirit of enterprise which hardly left room for anti-Parisian regionalism. The North of France worked – it was almost a slogan; it ran the French economy.

And the Midi, so it was said, governed France. How are we to take this statement? Let us leave aside Bouches-du-Rhône and Alpes Maritimes, rising rapidly but in a marginal geographical situation, and let us turn to the series of departments known collectively as Languedoc. This vast region had gone into a steep decline. The industrial bourgeoisie still active in Bas-Languedoc at the end of the century, particularly in the Biterrois, was moving out of business and the regional banks were retreating before the advance of the national credit establishments.[38] Nowhere was the decline more striking or more established than in the Garonne area, where the old mixed farming by owner farmers had not been superseded by the cultivation on an industrial scale of the vine. Where this had indeed developed it had created an economy that produced enormous profits but was liable to sudden collapse on a saturated market affected by increasing competition from Algerian wines. All round, the area's economic structures were either in decay or extremely precarious. The marked, and premature, decline in the birth rate confirms this analysis. The Midi had been sacrificed on a large scale.

In compensation the southerners had found a new opportunity – the tertiary sector of the economy; hence the illusion that they governed the country via post-office employees, customs officers and teachers. Hence also their need for a good knowledge of French and possibly the strictness of the teachers, who forbade the use of the 'patois' in school. But in these departments, which were apt to be 'Red' and were decidedly anti-clerical, cultural traditions had remained very much alive: village customs had been all the better preserved since more than a tenth of Languedoc land was still collectively owned. Then there was the *langue d'oc* with its wealth of variants, whose sonority and grace contrasted sharply with the 'angular' tongue of the *pays d'Oil*. The *Langue d'oc* was the language of the people. It was spoken at home, at work and in the cafés. In the villages the local *félibres* (poets) sang of family events and neighbourhood scandals. And the *félibréen* movement, founded sixty years earlier by Mistral, who died in 1914, succeeded in making people recognize its poetic power. But is it possible to discern in this taste for tradition and in these literary movements, which often expressed a folklorish social and political conformism, the basis of an anti-north regionalism or even of an Occitanian patriotism? Mistral, who tended to favour the right, was sensitive to this current, but the men of the left refused to have anything to do with it. And the left was in a majority in these departments. Ferroul, the mayor of Narbonne and the hero of 1907, was certainly a 'man of the Midi'; but he was also a clever politician who had no intention of cutting his region off from the north. The regionalism of the Midi was simply a longing for the cultural renaissance of the *pays d'oc*, and the desire to ensure an easy life for their inhabitants; the real reasons for the end of the economic dynamism were not perceived.

Another region whose difficulties formed a contrast with the expansion of the Parisian Basin and one with a strong character of its own was Breton-speaking Brittany. Devoid of industry except in the ports, over-burdened with children in spite of considerable emigration to Paris, Brittany had begun to create an intensive agriculture by dint of desperately hard work. But the small farmer found great difficulty in feeding his numerous family. In spite of the strength of traditions, the bases for an independence movement were practically non-existent: the prestige of the State that protected the fishermen and provided local work – the arsenals and the navy – was too great, and the need of the Parisian outlet for the surplus population was too keenly felt. But, unlike the Midi, Catholic and peasant Brittany, where the urban bourgeoisie had little influence, did not entertain the illusion of governing the country. As a result, the extreme regionalist movements, although without a mass base, took a more organized form than in the Midi. This was true whether they turned completely towards a Celtic, feudal past, like the Breton Regional Union (1893–1911), or were rather run by disputatious *petit-bourgeois* elements, like the Breton Nationalist Party (founded in 1911). The Breton socialists themselves maintained a confederation among themselves when five departmental federations were created in 1907 in conformity with the statutes of the *SFIO*. And in 1909 the radical deputy for Lorient, Paul Guieysse, asked (in vain) for the introduction of the teaching of Breton. On the eve of the Great War there were signs of a certain national consciousness.

Space – and even more the necessary information[39] – is lacking to indicate the abyss that yawned between northern France and the highlands of the Massif Central, or the way in which the proud Lyon region hesitated between its past and its future. The growing inequality of development does not seem to have affected national unity, which in the eyes of the masses seemed rather to be a way out. However, at bottom the whole nation was impoverished by this uneven development and there were various signs of a certain disquiet at an alienating cultural centralism, and of a new interest in a regional approach.

A society of citizens

Citizens! The word, common to radicals and socialists, united the devotees of universal suffrage but excluded those who did not participate in it – foreigners, women, the young.

The immigrants – there were 1,160,000 of them, or 2.9 per cent of the population – belonged to two categories that sometimes overlapped. First there were the political refugees, whom the Republic welcomed. Militant Russians and Russian Jews forced out by the pogroms accounted for a considerable proportion of these. At the beginning of the century they probably numbered between 25,000 and 40,000. They settled mainly in Paris, but also in the provincial university towns, Montpellier in particular. They lived in the same quarters – in Paris the *IVe* and *XIe arrondissements* and the hill of Montmartre were peopled by Jewish cap-makers and furriers, and the *Ve* and *XIVe arrondissements* were also 'Slav' – and had their own newspapers, their own political connections and their own cheap restaurants. The police were somewhat baffled by the complexity of these groups; they regarded the Bolsheviks as 'more moderate' than the anarchists and Mensheviks. The immigration or urban and rural workers was on a larger scale. Over a third – 36 per cent – of these immigrants were Italian and a quarter were Belgian. The Spaniards, Germans and Swiss came a long way behind. In 1906 the Poles began to arrive. Some of these immigrants wanted to settle permanently in France; such was the case with many Spaniards in Languedoc. Bertillon deplores the laxity of the naturalization process since 1891. In the Longwy area the workers in the mines and in the iron and steel works were largely immigrants. In 1910 some 10,000 Belgians and as many Germans were working there, not to mention 28,000 Italians whom socialist militants from their own country helped to organize. They all bought their provisions at the store run by the employers and slept two or three to a bed. After a few years, if they survived – many young slag-crushers died in a few months – they returned to their own country. Finally, numerous agricultural workers came just for the season; in the big farms of Brie, Flemings were to be seen – left to fend for themselves – and the Poles accompanied by their parish priest.

The attitude of the French to these immigrants has never been seriously studied. Demonstrations of hostility in working-class circles seem to have been less numerous than in the 1880s, probably because unemployment had diminished. But most of the bills introduced concerning them were discriminatory in character: the Millerand decrees of 10 August 1899 fixed a maximum percentage of foreigners in work carried out for the State. The working classes were liable to accuse them of being clericals or of breaking strikes: this was a working-class reaction rather than a nationalist one, but it could easily be exploited by nationalism. On the whole, few people were concerned about these workers, who did not vote and did not strike.

The Frenchman himself did not acquire full citizenship until the age of twenty-one. The adolescent was excluded even when he was working as an adult. In southern rural societies the youth group, the *jovent*, traditionally occupied a central position: for example, to preserve the balance of the sexes it had the 'right' to veto the departure of girls or to prevent the settlement of a stranger. Urban life meant that such customs disappeared, along with the autonomy of the young: the young worker had neither the rights of an adult nor the customary privileges of adolescence. The almost total disappearance of apprenticeships meant that he received low wages and the adult worker saw him as a competitor, a sort of foreigner. In addition, his family kept him on a tight rein: he had to contribute in his turn to feed those who had fed him. The moving and funny account that René Michaud has left us of his early days sounds like the famous remarks of La Maheude a quarter of a century earlier in *Germinal*.[40] At the beginning of the century students alone formed a group which snowballed – there were 42,000 of them in 1914 as opposed to fewer than 30,000 in 1900 – and which was given some kind of structure by well-organized secular, Christian or collectivist associations: 'Outside student circles there are no young men; only men who are young.'[41]

What about the position of women in society? These silent, passive creatures had never drawn so much attention to themselves as at the dawn of the twentieth century. The representations of women, the images of them to be found in literature, publicity, and the pronouncements of employers, whether clerical or radical, certainly remained very traditional: they oscillate between the theme of the sweet-and-fragile-woman-object-of-man's-desire and that of the mother-of-the-family-real-head-of-the-household whose 'far-seeing and instinctive prudence' fortunately deters the husband from striking.[42] Work outside the home was still considered a crime of feminine treason, and at the very least as a temporary phenomenon on which it was not worthwhile to dwell too long. The gap between words and reality was here at its greatest: the proportion of female labour in the working population had never been so large – 37 per cent – and in Paris alone in 1911 there were over 10,000 workers' widows burdened with more than three children. But the stereotypes made it possible to conceal the way in which employers put men and women in keen competition with each other. The enquiry carried out by the Office du Travail between 1891 and 1897 showed that in the provinces, while the average wage for a man was 3.24 francs, that for a woman was only 2.01 francs; and in the Seine area the gap was much greater: a man's wage, 6.30 francs, was double that of a woman's, 3.24 francs.[43] This was because female labour was employed for preference in fairly unskilled trades and jobs. But even for equal work women almost never received an equal wage.

However, it was not in the female industrial worker that people were interested on the eve of the Great War. Women's problems arose essentially from the advent of a new sector of women's work, the tertiary sector. The professions of typist, postal employee, saleswoman and schoolmistress were regarded as conferring a higher status. The real star jobs were those in the liberal professions or in scientific work. In 1914 there were some hundreds of women doctors, but a law was needed to give women access to the bar. The years 1906–13 were decisive: Mme Curie taught physics at the Sorbonne from 1906; in 1911 the Grand Prix de Rome for sculpture went to a woman; in 1912 Maria Vérone pleaded for the first time in an assize court and a woman – horror! – came first in the male *agrégation* examination in grammar. The great 'masculine' press reported these exploits with an amused air, and the problem of the professions that one could advise girls to enter became the subject of discussion.

Yet for the first feminists the problem of work was not the essential point. The movement was formed in the 1880s to obtain civil equality and, so far as the most enthusiastic members were concerned, political equality. The implementation of the right to vote dominated the suffragette movement, a decidedly free-thinking organization, from Hubertine Auclert to Marguerite Durand and Madeleine Pelletier. But many organizations that claimed to defend the rights of women confined themselves to their civil rights; two examples were the French League for the Rights of Women and the National Council of French Women, which was organized by Protestant women. Attempts to form a working-class, revolutionary feminist movement remained isolated, in spite of the efforts of Nelly Roussel and Gabrielle Petit. Nevertheless, by 1914 some progress had been made: the suffragette movement had expanded, for the first time the *CGT* gave a place of their own to the problems posed for the revolutionary movement by working women, and finally a handful of feminist, trade unionist schoolmistresses formed a group whose audience among teachers and workers was to go on growing after the Great War.

'This drama whose heroes are the classes'

Let us now examine how the end of the Belle Epoque was changing the social classes in themselves. The Republic of Gambetta had declared that it was based on the 'new strata'. In the days of the Bloc, the radicals leaned on 'the people'. In 1914 the Republic, in the running of which the radicals played a part without holding all the key posts, liked to say that it was supported by the middle classes, whose virtues were praised at congresses and banquets. What did this mean? First of all there was a paradox in the employment not only by sociologists and students of politics but also by radical politicians of a class vocabulary the practical application of which they elsewhere denied: 'I refuse', Herriot was to say, 'to believe that the class theory applies to a country like France, where conditions are so varied, property so split up and craftsmanship so highly developed.'[44] The point was that these middle classes looked like an absence of class; they played no common rôle in production and there was infinity of imperceptible, or barely perceptible, transitions by which, so it was said, their members passed from being workers to being employers. There was agreement at that time on the social categories embraced by the concept of middle classes: craftsmen and small employers, tradesmen, members of the liberal professions, civil servants, clerks and people living on small unearned incomes. There was hesitation on one point: should small and middle-sized landowners, the 'rural democracy', be included? We shall include them when they lived on the proceeds from leased farms and we shall exclude them when they tilled the soil themselves.

What the middle classes had in common was their concern not to work with their hands – either oily hands or earthy hands. Their members were fairly well off or at any rate they had a permanent job which protected them against those two obsessions, old age and unemployment. The concern for respectability was evident and urban life strengthened it. It implied a fairly high rent, the employment of a servant and a big effort to educate the children. The daily diet could be frugal, the clothes constantly 'tidied up' but decent, amusements few; holidays abroad had not yet become a normal part of life. Budgets were very carefully managed and savings were regarded as a duty. The extraordinarily low rate of taxation helped them. One can understand that the middle classes did not fight very hard for the introduction of income tax. One felt, too, in these circles, a real confidence in the future and progress, and often in a régime that brought individual successes.

The professional diversity of these circles was extreme and incomes were totally lacking in homogeneity. Moreover, the distribution of the layers of the population which made up the middle classes had changed perceptibly in the previous thirty years. The shop and the small business had been the traditional bases of the middle classes. The number of licensees had distinctly increased – there were 1.7 million of them in 1911 – especially that of the proprietors of *bistrots*, who amounted to nearly half a million.[45] Another ancient pillar of the middle-classes was formed by those who lived only on unearned income; of 550,000 people living in this way 500,000 could be assigned to the middle classes (see J.-B. Duroselle, Biblio. no. 36). The product of land rents had declined substantially during the great depression; many small landowners who did not work their own land had consequently sold up and put their money into property. Many men in full vigour stopped productive work when they reached the age of fifty and lived 'on their income'. On the other hand, although the liberal professions carried great weight their numbers were derisory. The number of lawyers was stable – 6,500 barristers and 8,500 notaries – but that of doctors had more than doubled in forty years. Apart from the growing number of clerks in the private sector – it had easily doubled in thirty years – the big change that had transformed the composition of the middle classes was the rise of the civil service. If we include tobacconists, local government officials and all the career soldiers and sailors, we reach the figure of 1,300,000 in 1913. The small posts were still much sought after in spite of the low salaries. S far as the middle ranks of the civil service were concerned, where hierarc' prevailed to an extraordinary degree, conservative tendencies won the ay all the more easily since the job, long coveted, often brought only very average financial rewards and social status.[46] Periodically snubbed, trade unionism made only slow progress in these quarters.

It has been estimated that some five million Frenchmen were members of the middle class. The figure is naturally debatable,[47] but it does not seem improbable. Where did the middle classes draw their recruits from? The Republic professed to ensure the regular rise of deserving wage-earners from the primary and secondary sectors and that of their children, as soon as they had set foot on the lowest rung of the *petit-bourgeois* ladder. And there was much truth in this claim. The privileged instrument of this promotion in status was the academic system. Scholarship winners from the ranks of the people were numerous in the teaching profession. Of those teaching in secondary schools between 1900 and 1914, 14 per cent were the sons of farmers, 9 per cent the sons of workers and 15 per cent the sons of schoolmasters.[48] The practical schools of commerce and industry, especially the national professional schools, facilitated access to the master craftsman's certificate and even to the responsibilities of the engineer. But the academic system was far from operating systematically in favour of social advancement. First, because it comprised two streams; there was the primary school stream, which led to the higher primary schools and the *brevet*; and there was the stream formed by the elementary classes of the *lycées* and *collèges*, which led to secondary education, the producer of 'bachelors'. Moreover, the advancement of adults was reduced to little more than the training of apprentices. Finally – and this has been studied where the universities are concerned – the levelling effect exerted by academic selection did not cancel out 'at any level of the profession's intellectual hierarchy the effect of social inequalities'.[49] The effect of social advantages and disadvantages was cumulative in each case.

However, the place occupied by the sons of the 'rural democracy' in this outline of social mobility is not negligible. The somewhat vague term includes all small farmers, whether they owned their land or not. Those who held out at the time of the great depression, when very small properties finally disappeared, had been able to round out their holding or at the very least acquire a small plot by profiting from the drop in the price of land and, at the beginning of the century, from the rise in agricultural prices. Of all farmers – 2.7 million in 1906 – the small owners and in particular the tenant farmers managed to do better than the share-croppers. This could be noted in Aquitaine, in Loir-et-Cher, in the Pays d'Auge and – vice versa – in the Bourbonnais, where during the course of a few years 1,800 share-croppers joined the Federation of Agricultural workers. The price paid for the progress thus achieved by the least deprived was heavy: their style of life was not much improved, and in the absence of hospitals or hospices the old man who had to stop working became a burden on his children. The hardness which he had inculcated in them was often turned against him.

The peasants were also the day-labourers and full-time farm servants. In 1906 there were still 2.6 million of them. Their place in the chain of production put them basically in the same class as the industrial workers, of whom there were over five million (to whom must be added one million servants). Moreover, in the fields and in the factories wages moved according to the same rhythm; they rose continually, especially from 1895, and real wages rose too until 1910; at that point the cost of living rose so sharply that real wages declined, as they did all over Europe. For all these people life was insecure. Their housing conditions were often squalid,[50] 60 per cent to 70 per cent of their wages went on food, and their clothes amounted to rags. The housing instability bears witness to the poor social integration of the working class of which we have other evidence and against which the activities of the Union Sacrée were not to prevail – but that is another story.

It was thus a separate class but also an extremely diverse one. The scale of wages has been calculated on the basis of the enquiry of 1891–7; they ranged from one franc per day for a female manual worker in the chemical industry in the provinces to twelve francs a day for a male foreman in mechanical engineering in Paris. Parisian wages were much higher but also much more rigid. They differed in the same industry according to whether the labour force was male or female. There were sectors – chemistry, linen – where misfortune reigned and others – metallurgy – in which people got on. By 1914 the organization of working-class labour was the result of the big changes imposed by the development of mechanization and of the division of work introduced by the employers to raise production. Payment by time, which is normally applied to unskilled labour or, at the other end of the production chain, to the qualified professional trained as a craftsman, was perhaps still received by the majority of men. By the end of the nineteenth century it was no longer the case with women. The young proletarian was paid more and more often on the piece-work system: this kind of organization is suited to specialized workers who have only to repeat a few simple operations. On the eve of the Great War attempts to superimpose on it certain aspects of 'Taylorism' (a set of techniques to raise production), in particular time-monitoring, heralded changes that were to become decisive in the 1920s.

Even though the effect of this phenomenon was reduced by the ambiguous position of the small owner–workers – in 1892 nearly half the labourers were in this position – the proletariat did not benefit much from the seductive possibilities of social advancement and, with exceptions, neither its members nor the small owners had any part in the formation of capital. The links between the middle classes and the ruling classes were of another kind. It was not a question simply of the real possibility, when one knew the twists and turns of the labyrinth, of moving from management functions to more prestigious and profitable posts of responsibility. The *petite bourgeoisie*, while refusing to admit the existence of classes, participated in the formation of capital and thus found itself bound to it by a complicity, the consequences and certainly the consciousness of which it was able partly to evade by its mistrust of 'the big-wigs'. Among its members those who lived on modest unearned incomes were not the only ones to own stocks and shares. As for the small employer who lived on familiar terms with his workers, it was from their work that he benefited, and thanks to whom his business prospered. Thus a large proportion of the middle classes found themselves bound by myriad ties to the men who held the keys to big business, even though they traditionally opposed these people politically.

These big capitalists had won a dominant position in the ruling classes. They were the real leaders of these privileged circles – possibly some 200,000 heads of families – much more than the nobles with their country houses and drawing-rooms. However, many links had been forged between the two groups. At the time of the great depression landed proprietors had sold all or part of their lands and reinvested their money in business, while part of the Parisian *haute bourgeoisie* bought the big farms of the Ile-de-France where they then introduced capitalist methods. The two groups mingled in the army, the diplomatic service and the upper echelons of the civil service. These new links must be interpreted in connection with the rise of nationalism and the return in force of Catholicism as the ideology of the bourgeoisie. The frontier between those who lived 'aristocratically' and the rich bourgeoisie had been crossed, but the initiative lay more and more with the industrialists and the bankers, and although they no longer held the monopoly as political rulers they had managed to retain considerable influence in affairs of State.

1914

The France of the Belle Epoque, with its well-established form of government, its dynamic economy and its many confused tensions, was about to embark on war. There are few stranger moments in its history than this year of 1914 which was going to bring about the massacre of a whole generation. Before describing the tragic chain of events of that fine summer we must earmark the political polarities, more apparent than real, which had appeared since the three-year law was passed, on 19 July 1913 in the Chamber and on 7 August in the Senate. Secured after four months of passionate debate, this vote marked a turning-point – but how big? – in the political life of the nation.

The nationalists

The debate and its conclusion brought to light the strength of the nationalist current in Parliament and in the country, and its capacity to unite when it could see a sufficiently strong motive. The extension of military service turned out to be just such a motive. Presented as a riposte to Germany's rearmament plans,[51] it was demanded by the Conseil Supérieur de la Guerre, dominated by Colonel de Grandmaison and the advocates of all-out offensive, and by Joffre, a 'republican' appointed Chief of the General Staff in 1911. The new President of the Republic also was such a keen advocate that later on he was ready to make many 'political sacrifices' to safeguard 'his' law. From *Le Temps* to *La Libre Parole*, from *La Croix* to *Le Matin*, and from *La République française* to *L'Echo de Paris*, a panic campaign of extreme violence was launched: neither the secret Russian funds, so it was said, nor the merchants of cannon were mythical. For a few weeks Frenchmen might have thought that war was going to break out the next day. The debate which involved the whole country, made possible a huge re-grouping round the nationalist leaders. Numerous radicals came down in favour of the law, as did Catholics of the old stamp such as Albert de Mun or newly converted – and hence all the more ardent – ones like Psichari. Péguy, saying 'I am an old republican, I am an old revolutionary', and invoking the Convention, allied himself with the anti-semitic fathers of *La Croix*, and Maurras allied himself with Briand. Matters of security were presented as things that should remain outside 'political questions': that was the key phrase, to which the alliance achieved gave a certain credibility.

The movement seemed subsequently to continue and even to grow louder among the young men of the *écoles*, but once the law had been passed disagreements appeared in the nationalist camp. They were caused by the absence of any grave diplomatic crisis, by the problems posed by the financing of the law and by the pressure exerted – in vain – by the forces of the anti-parliamentary right, which urged Poincaré to adopt a political attitude showing little respect for constitutional law. Moreover, woolly as the Fédération des Gauches was – a jelly-faced masterpiece invented by Briand, Millerand, Etienne and a few others – the electoral campaign of April–May 1914 was only moderately favourable to the shared front of laymen and 'the parish priests'. The big nationalist demonstrations round the statue of Strasbourg, draped in mourning, in the place de la Concorde, and the procession organized for the festival of Jeanne d'Arc on 24 May attracted a smaller crowd than the one which had been madly enthusiastic in the spring of 1913 for the 'three years'. And when, for the seventh centenary of Bouvines, the government in June finally gave permission for the organization of a festival in honour of the victory of Philippe Auguste over the German emperor Otto, it was on the express condition that no priests would be seen at it.[52]

The left gets a grip on itself

The reason was that on the left the political counter-offensive had begun and forces separated or even opposed since the crisis of 1905–7 were in the process of drawing closer to one another. The impetus was provided by the mass campaign against the three-year law. The socialists played a decisive part in its organization: their popular petition had secured 700,000 signatures by the end of June. There were serious incidents in the barracks when it was announced that the class due for release would be retained with the colours. The *SFIO* was able to capitalize on the results of the long struggle for peace conducted mainly by Jaurès. It seemed like the only organized force capable of stimulating actions inspired by ethical and political militancy and of taking effective initiatives. The number of its members increased rapidly – it was to be close on 90,000 in July 1914 – and for the first time for many years young literary reviews turned to the party and intellectuals kept at a distance by its 'parliamentarization' joined it.

The socialist dynamism some months before the elections contrasted with the radicals' majority vote for the three-year law. It worried them and provoked reflection on the structural weakness of the radical party. At the congress of Pau (16–19 October 1913) the party sought to assert itself as an organization: the new statutes obliged deputies to belong to the parliamentary group of the radical and radical-socialist party if they wished to run on the profitable radical ticket at the next elections, and voting discipline was imposed for divisions endangering the existence of the government. Above all, the party gave itself a new leader, Joseph Caillaux, whose evolution into a radical was recent, but whose attachment to peace and to the tax on income was well known. Obviously there was no question of bringing radicalism closer to the people. With Caillaux a new sector of business took over – this time officially – the running of the party: the days when big business ran the government from the wings and Pelletan innocently thought that he was in charge were over. One generation had been succeeded by another. The pacifist banks were in power and Caillaux was at the tiller.

This change led to a rapprochement with the socialists. For the first time since 1902 withdrawals between socialists and radicals in the parliamentary elections (26 April–10 May 1914) signified a common party line. The nationalists were beaten and Briand's group was made to look ridiculous. With 103 seats and 1,400,000 votes, the *SFIO* came out as the great victor in the working-class regions and more and more in the country districts. As for the radicals, of 238 successful candidates who called themselves radicals, only 172 paid their respects in the rue de Valois, but the party retained a number of seats superior to that of the *SFIO*. Was a Caillaux–Jaurès government probable at that point? We know of the concrete plan through the account given by Charles Paix-Séaille, but it is made not very credible by other evidence,[53] as also by the statutory position, constantly reasserted, of the *SFIO*.

Jaurès himself had a wider conception of unity: he had always attached fundamental importance to that of the proletariat. Concretely, in France, that meant a free agreement between the *SFIO* and the *CGT*. During the anti-three-year campaign the *CGT* agreed to participate in common meetings. After the elections Jouhaux, in *La Voix du Peuple*, applauded the success of the socialist party and described it as 'the consequence of the trade union movement of the last fifteen years'. To accelerate this process Jaurès is said to have envisaged choosing Dormoy, the secretary of the

Seine federation, well known for his pro-CGT attitude, as successor to Dubreuilh in the party secretariat.

The weaknesses of the 'rassemblement à gauche'

The coalition of the left was in reality much less strong than it looked, first of all because of the weakening of some of its component parts. The *CGT*, for example: its 'crisis' no doubt reflected the changes taking place in the structure of the working class. The failure of the general strike against war on 16 December 1912 and the campaign against Merrheim, the secretary of the Metal Federation, underlined its ebbing vitality. As for the *SFIO*, its rapid development took place amid the silence or the support of those who not long before had formed its extreme left. Above all, the ambiguities in the radical party had by no means been eliminated. The party had not been transformed in a day just because it had received the benediction of Caillaux. Some of its deputies, to retain their seats, had not opposed the law – Messimy, for example; twenty-nine of them, all told – while others had put down its abolition in their programme, but not in their voting intentions. Then there were the 'non-radical' radicals – about a hundred in number – and some thirty 'non-socialist' socialists on whom any majority depended: out of 602 deputies, 325 altogether had declared themselves favourable to the law and only 227 had demanded the immediate or gradual return to the two years. In short, on this point, which the situation had made fundamental, the left remained in a minority and incoherent, essentially because of its complex links with the middle classes. It should be added that Caillaux had had to renounce any idea of a government post after his wife shot dead the editor of *Le Figaro*, Gaston Calmette, who had been conducting against Caillaux a campaign carefully orchestrated by Briand and certainly tolerated by Poincaré.

Moreover, the left had no theoretical analysis at its disposal; that is one of the reasons why in 1914 it did not believe in the imminence of war. The most clear-headed socialists liked to persuade themselves, when diplomatic tensions decreased, that the international trusts wanted peace and that the essential point was to check the imprudent behaviour of government, while preparing for the future the international education of the working class and its recourse to the preventive strike. Thus for the time being they put their trust in arbitration and the Franco-German parliamentary meetings in which numerous radicals also took part. However, their challenge to the effectiveness of the three-year law sufficed to make people accuse them of treason. Was this a sincere emotion or one orchestrated by property owners more worried by the rise of the socialists than tortured by the thought of Strasbourg in German hands? The weakness – well known to the police – of the genuinely anti-militarist organizations inclines us to the latter hypothesis.[54]

These ambiguities were reflected in the curiosities of parliamentary life immediately after the elections. After Ribot had made a ridiculous circuit of the track (9–13 June), Poincaré entrusted the task of forming a government to Viviani, a republican-socialist. He formed a cabinet that was more to the left than any that France had had since 1911, promised to tackle the question of a tax on income but declared that there was no question of changing the military law immediately. For the nationalists the essential point was safe. In view of the disastrous financial situation the Senate finally agreed in June to accept the tax on income in the final form proposed by René Renoult. The finance law in which it was incorporated was passed on 15 July.

A fine summer

With the distant assassination of a not very well known archduke (Sarajevo, 28 June), the French entered the arena. But for nearly a month no one suspected it. A very serious stock exchange crisis – did it herald the end of a cycle? – shook Paris, Berlin and St Petersburg. London seemed to be less affected. But the masses were no more aware of it than of the approach of war. What occupied people's minds was the arrival of the income tax, feared for twenty years by property owners and finally tolerated in exchange for the three-year law; the special congress of the *SFIO* which passed the motion of Jaurès in favour of the preventive workers' strike, organized on an international scale, with a view to the congress of the International – not with a view to a serious European crisis; the holidays for the rich and the harvests for the peasants. What was one more Balkan crisis? the others had been solved; why not this one?

Should Poincaré be credited with greater perception? At bottom, the question is secondary. Supposing that he was, it is the use he made of it that assumes importance. The fact is that during his official visit to Russia with Viviani, on 15 July, the President of the Republic does not seem to have advised his major ally to be cautious. Yet the strengthening of the military, diplomatic and, in particular, financial links between Paris and St Petersburg would have given great weight to any advice in this direction. Did Poincaré go as far as giving the Tsar formal assurances? At any rate, apart from the quest for a favourable solution to a series of questions to which French businessmen attached the greatest importance, was his principal concern, in this period when decisions were maturing, the consolidation of the alliance at the price of resolute support for the ally? All the more resolute, perhaps, since it was necessary to erase the displeasure which had arisen recently in Russia as a result of the seizures by French firms.[55] On 23 July, when the Austrian ultimatum to Serbia, encouraged by Wilhelm II, became known and when the risk of war suddenly became apparent to everyone, the French government promised Russia 'to fulfil the obligations of the alliance', that is, to intervene militarily if Germany supported Austria–Hungary. On 29 July the Head of State and the Prime Minister returned to Paris. It was now very late for France to take any initiative. The very next day Russia mobilized against Germany in spite of a somewhat late appeal for caution from Viviani. On 31 July came the German ultimatum to Russia and to France as well. That evening Jaurès, who had just decided to 'absolve the party from responsibility', was assassinated in the Café du Croissant. On 1 August, the French government having replied to Berlin that France would act 'in accordance with her interests', the country was covered with the white notices of general mobilization. On 3 August Germany declared war on France.

There can be no question here of dealing with the problem of 'responsibility'. It is true that the working class did not do much. The Second International revealed not only its impotence but also its incapacity to act and its illusions: on the evening of 30 July the leaders of the *SFIO* and of the *CGT*, which had adopted the party's position, decided to organize a great proletarian meeting ... on 9 August for the opening in Paris of the congress of the International. Nor did the assassination of Jaurès trigger off the revolt feared by Malvy, the Minister of the Interior, and the latter, well informed as he was, could afford not to implement the decisions foreseen for *carnet B*. The peasantry displayed in turn stupefaction, resignation and confidence, but only on 1 August.[56] On the national level, there was no great wave of nationalism. A genuine affection, encouraged by the schools, for a Republic equipped with all the virtues had long led to the perversion – rather than the submersion – of class consciousness by the consciousness of belonging to a nation so worthy of being defended. No doubt all this was foreseeable. But who foresaw it?

In any case, it was the rulers who ruled: the politicians, the ruling classes. Historians have no proof of war-mongering intervention in the middle of the crisis by any business circle or circles. Moreover, we know that they were divided. But their collusion is not a myth invented by the Marxists, and the connections between one man and another, the connections between ministers' offices and boards of directors, the precise interests granted political support – all these things were also part of the French Republic. The Union Sacrée had already been there in embryo since Poincaré had called on Viviani after the elections. It was not Maurras who was president of the Republic, but a company lawyer, a republican in the traditional sense of the term, that is an anti-clerical Dreyfusard who had become, or again became, a moderate nationalist; and it was not Jaurès who was prime minister but a former socialist, in short someone who was 'acceptable'. For the rest, it was not France alone that was concerned and it

was probably not her political opinion or her government or her businessmen who at the last minuted played a decisive part in the misfortunes about
to descend. The responsibilities went back further. 'Chaque peuple paraît,
à travers les rues de l'Europe, avec sa petite torche à la main, et maintenant
voilà l'incendie.'[57]

Conclusion to Part II

There are many ways of approaching an epoch. It can be judged by what it did, by what it said about itself, or by what it led to. It can be judged by looking at it in the long term or by sticking to the dates which define it, according to its events or its structures. In our survey of the Belle Epoque we wanted to start with the political dimension, because from 1898 to 1906–7 the life of the French was passionately political, as political as the life of a people can be in a non-revolutionary period. It was during those years that the radical Republic settled in. Subsequently the political debate proper tailed off in the towns and villages. Except for the socialists, the political groups broke up and the newspapers lost their keenness. The foreground was occupied by structures: bourgeois prosperity, the rise of big business and first and foremost the banks, the dangerous revival of colonial expansion and the exploitation by business of certain colonies and semi-colonies. Can we nevertheless say that it was then and only then that the question mark appeared after the word radical in the phrase 'radical republic'? To ask this question is to wonder about the part played by the radical party at the beginning of the century. It seems to have been a distinguished part. Radicalism, like Gaullism at a later point in French history, had carried the country safely through to different horizons. The radicals, by winning the leadership of the State and of local government, by putting in their men, by multiplying committees and by heading the civil service, had been able to induce their rural and *petit-bourgeois* grass-roots supporters to accept colonial expansion as an interesting necessity and expansion in general as a virtue. They had enabled the major economic work begun under the Second Empire – the entry of France into capitalism – to be confirmed by those who for one reason or another had remained hostile or indifferent to it in the time of Napoleon III. They had won over those strata of the population which benefited – and, even more, thought they benefited – from expansion and stability, and they had coloured both these things with the very bright and very real colours of secularization. The year in which Herriot became mayor of Lyon and Daladier sat the *agrégation* in history – 1905 – their rôle was already in all essentials over. In

1914, they had been out of power for some years. Yet radicalism was not dead; Herriot and Daladier were to turn up again. But it was a bit like Gaullism after de Gaulle. The men were there; the institution still worked; and even the ideas were not necessarily absent. But their function had been fulfilled.

It was the shadow of radicalism that hung over not only the great massacre but also the profound crisis in cultural and political values and the social crisis, all the basic elements of which were already present before 1914. In this respect the break imposed by the Great War was not very pertinent. It accelerated more things than it created. And it was the period of the radical Republic that sowed the seeds of the tragic world, the world in conflict experienced by the sons of the radicals of the beginning of the century.

Notes

1. The end of the notables, 1871–1879

1 Out of 753 seats, 78 were not filled because of the multiple elections. The seats belonging to the departments annexed also have to be deducted. See R. Rémond, Bibliography, no. 102.

2 His *Journal politique*, Biblio. no. 10, remains one of the best sources for information on the National Assembly, like the *Souvenirs politiques* (1871–7) of Montalembert's son-in-law, the vicomte de Meaux.

3 The republican terms 'representatives' and 'National Assembly' were not adopted.

4 Quoted by M. Prélot, *Institutions politiques et Droit constitutionnel* (Paris, 1969), p. 450.

5 It should not be forgotten that Bismarck, engaged in the *Kulturkampf*, did not much like the declarations of the French ultramontanes in 1873. In the spring of 1875, confronted with a French law which enlarged the cadres of the army, he brandished the threat of a preventive war. He favoured the republicans, who, he thought, would find it more difficult to enlist allies in Europe than the monarchists.

6 The number of non-registered citizens was 12.8 per cent of the potential electorate. The non-registered were particularly numerous in Seine-Inférieure, Nord, Paris, Lyon and Marseille. This fact was due principally to the migrations occasioned by urbanization. See A. Lancelot, *l'Abstentionnisme électoral en France* (Paris, 1967).

7 The two chambers returned to Paris in 1879, but it remained the custom to hold the Congress at Versailles.

8 See the unpublished thesis of Rosemonde Sanson, 'La Célébration de la fête nationale sous la IIIe République (1880–1914), Paris, 1970.

9 Quoted by *L'Année politique*, 1880, p. 285 (Biblio. no. 5).

10 Avant-propos of the third volume of G. Hanotaux's *Histoire de la France Contemporaine* (Biblio. no. 37).

11 Abbeville, 10 June 1877, quoted by P. Barral, Biblio. no. 93, p. 235.

12 In Lille, 15 August 1877, *ibid.*

13 *Souvenirs et réflexions politiques* (2 vols., Paris 1886), vol. II, p. 38.

14 See the admirable book by Roger Thabault, Biblio. no. 74.

15 *L'Univers* of 8 January. A series of very detailed articles studies 'radical propaganda' in the rural areas.

2. Economy and society

1 See G. Garnier, *Bulletin du Centre d'histoire économique et sociale de la région lyonnaise*, 2, 1972.

2 See M. Perrot, 'Les rapports des ouvriers français et des ouvriers étrangers, 1871–1893', *Bulletin de la Société d'histoire moderne*, 1, 1960.

3 In the next decade the figures were 61 per cent and 41.1 per cent, respectively.

4 J. Marczewski, *Introduction à l'histoire quantitative* (Geneva, 1965), p. 125.

5 R. Cameron, *Annales*, September–October 1970, p. 1,421.

6 See P. Léon, 'La région lyonnaise dans l'histoire économique et sociale de la France', *Revue historique*, January–March 1967, p. 52.

7 See R. Trempé, 'Le réformisme des mineurs français à la fin du XIXe siècle', *Le Mouvement social*, October–December 1968, pp. 93–106.

8 See A. Chatelain, *Annales*, July–September 1958, pp. 573–85.

9 We have adopted the conclusions reached by J. Rougerie after an analysis which is a model of critical rigour: 'Remarques sur l'histoire des salaires à Paris au XIXe siècle', *Le Mouvement social*, April–June 1968.

10 As is noted by G. Dupeux, *La Société française, 1789–1960* (Paris, 1966), p. 194.

11 The most accurate summary of all this is still that of Levasseur, Biblio. no. 120.

12 See M. Gillet, 'Aux origines de la première convention d'Arras', *Revue du Nord*, 1957, pp. 111–23.

13 This section is largely based on the attempt at the classification of rural societies by P. Barral, Biblio. no. 107.

14 Cf. J. Fauvet and H. Mendras, *Les Paysans et la Politique dans la France contemporaine* (Paris, A. Colin, 1957), p. 396.

15 See R. Leveau, *Le Mouvement social*, April–June 1969.

16 See Ph. Gratton, 'Mouvement et physionomie des grèves agricoles (1820–1935)', *ibid.*

17 See A. Daumard, 'L'évolution des structures sociales en France à l'époque de l'industrialisation', *Revue historique*, April–June 1972.

18 See V. Wright, 'L'épuration du Conseil d'Etat, juillet 1879', *Revue d'histoire moderne et contemporaine*, October–December 1972, p. 643.

19 See J. Bouvier, 'Une dynastie d'affaires lyonnaise au XIXe siècle, les Bonnardel', *Revue d'histoire moderne et contemporaine*, 2, 1955, pp. 185–205.

20 See Jean Bouvier's discussion of J. Toulemonde, *Naissance d'une métropole. Roubaix et Tourcoing au XIXe siècle* (Tourcoing, 1966), in the *Revue du Nord*, January–March 1967, p. 239.

21 See R. Talmy, *L'Association catholique des patrons du Nord (1884–1895)* (Lille, 1962).

22 The table of incomes by categories inserted by Doumer in his draft tax on incomes in 1894–5 gives the following figures established by an extra-parliamentary commission (cf. E. Levasseur, Biblio. no. 120, p. 619):

Category of income	No. of incomes by category	Total of incomes by category
2 500 F and less to	9 509 800	12 342 000 000
2 501 to 3 000 F	563 000	1 597 000 000
3 001 to 5 000	446 000	1 735 000 000
5 001 to 10 000	294 000	2 109 000 000
10 001 to 20 000	123 400	1 898 000 000
20 001 to 50 000	51 000	1 573 000 000
50 001 to 100 000	9 800	674 000 000
100 001 and more	3 000	572 000 000
Total:	11 000 000	22 500 000 000

23 An enquiry by the Ministry of Finance in 1899 covering 342,000 civil servants revealed that 89.5 per cent of salaries were less than 3,000 francs, that 10.43 per cent ranged from 2,000 to 20,000 francs and that 0.07 per cent were more than 20,000 francs (cited by Levasseur, Biblio. no. 120, p. 623).

3. The period of Jules Ferry, 1879–1885

1 A. Rivet, 'Les Débuts de la IIIe République en Haute-Loire', *thèse de troisième cycle*, Lyon, 1972.

2 See J.-T. Joughin, *The Paris Commune in French Politics, 1871–1880. The History of the Amnesty of 1880* (2 vols., Baltimore, 1955).

3 Cf. the article by Michelle Perrot, 'Le premier journal marxiste français: *L'Egalité* de Jules Guesde, 1877–1883', *Actualité de l'histoire*, July–September 1859.

4 Mermeix, in his *France socialiste*, in 1886, ascribes about 200 determined militants to the Central Revolutionary Committee.

5 Letter to Ranc of 24 December 1874, quoted by D. Halévy and E. Pillias, Biblio. no. 9.

6 53,216,074 francs in 1872, 52,408,162 francs in 1880.

7 See P. Zind, *L'Enseignement religieux dans l'instruction primaire publique en France, 1850–1875*, Lyon, 1971; the author gives a marvellous description of the way in which religion was taught under the auspices of the Falloux law.

8 See the article by A. Prost and C. Rosenzveig, which has wide methodological implications: 'La Chambre des Députés (1881–1885). Analyse factorielle des scrutins', *Revue française de science politique*, February 1971, pp. 5–50.

9 Letter quoted by D. Halévy and E. Pillias, Biblio. no. 9.

10 This clause disappeared in 1907. The government had wanted to make religious ceremonies subject to this law, since Catholics rejected the *associations cultuelles*. But they showed the same hostility to the prior declaration, which was then abolished.

11 See V. Wright, 'L'épuration du Conseil d'Etat, juillet 1879', *Revue d'histoire moderne et contemporaine*, October–December 1972, p. 643.

12 In the phrase used by Littré in his penetrating book, *De l'établissement de la IIIe République* (Paris, 1880), a reprint of articles that had appeared in the *Revue de philosophie positive*, pp. 489–508. Littré made it an argument for opposing the granting of exceptions.

13 Cf. Maurice Sorre, 'Les pères du radicalisme', *Revue française de science politique*, October 1951.

14 Speech of 2 July 1882, reprinted in the *Revue internationale de l'enseignement*, July–December 1882, p. 104.

15 Freycinet to the Senate in July 1879, *L'Année politique*, 1879, Biblio. no. 5, p. 248.

16 In March 1878, *L'Année politique*, 1879, p. 84.

17 On all this, see J. Bouvier, Biblio. no. 108.

18 In the words of the *Année politique*, 1882, p. 181.

19 See Y. Gonjo, Biblio. no. 117, and the *Année politique*, 1883, pp. 116–21.

20 F. Crouzet, discussing the thesis of F. Caron on the Northern Railway Company, *Revue historique*, April–June 1970, p. 526; et Y. Gonjo, Biblio. no. 117.

21 As J. Chastenet rightly notes (vol. III), p. 129 (Biblio. no. 33).

22 Cf. R. Girardet, Biblio. no. 55, p. 85; J. Valette, 'Note sur l'idée coloniale vers 1871', *Revue d'histoire moderne et contemporaine*, April–June 1967, pp. 158–72.

23 See Charles A. Julien's study in *Les Politiques d'expansion impérialistes* (Paris, 1949); and J. Ganiage, Biblio. no. 45.

24 See J. Valette, 'L'expédition de Francis Garnier au Tonkin à travers quelques journaux contemporains', *Revue d'histoire moderne et contemporaine*, April–June 1969, pp. 189–220.
25 See Charles Fourniau, 'La genèse et l'évolution de l'affaire du Tonkin', *Revue historique*, October–December 1971, pp. 377–408.
26 The minority comprised 94 republicans and 176 deputies of the right. Among the six members who abstained was Albert de Mun. Mgr Freppel, Bishop of Angers, was the only member of the right to vote with the majority.
27 See John Laffey, 'Les racines de l'impérialisme français en Extrême-Orient', *Revue d'histoire moderne et contemporaine*, April–June 1966, pp. 288–9.
28 He wished to rest, he wrote in his will, 'opposite the blue line of the Vosges, whence the touching lament of the conquered rises up to my faithful heart'.
29 Preface to the book, *Le Tonkin et la Mère Patrie*, 1890.

4. Beliefs and cultures

1 In *Le Régime moderne*, the last volume of *Origines de la France contemporaine*.
2 See the important article by Y.-M. Hilaire, 'La pratique religieuse en France de 1815 à 1878', *L'Information historique*, pp. 57–69.
3 See Abbé E. Parinet, 'Paysan et maçon émigrant de la Marche (Creuse)', *Les Ouvriers des deux mondes* (Paris, 1888), pp. 220–44.
4 See Fernand Boulard, 'La "déchristianisation" de Paris, l'évolution historique du non-conformisme', *Archives de sociologie des religions*, 31, 1971, pp. 69–98.
5 See Y. Daniel, *l'Equipement paroissial d'un diocèse urbain: le diocèse de Paris* (Paris, 1957).
6 See Y.-M. Hilaire, *L'Information historique*.
7 See F. Boulard, *Essor ou Déclin du clergé français* (Paris, Le Cerf, 1950).
8 The Protestants of the Cévennes under the Third Republic, in *Visages du protestantisme français* (Paris, Plon, 1945).
9 See C. Mesliand, 'Contribution à l'étude de l'anticléricalisme à Pertuis de 1871 à 1914', *Archives de sociologie des religions*, 10, 1960, pp. 49–62.
10 See A. Bouton, *Les Luttes ardentes des francs-maçons manceaux pour l'établissement de la République* (Le Mans, 1966).
11 See A. Prost, Biblio. no. 66, to whom great credit is due for bringing to light a publication whose great riches sweep away accepted ideas about the sclerotic condition of higher education a century ago.
12 Lavisse paid exceptional homage to him in the *Revue internationale de l'enseignement*, 1884.
13 See M. Leblond, 'La scolarisation dans le département du Nord au XIXe siècle', *Revue du Nord*, July–September 1970, pp. 387–98.
14 A woman with burning body
And breast swelling with independence ...
The Frenchmen's own mistress
Responds to the name of Marianne.
Le Cri patriotique of 1882; one of the many songs composed in honour of the Republic.
15 As George Fonsegrive notes in *De Taine à Péguy. L'évolution des idées dans la France contemporaine* (Paris, 1917).
16 H. W. Paul, 'The Debate over the Bankruptcy of Science in 1895', *French Historical Studies*, 3, 1968, pp. 299–327.
17 See J. Chastenet, vol. III, p. 233 (Biblio. no. 33).

5. The Republic confronted by nationalism and socialism

1 After 1919 this term was to denote the union of the radicals and the centre right; in short, a combination of centres as opposed to the alliance with the socialists.

2 Declaration by 76 retiring deputies belonging to the right, *L'Année politique*, 1885, p. 198.

3 Jacques Néré in his unpublished thesis (Biblio. no. 161) has made a significant contribution to our knowledge on this point. (Jaurès was the general editor of the *Histoire socialiste* but J. Labusquière was responsible for the volume devoted to the Third Republic.)

4 See R. Girardet, 'La Ligue des patriotes dans l'histoire du nationalisme français', *Bulletin de la Société d'histoire moderne*, 3, 1958.

5 After the passage of the law of 22 June 1886, forbidding the heads of the royal and imperial families to stay in France, authorizing the expulsion of the other members of those families and prohibiting them from holding any post or elected position.

6   As for me, I could only admire
     Our fine General Boulanger.

7 Bernard Lavergne, *Les Deux Présidences de Jules Grévy, 1879–1887* (Paris, Fischbacher, 1966), p. 422 (Biblio. no. 11). The deputy for Tarn is reporting the remarks made to him by the President of the Republic, whose trusted friend he was.

8 Seignobos has noted this as the first example of a practice peculiar to French governments, which is to take account, in the case of a vote of confidence, only of republican majorities. Loyal to this tradition, in 1954 Pierre Mendès-France rejected the Communist votes...

9   He will return when the drum beats,
     When the foreigner threatens our frontier.
     He will return and everyone will follow him
     He will have all France behind him.

10 Adrien Dansette has shown this to be true, confirming the revelations of Mermeix in *Les Coulisses du Boulangisme*, published in 1889.

11 Then at the beginning of a long career; it was he who was to reveal the Panama scandal; he finished up in the Action Française.

12 With proportional representation it would have won 52 fewer seats; we are here following G. Lachapelle, *Les Régimes électoraux* (Paris, A. Colin, 1934), p. 78.

13 Votes for Boulanger were cancelled and the Chamber, declining to quash the election, declared Joffrin elected.

14 *Le Figaro*, 3 February 1890. Boulanger was at that time in exile in Jersey.

15 For all that follows, see the thesis of Claude Willard, no. 163.

16 To use the words of J. Howorth, 'La propagande socialiste d'Edouard Vaillant pendant les années 1880–1884', *Le Mouvement social*, July–September 1970.

17 See M. Winock, 'La scission de Châtellerault et la naissance du parti allemaniste (1890–1891)', *Le Mouvement social*, April–June 1971.

18 Y. Lequin, 'Classe ouvrière et idéologie dans la région lyonnaise à la fin du XIXe siècle', *Le Mouvement social*, October–December 1969.

19 *Ibid.* Sometimes described as 'independent revolutionaries'.

20 M. Prélot, *l'Evolution politique du socialisme français* (Paris, Spes, 1939). This penetrating essay has not become well known because of its date of publication.

21 Benoît Malon, 'Le socialisme intégral,' *La Revue socialiste*, 1891, pp. 141 and 203, quoted by M. Prélot, *l'Evolution politique*, p. 106.

22 It was less than 141,000. Cf. P. Sorlin, p. 297.

23 See J. Julliard, 'Fernand Pelloutier et les origines du syndicalisme d'action directe', *Le Mouvement social*, April–June 1971.

6. The moderate Republic, 1889–1898

1 Reprinted as a book in 1897, with an introduction by Jaurès.
2 The Treaty of Frankfurt had granted Germany 'most favoured nation' status. The duties on German products could not be higher than the duties fixed by a treaty with another State. Industrialists complained of German competition.
3 Quoted by Lecanuet, *Les Premières Années du pontificat de Léon XIII* (Paris, 1931), p. 580.
4 See M. Rebérioux, 'Jaurès et les étudiants parisiens au printemps de 1893', *Bulletin de la Société d'études jaurésiennes*, July–September 1968. Seignobos remarks that Dupuy was suspected of having provoked the riot in the Latin quarter in order to have a pretext for the occupation of the *bourse* by the troops.
5 2,914,985 votes (the Boulangist votes, 709,223, are not included in this figure). In 1893 the *ralliés* obtained 458,416 votes and the monarchists 1,000,381. The revisionist votes, which certainly cannot all be ascribed to the right, were 171,626 in number. See M. Fournier, *Revue politique et parlementaire*, June 1898, p. 491.
6 See J.-M. Mayeur, 'Droites et ralliés à la Chambre des députés au début de 1894', *Revue d'histoire moderne et contemporaine*, April–June 1966, pp. 117–35.
7 Subsequently published in book form: *Solidarité* (Paris, A. Colin, 1897).
8 *Le Comte Albert de Mun* (Paris, Spes, 1925), p. 176, and *Le Ralliement* (Paris Spes, 1928), p. 60.
9 Quoted by Lecanuet, *Les Signes avant-coureurs de la séparation* (Paris, 1930), p. 110.
10 Appeal by the Republican Central Action Committee, 1894.
11 *La IIIe République* (Paris, Fayard, 1935), pp. 153–5.
12 Cf. on all this P. Renouvin's illuminating restatement of events (Biblio. no. 46).
13 The capital lent to Russia by French savers amounted to 1.4 milliards on 1 January 1889, 5.7 milliards on 1 January 1892 and 10.6 milliards on 1 January 1895. See R. Girault, 'Sur quelques aspects financiers de l'alliance franco-russe', *Revue d'histoire moderne et contemporaine*, January–March 1961.
14 'The English . . . are the real beneficiaries of the situation created by the question of Alsace', said the *Bulletin du Comité de l'Afrique française* in 1898. The *Bulletin* suggested 'looking within this continent' for security or even support in order to avoid 'dangerous adventures' in Asia and Africa.
15 See Herward Sieberg, *Eugène Etienne und die französische Kolonialpolitik (1887–1904)* (Cologne, 1968).
16 According to Mgr Baunard, *Un siècle de l'Eglise de France*, p. 433, there were 70,114 French missionaries, 17,184 of them men.
17 Marchand took Fashoda on 10 July 1898.

Summary of the period 1871–1898

1 See the work of M. Dogan and especially his important article, 'Les filières de la carrière politique en France', *Revue française de sociologie*, October–December 1967, pp. 468–92.

7. The Dreyfus affair

1 Marcel Thomas: see Biblio. no. 182. Henri Guillemin: *L'Enigme Esterhazy* (Paris, Gallimard, 1962).

2 In particular after the publication of the *Journal de l'affaire Dreyfus*, by Maurice Paléologue (Paris, Plon, 1955), a book which in many ways is so convincing.

3 R. Martin du Gard speaks in the second part of *Jean Barrois* of the 'wild cry of triumph' with which the news was welcomed in Dreyfusard circles.

4 Jeanne Siwek-Pouydesseau, *Le Corps préfectoral sous les IIIe et IVe Républiques* (Paris, A. Colin, 1969).

5 In January 1898 Jaurès stated in the review *Cosmopolis* that socialism would be victorious in ten years, and Guesde declared at Tourcoing in December 1897: 'The beginning of the next century will be the beginning of the new era.'

6 F. Bédarida has had access to two memorandums of February 1876 and autumn 1878; they are real card-indexes of the senior officers. See 'L'armée et la République', *Revue historique*, July–September 1964.

7 The list of subscribers, classified by profession, was published in 1899, under the Stock imprint, by P. Quillard, under the title *Le Monument Henry*. Among the numerous officers one may note, as well as five generals on the active list, the name of Captain Weygand.

8 They were not alone. The *Dépêche* saw the appellation, and the initiative, as a disquieting sign of élitism.

9 M. Launay, 'Jaurès, la Sorbonne et l'affaire Dreyfus', *Bulletin de la Société d'études jaurésiennes*, July–September 1967.

10 See J.-P. Peter, 'Dimensions de l'affaire Dreyfus', *Annales ESC*, November–December 1961.

11 Janine Ponty, 'La France devant l'affaire Dreyfus. Contribution à une étude sociale d'opinion publique', *Ecole pratique des hautes études*, 1971 (*thèse de troisième cycle*, still unpublished).

12 Eugen Weber, *Satan franc-maçon* (Paris, Julliard, 1964).

13 This, it is believed, was supposed to be the cult of Satan, restricted to the highest masons of all rites and all countries.

14 Elizabeth Cazenave, 'L'affaire Dreyfus et l'opinion bordelaise', *Annales du Midi*, January–March 1972.

15 Cf. Charles-Robert Ageron, 'Jaurès et la question algérienne', *Le Mouvement social*, January–March 1963.

16 L. Poliakov, *Le Mythe aryen* (Paris, Calmann-Lévy, 1971), Part 2, chapter 5.

17 Patrick Dumont, *La Petite Bourgeoisie vue à travers les contes quotidiens du Journal (1894–1895)* (Paris, Minard, 1973).

18 Péguy, *Oeuvres en prose* (2 vols., Paris, Gallimard, 1959–61), vol. II, p. 538.

19 Cf. Waldeck-Rousseau's speech at Toulouse on 28 October 1900: 'The meetings which organized the following day's riots have ceased, and the street has become once again an animated, peaceful avenue no longer filled with the clamour of processions.'

8. The France of the left-wing Bloc and the rise of radicalism

1 It was different with the Obédience du Droit Humain, mixed since its creation in 1893–4.

2 According to J.-P. Roux, who is writing a thesis on the League for the Rights of Man.

3 Doizié's amendment to the charter of Free Thought (Rome, September 1904).

4 This was an anagram of G. Béret, a former contributor to the *Revue socialiste*.

5 Art. 1 of the regulations approved at the Marseille congress in 1903.

6 A. Huc was to have this point out in the *Dépêche* of 5 March 1908.

7 E. Davesne, *Le Comité républicain de commerce, de l'industrie et de l'agriculture* (Nevers, 1912). The rural notables joined in 1908.

8 P. Mansire, 'La presse et les élections de 1902 en Seine-Inférieure', in J. Kayser (ed.), Biblio. no. 143.

9 G. Dupeux makes it start in 1903 in Loir-et-Cher, Biblio. no. 71.

10 In particular H. Lerner's *thèse d'Etat* on 'La Dépêche de Toulouse, contribution à l'étude du radicalisme français'; R. Vandenbussche's article, Biblio. no. 199; and the work by D. and G. Fabre on *L'Implantation du radicalisme dans la Haute-Garonne, 1870–1914* (Toulouse, 1973).

11 Declaration by the parliamentary radical and radical-socialist group, 30 March 1898.

12 At the session of Easter 1905, only 17 general councils voted in favour of Separation; most abstained.

13 Cf. the enquiry of the *Siècle* summarized by J.-M. Mayeur, Biblio. no. 193.

14 Although just after his accession, in August 1903, he had shown a spirit of conciliation.

15 Papal note concerning the presence of the nuncio in France; summoning of two French bishops before the Holy See.

16 The Allard amendment, which defended their point of view, received 59 votes.

17 He was accused of tactlessly denying the sacred character of the French national heroine.

18 Louis Martin, *Bulletin du parti radical*, 3 May 1905.

19 Editorial of the *Bulletin du parti radical*, 8 March 1905.

20 J. Siwek-Pouydesseau, *Le corps préfectoral sous les IIIe et IVe Républiques* (Paris, A. Colin, 1969).

21 Decrees of 28 September 1899 and 9 January 1900.

22 Suggestions made in 1903 by the Clermont-Ferrand lodge, the Enfants de Gergovie.

23 Decrees of 20 July and 18 November 1901; and especially the decree of 30 May 1902.

24 G. Leygues, Chamber of Deputies, 14 February 1902.

25 'The classical spirit', the minister declared, 'belongs to all ages and all countries, because ... it is the cult of clear, free reason, the disinterested quest for beauty.'

26 See the unpublished thesis of A. Tramoni, 'Idéologies ouvrières et patronales à travers l'enquête de l'Office du travail (1901)', University of Provence, 1970.

27 This plan was to come to nothing. It was firmly rejected by trade unionists, who felt that receiving the right to possess property was an encouragement to undertake profit-making activities – that is, an encouragement to behave like the bourgeoisie.

28 The decree of 1 September 1899 laid down that a third of its members should be nominated by the workers' unions and a third by the employers. The remaining third were members by right or were appointed by the government.

29 This plan was to be rejected on 22 December 1904.

30 R. Trempé, 'Le réformisme des mineurs français à la fin du XIXe siècle', *Le Mouvement social*, October–December 1968.

31 'La République et les élections de 1902', *Revue politique et parlementaire*, October 1901.

32 Jules Huret, 'Les Grèves', *Revue Blanche*, Paris, 1902 (preface by A. Millerand).

9. Crises and death of the Bloc, 1904–1907

1 These descriptions are drawn from J.-M. Mayeur, Biblio. no. 193. See also J.-M. Mayeur, Biblio. no. 206. (See also 201.)

2 P. Grunebaum-Ballin was later to suggest that 'this incredible document' may have been the work of an *agent provocateur* (*Cahiers laïques*, January–February 1956).

3 See Marc Sangnier's speech to the learned societies on 9 February 1906, *Discours* (Paris, Bloud et Gay, 1910), book 1, pp. 459–94.

4 The anecdote is well known. Sarrien – Ça Rien, as the enemies of the member of Saône-et-Loire called him – passes the refreshments to his future colleagues, who had met at his house. 'What will you have?' he says to Clemenceau. 'The Ministry of the Interior'.

5 C. Geslin, 'Provocations patronales et violence ouvrières; Fougères', *Le Mouvement social*, January–March 1973.

6 J.-M. Laux, 'Travail et travailleurs dans l'industrie automobile jusqu'en 1914', *Le Mouvement social*, October–December 1972.

7 There were woodcutters' strikes in 1892–4 and the victorious episode of the barrel-makers of Saint-Yrieix in 1901.

8 Words quoted in P. Vilar's preface to Ph. Gratton's book, Biblio. no. 203.

9 R. Dugrand, Biblio. no. 287, and R. Pech, *Entreprise viticole et capitalisme en Languedoc-Roussillon* (University of Toulouse-le-Mirail, 1975).

10 H. Chardon, *L'Administration de la France* (Paris, Librairie académique Perrin, 1908).

11 Combes's speech at Tréguier on 13 September 1903 at the unveiling of the statue of Renan.

12 This is what he wrote to the Italian socialist Andrea Costa in September 1902, in a letter that soon became famous.

13 This tragic episode has been not only described but also analysed by J. Julliard, Biblio. no. 204.

14 G. Clemenceau, *Lettres à une amie, 1923–1929* (Paris, Gallimard, 1970).

15 Cf. the speech by Estier, president of the general council of Bouches-du-Rhône, at the closing banquet of the first annual congress of the radical and radical-socialist party of the south-east (Nice, April 1906). In it Clemenceau is denounced for his softness and his readiness to accommodate the united socialists.

10. The days of imperialism

1 The 1911 census must be used very cautiously.

2 This is what happened in 1904–5 with the producers of rails: cf. F. Caron, *Revue d'histoire de la sidérurgie*, 1963.

3 The Société des Mines de Lens had 6,000 shareholders in 1900 and 10,464 in 1904: a whole world of small and medium savers.

4 Thus on the eve of the Great War it was in the joint-stock banks that money deposited earned least: the rate of profit of the Crédit Lyonnais was 16.6 per cent in 1914, as against 35 per cent for Paribas.

5 According to F. Divisia, *La Géographie des banques en France* (Dunod, 1942).

6 E. Aynard (banker and deputy for Lyon), quoted by J. Labasse, *Les Capitaux et la Région. Essai sur le commerce et la circulation des capitaux dans la région lyonnaise* (Paris, A. Colin, 1956).

7 Phase A: an expression designating that period of prosperity in the late nineteenth century characterized by a rise in prices and profits.

8 The loan of April 1906, made at a time when the revolution was not yet over, enabled French capitalists to gain a dominant position in Russia to the detriment of their competitors.

9 The Radicals were very keen on demanding it: 'French capital must take French industry and the French proletariat with it wherever it goes' *Le Radical*, 10 March 1911.

10 J. Thobie has studied the conditions in which the Ottoman loan of 1910 was refused in France: *Revue historique*, April–June 1968.

11 See J. Suret-Canale, *Afrique noire (Occidentale et centrale)* (Paris, Editions sociales, 1968), vol. 1, pp. 296–304.

12 See G. Jacobet and F. Koerner, 'Economie de traite et bluff colonial: la Compagnie Occidentale de Madagascar (1895–1934)', *Revue historique*, October–December 1972.

13 See M. Brugière, Biblio. no. 215, for a good account of his career.

14 H. Lorin, professor of commercial geography at the university of Bordeaux, praises him for this particularly in the *Revue politique et parlementaire* for December 1901.

15 In 500 km of railway the plan provided for 7.3 viaducts, bridges or aqueducts per km and that in a totally deforested area.

16 An analysis and precise calculations will be found in Ch.-R. Ageron, Biblio. no. 211.

17 See Ch. Poitevin, Biblio. no. 236. Between 1901 and 1904 Couitéas acquired a huge estate in more than dubious circumstances and when the protests of the natives provoked an enquiry he presented himself as a victim of arbitrary behaviour over the colonies (1908–1912).

18 See P. Soumille, *Européens de Tunisie et questions religieuses (1892–1901)* (Paris, Éditions du CNRS, 1973).

19 'La crise du parti radical', *La Revue*, 5 May 1909.

20 In the Caillaux bill, besides the general tax on income which affected taxable incomes divided into seven categories (the schedules), a 'complementary tax' was foreseen; its rate was progressive and it was to be paid by those with an annual income of over 5,000 francs, that is, more than a young university teacher earned, less than a country doctor earned.

21 On 11 January 1910 Arthur Huc compared the Bloc to Roland's mare – equipped with every quality except life.

22 The declaration by the cardinals and archbishops of 12 September 1908 called for a watch on state schools – teachers, timetables and books – and demanded that they should be kept strictly 'neutral'.

23 Henry Bérenger, for example, editor first of *L'Action* then of the *Siècle*.

24 Emile Macquart, *Revue politique et parlementaire*, October 1901.

25 The book which he published under this title in 1896 found echoes for some years in many articles and meetings; cf. the Congress of Social Education which was held in Paris from 26 to 30 September 1900.

26 Editorial of *L'Action libérale populaire*, 14 February 1906.

27 Cf. the debate, at the Geneva congress of June 1906, studied by J. Baubérot (Biblio. no. 242).

28 Cl. Liauzu, 'Jalons pour une étude des Biribi', *Cahiers de Tunisie*, nos. 73 and 74 (1971).

29 G. Leygues, Minister of Education, in the Chamber on 14 February 1902.

30 See F. Amaury, *Histoire du plus grand quotidien de la IIIe République, le Petit Parisien, 1876–1944* (Paris, PUF, 1972).

32 A. Robinet, *Péguy entre Jaurès, Bergson et l'Eglise* (Paris, Seghers, 1968).
33 E. Weber, 'Le renouveau nationaliste en France et le glissement vers la droite, 1905–1914', *Revue d'histoire moderne et contemporaine*, April–June 1958.
34 Preface by René Henry, professor at the School of Political Science, to the thesis by R. Baldy on Alsace-Lorraine (1912). Text published by R. Girardet, *Le Nationalisme français (1871–1914)* (Paris, A. Colin, 1966).
35 M.-Th. Borrelly, 'L'image de l'Alsace-Lorraine à travers quelques oeuvres littéraires françaises, 1871–1914', Centre de Recherches de l'Université de Metz, *Travaux et Recherches*, 1973.
36 Remarks of Captain H. de Malleray, on pilgrimage at Bouvines in 1905.
37 The colonial group recruited its members mainly from the centre. It also included some well-known *ralliés* and more and more radicals.
38 'L'implantation de Schneider au Maroc', *Revue d'histoire diplomatique*, 1965.
39 R. Girault, 'Sur quelques aspects financiers de l'alliance franco-russe', *Revue d'histoire moderne et contemporaine*, January–March 1971.
40 D. Watson, 'Clemenceau, Caillaux and Pichon: la politique étrangère du premier gouvernement Clemenceau (1906–1909)', Université de Metz, *Travaux et Recherches*, 1973.
41 Cf. J. Thobie, *Revue historique*, April–June 1968.
42 Cf. M. Bastid, 'La diplomatie française et la révolution chinoise de 1911', *Revue d'histoire moderne et contemporaine*, April–June 1969.

11. The avant-garde movements

1 For example, in March 1911. The play was *Après moi*, by Bernstein.
2 Thanks mainly to the big book by J. Caron, Biblio. no. 249.
3 Examined by M. Launay in the *Revue Historique*, April–June 1971.
4 Such is the hypothesis of M. Barthélémy-Madaule, Biblio. no. 83.
5 See the article by J.-M. Mayeur, 'Catholicisme intransigeant, catholicisme social, démocratie chrétienne', *Annales ESC*, March–April 1972.
6 Cf. the *Lettres d'un curé de campagne* by Yves Le Querdec (Georges Fonsegrive).
7 Cf. E. Poulat, *Intégrisme et Catholicisme intégral. Un réseau secret international antimoderniste:la Sapinière (1909–1921)* (Paris, Casterman, 1969).
8 Not always: two Guesdist deputies, Ghesquière and Compère-Morel, openly attacked the methods of the *CGT* in the Chamber on 2 December 1911, and the socialist congress held at Lyon two months later did not disown them.
9 See the tables drawn up by J.-J. Fiechter, *Le Socialisme français de l'affaire Dreyfus à la Grande Guerre* (Geneva, Droz, 1965).
10 See J. Baubérot, 'L'évolution des courants chrétiens sociaux du protestantisme français de 1906 à 1914', *Parole et Société*, no. 1, 1974.
11 Edgard Milhaud and Albert Thomas made themselves the prophets of these ideas, while the Guesdists made ironical remarks about municipal monopolies, the 'skirts and knickers of socialism'.
12 Ch. Gras, in his thesis on *Alfred Rosemer*, points convincingly to the links established between the 'kernel' of *La Vie ouvrière*, the leadership of the Confédération and the currents which, especially in the United States, England and Italy, but also in Holland, Belgium and the Scandinavian countries, laid claim to revolutionary trade unionism.
13 The socialist-feminist group formed in 1899 by E. Renaud and L. Saumoneau disappeared about 1904.
14 Cf. P. Robin and his 'League of Human Regeneration'. Cf. also the popular song of Montéhus, *The mothers' strike*.

15 This is the point of view expressed by Francis de Pressensé at the socialist congress of Brest in March 1913.

16 The most complete analysis of this is that of J.-J. Becker, Biblio. no. 276.

17 J. Maitron has shown that the movement 'almost doubled its influence from 1893 to 1913', *Le Mouvement social*, April–June 1973.

18 This was the mandate which the socialist federation of Côtes-du-Nord gave its delegates to the national council on 20 December 1908.

19 Cf. Ch. Pawlowski, *Tony Garnier et les Débuts de l'urbanisme fonctionnel en France* (Centre de Recherche d'Urbanisme, Paris, 1967).

20 In particular with Harnack, whose lectures of 1900 on 'The essence of Christianity' were partly at the origin of *l'Evangile et l'Eglise*.

21 Abbé J. Rivière, *Le Modernisme devant l'Eglise* (Paris, Letouzey, 1929).

22 This is what is shown by the correspondence of M. Blondel with Father A. Valensin (1899–1947) (3 vols., Paris, Aubier, 1957).

23 Evidence of this is provided by the controversy in 1903 in the *Revue de synthèse historique*, and later in *L'Année sociologique* between Seignobos and Mantoux, Lacombe and Simiand.

24 Cf. J. Bouvier, 'Feu François Simiand?', *Annales ESC*, September–October 1973.

25 Durkheim obtained a chair at Bordeaux in 1887, when he was less than thirty years old, and the chair of the science of education at the Sorbonne to which he was appointed in 1902 became an independent chair of sociology in 1913.

26 H. Poincaré, *La Science et l'Hypothèse* (Paris, Flammarion, 1902); *La Valeur de la Science* (Paris, Flammarion, 1918); *Science et Méthode* (Paris, Flammarion, 1908).

27 See the study by J. Guillerme, in *l'Année 1913*, Biblio. no. 246.

28 See R. Moulin, *Le Marché de la peinture en France* (Paris, Editions de Minuit, 1967).

29 Cf. the still unpublished thesis of A. Danglès, 'La NRF: la formation du groupe et les années d'apprentissage, 1890–1910', Paris, 1973.

30 The phrase is Michel Zeraffa's.

31 The term is a routine one in sociology, for example in the works of the socialist Lucien Lévy-Bruhl.

32 Yet the Futurist exhibition which opened on 5 February 1912 in the gallery of Bernheim junior, and which was to be so successful in Italy and Russia, was coolly received in Paris.

33 Cf. the article by R.-J. Smith, 'L'atmosphère politique à l'ENS (fin du XIXe siècle)', *Revue d'histoire moderne et contemporaine*, April–June 1973.

34 *Revue de l'enseignement primaire et primaire supérieur*, 11 July 1909.

35 There was one exception: the marvellous *Philémon, vieux de la vieille*, which Descaves published in 1913; what *Le Chagrin et la Pitié* is to the Resistance, *Philémon* is to the Commune.

36 One of the building union leaders, Raymond Péricat, launched this appeal from prison (*Bataille syndicaliste*, 12 October 1911).

12. France in 1914

1 M. Agulhon has found a statue in one out of every six village squares in the departments of Var and Bouches-du-Rhône: 'Pour une archéologie de la République. L'allégorie civique féminine', *Annales ESC*, January–February 1973.

2 J. Valdour, *L'Ouvrier agricole, la vie ouvrière* (Paris, A. Rousseau). The book did not appear until 1919.

3 The Ministry of the Interior was responsible among other things for the protection of literary works and the appointment of the staff of prisons.

4 The *CGT* asked how many workers were still alive at sixty-five.

5 Those available to Briand are said to have been responsible for the fact that the Senate finally passed the law on pensions, on 22 March 1910.

6 1.8 per cent between 1896 and 1913 according to J.-J. Carré, P. Dubois, E. Malinvaud, Biblio. no. 217.

7 According to the estimates of the *Statistique agricole* (1912).

8 F. Crouzet, Biblio. no. 285. See also *Revue du Nord*, July–September 1972.

9 A decidedly lower figure than the one arrived at by M. Lévy-Leboyer.

10 According to the most recent calculations, Biblio. no. 217.

11 Cf. the distinction, already classical, applied by J. Marczewski.

12 P. Fridenson, 'Une industrie nouvelle: l'automobile en France jusqu'en 1914,' *Revue d'histoire moderne et contemporaine*, October–December 1972.

13 J.-M. Laux, 'Travail et travailleurs de l'industrie automobile jusqu'en 1914', *Le Mouvement social*, October–December 1972.

14 He published his results in October 1914 in the *Bulletin de la statistique générale de la France*.

15 In 1914 it had 3000 branches and 140,000 members.

16 E. Morel noted in 1908, in a big, well-documented book, that in the provinces the average number of books borrowed annually per inhabitant was 0.1 (*Essai sur le développement des bibliothèques publiques et de la librairie dans les deux mondes* (2 vols., Paris, Mercure de France, 1908).

17 At its congress in Lyon (February 1912), the *SFIO* decided against asking its members to quit masonry, in spite of Guesdist pressure.

18 See P. Gerbod, 'Associations et syndicalismes universitaires de 1828 à 1928', *Le Mouvement social*, April–June 1966.

19 This is the advice given, via the pen of A. Balz, in *La Revue universitaire* in 1907.

20 Teachers in *lycées*, teachers in communal *collèges*, assistant teachers in *lycées*, principals, general supervisors, vice-principals, bursars and so on – they all had their associations.

21 See Biblio. no. 292, and in particular the astonishing 'Testament syndical' left by E. Duport, the administrator of the most dynamic union, that of the south-east.

22 This was the Fédération Nationale de la Mutualité et de la Coopération Agricole, known as the organization 'in the boulevard Saint-Germain'.

23 Dr A. Beauvy, 'Tuberculose et vie urbaine', *Revue de Paris*, 9 January 1909.

24 E. Rist, *Vingt-cinq portraits de médecins français, 1900–1950* (Paris, Masson, 1955).

25 Gide went to Biskra for his health and brought back with him *L'Immoraliste*.

26 'Father has come in full of absinthe and they're busy upstairs', says the concierge of the Ménilmontant furnished lodgings which Léon Frapié describes in *La Maternelle*.

27 L. Hersch, 'Mortalité différentielle à Paris, *Revue d'économie politique*, 1920. The conclusions of this article are adopted and enlarged by A. Armengaud, *Démographie et Sociétés* (Paris, Stock, 1966).

28 In Lot-et-Garonne, if a second child was born people came to condole with the couple. The most friendly tried to excuse the husband.

29 In the present state of the literature on this subject, see R.-H. Guerrand, *La Libre Maternité* (Paris, Casterman, 1971).

30 However, the principal leaders of the *SFIO* did not favour Malthusianism.

31 Cf. the replies to the enquiry organized in 1909 by Humbert's paper, *Génération consciente*.

32 It was in 1910 that Alfred Binet published *Les Idées modernes sur les enfants* (Paris, Flammarion).

33 It seems that one must regard with suspicion Lyon censuses, which probably overestimated by 5 per cent; cf. J. Bienfait, 'La population de Lyon à travers un quart de siècle de recensements douteux, 1911–1936', *Revue de géographie de Lyon*, 1968.

34 A multi-racial city, too, containing refugees from the whole world: Turks, Egyptians, Persians, Vietnamese, Chinese, Hungarians and of course, Russians.

35 M. Perrot, *Les Ouvriers en grève, France 1871–1890* (vol. 1, Paris, Mouton, 1974), p. 220.

36 Yet in connection with this area people have been able to speak of 'growth without development'.

37 M. Gillet has shown how the mine owners divided France up into zones, each of which was systematically conquered.

38 Such was the case in 1912 with Armand Gaidan of Nîmes, a member of the Protestant bourgeoisie who had run the Comptoir Commercial d'Escompte since 1893.

39 The information is assembled, for the Massif Central, by A. Fels, Biblio. no. 290, and summarized for the Lyon region in an article by P. Léon, 'La région lyonnaise dans l'histoire économique et sociale de la France', *Revue historique*, January–March 1967.

40 R. Michaud, *J'avais vingt ans* (Paris, Éditions syndicalistes, 1967).

41 Ph. Béneton, 'La génération de 1912–1914', *Revue française de science politique*, October 1971.

42 Cf. among many others, the speech of the president of the PLM, Noblemaire, at the annual assembly of the Association Fraternelle des Agents de la Cie (July 1899), reprinted in *Hommes et Choses des chemins de fer* (1905), p. 273.

43 This enquiry has been put to good use in a *mémoire de maîtrise* submitted at Nanterre in 1973 by J. Desruelles.

44 *Jadis* (Paris, Flammarion, 1948), p. 146. Herriot explains why he did not run on the socialist ticket when he was a candidate for the municipal council of Lyon in 1904.

45 All attempts to increase taxes on the drink trade came up against the effective defences of this very much united profession.

46 Nevertheless, there were perceptible differences between secondary teaching – 6,000 to 7,000 candidates at the *agrégation* every year for about a hundred posts – and the administration properly so called, where it seems that from 1911 onwards there was a real recruitment crisis.

47 It is the one adopted by J.-B. Duroselle, Biblio. no. 36.

48 G. Vincent, 'Les professeurs du second degré au début du XXe siecle', *Le Mouvement social*, April–June 1966.

49 V. Karady, 'Note sur l'origine sociale et la réussite d'une profession intellectuelle', *Revue française de sociologie*, 1972.

50 Cf. in particular Dr Dumesnil's enquiry in 1899.

51 Yet the campaign began in May 1912, whereas the German General Staff's proposals date from January 1913.

52 G. Duby, *Le Dimanche de Bouvines* (Paris, Gallimard, 1973), p. 226.

53 In particular that of Paul-Boncour (*Encyclopédie permanente de l'administration française*, June 1963), who asserts that Jaurès always refused to dine at the same table as Caillaux.

54 Cf. the small number of people recorded in the *carnet B* and the poor audiences noted in Languedoc for the most convinced anti-militarist groups.

55 R. Girault has published in his thesis a note prepared by the Quai underlining the delicacy of this mission.

56 Cf. J.-J. Becker, 'L'appel de guerre en Dauphiné' in *Le Carnet B*, Biblio. no. 276.
57 'Each nation has taken to the streets of Europe brandishing a lighted torch, and now the fire is raging' (Jean Jaurès).

Bibliography

The French bibliography has been updated for this edition, and a supplementary bibliography of works in English has been added.

WORKS IN FRENCH (AND GERMAN)

Unless otherwise stated the place of publication is Paris.

A. Principal sources, works of reference and general studies

I. Atlases

1 *Atlas historique de la France contemporaine, 1800–1965*, edited by René Rémond. A. Colin, 1966
2 *Atlas pittoresque de la France*, edited by O. Reclus. Attinger, no date (1913)
3 Goguel, F. *Géographie des élections françaises*. New edition, A. Colin, 1970

II. Chronicles

4 Bonnefous, G. *Histoire politique de la IIIe République*. Vol. I: *L'Avant-guerre (1906–1914)*, PUF, 1956
5 Daniel, A. *L'Année politique*. Perrin (up to 1905)

III. Biographical dictionaries

6 *Catholicisme* (encyclopaedia), edited by G. Jacquemet. Letouzey, n.d.
7 *Dictionnaire biographique du mouvement ouvrier français*. Third part: *1871–1914*, edited by Jean Maitron. 6 vols., Editions ouvrières, 1973–7
8 *Dictionnaire des parlementaires français*, edited by Jean Jolly. 8 vols., PUF, 1960–77. The first volume contains a list of all the ministers from 1889 to 1940

IV. Letters, memoirs, collections of texts

(for Part I)

9 Gambetta. *Lettres*, edited by D. Halévy and E. Pillias. Grasset, 1938
10 Lacombe, Charles de. *Journal politique*. 2 vols., A. Picard, 1907 and 1908. Essential on the National Assembly.

11 Lavergen, Bernard. *Les Deux Présidences de Jules Grévy, 1879–1887*. Fischbacher, 1966. Notes and commentary by J. Elleinstein.
12 Rémusat, Charles de. *Mémoires de ma vie*, edited by Ch.-H. Pouthas. 5 vols., Plon, 1967

(for Part II)

13 Barrès, M. *Mes cahiers*. II to X, Plon, 1929–38
14 Bouglé, C. *Syndicalisme et démocratie*. Rieder, 1908
15 Brisson, H. *La Congrégation. Opinions et discours, 1871–1901*. Cornély, 1902
16 Caillaux, J. *Mes mémoires*. I and II (3 vols.), Plon, 1942
17 Cambon, P. *Correspondance, 1870–1924*. 3 vols., Grasset, 1940
18 Combes, E. *Une campagne laïque*. Simonis, Empis, 1904
19 France, A. *Trente ans de vie sociale*. 3 vols., Emile-Paul, 1949–63
20 Goyau, G. *Autour du catholicisme social*. 5 vols., Perrin, 1897–1912
21 Halévy, D. 'Apologie pour notre passé', *Cahiers de la quinzaine*, 1910
22 Jaurès, J. *Oeuvres*. I to IX, Rieder, 1931–9
23 Maurras, Ch. *Oeuvres capitales*. Flammarion, 1954
24 Paul-Boncour, J. *Entre deux guerres*. Vol. I: *Les Luttes républicaines, 1877–1918*, Plon, 1945
25 Péguy, Ch. *Oeuvres en prose*. I and II, Gallimard, 1959–61
26 Portis, L. *Georges Sorel: Présentation et textes choisis*. Maspero, 1982

V. Basic bibliographies

27 Maitron, J. *Histoire du mouvement anarchiste en France*. Maspero, reissued 1975. On anarchism.
28 Mayeur, J.-M. *Un prêtre démocrate, l'abbé Lemire, 1853–1928*. Casterman, 1968. On religious questions.
29 Sorlin, P. *Waldeck-Rousseau*. A. Colin, 1966. On political problems.
30 Willard, Cl. *Le Mouvement socialiste en France, les guesdistes*. Editions sociales, 1965. On socialism.

VI. Works of reference and general studies

31 Agulhon, M., Désert, G. and Specklin, R. *Histoire de la France rurale*. Vol. III: *1789–1914*. Editions du Seuil, 1976
32 Bougin, G. *La IIIe République (1871–1914)*. Revised by J. Néré, A. Colin, 1967
33 Chastenet, J. *Histoire de la IIIe République*. Paris, Hachette
    I. *L'Enfance de la IIIe République, 1870–1879*, 1952
    II. *La République des républicains*, 1879–1893, 1954
    III. *La République triomphante, 1893–1906*, 1955
34 Dansette, A. *Histoire religieuse de la France contemporaine*. Flammarion, 1965
35 Duby, G. *Histoire de la France*. Vol. III, Larousse, 1972, contributions from J. Bouvier, G. Dupeux, P. Joutard
36 Duroselle, J.-B. *La France de la Belle Epoque. La France et les Français, 1900–1914*. Editions Richelieu, 1972
37 Hanotaux, G. *Histoire de la France contemporaine (1871–1900)*. Combet, 1908
    I. *Le Gouvernement de M. Thiers*
    II. *La Présidence du maréchal de Mac-Mahon. L'échec de la monarchie*
    III. *La Présidence du maréchal de Mac-Mahon. La constitution de 1875*
    IV. *La République parlementaire*
    Based on numerous oral testimonies and many private archives, these works remain essential for an understanding of the beginnings of the régime.

38 Machelon, J.-P. *La République contre les libertés*, Presses de la FNSP, 1976
39 Mayeur, J.-M. 'La France bourgeoise devient laïque et républicaine', contribution to vol. V of the *Histoire du peuple français*. Nouvelle Librairie de France, 1964
40 Seignobos, Ch. *Le Déclin de l'Empire et l'établissement de la IIIe République, 1859–1875*. Hachette, 1921
41 Seignobos, Ch. *L'Evolution de la IIIe République, 1875–1914*. Hachette, 1921. Nos. 40 and 41 are vols. VII and VIII of the *Histoire de la France contemporaine*, edited by E. Lavisse. They are still essential reading.
42 Sorlin, P. *La Société française*. Vol. I: *1840–1914*, Arthaud, 1969
43 Zeldin, Th. *Histoire des passions françaises*. Vols. I and II, Recherches, 1978

VII. International relations and colonial expansion

44 Brunschwig, H. *Mythes et Réalités de l'impérialisme colonial français, 1871–1914*. A. Colin, 1960
45 Ganiage, J. *L'Expansion coloniale de la France sous la IIIe République, 1871–1914*. Payot, 1968
46 Renouvin, P. *Histoire des relations internationales*. Vol. VI: *Le XIXe siècle, de 1871 à 1914*, Hachette, 1955
47 Thobie, J. *La France impériale*, Mégrelis, 1982

VIII. Political problems and forces

48 Ageron, Ch.-R. *France coloniale ou parti colonial?* PUF, 1978
49 Beau de Loménie, E. *Les Responsabilités des dynasties bourgeoises*. Denoël
   I. *De Bonaparte à MacMahon*, 1943
   II. *Du maréchal MacMahon à Poincaré*, 1947
   The author's thesis is not always convincing.
50 Chevalier, J.-J. *Histoire des institutions et des régimes politiques de la France de 1789 à nos jours*. New edition, Dalloz,1971
51 Dansette, A. *Histoire des présidents de la République. De Louis-Napoléon Bonaparte à Vincent Auriol*. Amiot-Dumont, 1953
52 Digeon, C. *La Crise allemande de la pensée française, 1870–1914*. PUF, 1959
53 Estebe, J. *Les ministres de la République*. Presses de la FNSP, 1982
54 Girardet, R. *Le Nationalisme français, 1871–1914*. A. Colin, 1966
55 Girardet, R. *L'Idée coloniale en France*. La Table ronde, 1971
56 Goguel, F. *La Politique des partis sous la IIIe République*. Le Seuil, 1946
57 Kayser, J. *Les Grandes Batailles du radicalisme, des origines aux portes du pouvoir, 1820–1901*. Rivière, 1962
58 Lefranc, G. *Le Mouvement socialiste sous la IIIe République, 1875–1940*. Payot, 1943
59 Prost, A. *Vocabulaire des proclamations électorales de 1881, 1885 et 1889*. PUF, 1974
60 Rémond, R. *Les Droites en France*. Aubier, 1982
61 Sternhell, Z. *La Droite révolutionnaire, 1885–1914*. Le Seuil, 1978

IX. Religious questions

62 Dansette, A. *Histoire religieuse de la France contemporaine*. New edition, Flammarion, 1965
63 Latreille, A., and Rémond, R. *Histoire du catholicisme en France*. III, Spes, 1962
64 Rémond, R. *L'Anticléricalisme en France de 1815 à nos jours*. Fayard, 1976

X. Education

65 Mayeur, F. *L'Enseignement des jeunes filles sous la IIIe République.* Presses de la
    FNSP, 1977
66 Prost, A. *L'Enseignement en France, 1800–1967.* A. Colin, 1968

XI. The army

67 Girardet, R. *La Société militaire dans la France contemporaine.* Plon, 1963. See also
    Works in English: Ralston.

XII. Regional monographs

68 Barral, P. *Le Département de l'Isère sous la IIIe République, 1870–1940.* A. Colin,
    1962
69 Bois, P. *Paysans de l'Ouest.* Flammarion, 1971. Abridged version of the thesis
    published in 1960.
70 Corbin, A. *Archaïsme et Modernité en Limousin au XIXe siècle, 1845–1880.* 2 vols.,
    Rivière, 1975
71 Dupeux, G. *Aspects de l'histoire sociale et politique du Loir-et-Cher, 1848–1914.*
    Mouton, 1962
72 Siegfried, A. *Géographie électorale de l'Ardèche sous la IIIe Rèpublique.* A. Colin, 1949
73 Siegfried, A. *Tableau politique de la France de l'Ouest sous la IIIe République.* A.
    Colin, 1964. Anastatic reprint – an admirable classic.
74 Thabault, R. *1848–1914. L'ascension d'un peuple. Mon village. Ses hommes. Ses routes.
    Son école.* Delagrave, 1945, reprinted 1982.

XIII. Biographies

(for Part I)
75 Chastenet, J. *Gambetta.* Fayard, 1968
76 Goldberg, H. *Jean Jaurès. La biographie du fondateur du parti socialiste.* Fayard, 1970
77 Mayeur, J.-M. *Un prêtre démocrate, l'abbé Lemire, 1853–1928.* Casterman, 1968
78 Miquel, P. *Poincaré.* Fayard, 1961
79 Molette, C. *Albert de Mun.* Beauchesne, 1970
80 Sorlin, P. *Waldeck-Rousseau.* A. Colin, 1966
81 Reclus, M. *Jules Ferry.* Flammarion, 1947
(for Part II)
There is no *good* biography of several big radical leaders – Brisson, Buisson, Pelletan
– or of Briand. [The volumes of G. Suarez must be read critically.]
82 Allain, J. C. *Joseph Caillaux, Le défi victorieux, 1863–1914,* Imprimerie nationale,
    1978
83 Barthélémy-Madaule, M. *Marc Sangnier (1873–1950).* Ed. du Seuil, 1973
84 Droulers, P. *Politique sociale et Christianisme: le père Desbuquois et l'Action populaire.*
    Ed. Ouvrières, 1969
85 Goldberg, H. *Jean Jaurès.* Fayard, 1970
86 Goriély, B. *Le Pluralisme dramatique de Georges Sorel.* Rivière, 1962
87 Howorth, J. *Edouard Vaillant, la creation de l'unité socialiste en France.* EDI, 1982
88 Lindenberg, D. and Meyer, P. A. *Lucien Herr, le socialisme.* Calmann-Lévy, 1977
89 Miquel, P. *Poincaré.* Fayard, 1961
90 Rabaut, J. *Jaurès.* Librairie académique Perrin. 1971

91 Schaper, B. W. *Albert Thomas*. PUF, n.d.
92 Sternhell, Z. *Maurice Barrès et le Nationalisme français*. A. Colin, 1972

B. Specialized studies, by chapters

(for Part I)

1. The end of the notables, 1871–1879

93 Barral, P. *Les Fondateurs de la IIIe République*. A. Colin, 1968
94 F. Bédarida, 'L'armée et la République: les opinions politiques des officiers français en 1876–1878', *Revue historique*, July–September 1964, pp. 119–64
95 Castries, Duc de. *Le Grand Refus du comte de Chambord*. Hachette, 1970. Penetrating and fresh, thanks to recourse to private archives.
96 Gadille, J. *La Pensée et l'Action politique des évêques français au début de la IIIe République, 1870–1883*. 2 vols., Hachette, 1967
97 Gouault, J. *Comment la France est devenue républicaine. Les élections générales et partielles à l'Assemblée nationale, 1870–1875*. A. Colin, 1954
98 Halévy, D. *La Fin des notables*. Le livre de poche, 1972
99 Halévy, D. *La République des ducs*, Paris, Le livre de poche, 1972. Nos. 98 and 99 are two classics, fortunately reprinted.
100 Lajusan, A. 'A. Thiers et la fondation de la République, 1871–1877', *Revue d'histoire moderne*, November–December 1932, pp. 451–83; January–February 1933, pp. 36–52. Precise and subtle reassessment.
101 Pisani-Ferry, F. *Le Coup d'Etat manqué du 16 mai 1877*. Laffont, 1965
102 Rémond, R. *La Vie politique en France depuis 1789*. A. Colin. II. *1848–1879*, 1969
103 Rothney, J. *Bonapartism after Sedan*. New York, Cornell University Press, 1969. An important study which demonstrates the persistence of Bonapartist traditions.
104 Schnerb, R. 'La politique fiscale de Thiers', *Revue historique*, April–June 1949, pp. 186–213; October–December 1949, pp. 184–220

2. Economy and society

105 Armengaud, A. *La Population française au XIXe siècle*. PUF, 1971
106 Augé-Laribé, M. *La Politique agricole de la France de 1880 à 1940*. PUF, 1950
107 P. Barral, *Les Agrariens français, de Méline à Pisani*, A. Colin, 1968
108 Bouvier, J. *Etudes sur le krach de l'Union générale*. PUF, 1960
109 Bouvier, J. *Naissance d'une banque: le Crédit lyonnais*. Flammarion, 1968. Abridged version of the thesis published in 1961.
110 Bouvier, J., Furet, F., Gillet, M. *Le Mouvement du profit en France au XIXe siècle. Matériaux et études*. Mouton, 1965
111 Cameron, R. *La France et le Développement économique de l'Europe*. Le Seuil, 1971
112 Caron, F. *Histoire de l'exploitation d'un grand réseau français la Compagnie du chemin de fer du Nord 1846–1937*. Mouton, 1973
113 Codaccioni, F. *Lille, 1850–1914. Contribution à une étude des structures sociales*. Université de Lille, 1971
114 Crouzet, F. 'Essai de construction d'un indice de la production industrielle française au XIXe siècle', *Annales*, January–February, 1970, pp. 56–99
115 Crouzet, F. 'Encore la croissance économique française au XIXe siècle', *Revue du Nord*, July–September 1972, pp. 271–89. Very clear reassessment, which gives all the essential bibliographical references.

116 Gillet, M. 'Le bassin houiller du Nord et du Pas-de-Calais de 1815 à 1914, étude économique et sociale', *Revue du Nord.* July–September 1971, pp. 509–23. Thesis presentation.

117 Gonjo, Y. 'Le plan Freycinet, 1878–1882: un aspect de la "grande dépression économique" en France', *Revue historique*, July–September 1972, pp. 49–79

118 Lambert-Dansette, J. *Quelques familles du patronat textile de Lille-Armentières, 1789–1914.* Lille, Raoust, 1954

119 Lefranc, G. *Le Mouvement syndical sous la IIIe République.* Payot, 1967

120 Levasseur, E. *Questions ouvrières et industrielles en France sous la IIIe République.* Rousseau, 1907. Remains a basic book.

121 Lévy-Leboyer, M. 'La croissance économique en France au XIXe siècle. Résultats préliminaires', *Annales*, July–August 1968, pp. 788–807

122 Lévy-Leboyer, M. 'La "décélération" de l'économie française dans la seconde moitié du XIXe siècle, *Revue d'histoire économique et sociale*, 4, 1971, pp. 485–507

123 Lhomme, J. *La Grande Bourgeoisie au pouvoir, 1830–1880.* PUF, 1960

124 Palmade, G. P. *Capitalisme et Capitalistes français au XIXe siècle.* A. Colin, 1961

125 Perrot, M. *Le Mode de vie des familles bourgeoises.* A. Colin, 1961, reprinted by Presses de la FNSP, 1982.

126 Rougerie, J. 'Remarques sur l'histoire des salaires à Paris au XIXe siècle', *Le Mouvement social*, April–June 1968

127 Siegfried, A. *Mes souvenirs de la IIIe République. Mon père et son temps. Jules Siegfried 1836–1922.* PUF, 1952. Penetrating sketch.

128 Trempé, R. *Les Mineurs de Carmaux, 1848–1914*, 2 vols., Editions ouvrières, 1971

3. The period of Jules Ferry, 1879–1885

129 Brötel, D. *Französischer Imperialismus in Vietnam. Die koloniale Expansion und Errichtung des Protektorates Annam-Tongking 1880–1885.* Fribourg, 1971

130 Capéran, L. *Histoire contemporaine de la laïcité française*, 3 vols., 1957–61

131 Dietz, J. 'Jules Ferry et les traditions républicaines', *Revue politique et parlementaire*, 1934–36. An excellent series of articles.

132 Ganiage, J. *Les Origines du protectorat français en Tunisie.* PUF, 1959

133 Julien, C.-A. 'Jules Ferry', dans les *Politiques d'expansion impérialistes.* PUF, pp. 11–72

134 Pisani-Ferry, F. *Jules Ferry et le Partage du monde.* Grasset, 1962

135 Reinach, J. *Le Ministère Gambetta – Histoire et doctrine (14 novembre 1881–26 janvier 1882).* Charpentier, 1884. Remains essential; a great contemporary history.

136 Vaucelles, L. de '*Le Nouvelliste' de Lyon et la défense religieuse, 1879–1889.* Les Belles Lettres, 1971

4. Beliefs and cultures

137 Albert P. *et alii. Histoire générale de la presse française.* III. *De 1871 à 1940*, PUF, 1972

138 Barbier, P., Vernillat, F. *Histoire de France par les chansons.* Gallimard, 1961

139 Bonheur, G. *Qui a cassé le vase de Soissons? L'album de famille de tous les Français.* 1963

140 Bonheur, G. *La République nous appelle. L'album de famille de Marianne.* Laffont, 1965. Nos. 139 and 140 are two penetrating introductions to the primary school's scale of values.

141 Gerbod, P. *La Condition universitaire en France au XIXe siècle.* PUF, 1965.

142 Griffiths, R. *Révolution à rebours. Le renouveau catholique dans la littérature en France de 1870 à 1914*. Desclée de Brouwer, 1971

143 Kayser, J. (ed.) *La Presse de province sous la IIIe République*. A. Colin, 1958

144 Le Bras, G. *Etudes de sociologie religieuse*. 2 vols., PUF, 1955, 1956

145 Léonard, E.-G. *Le Protestant français*. PUF, 1953

146 Lethève, J. *Impressionnistes et Symbolistes devant la presse*. A. Colin, 1959

147 Ligour, D. *Frédéric Desmons et la Franc-maçonnerie sous la IIIe République*. Gedalge, 1966

148 Marcilhacy, C. *Le Diocèse d'Orléans sous l'épiscopat de Mgr Dupanloup*. Plon, 1962

149 Marrus, M. *Les Juifs de France à l'époque de l'affaire Dreyfus*. Calmann-Lévy, 1972

150 Ménager, B. *La laïcisation des écoles communales dans le département du Nord, 1879–1899*. Université de Lille, 1971

151 Molette, C. *L'Association catholique de la jeunesse française, 1886–1907*. A. Colin, 1968

152 Montuclard, M. *Conscience religieuse et Démocratie. La deuxième démocratie chrétienne en France, 1891–1902*. Le Seuil, 1965

153 Ozouf, M. *L'Ecole, l'Eglise et la République, 1871–1914*. A. Colin, 1963

154 Poulat, E. *Le 'Journal d'un prêtre d'après-demain' de l'abbé Calippe*. Casterman, 1961

155 Rémond, R. *Les Deux Congrès ecclésiastiques de Reims et de Bourges, 1896, 1900*. Sirey, 1964

156 Robert, D. and Mours, S. *Le Protestantisme en France du XVIIIe siècle à nos jours*. Librairie protestante, 1972

157 Sorlin, P. *'La Croix' et les Juifs*. Grasset, 1968

158 Thibaudet, A. *Histoire de la littérature française de 1789 à nos jours*. Gallimard, 1936

5. The Republic confronted by nationalism and socialism

159 Dansette, A. *Le Boulangisme*. Fayard, 1946

160 Julliard, J. *Pelloutier et les Origines du syndicalisme d'action directe*. Le Seuil, 1971

161 Néré, J. 'La Crise industrielle de 1882 et le Mouvement boulangiste', *thèse dactylographiée*, 1959

162 Néré, J. *Le Boulangisme et la Presse*. A. Colin, 1964

163 Sternhell, Z. *Maurice Barrès et le Nationalisme français*. A. Colin, 1972

164 Willard, C. *Le Mouvement socialiste en France, 1893–1905. Les guesdistes*. Editions sociales, 1965

6. The moderate Republic, 1889–1898

165 Bouvier, J. *Les Deux Scandales de Panama*. Julliard, 1964

166 Dommanget, M. *La Chevalerie du travail française*. Lausanne, Rencontre, 1967

167 Dubief, H. *Le Syndicalisme révolutionnaire*. A. Colin, 1969

168 Girault, R. *Emprunts russes et Investissements français en Russie, 1887–1914*. A. Colin, 1973

169 Lachapelle, G. *Le Ministère Mèline. Deux années de politique intérieure et extérieure, 1896–1898*. 1928. The work of a close collaborator of Méline.

170 Montclos, X. de *Le Toast d'Alger. Documents*. De Boccard, 1966

171 Maitron, J. *Histoire du mouvement anarchiste en France*. Su del, 1951

(for Part II)

7. The Dreyfus affair

172 Charle, Ch. 'Les écrivains et l'affaire Dreyfus', *Annales ESC*, March–April 1977

173 Gautier, R. *Dreyfusards!* Julliard, 1965
174 Girardet, R. *La Société militaire dans la France contemporaine.* Plon, 1963
175 Marrus, M. *Les Juifs de France à l'époque de l'affaire Dreyfus.* Calmann-Lévy, 1972
176 Pierrard, P. *Juifs et Catholiques français.* Fayard, 1970
177 Ponty, J. 'La presse quotidienne et l'affaire Dreyfus en 1898–1899', *Revue d'Histoire moderne et contemporaine,* 1974
178 Rebérioux, M. 'Histoire, historiens et dreyfusisme', *Revue historique,* 1976
179 Rioux, J.-P. *Nationalisme et conservatisme. La ligue de la Patrie française, 1899–1904.* Beauchesne, 1977
180 Sée, H. *Histoire de la Ligue des Droits de l'homme.* 1927
181 Sorlin, P. *La Croix et les Juifs.* Grasset, 1967
182 Thomas, M. *L'Affaire sans Dreyfus.* Fayard, 1961
183 Verdès-Leroux, J. *Scandale financier et Antisémitisme catholique.* Le Centurion 1969
184 'Les intellectuels dans la société française contemporaine', special number of the *Revue française de science politique,* December 1959

8. The France of the left-wing Bloc and the rise of radicalism

185 Baal, G. 'Combes et la République des comités', *Revue d'histoire moderne et contemporaine,* April–June 1977
186 Bruhat, J. 'Anticléricalisme et mouvement ouvrier avant 1914', *Le Mouvement social,* October–December 1960
187 Buisson, F. *La Politique radicale.* Giard et Brière, 1908
188 Derfler, L. *Alexandre Millerand, The Socialist Years.* The Hague–Paris, Mouton, 1977
189 Dintzer, L. *et al.,* 'Le mouvement des Universités populaires', *Le Mouvement social,* April–June 1961
190 Kayser, J. *Les Grandes Batailles du radicalisme.* Rivière, 1962
191 Lévêque, P. 'Libre pensée et socialisme', *Le Mouvement social,* October–December 1966
192 Ligou, D. *F. Desmons et la Franc-Maçonnerie sous la IIIe République.* Gedalge, 1966
193 Mayeur, J.-M. *La Séparation de l'Eglise et de l'Etat.* Julliard, 1966
194 Millerand, A. *Le Socialisme réformiste.* Bibliothèque socialiste, 1903
195 Nordmann, J.-Th. *Histoire des radicaux, 1820–1973.* La Table ronde, 1974
196 Ozouf, J. *Nous, les maîtres d'école.* Julliard, 1967
197 Rebérioux, M. *Le socialisme français.* Vol. II of the *Histoire générale du socialisme,* PUF, 1974
198 Ruby, M. *Le Solidarisme.* Gedalge, 1971.
199 Vandenbussche, R. 'Aspects de l'histoire politique du radicalisme dans le département du Nord (1870–1905)', *Revue du Nord,* April–June 1965

9. Crisis and death of the Bloc, 1904–1907

200 Augé-Laribé, M. *La Viticulture industrielle du Midi de la France.* Giard et Brière, 1907
201 Brécy, R. *La Grève générale en France.* EDI, 1969
202 Dommanget, M. *Histoire du 1er mai.* SUDEL, 1953
203 Gratton, Ph. *Les Luttes de classes dans les campagnes.* Anthropos, 1971
204 Julliard, J. *Clemenceau briseur de grève.* Julliard, 1965
205 Launay, M. 'Aux origines du syndicalisme chrétien en France', *Le Mouvement social,* July–September 1969

206 Mayeur, J.-M. 'Géographie de la résistance aux Inventaires', *Annales ESC*, November–December 1966
207 Michel, J. 'Syndicalisme minier et politique dans le Pas-de-Calais: le cas Basly, 1880–1914', *Le Mouvement social*, April–June 1974
208 Molette, C. *L'Association catholique de la Jeunesse française, 1886–1907.* A. Colin, 1968
209 Sieburg, H. O. *Die Grubenkatastrophe von Courrières 1906*, Wiesbaden, Steiner, 1967
210 Tartakowksy, D. *La Grève des postiers de 1909.* Sorbonne, 1969, unpublished master's thesis.

10. The days of imperialism

211 Ageron, Ch.-R. *Les Algériens musulmans et la France, 1871–1919*, I and II, PUF, 1968
212 Astier-Loufti, M. *Littérature et Colonialisme. L'expansion coloniale vue dans la littérature romanesque française, 1871–1914.* Mouton, 1971
213 Bouvier, J. *Un siècle de banque française.* Hachette-Littérature, 1973
214 Bouvier, J., Furet, F., Gillet, M. *Le Mouvement du profit en France au XIXe siècle.* Mouton, 1965
215 Brugière, M. 'Le chemin de fer du Yunnan. Paul Doumer et la politique d'intervention française en Chine (1899–1902)', *Revue d'histoire diplomatique*, July–September 1963
216 Caron, F. *Histoire de l'exploitation d'un grand réseau français. La Compagnie de chemin de fer du Nord de 1846 à 1936.* Mouton, 1973
217 Carré, J.-J., Dubois, P., Malinvaud, E. *La Croissance française. Essai d'analyse économique causale de l'après-guerre.* Editions du Seuil, 1972
218 Coquery-Vidrovitch, C. *Le Congo au temps des grandes compagnies concessionnaires, 1898–1930.* Mouton, 1972
219 Crubellier, M. *Histoire culturelle de la France.* A. Colin, 1974
220 Daumard, A. 'L'évolution des structures sociales en France à l'époque de l'industrialisation, 1815–1914', *Revue historique*, April–June 1972
221 Dezès, M.-G. 'Participation et démocratie sociale: l'expérience Briand de 1909', *Le Mouvement social*, April– June 1974
222 Frajerman, M. and Wincock, D. *Le Vote de l'impôt général sur le revenu, 1907–1914.* Microéditions, 1973
223 Ganiage, J. and Hémery, D. *L'Expansion coloniale de la France sous la IIIe République (1871–1914).* Payot 1968
224 Gillet, M. *Les Charbonnages du Nord de la France au XIXe siècle.* Mouton, 1973
225 Girardet, R. *L'Idée coloniale en France de 1871 à 1962.* La Table Ronde, 1972
226 Girault, R. *Emprunts russes et Investissement français en Russie, 1887–1914.* Mouton, 1973
227 Griffiths, R. *Révolution à rebours. Le renouveau catholique dans la littérature en France de 1870 à 1914.* Desclée de Brouwers, 1971
228 Guillen, P. *L'Allemagne et le Maroc de 1870 à 1905.* PUF, 1967
229 Guillen, P. 'Les questions coloniales dans les relations franco-allemandes à la veille de la Première Guerre mondiale', *Revue historique*, July–September 1972
230 Haupt, G. and Rebérioux, M. *La Deuxième Internationale et l'Orient.* Cujas, 1967
231 Hirtz, C. *L'Est Républicain, 1899–1914*, Presses universitaires de Grenoble, 1973
232 Le Thanh Khoi, *Le Vietnam, histoire et civilisation.* Editions de Minuit, 1955

233 Michalet, Ch.-A. *Les Placements des épargnants français de 1815 à nos jours.* PUF, 1968

234 Milza, P. *Les Relations internationales de 1871 à 1914.* A. Colin, 1968

235 Poidevin, R. *Les Relations économiques et financières entre la France et l'Allemagne de 1898 à 1914.* A. Colin, 1969

236 Poitevin, Ch. 'Les Spoliations coloniales en Tunisie au début du XXe siècle', mémoire de maîtrise, 1973, University of Paris

237 Renouvin, P. *La Politique extérieure de Th. Delcassé 1898–1905.* Tournier et Constant, 1954

238 Sadoul, G. *Histoire du cinéma mondial des origines à nos jours.* Flammarion, 1949

239 Sieberg, H. *Eugène Etienne und die Französische Kolonial-Politik, 1887–1904.* Cologne, 1968

240 Thobie, J. *Les Intérêts économiques, financiers et politiques français dans la partie asiatique de l'Empire ottoman de 1895 à 1914.* Publications de la Sorbonne, 1975

11. The avant-garde movements

241 Anglès, A. *André Gide et le premier groupe de la NRF.* Gallimard, 1978

242 Baubérot, J. *Un christianisme profane?* PUF, 1978

243 Bertrand, G. *L'Illustration de la poésie a l'époque du cubisme.* Klincksieck, 1971

244 Bonnet, S. *L'Homme du fer.* Metz, SMEI, 1975

245 Bonnet, S., and Humbert, R. *La Ligne rouge des Hauts-Fourneaux.* Denoël, 1981

246 Brion-Guerry, L. (ed.). *L'Année 1913.* 2 vols., Klincksieck, 1971

247 Cabanne, P., and Restany, P. *L'Avant-garde au XXe siècle.* A. Balland, 1969

248 Carassus, E. *Le Snobisme et les Lettres françaises: de Bourget à Marcel Proust.* A. Colin, 1966

249 Caron, J. *Le Sillon et la Démocratie chrétienne 1894–1910.* Plon, 1967

250 Cazals, R. *Avec les ouvriers de Mazamet.* Maspero, 1978

251 Chatelet, F. *Histoire de la philosophie.* Vol. VIII, Hachette-Littérature, 1973

252 Decaudin, M. *La Crise des valeurs symbolistes.* Toulouse (privately printed), 1960

253 Devillers, C., and Huet, B. *Le Creusot. Naissance et développement d'une ville industrielle 1782–1914.* Le Creusot, Milieux–Champ Vallon, 1981

254 Francastel, P. *Peinture et Société.* Gallimard, 1950

255 Guilbert, M. *Les Femmes et l'Organisation syndicale avant 1914.* CNRS, 1966

256 Jaurès, J. *Histoire socialiste de la Révolution française.* Rouff, 1901–4

257 Julliard, J. *Fernand Pelloutier et les origines du syndicalisme d'action directe.* Editions du Seuil, 1971

258 Laude, J. *Les Arts de l'Afrique noire.* Livre de poche, 1968

259 Le Bot, M. *Peinture et Machinisme.* Klincksieck, 1973

260 Lequin, Y. *Les Ouvriers de la région lyonnaise.* 2 vols., Presses universitaires de Lyon, 1977

261 Pennetier, C. *Le Socialisme dans le Cher 1851–1921.* MSH, 1982

262 Poulat, E. *Histoire, Dogme et Critique dans la crise moderniste.* Casterman, 1962

263 Rebérioux, M. 'Avant-garde esthétique et avant-garde politique', *Esthétique et Marxisme,* Plon, 1974

264 Rebérioux, M. *Les Ouvriers du Livre et leur Fédération.* Temps actuels, 1981

265 Sagnes, J. *Le Mouvement ouvrier du Languedoc.* Toulouse (privately printed), 1980

266 Weber, E. *L'Action française.* Stock, 1962

267 Zylberberg-Hocquard, M.-H. *Féminisme et syndicalisme en France.* Anthropos, 1978

268 'Critique littéraire et socialisme au tournant du siècle', special issue of *Le Mouvement social,* April–June 1967

269 *Les Sources du XXe siècle*. Catalogue of the exhibition at the Museum of Modern Art, 1960–1

12. *France in 1914*

270 Ariès, Ph. *Histoire des populations françaises*. Editions du Seuil, 1971
271 Armengaud, A. 'Mouvement ouvrier et néo-malthusianisme au début du XXe siècle', *Annales de démographie historique*, 1966
272 Armengaud, A. *La Population française au XIXe siècle*. PUF, 1971
273 Augé-Laribé, M. *La Politique agricole de la France, de 1880 à 1940*. PUF, 1950
274 Barral, P. *Le Département de l'Isère sous la IIIe République 1870–1940*. A. Colin, 1962
275 Bastié, J. *La Croissance de la banlieue parisienne*. PUF, 1964
276 Becker, J.-J. *Le Carnet B*. Klincksieck, 1973
277 Becker, J.-J. *1914: comment les Français sont entrés dans la guerre*. Presses de la FNSP, 1977
278 Bertillon, J. *La Dépopulation de la France*. Alcan, 1911
279 Bonneff, L. and M. *La Vie tragique des travailleurs*. Rouff, 1908
280 Bonnet, S., Santini, Ch., Barthélémy, J. 'Les Italiens dans l'arrondissement de Briey', *Annales de l'Est*, 1962
281 Brelot, C. I., and Mayaud, J. L. *L'Industrie en sabots*. Garnier-Pauvert, 1982
282 Brun, Ch. *Le Régionalisme*. Bloud, 1911
283 Brunet, R. *Les Campagnes toulousaines*. Toulouse (privately printed), 1965
284 Chardon, H. *Le Pouvoir administratif*. Perrin, 1910
285 Crouzet, F. 'Essai de construction d'un indice de la production industrielle française au XIXe siècle', *Annales ESC*, January–February 1970. See also *Revue du Nord*, July–September 1972
286 Crubelier, M. *L'Enfance et la jeunesse dans la société française*. A. Colin, 1979
287 Dugrand, R. *Villes et Campagnes en Bas-Languedoc. Le réseau urbain du Bas-Languedoc méditerranéen*. PUF, 1963
288 Fabre, D., and Lacroix, J. *La Vie quotidienne des paysans du Languedoc au XIXe siècle*. Hachette-Littérature, 1973
289 Fay-Sallois, F. *Les Nourrices à Paris au XIXe siècle*. Payot, 1980
290 Fels, A. *Les Hautes Terres du Massif-central. Tradition paysanne, économie agricole*. PUF, 1962
291 Fridenson, P. *Histoire des usines Renault*. I. *Naissance de la grande entreprise, 1898–1939*. Editions du Seuil, 1972
292 Garrier, G. *Paysans du Beaujolais et du Lyonnais, 1800–1970*. 2 vols., Presses universitaires de Grenoble, 1974
293 Guizal, P., and Thuillier, G. *La Vie quotidienne des domestiques en France au XIXe siècle*. Hachette, 1978
294 Guizal, P., and Thuillier, G. *La Vie quotidienne des professeurs de 1870 à 1940*. Hachette, 1982
295 Halévy, D. *Visites aux paysans du Centre*. Le livre de poche, reprinted 1978
296 Hatzfeld, H. *Du paupérisme à la Sécurité sociale, 1850–1940*. A. Colin, 1971
297 Kayser, B. *Campagnes et villes de la Côte d'Azur. Essai sur les conséquences du développement urbain*. Monaco, 1960
298 Kriegel, A., and Becker, J.-J. *1914. La Guerre et le Mouvement ouvrier français*. A. Colin, 1964
299 Lévy-Leboyer, M. 'La croissance économique en France au XIXe siècle', *Annales ESC*, July-August 1968
300 Markhovitch, T.-J. 'L'industrie française de 1789 à 1964. Sources et méthodes', *Cahiers de l'ISEA*, 1965

301   Martin-Fugière, A. *La Place des bonnes. La domesticité féminine à Paris en 1900.* Grasset, 1979

302   Masson, E. *Les Bretons et le socialisme.* Maspero, 1972

303   Moscovici, S. *L'Age des foules.* Fayard, 1981

304   Ozouf, M. *L'Ecole, l'Eglise et la République.* A. Colin, 1963

305   Perrot, M. *Le Mode de vie des familles bourgeoises.* A. Colin, 1961, reissued FNSP 1982

306   Phlipponeau, M. *La Vie rurale dans la banlieue parisienne.* A. Colin, 1956

307   Pinchemel, Ph. *Structures sociales et dépopulation rurale dans les campagnes picardes de 1836 à 1936.* A. Colin, 1957

308   Ronsin, F. *La Grève des ventres.* Aubier, 1980

309   Siegfried, A. *Géographie électorale de l'Ardèche sous la IIIe République.* A. Colin, 1949

310   Siegfried, A. *Tableau politique de la France de l'Ouest.* A. Colin, reissued 1964

311   Sutet, M. *Montceau-les-Mines.* Roanne, Horvath, 1981

312   Trempé, R. *Les Mineurs de Carmaux, 1848–1914.* Editions ouvrières, 1971

313   Vincent, G. 'Les professeurs de l'enseignement secondaire dans la société de la Belle Epoque', *Revue d'histoire moderne et contemporaine,* January–March 1966

314   '1914: la guerre et la classe ouvrière européenne', *Le Mouvement social,* October–December 1964, special issue

315   'Droite et gauche de 1789 à nos jours', *Actes du Colloque de Montpellier 9–10 June 1973,* Montpellier, Université Paul Valéry, 1975

316   'Travaux de femmes dans la France du XIXe siècle', *Le Mouvement social,* October–December 1978, special issue

317   'Petite entreprise et politique', *Le Mouvement social,* January–March, 1981, special issue.

SUPPLEMENTARY BIBLIOGRAPHY OF WORKS IN ENGLISH

Agulhon, Maurice. *Marianne into Battle. Republican Imagery and Symbolism in France 1789–1880.* Cambridge University Press, 1981

Anderson, Malcolm. *Conservative Politics in France.* London, Allen and Unwin, 1974

Anderson, R.D. *France 1870–1914. Politics and Society.* London, Routledge and Kegan Paul, 1977

Andrew, Christopher. *Théophile Delcassé and the Making of the Entente Cordiale.* London, Macmillan, 1968

Brabant, F.H. *The Beginning of the Third Republic in France.* London Macmillan, 1940

Brogan, D.W. *The Development of Modern France (1870–1939).* London, Hamish Hamilton, new edn, 1967

Brunschwig, Henri. *French Colonialism 1871–1914. Myths and Realities.* London, Pall Mall Press, 1966

Bury, J.P.T. *France, 1814–1940.* London, Methuen, 4th edn, 1969
    Gambetta and the Making of the Third Republic. London Longman, 1973
    Gambetta's Final Years. 'The Era of Difficulties' 1877–1882. London, Longman, 1982

Byrnes, R.F. *Antisemitism in Modern France. 1. The Prolog to the Dreyfus Affair.* New Brunswick, 1950

Caldwell, T.B. 'Workers' Institutions in France, 1890–1914', Ph.D. thesis, University of Leeds, 1962

Campbell, Peter. *French Electoral Systems and Elections since 1789.*

Caron, François. *An Economic History of Modern France.* London, Methuen, 1979

Carroll, E.M. *French Public Opinion and Foreign Relations 1870–1914.* New York, Century, 1931

Chapman, Guy. *The Dreyfus Case. A Reassessment.* London, Hart-Davis, 1955

Charvet, P.E. *A Literary History of France.* Vol. V: *The Nineteenth and Twentieth Centuries 1870–1940,* London, Ernest Benn, 1967

Cobban, Alfred. *A History of Modern France.* Vol. III: *1871–1962,* London, Penguin, 1965

De Tarr. *The French Radical Party.* London, 1961.

Evenson, Norma. *Paris. A Century of Change 1878–1978.* New Haven and London, University Press, Yale 1979

Gimpl, M.C.A. *The 'Correspondant' and the Founding of the French Third Republic.* Washington, 1959

Goldberg, Harvey. *The Life of Jean Jaurès.* Madison, University of Wisconsin Press, 1962

Halévy, Daniel. *The End of the Notables.* Middleton, Conn., Wesleyan University Press, 1974

Halls, W.H. *Education, Culture and Politics in Modern France.* Oxford, Pergamon Press, 1976

Headings, M.J. *French Freemasonry under the Third Republic.* Baltimore, 1949

Hutton, P.H. *The Cult of the Revolutionary Tradition. The Blanquists in French Politics, 1864–1893.* Berkeley, University of California Press, 1976

Johnson, Douglas. *France and the Dreyfus Affair.* London, Blandford Press, 1966

Joughin, Jean T. *The Paris Commune in French Politics 1871–1880.* Baltimore, Johns Hopkins University Press, 1955

Judt, Tony. *Socialism in Provence 1871–1914.* Cambridge University Press, 1979

Kanya-Forstner, A.S. *The Conquest of the Western Sudan.* Cambridge University Press, 1969

Kindleberger, Charles P. *Economic Growth in France and Britain 1851–1950.* Cambridge, Mass., Harvard University Press, 1964

Larkin, Maurice. *Church and State after the Dreyfus Affair.* London, Macmillan, 1974

Lichtheim, George. *Marxism in Modern France.* New York, Columbia University Press, 1966

Locke, R.R. *French Legitimists and the Politics of Moral Order in the Early Third Republic.* Princeton University Press 1974

McManners, John. *Church and State in France 1871–1914.* London, Church Historical Society, 1972

McMillan, James F. *Housewife or Harlot. The Place of Women in French Society 1870–1940.* New York, St Martin's Press, 1981

Mitchell, Allan. *The German Influence in France after 1870.* Chapel Hill, University of North Carolina Press, 1979

Moss, Bernard H. *The Origins of the French Labour Movement 1830–1914.* Berkeley and London, University of California Press, 1976

Noland, Aaron. *The Founding of the French Socialist Party 1893–1905.* Cambridge, Mass., Harvard University Press, 1956

Osgood, Samuel M. *French Royalism since 1870.* The Hague, M. Nijhoff, 1970

Papayannis, N. 'Alphonse Merrheim and the Strike of Hennebont: the struggle for the eight-hour day in France', *International Review of Social History,* vol. XVI, 1971, second part

Porch, Douglas. *The March to the Marne, the French Army 1871–1914.* Cambridge University Press, 1981

Price, Roger. *An Economic History of Modern France 1730–1914.* London, Macmillan, revised edn, 1981

Ralston, D.B. *The Army of the Republic. The Place of the Military in the Political Evolution of France, 1871–1914.* Cambridge, Mass., 1967

Rémond, René. *The Right Wing in France from 1815 to de Gaulle*. Philadelphia, Univ. of Pennsylvania Press, 2nd edn, 1966

Ridley, F.F. *Revolutionary Syndicalism in France*. Cambridge University Press, 1970

Rothney, John. *Bonapartism after Sedan*. Ithaca, New York, Cornell University Press, 1969

Seager, Frederic H. *The Boulanger Affair, Political Crossroad of France 1886–1889*. Ithaca, New York, Cornell University Press, 1969

Sedgwick, Alexander. *The Ralliement in French Politics*. Cambridge, Mass., Harvard University Press, 1965

Shattuck, Roger. *The Banquet Years. The Origins of the Avant-Garde in France, 1885 to World War I*. London, Jonathan Cape, revised edn, 1969

Shorter, Edward, and Tilly, Charles. *Strikes in France 1830–1968*. Cambridge University Press, 1974

Soucy, Robert. *Fascism in France, the Case of Maurice Barrès*. Berkeley, University of California Press, 1972

Stafford, D. *From Anarchism to Reformism. A Study of the Political Activities of Paul Brousse within the First International and the French Socialist Movement 1870–1890*. London, Weidenfeld and Nicolson, 1971

Stearns, P.N. *Revolutionary Syndicalism and French Labor. A Cause without Rebels*. New Brunswick, 1971

Sutcliffe, Anthony. *The Autumn of Central Paris, the Defeat of Town Planning, 1850–1970*. London, Edward Arnold, 1970

Swart, Koenraad W. *The Sense of Decadence in Nineteenth-Century France*. The Hague, M. Nijhoff, 1964

Thabault, Roger. *Education and Change in a Village Community*. London, Routledge and Kegan Paul, 1971

Thomson, David. *Democracy in France since 1870*. Oxford University Press, 5th edn, 1969

Watson, D.R., *Georges Clemenceau, a Political Biography*. London, Methuen, 1974

Weber, E. *Peasants into Frenchmen, the Modernization of Rural France 1870–1914*. London, Chatto and Windus, 1977

   The National Revival in France 1905–1914. Berkeley, University of California Press, 1959

Williamson, Sam R. *The Politics of Grand Strategy. Britain and France Prepare for War 1904–14*. Cambridge, Mass., Harvard University Press, 1969

Wilson, N. *Bernard-Lazare*. Cambridge University Press, 1978

Wilson, Stephen. *Ideology and Experience. Antisemitism in France at the Time of the Dreyfus Affair*. London, Associated University Press, 1982

Zeldin, Theodore. *France 1848–1945*. 2 vols., Oxford, Clarendon Press, 1973–7

Index